Gerald Henry Rendall

The Emperor Julian, paganism and Christianity, with genealogical, chronological and bibliographical appendices

Being the Hulsean essay for the year 1876

Gerald Henry Rendall

The Emperor Julian, paganism and Christianity, with genealogical, chronological and bibliographical appendices
Being the Hulsean essay for the year 1876

ISBN/EAN: 9783337263058

Printed in Europe, USA, Canada, Australia, Japan

Cover: Foto ©ninafisch / pixelio.de

More available books at **www.hansebooks.com**

THE
EMPEROR JULIAN

PAGANISM AND CHRISTIANITY

WITH GENEALOGICAL, CHRONOLOGICAL AND
BIBLIOGRAPHICAL APPENDICES.

BEING THE HULSEAN ESSAY FOR THE YEAR 1876.

BY

GERALD HENRY RENDALL, M.A.

FELLOW OF TRINITY COLLEGE, CAMBRIDGE.

Cambridge:
DEIGHTON, BELL, AND CO.
LONDON: GEORGE BELL AND SONS.
1879

PATRI CARISSIMO

CVI REFERO ACCEPTVM

SI QVID VEL POTVI VEL POTERO

HAS DEDICO PRIMITIAS

PREFACE.

I OWE it to the indulgence of the Trustees of Mr Hulse's benefaction that I have been enabled to mend and finish much that was faulty and imperfect in this Essay as submitted more than two years ago to the Examiners. The *Introduction*—which makes no pretension to research and merely gathered up some thoughts suggested by preliminary reading—has been abridged, and rigorously stripped of all expansions and unnecessary illustrations. What remains of it I have spared rather from tenderness for its prescriptive right to appear in print than from any sense of its intrinsic worth. The body of the work has been treated to pruning here and readjustment there, and to more of augmentation than either. I have not stinted fulness of treatment, more sanguine of making my Essay thorough and true, than popular or entertaining. *Chapters* III. and VII. have been so rewritten as to be almost new, and the same may be said of much of the last *Chapter*. The *Appendices*, though prepared in germ, were of course not inflicted upon the first readers of the Essay, and aspire only to be serviceable to this or that special student.

Ancient and modern authorities—as the closing *Appendix* may attest—furnish wide fields for the student of Julian's acts and motives. Through by far the greater part of these I have found time and opportunity to roam. Much as I am in debt to judgments passed by other minds on materials open to all, I trust that no facts are now imported into this Essay which do not find warrant in the pages of the old writers. Whatever in the first scramble of Prize Essay writing I jotted down at second hand, I have since been able to verify, and according to its proper weight and context co-ordinate or exclude. References to the prime authorities—to Julian's own works in the margin, to the writings of others in the foot-notes—I have appended freely, but—except where conscious of a direct debt in thought or expression—have not been at ill-spent pains to multiply corroborative citations from later critics.

Two hundred years ago the Apostate's career furnished English Pamphleteers with food for piquant and voluminous controversy. A century has run since the great author of *The Decline and Fall* compiled his masterly narration of Julian's successes and failures: it must remain the wonder and despair of rivals. It seems indeed to have scared competitors from the field. French brilliance, German thought, Danish imagination have all had their say, but Gibbon's countrymen have honoured their greatest by silence. It needed some external impulse to call out a successor, and a gentle violence to drive him into print. I can only be grateful that *Alma Mater* has supplied both incentives for work that has been full of pleasure in the execution.

To De Broglie preeminently among Frenchmen, to Neander, to Mücke, to Strauss, and in a less degree to Rode, Semisch and the like among Germans, I tender thanks for the suggestive labours of which I have reaped the fruits, the value and helpfulness of which I inadequately requite by this general acknowledgment.

I must close with thanking my friend and brother-fellow Rev. V. H. Stanton of Trinity College for his kindness in reading my proofs as they passed the Press, and aiding me with wise corrections and suggestions.

G. H. R.

TABLE OF CONTENTS.

Introduction　　　　　　　　　　　　　　　　　　*pages* 1—22

CHAPTER I.
Religious Policy of Constantine and Constantius　　　　25

CHAPTER II.
Julian's Boyhood, Youth, Education, and Cæsarship　　　35

CHAPTER III.
Neo-Platonism　　　　　　　　　　　　　　　　　　62

CHAPTER IV.
Julian's Theology　　　　　　　　　　　　　　　　74

CHAPTER V.
Julian's Idea of Religion　　　　　　　　　　　　　103

CHAPTER VI.
Julian's Personal Religion　　　　　　　　　　　　127

CHAPTER VII.
Julian's Administration　　　　　　　　　　　　　150

CHAPTER VIII.
Persecution under Julian　　...　　...　　...　　176
　　Section I.　Acts of Persecution, p. 176—203.
　　Section II.　Educational Policy, p. 203—216.
　　Section III.　Estimates of Julian, p. 216—227.

CHAPTER IX.
Julian and Christianity ... 228

CHAPTER X.
Julian and Hellenism ... 240

CHAPTER XI.
Vicisti Galilaee! ... 264

Appendix A. Genealogical Table of the family of Constantius Chlorus ... 280

Appendix B. Chronological Tables of Julian's life ... 281

Appendix C. Synopsis of Literature upon Julian ... 291

INTRODUCTION.

INTRODUCTION.

§ 1. *Roman Religion.*

THE birth of Christ sounded the knell of Paganism. Though from distant and despised Judæa the wailing of the banshee was inaudible to Roman Paganism, at almost the same time the ancient religion of Rome underwent a final revolution. Old faiths had long been refluent. At the close of the Republic they were abandoned and replaced by new. The inauguration of the Empire of Rome synchronizes in some sort, and by no means accidentally, with an abdication of Empire by the old gods. Amid the varying types of Paganism, representing sometimes Greek æstheticism, sometimes Scythian savagery, sometimes Oriental sensuousness, sometimes Egyptian repose, it had been the pride of Roman Paganism to be above all else patriotic. Lacking the exuberant richness of Hellenic art and poetry, spurning alike the mystic piety and the voluptuous self-abandonment of the hot East, it strove with characteristic earnestness and consistency to be intensely national. Even before the Republic fell the power and the genius of the primitive religion died utterly out. Rome haughty, self-reliant, mistress of the world, needed no longer the aid of gods to win her victories; the soul of Roman religion had evaporated, and the young Empire proclaimed its disappearance. Before imperialism and cosmopolitanism the very conception of patriotism had withered: it could not breathe or live in that atmosphere.

Next after being patriotic Roman religion had been moral: it had personified (such was its one effort of imagination) the moral virtues, and set these personified abstractions to superintend every sphere and occupation of life. But in an age of much superficial culture and still more of vast material civilisation, bringing with it luxury and enervation and their habitual concomitants widespread social and personal immorality, the homeliness and simplicity of the old faith had been abandoned. Faith, early cramped by the pedantry of a fatuous theology, had first degenerated into formalism, and then fallen an easy prey to rationalism, scepticism or all-pervading Hellenism. As a system of faith extinct, as an agent of morality powerless, as a lever of patriotism decayed, it was chiefly as a political mechanism that the ancient religion survived. Augur could not face augur without a smile, but neither was the worse augur for that. The old forms were of service still. They subsisted on the strength of their weakness. They were too harmless to evoke opposition: they were too useful to invite abandonment. They answered their purpose sufficiently well, and to supply their place would have been tiresome.

Imperialism and Religious Revival.

To the consolidation of Imperial government corresponded a consolidation, so to say, of State religion. We are astonished to find Augustus actually taking in hand a religious revival; and emperor after emperor follows in his suit. Strange to say, when religion seemed most dead, there was a general restoration of temples, a new importance attached to worship and ceremonial, a higher regard for the sacred offices, a refreshed reverence paid to the Gods. This did not mean that the old faith was repossessing its lost dominion, but that a revolution in religion had occurred. Achieved facts received recognition, and religion was openly remodelled in accordance with their teaching. Imperial religion presents as necessary and violent a contrast to the religion of primitive Rome, as Imperialism itself to senatorial rule. Its sole unity was of a political character. The Emperor's power needed every support that it could find, and religion promised to be one of the most valuable. It was effective as a police agent; it could be conveniently turned to a moral purpose, where policy and morality went hand in hand; and in a few

Nature of the Revival.

cases its time-honoured prerogatives enabled it to discharge as effectively and less offensively a censorship which required something more than a statutory sanction. When the monarch became the fountain-head of law and authority, religion contributed its quota to his elevation. It was not enough that the Emperor should be Pontifex Maximus, the head of the religion; not enough that a lineal connexion should be established between the mythical Gods and the Imperial house; the Emperor was made the object of religion as well. The deification of the Emperors proved a project as happy in result as it was audacious in conception. It was no wonder that Emperors should foster religion which, more than anything else, conferred on them a prestige literally supernatural. In a manner, too, religion by this very step retained in a changed dress its old characteristic of nationality. Patriotism proper had of course died out; cosmopolitanism had transformed it into submission instead of self-sacrifice; loyalty to the State had become obedience to the Emperor. As patriotism has been the ruling element in the old religion, so in the new the key-stone of the whole was reverence clustering round the person of the Emperor.

But the fossilisation of the old State religion, and its virtual abandonment of all religious pretensions, could not kill the religious instinct. That remained active as ever, and needed to be provided for. This was done in the simplest and at the same time most comprehensive way, by giving it free scope. Every trace of the old jealous exclusiveness was forgotten. Just as the constitution of Rome swelled from city to state and from state to world-embracing empire, so religion became as broadly cosmopolitan as the Empire itself. Henceforth Roman Paganism loses all unity except that of political allegiance already described. Strictly speaking it does not admit of treatment as a single whole. It breaks into innumerable forms of faith and worship, which alike by their complexity and independence defy analysis. But this multitudinous assemblage of creeds was constantly subjected to the action of various forces, intellectual, emotional, spiritual and mystical, the general drift of which can be roughly

Provision for religious needs.

measured and traced. This we will attempt to do, at least in the case of those which bore most directly on the state of things preceding the era of Julian.

§ 2. *Philosophies Old and New.*

The intellectual currents of the time are mirrored in the fortunes of the more conspicuous schools of philosophy. Stoicism has first claim upon our attention. It produced its noblest representatives from a soil with so little outward promise as the Empire. Almost alone among the sages of antiquity, does Marcus Aurelius, the Roman Emperor, with Epictetus, the Roman slave, deserve the epithet of 'holy,' not unjustly accorded by Pagans to his colleague and father-in-law Antoninus.

The influence of Stoicism was necessarily very partial: it was congenial only to the narrow circle of minds of a tone so pure and elevated and self-sufficing as to cherish virtue for the innate love and reverence they had for it. Through them it influenced others, but indirectly and imperfectly. For Stoicism, aiming at perfect ἀπάθεια, and inculcating an ideal of unapproached severity, provided neither lever nor fulcrum to lift earth-bound souls to the 'toppling heights of duty' set before them. On the religious side it never soared like Platonism, for its conception of religion was limited to duty and conduct. Neither transporting the emotions, nor kindling the imagination, it failed in effectiveness of appeal to the individual and unregenerate soul: it could not work conversions. Its thinly masked materialism, its pantheistic degradation of the deity, its dreary fatalism, all combined with its forbidding severity to narrow and restrict its influence. It was, and was found out to be, wanting. It imparted to the best of its disciples a profound undertone of sadness and desolation. True it nerved a Thrasea Paetus here and a Helvidius Priscus there, fired a Lucan or embittered a Persius, but it never, for good or for evil, so much as touched the common crowd. For them it was useless. It provided no personal God; it offered no explanation of pain or misery or present evil; it promised no release from sin, no mode of sanctification; it enunciated that he who offended in one point was guilty of all; and yet in its entire annals it could not find[1] one ideal wise man to satisfy the requirements of its law, and be the exemplar of them that came after: finally, it cut off hope in denying immortality[2]. For such defects not even its lofty universalism could atone.

Introduction.

The first centuries of the Christian era show Stoicism becoming forlornly conscious of its own inadequacy. It ceased either to originate or refute. Its constructive and scholastic age alike were past. Wearied with fruitless disputation, hopeless of a sound criterion of truth, baffled or else satisfied in its researches into nature, it elaborated no further its treatises on formal logic or metaphysics, abstained from multiplying or exploding new theories of physics, and devoted itself to ethics alone. *Facere docet philosophia non dicere*, 'Conduct not theory is the end of philosophy,' writes Seneca; while Musonius, in the same spirit, reduced philosophy to the simplest moral teachings. Even here it had no heart to argue longer, and refine upon the relations or interdependence of differing forms of virtue. In an age of flat unbelief and timorous superstition, of hopeless dissatisfaction and of passionate longing after securer truth, Stoicism despairingly conscious of universal and increasing degeneracy, fruitlessly battling against sin within and without, ceased to teach didactically, and wearily addressed itself to preach its gospel of sad tidings, or sadly to commune with its own soul and be still. Its very sternness became strangely and wistfully indulgent towards human frailty. Its great doctors become homilists or devotional writers, throwing themselves with vehemence or tenderness or importunate appeal upon the promptings of man's inner self, not endeavouring to con-

Transformation of Stoicism.

Stoic preaching.

---

[1] In despair it sometimes cited Cato (Zeller, *Stoics* &c., p. 257 n.), or again Antoninus. Cf. Merivale, *Boyle Lectures*, p. 96.

[2] So at least earlier Stoics; and so too, to the popular understanding at any rate, M. Aurelius; though the convergence of Stoicism towards Platonism, represented by Seneca, taught a future life with Purgatory and Elysium, and indeed a quasi-immortality. Zeller, *Stoics Epicureans and Sceptics*, pp. 206—209.

vince the intellect but to move the heart. In its old age Stoicism fathomed new deeps in its vaunted "conformity to nature."

To Paganism Stoicism was not antagonistic. It did indeed in its esoteric teaching scornfully reject the current mythologies, and deny the efficacy of prayer or ceremonial worship, but even here, by virtue of free allegorizing of ancient myths, of faith in prophecy dreams and divination (to which a doctrine of predestination was made to lend some rational support), and of belief in δαίμονες and guardian genii, the Stoic philosopher found various points of approximation to the popular beliefs. In its exoteric utterances however it went far beyond this. In the supposed interests of morality Stoicism pertinaciously upheld existing modes of faith and worship, and strove to confirm by a religious sanction individual conscientiousness and public virtue. Thus Marcus Aurelius, an Agnostic as regards his personal convictions, was yet as Emperor careful to observe all ancestral religious rites: and this not from simple indifference or sheer hypocrisy. The Stoic Pantheist discerned in Polytheism the popular expression of his own more enlightened Pantheism, and believed that the manifold Gods of the heathen were but partial, and, as it were, fractional representations of the unknown One, whom he had learned dimly to apprehend.

Towards Christianity, in so far as it differentiated that religion from other cults, Stoicism felt very differently. When in the person of Antoninus Stoicism mounted the throne of the world, both from the vigorous suppression of malicious sycophants, and from the tolerance accorded to the most pronounced Scepticism, the Christians hoped much. But neither petitions nor complaints availed to justify their expectations. Under the just and gentle sway of Marcus Aurelius persecution waxed fiercer than before. Martyrdoms for the first time became numerous: torture apparently was now first employed to enforce apostasy. The records of the churches of Smyrna, of Lyons, of Autun, and of Vienne all testify the same tale. The ribald calumnies of detractors, and the defiant taunts of Christian Apologists, may have whetted the philosopher's dislike, but from the first Christianity must have roused his aversion rather than his sympathy. The stern Stoic could have little tenderness for these stubborn and rebellious nonconformists. In favour of their religion they could claim neither the ancestral sanction of Paganism, nor the prescriptive liberties of philosophic Scepticism. It was an impertinence for ignorant rustics and untaught artisans obstinately, contemptuously to spurn rites to which the cultivated philosopher yielded at least outward respect. Stoicism, in spirit if not in theory, was too exclusive and aristocratic to suffer *common* folk to share that intellectual freedom, that elevated atheism, which was the monopoly of the initiated few. Of the inward purity and loftiness of Christian morality Stoicism knew nothing; the inscrutable courage and resolution imparted by it was imputed to sheer perversity[1]; while the irrepressible *Schwärmerei* of Christians, their enthusiasm and fanaticism, their infatuation and aggressiveness, their superstition and their bigotry, were as repulsive as they were unaccountable to the Stoic.

Introduction.

Epicureanism—and a wide latitude may be accorded to the term—deserves consideration next. In numbers, it distanced Stoicism hopelessly: no philosophy was so popular; it seemed to many the only philosophy that could strictly be said to survive[2]. Intellectually however it was in stagnation. Throughout the Imperial epoch it produced not one exponent of first or even second-rate capacity. In his auction of philosophers Lucian lets Epicurus go for two *minae*: Sceptics and Cynics alone fetch a lower price. For many years before Julian's accession Epicureanism was the one historic school unrepresented amid the chairs of Athens University. The inspired intensity of its great poet-apostle had rapidly burnt out. Men cared as little for the Atomic Theory, as the Gods of Epicurus cared for men. Epicureans, like Stoics, abandoned physics and metaphysics, and found no ethics worth

Epicureanism.

[1] κατὰ ψιλὴν παράταξιν, ὡς οἱ Χριστιανοί.—M. Aurel. *Medit.* XI. 3.
[2] Diog. Laert. x. 9.

teaching; dilettantes, with a thin veneer of spurious Hellenism, anxiously flattering themselves that they lived after some theory, they enlisted under Epicureanism as giving the most comfortable account of this life and the most absolute assurance that there was no life to come. As tutors, rhetoricians, barristers and wits they leavened society.

Epicureanism and Paganism.

Epicureanism derived much amusement from attacks on the popular religion. It derided its superstitions, chuckled over its immoralities, and poked fun at its Gods. In the abandoned flippancy of its attacks it proves how completely religion had lost its hold on the upper classes of society. It did not attempt any semblance of reconstruction; for by the Epicurean the religious instinct was declared not to exist, and where created or inculcated to be bad and deserving of eradication alone. By exposing charlatanism, jeering at faith and ridiculing enthusiasm, he served partly to discredit, and still more to debase sinking Paganism.

Epicureanism and Christianity.

Against Christianity Epicureanism felt no peculiar spite. Christians were possibly more simple and gullible than other denominations, but apart from that were well-meaning good-natured people, by no means adapted to make much stir in the world.

Scepticism.

The Sceptic Philosophy proper was far too sterile and negative to be widely influential under the Empire or at any other time. Still small coteries went on thrashing chaff and demonstrating doubt, the certainty and desirability of which Sextus Empiricus among others syllogised in formal tropes, with the solitary flaw that logical demonstration was by his own showing proved impossible. Of dogmatic theology, Pagan Hellenistic or Christian, they said as of other things, that God and belief in God were equally probable, equally true, and equally untrue as any other hypothesis.

New Systems.

Such is the unattractive spectacle presented by the old philosophies. It is no marvel that efforts were made after new systems. From the inauguration of the Empire, and even earlier, Eclecticism—witness from very different sides Seneca and Lucian—was everywhere rampant. The new philosophies—if theosophies is not the more appropriate appellation—were eclectic attempts to harmonise more intelligently faith and reason. *Introduction.*

Of these sects the Neo-Pythagoreans need very passing mention; they endeavoured to reconcile polytheistic beliefs and practices with the transcendental conception of a supreme Being too exalted to be honoured by sacrifices or named in words, and only to be dimly apprehended by pure reason as darkly prefigured or occultly manifested in the mystic symbols and numbers of Pythagoreanism. *Neo-Pythagoreanism.*

A kindred but less abortive attempt presents itself in revived Platonism. The School of Plutarch, Apuleius, Galen, Celsus and Numenius flourished until merged in third-century Neo-Platonism. Men of piety conjoined with culture, dissatisfied alike with vulgar superstitions and with current intellectual negations, they sought in the defaced traditions of antiquity a record of the primitive revelation vouchsafed to man. With this view national beliefs were reverently but closely scrutinised. The result was the recognition of a supreme eternal invisible God, pure and passionless, and also of the immortality of the soul, whose proper aim was moral assimilation to God. Subordinate to the supreme deity were ranged superhuman powers and activities, who controlled the forces of nature, and regulated the affairs of men. Beneath these again were unnumbered δαίμονες, peopling the universe and the *intermundia*, the authors of health and sickness, weal and woe: to them it was that prayers and sacrifices were offered, as the appointed mediators between God and man. *Platonism.*

The truth of religion in Plutarch's view was irrefragably proved by the testimony of antiquity, by the evidences of prophecy and oracles, by miracles of mercy and visitations of judgment, by the efficacy of prayer and the revelations of the inner consciousness. He appealed alike to historical evidence and to individual experience. His sympathies were singularly wide: he gladly recognised the soul of goodness in the thousand creeds and formulas of Paganism. Amid all the characteristic diversities of development he pointed to the central and animating truth which they with more or less of faithfulness represented. By their aid he strove to recon- *Plutarch.*

cile the supernatural with the rational, disarming the infidel by the same argument with which he refuted superstition. "The true priest of Isis is he who, having been taught by law the rites and ceremonies that pertain unto the Gods, examines the same by reason and philosophises on the truth that they enshrine[1]." These principles he faithfully applied to the fabric of existing religions. Omens, for instance, were defended by a theory of predestination, a kind of ordered or pre-arranged harmony whereby for the believer the signs were brought into correspondence with the event signified. The eccentricities and imperfections of prophecies and oracular verses, out of which scoffers made great capital, were accounted for by distinguishing between what has been called dynamic and mechanical inspiration. 'Not the language, nor the tone nor the expression nor the measure of the verse proceeds from the God;—all this comes from the woman. God but supplies the intuition and kindles in the soul a light for that which is to come.' Similarly the rationale of prayer, that is the converse of man with God, was to be found in its subjective effect. Images could only be defended as representations and reminders of the invisible deities, and such indeed in their origin they were, until an idle superstition perverted them from symbols into actual gods.

Thus there was at least one philosophy, which assailed the rationalism of Euhemerus and the atheistic materialism of Epicurus as sincerely and unsparingly as it denounced the credulity of superstition; which recognised in infidelity the counterpart and twin brother of superstition; and which endeavoured to enlist against both the higher promptings alike of reason and of conscience. But while philosophy timidly conserved old faiths, or despondently proffered bare negations, the religious instincts of men carved for themselves more convenient channels in which to flow.

[1] Plut. *To priestess of Isis*, c. III.

§ 3. *Hellenism and Mystery Worship.*

Hellenism.

Greek religion, originally derived from the East, had wholly changed the conceptions from which it took its origin. Repelled artistically by the grotesque ugliness of Phœnician religion both in its inward conceptions and outward representations, too full of joyfulness to bear with the cruelties of a Moloch worship or offerings of human blood, the Greek genius with a splendid imaginativeness recast the whole of its religion in an anthropomorphic mould. By a series of magnificent metamorphoses it repudiated a debased Fetichism, and substituted a graceful anthropolatry. As Egypt and the East were the home of symbol-worship, Greece was the nursery of myths. Such as they were, teeming with grace and beauty and gladness, yet as a religion destitute enough of moral elevation or depth of insight, Greek forms of belief attained a strong external and literary hold upon the people who professed them.

Its adaptability.

From its defects as a religion hardly less than its merits as a mythology, Hellenism possessed unique power of adaptation to the taste or instincts of foreign nations. Everywhere commended by the supreme intellectual ascendancy of the Greek mind, everywhere communicated by the conquests of Alexander, it eventually not only naturalised itself in the religion of Rome, but spread from town to town throughout the East, from the shrine of Jupiter at Ammon or Venus at Dendera to the mouths of the Danube and Borysthenes, or the banks of the Indus and Jaxartes, until "Ἕλληνες became in the East the generic name for Pagans. Sometimes supplanting, sometimes transfiguring, sometimes combining with pre-existing faiths, Hellenism triumphed gloriously. But having neither moral depth nor historical foundation, it was as a religion helpless in battling against Scepticism. It yielded on the intellectual ground after strangely ineffective pretences at resistance, and fell back for influence and self-maintenance on the innate richness of its mythology, the wealth of its literature, the products of its art, the beauty and joy-

Introduction.

Mystery-Worship.

Its relations with Greek religion.

With Roman religion.

Growth and function of Mystery-Worship.

ousness of its cults. These were calculated to command every admiration short of worship, from high and low together.

The moral and religious element, which had disappeared from Roman and had scarcely found a place in Greek religion, was supplied by the mysticism of the East. The irreligious religion of Greece had been from the first supplemented by various forms of mystery-worship, and the more as its failure to meet the religious instinct of men became increasingly apparent. The Greeks, we have seen, reconstructed their mother religions on an anthropomorphic basis; pretty and captivating as was the result, it necessarily fell, so far as its truth was concerned, before the advances of philosophy and science, though the beauty of the design secured it to the last wide popularity alike from the literary side and from that of external observance. But the spiritual side having fallen into abeyance, the parent religion began forthwith either Kronos-like to devour its own offspring, or else harmoniously to adopt it as partner of the same hearth and home. Roman religion, on the other hand, with its deeply religious sense, forbade all mystery-worship, and for long successfully kept it at bay: as Roman faith failed, and became enfeebled in moral aspiration and ideals, various forms of mysteries began to intrude. Full license was not accorded, until the public renunciation of national faith was formally announced in the deification of the Emperors, and the public advertisement given that the old gods were defunct. Plain folk could no longer believe in state Gods, when asked to recognise in the person of Cæsar a God, a priest, an atheist all in one. The declaration of atheism was so explicit, that gods had to be sought elsewhere.

At a time when the oracles were wholly dumb, and faith burned very low, when men looked fondly back to 'the dear dead light' of at least a sincere Paganism, when they saw the dishonoured corpse of the old faith, for all its splendid trappings, simply the mark of ridicule and insult, when poor souls all the world over, utterly to seek for a Saviour or an exemplar or a divine voice of guidance, groped in darkness, what wonder that at such a time mystery-worship grew rampant? The mysteries of Mithras, Isis, and Serapis, the strange rites of *Taurobolia* and *Kriobolia* with their mystic interment of the neophyte and baptism of blood, professed at least to unveil the secrets of the hidden world, and supply a link between the unseen and the seen. Reinterpreting the ancient myths probably in a pantheistic sense, they at least averred that the world was not wholly forsaken of God, and in symbolic deed and word set forth the hope of immortality. In some particulars they furnish a strange and hardly accidental parody of the most sacred mysteries of Christianity. Not only was a long and painful preliminary training required of the catechumens of Mithras, the initiation of water, of fire, of fasting, and of penance, whereby as in the Christian Church the initiated (τέλειοι) might become first hearers, then worshippers, then illuminated or elect, and so pass into the body corporate of those admitted to the full esoteric revelation, but there were more direct imitations of Christian rites. There was baptism for the purification of sins, the unction of holy oil for the sanctification of life, and the oblation of bread and wine to serve as the bond of brotherhood.

But coupled with these rites were baser forms of worship, pandering to curious and diseased superstition. Magic, miraculous phenomena, invocation of the dead, visible apparitions of spiritual powers, were the unfailing accompaniment of all modes of mystery-worship. These brought in their train not only soothsaying and magic, demonolatry and necromancy, and all the arts called black, but came with their plague of lice as well as their plague of darkness: lewd and abominable rites, foul phallic emblems were employed to stimulate and satisfy the cravings of diseased minds. Thus shamefully prostituting the higher mission that they undertook, they at once degraded the intellect and polluted the soul.

Its immorality.

§ 4. *Christianity.*

Amid the fatigue of old faiths and philosophies, the tedious travail of new systems, and the invasion of pernicious superstitions, one only, faith philosophy or superstition, pressed steadily forward. Confounded at first with Judaism, Christianity soon shook itself free, and set out on its career of progress. It shunned publicity; it did not court the notice of the educated or the powerful; yet at the opening of the second century, even high officials became aware that there was 'a new superstition' abroad in the world; so novel indeed in kind, so strangely inoffensive and staid, so suspiciously loving and worshipful, as to call for the wisdom of an emperor[1] fitly to discountenance it. Its devotees were pronounced so far unblameable as to deserve punishment only when prosecuted, not inquisition for prosecution's sake. The next emperor[2] has ascended the throne, and Christianity is found to have made a new step in advance. The new religion is infecting the wise as well as the foolish; is adopting a philosophic guise, is entering the field of literature, and pressing for at least a fair hearing of its claims. Christianity denounced as atheistic, as revolutionary, as immoral, busily refutes these charges. It is the age of the Apologists. Gradually it abandons defence; the calumnies have become too stupid and flat to deserve reply; and Christian writers are engaged in co-ordinating Christian truth and doctrine with the lore of philosophers and the varied wisdom of the past. Christianity is in contact with the court; bishops are presented; Christian teachers are in correspondence with the Imperial family; nay, the Emperor himself is suspected of leanings towards the religion[3]. A very few years more, and Christianity is a recognised[4] cult existing under Imperial sanction and legal protection. The rulers[5] of the Church have become influential potentates, with whom it is no condescension for courts to

---

[1] Sc. Trajan.   [2] Hadrian.
[3] Cf. Origen's correspondence with Mammaea; with the Emperor Philip, his wife and mother.
[4] Edict of Gallienus.   [5] E.g. Paul of Samosata.

intrigue. Not many years later we find the principal places in court about the Imperial person filled by Christians, amid whom are numbered the Emperor's wife and sister, and from whose ranks the shrewd Diocletian selects his own most confidential servants. Even numerically, Christianity at the accession of Constantine was the professed religion of a tithe of the inhabitants of the Empire.

Such in most rapid outline was its external progress: let us examine its relations to current religion, to society and to the State.

Paganism in its later stages has no more characteristic feature than the carelessness and prodigality of its polytheism. The spirit of cosmopolitanism, inaugurated by Caesar and consummated in the Edict of Caracalla, affected religion no less than all other parts of thought and life. Free-trade in religion was alike a recognised theory and an accomplished fact. It was a quite antiquated proceeding to chain the guardian gods to the walls of the beleaguered city. Greek enterprise conveyed with it the national gods to favour the disposition of its wares, and in return transported home the deities of the countries where it dealt. At the great centres of commerce, Alexandria, Antioch, and the like, there lived side by side the strangest medley of heterogeneous gods:—gods of all origins, gods of all shapes and sizes, gods of all sexes and colours, found equal honour or dishonour from crowds of speculative worshippers. Athens, the city of temples, for fear of forgetting some one, reared altars to the unknown gods. Rome solved the same problem by building the Pantheon. Such was the religious universalism of the day. The rival religions, prompted whether by generosity or indifferentism or the shrewdness of self-interest, conspired as a rule to favour and abet each other. One only excited universal opposition. Priests and false prophets at least, if none other, recognised the radical antagonism of Christianity to their pretensions. 'If there is any atheist, *Christian* or Epicurean here present, let him be cast out[1].' 'No Christian admitted' was on the door of their sanctuaries.

[1] Lucian *Alex.* § 38.

Introduction.

Christianity and Public Opinion. Unpopularity of Christianity.

Such was the obvious attitude for Pagan Clergy towards the new religion. To which side did public opinion incline?

Unpopularity beyond a doubt was one of the trials which the early Christians were called to face. Again and again they were the first victims of any general dissatisfaction. Not merely does Nero select them as the most agreeable sacrifices to popular rage; but if there was a plague, or an earthquake, an eruption or an eclipse, a famine or a fire, if the Tiber overflowed its banks or the Nile did not, the populace cried out, 'The Christians to the lions.' The jealousies of Pagan priests and mystagogues, the imperilled interests of certain classes of artisans and employés account in part for this: but still more the character and effect of the religion itself. Atheism was a charge no less natural than damaging. The fanaticism, eccentricity and apparent moroseness of Christians made fatally against them. The extravagance of individuals, for instance as criminals at the bar or as soldiers called on to take the military oath, discredited their faith: and dark charges of nightly license and strange sorceries of blood easily fanned prejudice into persecution. It was little by little and very slowly that the sterling virtue of Christians disarmed calumny and enforced respect. It cannot be safely said that before the time of Diocletian Christianity had ceased to be unpopular. But one among other things proved by his persecution is its strength in the affections of the people.

Christianity and the State.

The treatment of Christianity by the State is quite another question. Religious persecution was an idea altogether alien to the genius of the Roman Empire. Incidentally, to be sure, to suppress patriotism or bridle some dangerous and ruling hierarchy, it might become necessary; but such persecution was political not religious. Rational polytheism naturally if not necessarily assumes the validity of other forms of belief. The State did not profess any exclusive religious belief: the gods of each newly-conquered nation were duly catalogued without remonstrance among divinities: Olympus was open to all comers without competitive examination. Nay, it did not profess even a particular cult. In the solemn religious festival preceding the Marcomannic War Marcus Aurelius sent for priests from *all* quarters and of *all* cults, that *all* the gods might go with his arms. Rome attributed half her success to her impartial treatment of all deities. Universal Empire was the due guerdon of universalism in religion. The persecutions of Nero and Domitian sprang it would seem out of mere caprice and malice. These excepted, it is those emperors who first descried the *social* and *political* powers and perils latent in Christianity, in other words the wisest and the most far-sighted, a Trajan, a Hadrian, or a Marcus Aurelius, who head the roll of reasoning consistent persecutors. The commonest test imposed on recusant Christians was the essentially political, though nominally religious test of sacrifice to the genius of the Emperor. Persecution naturally enough grows more violent and more systematic in proportion as the politico-social power of Christianity is gradually realised. When Christianity was a provincial and plebeian affair, Trajan's gentle and limited persecution rescript is put forward as a remedy for local troubles and disaffections. Hadrian's edict bears the same impress: it is a salutary, if painful antidote, to relieve the pressure of local pain. Antoninus Pius explicitly ordains that Christians are to be punished when convicted of political crimes; while whoever accused them on the score of religion was liable to prosecution. In Marcus Aurelius there is more of settled dislike and consistent suppression. We are informed, he writes, that *the laws are violated* by those called Christians; let them be arrested and punished with divers tortures. The Church was rapidly consolidating its internal government, and daily becoming a more formidable social power. The next real epoch in persecution is that, when 'after long years the accursed monster arose, Decius, to vex the Church.' Government being awake or at least waking to the sense that Christianity was a world-wide force, persecution ceases to be local and is made general. The spasmodic fears of Decius become the settled policy of Valerian. For the first time an Emperor realised the full extent of the problem, foresaw that Christianity must either triumph or die. Sternly and thought-

Introduc- tion.

Strength of the adult Church.

fully he grappled with it. For the time the attack was foiled. It was renewed in almost precisely the same form, when forty years later the great tenth wave of persecution swept with overwhelming violence upon the devoted Church.

But the Diocletianic persecution proved that the Church need no longer plead for sufferance from the secular power, but could face it as an equal and make terms in virtue of its own strength. By that time the Christians had become not merely the Emperor's trustiest servants: they were also the backbone of the State. In the army entire legions were composed of Christians, in the great towns whole quarters were occupied by them. The time was gone by when they declined military service or official functions. From their numbers were recruited the most enterprising artisans, the most regular tax-payers, and the strength of the proletariate. The old Empire was growing decrepit: it was not yet bed-ridden, yet had small strength longer to walk abroad: it could but just totter about its own domains and warn off intruders. It could not long hold out against increasing physical inanition: the steady decrease of population alone threatened it with rapid mortification. Few now married: still fewer produced offspring; and of offspring produced an abnormally large percentage perished in infancy. Physically as well as morally the best hope of the Empire lay in the Christians. For the successors of Diocletian the sole alternative was dull protracted civil war or unification of Church and State. Constantine's choice and execution of the wiser course constitutes his claim to greatness.

§ 5. *Conclusion.*

It is worth while in conclusion to gather into one focus the results obtained, and to summarise the state of affairs at the accession of Constantine.

Paganism doomed.

The simpler, more unsophisticated Paganism of earlier ages is manifestly doomed. It might still indeed be seen sitting in its tomb like Charlemagne, clothed with insignia of pomp and the sceptre of power, but void now of the living soul that had given to those outward emblems all their significance. Greek Philosophy as a decomposing agent had signally succeeded: as a constructive power it had no less signally failed. It had finally degenerated into stale moralising. To the rescue of prevalent unbelief various forces had stepped forward—most conspicuously, mystery-worship and revived Platonism. The former appealed most effectively to the lower instincts, the latter lacked the historical foundations which it required and assumed. The world lay in ruins; current creeds and philosophies were like convicts piling and repiling heaps of waste shot. Probably nine out of ten educated men regarded faith as a thing of the past, scepticism as mistress of the future.

Yet signs of a very different kind were not wanting. Though the forms of religion had broken away, the spirit of religion was still quick; it had even developed: the sense of sin, an almost new phenomenon, began to invade Society and philosophy; and along with this, an almost importunate craving after a revelation. The changed tone of philosophy, the spread of mysticism, the rapid growth of mystery-worship, the revived Platonism, are all articulate expressions of this need. The old Philosophy begins not only to preach but to pray: the new strives to catch the revealed voice of God in the oracles of less unfaithful days[1]. If any religion was destined to prevail amid the downfall of all creeds and mysteries, it had become manifest that that religion was Christianity. The precise numerical strength of the Church is comparatively unimportant. Whether a fifth or a twentieth of Rome's subjects, the minority was formidable from its nature not its numbers. It was with the Church as with her martyrs. Be they counted by hundreds or by thousands, their blood was in either case the seed of the Church. It was a new and astounding phenomenon that a religion had come into the world capable of producing martyrs at all. Of what other religion could it be said that its devotees 'were only too ready to die'? In the teeth of an organised

[1] Porphyry's *Collection of Ancient Oracles*.

and concentrated despotism a new society had grown up, self-supporting, self-regulated, self-governed, a State within the State. Calm and assured amid a world that hid its fears only in blind excitement, free amid the servile, sanguine amid the despairing, Christians lived with an object. United in loyal fellowship by sacred pledges more binding than the *sacramentum* of the soldier, welded together by a stringent discipline, led by trained and tried commanders, the Church had succeeded in attaining unity. It had proved itself able to command self-devotion even to the death. It had not feared to assimilate the choicest fruits of the choicest intellects of East and West. The main danger lay in the decomposing forces that threatened it from within. Yet it bid fair to triumph over these. It would hardly have to battle with a temper more impetuous and strong than Tertullian, an intellect more commanding and subtle than Origen: yet the centripetal forces were stronger; Tertullian had died an heresiarch, and Origen but narrowly and somewhat of grace escaped a like fate. If rent with schisms and threatened with disintegration, the Church was still an undivided whole.

THE EMPEROR JULIAN

PAGANISM AND CHRISTIANITY.

CHAPTER I.

RELIGIOUS POLICY OF CONSTANTINE AND CONSTANTIUS.

WITH the triumph of Constantine over Maxentius Christianity entered on a new stage. The Edict of Milan was the formal rehabilitation of Christians in their rights as citizens. The favour extended to them was in the first instance political rather than religious: but little by little, partly of policy, partly of superstition, partly of sincere conviction, Constantine, while adhering to a policy of religious toleration, rendered more and more unequivocal adhesion to Christianity. The vague Deism with which he commenced proved untenable in the heat of the strife between the old faith and the new. A colourless tolerance was *ipso facto* impossible as a permanence, however wise and natural a stepping-stone to the era to come. Each accession of power made it more imperative upon him 'to make up his mind on the choice of a God[1].' A hundred years previously it had appeared to a Tertullian inconceivable, either that an emperor should be a Christian, or a Christian be made emperor. Now with no very obvious wrench either to the state or the individual the momentous change was effected, the incredible achieved. Changed religion indeed, as Constantine himself declared[2], could not but produce changed government. But the general policy of toleration, the sole policy possible for a statesman of Constantine's political tact, was not aban-

Constantine's Religious Policy.

---

[1] Eus. *Vit. Const.* I. 27.
[2] *Ep. ad Arium* in Eus. *Vit. Const.* II. 65.

doned. In much of the empire, eminently at Rome[1] itself, Pagan society was too strong, too aristocratic, too influential to be defied with impunity, and a policy of open persecution would have been plain suicide. But the effect of the open patronage of Christianity by the Court and the active discouragement of Paganism was enormous.

External Progress of Christianity. In externals Christianity went forward with rapid strides. Proselytes poured in on all sides. 'In town and country alike might be seen nothing but new converts breaking their idols of their own accord[2].' Churches sprang up in all directions with architecture of a new magnificence. Vying with palaces in splendour, they were fitly called *basilicas*. The clergy increased yet faster than the laity. Of bishops there were nigh 2000. The Churches of Carthage and Constantinople each counted its 500 priests: it became necessary actually to limit by law the numbers of the clergy: of the lower orders, deacons and readers, acolytes and exorcists, singers and doorkeepers, there was proportionate abundance; while armies of paid agents, *paraboluni* and *copiatae*, visited the sick or buried the dead. Hermits and anchorites, celibates and virgins, monks and sisterhoods, swarmed by thousands in the land. Nor is this surprising when we read of the rich endowments in territory or cash given to special churches; of official promotion of Christians; of privileges and exemptions accorded to clergy; immunities from taxation reserved for Christian citizens; presents of clothes or money awarded to converts; subsidies granted to poor churches from the fiscal revenue; relief funds distributed among the poor. Besides these substantial aids the whole weight and prestige of Court favour was freely thrown into the scale of Christianity. The Emperor entertained bishops, discoursed doctrine, confuted heresy, presided at councils. Fashion and advancement both followed in the wake of the new religion.

The internal effects on Christianity produced by the new

---

[1] Beugnot goes so far as to suppose that Constantine's fear of the ascendant Paganism of Rome was one motive for the transfer of his capital to Constantinople.

[2] Eus. *Vit. Const.* II. 18.

relations in which it stood to the State, present less bright *Internal state of Christianity.* It was unqualified gain that Christianity should be able to temper the savage traditions of Roman law, abolishing the barbarous practices of branding and crucifixion, facilitating the manumission of slaves, and imposing penalties upon infanticide, rape, and fornication. But the Church did not stop here: Constantine's reign furnishes the earliest precedent for the infliction of spiritual punishments on civil offences, and conversely spiritual offences are now first chastised as such by the arm of law. The dragon's teeth are sown which sprang up armed, whether as the Inquisition or as Ultramontanism. And this was but the least part of the general demoralisation of spiritual life, which invaded the Church at large, and which found a very partial and in some respects injurious remedy in the great ascetic and monastic reaction which it largely contributed to excite.

A sudden outburst of heresy is another symptom which *Increase of Heresy.* followed the advent of the Church to power. Schisms gained all at once a new vitality, and began to flourish with tropical rankness and luxuriance. Donatists and Circumcellions in the South, Arians in the East, made havoc of the peace of the Church. The history of Arianism attests how ineffectual a salve for the sore councils proved. This new prominence of heresy is directly due to the changed relations of Church and State. Partly the Church assimilated foreign and impure elements: partly the civil power was placed from the outset in a false position. The Emperor should never have been permitted, far less invited to preside at councils, to administer church discipline, to decide on questions of doctrine, to deal out chastisement or leniency to heretics. The Donatist troubles which so vexed Africa flowed directly from Constantine's hesitation and embarrassment. Arianism but for imperial vacillation might have died with its author. Nursed by Constantine's unwisdom, it became the war-cry of an ambitious talented faction, who crippled Christianity, stifled true religion, well-nigh extirpated orthodoxy, and who have been the means of ousting the faith of Christ for more than a thousand years from the greatest of the old-world continents. Probably no keener disappointment ever befel Constantine than that of which he was thus the immediate source. He had hoped and, as it would seem, expected to find in Christianity that principle of unity which might reintegrate the divisions of the Empire. It was this hope perhaps which chiefly led him in the first instance to adopt the Christian faith: he was persuaded—it is his own confession[1]—that could he be fortunate enough to bring all men to the worship of the same God, this change would produce another such in the government of State. To his intense chagrin, he found that far from resolving all discords and reuniting jarring interests of State, the Church proved incapable of keeping peace within its own borders. The most troublesome of seditions was that kindled and fanned by a Church feud.

Paganism under Constantine. When Christianity became the avowed religion of the State, naturally enough Paganism, if not forcibly suppressed, was openly discountenanced. Constantine, in the first flush of triumph, seems to have expressly prohibited the old religion, and made the exercise of pagan rites a penal offence. He hoped perhaps by a bold stroke to give the finishing blow to tottering Paganism. Meeting with unexpected resistance, and saved by Christian advisers or by his own political tact from proceeding to open persecution, he yet discouraged the old religions in the most unmistakeable way. The subsidies and exemptions accorded to Christians were practically fines and disabilities imposed on Pagans. And more direct discouragements were not wanting. The Emperor would not suffer his portrait to appear in Pagan temples: Pagan festivals were neglected, or adapted[2] to Christian cults: Pagan shrines were by special writ left incomplete: many were dismantled of their most precious ornaments, more were suf-

[1] *Ep. ad Arium* in Eus. *Vit. Const.* II. 65.

[2] This principle of adaptation was widely carried out, or sometimes baldly enough, e.g. the old procession to Serapis was retained, with the solemn deportation of the πῆχυς τοῦ Νείλου and other emblems; its goal alone was altered, and became the Church, in place of the temple of the God, Soz. 5. 3. 3. On the widespread paganisation of Christianity cf. Draper, *Conflict between Religion and Science*, p. 46, and *Intell. Devel. of Europe.* Ch. x.

fered to fall into disrepair: not a few, where licentious rites were practised, were openly suppressed. The sign of the Cross supplanted the emblems of the gods. Sunday by Sunday, while Christian soldiers attended divine service, their comrades paraded in camp to recite with military precision a prayer to the one true God. So far as Paganism possessed inward devotional life and spirit, its disaster was even more complete. Not only did Constantine, while retaining the title of Pontifex Maximus and submitting probably to the ceremony of a formal installation, systematically neglect the religious functions of the office, but beyond this the blow was more directly fatal. The Emperor, it must be remembered, was the chief deity of Paganism; his worship almost the sole common link which bound together its endless denominations. For the Emperor to avow himself a Christian was for God to descend from his own altar and proclaim his apostasy. The small practical effect produced by so stupendous a catastrophe, proves merely how inconceivably little of sincere faith in its own creed remained to Paganism.

Such was the general tenour of Constantine's endeavours after religious unity. But local conditions stepped in to modify the execution of this general policy. In the East, where Christianity had widest hold, Paganism succumbed, to the verge in many places of complete disappearance. In Constantinople, *par excellence* the Christian city of the empire, no heathen rite, nor altar, nor temple, was to be seen. In the West, on the other hand, pre-eminently at Rome, the central asylum or shrine of Polytheism, the old ceremonial remained untouched. There temples were restored: the Emperor was still sovereign Pontifex; augurs and flamens and vestal virgins retained their old privileges; the *haruspices* officially reported the significance of thunderbolts; '*Dii te nobis servent*' was the recognised military salute; coins still wore their pagan emblems; the Emperor himself remained 'divine,' the consort of Jupiter or Mars, of the unconquerable Sun or the Genius of Rome. The Divine Institutions of Lactantius survive to show with how living a spell Paganism still held in bondage the minds of men.

Constantine's Religious Policy.

Constantius and Paganism.

The death of Constantine overlaps by six years the birth of Julian. The first great political event which the future Apostate could remember was doubtless the death of his grandfather and the accession of Constantius. The new emperor's policy towards Paganism hovered between reluctant tolerance and legalised persecution. He inaugurated[1] his reign with a decree of persecution, suggested or approved by his Christian councillors. All superstitious worship was suppressed, and Pagan sacrifices expressly interdicted: though in favoured localities at any rate temples were suffered to stand as interesting monuments of antiquity, or as useful for the celebration of public games or ceremonies. That during the earlier part of his reign the edict was not literally carried out, may be considered certain. During the troubles with Magnentius, it was practically a dead letter, to judge by the edict issued almost immediately after the pretender's fall, prohibiting heathen nocturnal rites at Rome[2]; but no sooner did Constantius find himself in 353 A.D. securely seated on the throne of empire, than he reinforced his earlier enactments by a decree[3] commanding under heavy penalties the summary closing of all Pagan temples. A yet more stringent edict[4] in 356 made participation in idol-worship or sacrifice a capital offence; increasing crimes and tyranny produced a corresponding increase of suspicious fears, and the next eighteen months produced three decrees[5] for the legal infliction of the most horrible tortures, the rack and the hot iron, on all persons in connexion with the court who dared to take part in magic rites. But here again Constantius did not consistently carry out the policy prescribed on paper. At Rome he himself respected the privileges of the vestal virgins[6], as Pontifex Maximus distributed coveted sacerdotal offices among the patricians, and investigated with

---

[1] A.D. 341.   [2] Theod. Cod. xvi. x. 5.
[3] The actual publication of this law (Cod. Just. i. xi. 1) has been disputed, but on hardly sufficient grounds. Cf. Beugnot, p. 138 : against him Chastel, p. 78.
[4] Cod. Theod. xvi. x. 6.   [5] *Ibid.* ix. xvi. 4—6.
[6] Symmachus, *Epp.* x. liv. 7.

interest the origin and story of the more famous temples. And this on the full tide of ascendant fortune! At Rome society remained Pagan, and the aristocracy sturdily declined to sue royal favour at the expense of religious apostasy. The loss of caste involved would have been but poorly counterbalanced by court smiles and official patronage bestowed in compensation on the renegade. Without dissimulation or check, patricians, prefects, consuls and municipal magistrates of Rome wore the garb, retained the titles[1], and did the honours of the old cult with unabated zeal. Nor was Rome a solitary exception: at Alexandria too heathen worship was maintained in almost its ancient splendour. From this conflicting evidence, this stringency of letter combined with laxity of practice, the fair inference is that the law was never dangerously pressed, but only politicly employed, where circumstances permitted. It was the sheathed sword that could be drawn at pleasure; and it was in the East that it found most scope for action. In the West, whatever may have been the theory, in practice the Imperial policy amounted to almost complete religious toleration[2].

Ill policy of Constantius.

Constantius during his closing years lapsed gradually into a sort of political dotage: he became the tool of hypocritical and designing courtiers; he grew less, not more tolerant; he multiplied the demoralising exemptions accorded to Christians; he fostered still more effectually Church disputes; he intruded more audaciously into theological controversies; he pitched his pretensions not short of infallibility; he surrounded himself more closely with, and left himself more

---

[1] Beugnot, p. 161 ff., quotes numerous inscriptions in support of this position.

[2] Beugnot considers Constantius' *professed* policy to have been one of toleration; but in face of the laws above referred to, of the non-publication of which there is no satisfactory evidence, this cannot be maintained: in any case they would appear to represent the views of Constantius, even if these were not actually carried into effect: (cf. De Broglie, III. 364 n.). He also makes far too light of the evidence for actual spoliation and destruction of temples. The fact does not rest merely on rhetorical tropes of Libanius, but is incidentally supported by numerous occurrences of Julian's reign. Cf. Schröckh *Kirchengeschichte*, VI. pp. 8—11.

completely than his father at the mercy of despicable favourites. 'With his chamberlain' (the notorious Eusebius), writes Ammian[1], 'he possessed considerable influence:' he armed himself with spies innumerable: the '*Curiosi*' became a regular department of State, with fixed salaries and an official name. It is difficult to credit the numbers of those who, as dependents in the palace or as officials in the provinces, sucked the blood of the exhausted State. The eunuch, that parasite of Eastern despotism, was re-imported[2] to the West, to serve in the bedchamber, to sit at the table, to whisper in the ear, and to guide the councils of the Emperor. Constantius promoted to special honour this crew, of whom Christian and Pagan writers speak with the same contemptuous hate, these 'lizards and toads, creatures may be of the spring, but all unclean.' Men of learning found no place at Court. His councillors, Christians in name, were many of them bishops, but all or almost all made religion a mere stepping-stone to self-advancement.

Constantius' Councillors.

Christian Anarchy.

The Church was in the most indescribable confusion. From the time when the Council of Nicaea had delivered the final verdict of Christianity on the Arian heresy, Arians had ceased to be honest if misguided heretics, and had converted themselves into a turbulent political faction. At each episcopal election or expulsion the most exalted sees of Christendom, Constantinople, Alexandria, Antioch, furnished scenes that would have disgraced a revolution[3]: venerable confessors[4] were tortured into heresy upon the rack: orthodox prelates or clergy were exiled, starved, strangled, or beheaded[5]. The great Christian commonwealth seemed drifting into helpless anarchy. Bishops had become so many centres of confusion and ringleaders of heresy, who could

---

[1] Apud quem—si vere dici debeat—multa Constantius potuit.—Amm. M. XVIII. iv. 3. His favourites and officials were also all Christians, not, like Constantine's, of mixed creeds.

[2] Constantine's wisdom had discouraged what Diocletian's pride had introduced. Gibbon, c. xix., is admirably terso upon this subject.

[3] Cf. esp. the history of Bps. Macedonius, Gregory and George.

[4] e.g. Hosius of Cordova.

[5] Cf. among many Lucius Bp. of Hadrianople, Paul of Constantinople, and Liberius of Rome.

publicly inaugurate their reign with ribald blasphemies[1]. Arians in the East, or Sabellians[2] in the West, they met in council and counter-council to frame new creeds, or fulminate anathemas[3]. To and fro they galloped to this synod and to that, till the public posting service (at whose expense they travelled) threatened to succumb. Arians, semi-Arians, and Acacians found councils an unrivalled organisation for mischief; Homœan, or even Anomœan creeds, were put forth with reckless prodigality. From the time that Constantius became sole emperor, though the number of councils keeps pace with the number of years, not one supported orthodox Christianity. Constantius lived to see the work of subversion crowned with success, and orthodoxy virtually non-extant. He lived to see Athanasius a fugitive with a price upon his head, and to witness the Council of Ariminum at which, in the words of Jerome, 'the whole world groaned amazed to find itself Arian[4].' The fatal results of the policy adopted in Constantine's reign were making themselves manifest. In alleys and in the wilderness, out of sight of kings' palaces, the Church had thriven better than under shadow of the imperial upas-tree. The Emperor, surrounded by a greedy faction of Eusebian councillors, became semi-Arian by conviction. Thenceforth he acted sometimes as mouthpiece, sometimes as catspaw, of the Eusebians. His unreasoning arrogance suited him for either task. No hesitation or bashfulness hindered his usefulness. Ignorant, if not stupid, no problem awed him. His will, he said in open council of the Church, was as good as a canon[5]. He began to regard himself as above all human limitations, to style himself lord of the universe[6], to substitute for 'His

Constantius and Christian leaders.

Constantius' arrogance.

---

[1] Eudoxius at Constantinople. On taking the episcopal throne his first words were, 'The Father is ἀσεβής; the Son εὐσεβής.'

[2] Photinus.

[3] Cf. the rival councils of Sardica and Antioch.

[4] Ingemuit totus orbis, et Arianum se esse miratus est. In this paragraph the worst, *i.e.* the political, side of Arianism is depicted. There is no intention to prejudge controversial rights or wrongs.

[5] ὅπερ ἐγὼ βούλομαι τοῦτο κανών, ἔλεγε, νομιζέσθω.—Athan. *Hist. Ar. ad Mon.* i. 33, p. 732 c.

[6] Amm. Marc. xv. i. 3.

Majesty' a new title 'His Eternity,' and having scaled the heights of solitary pre-eminence to assert like dominion in Church as in State. In return for the aggrandisement and privileges he conferred upon the Church, he claimed a sole jurisdiction within it[1]: and the more worldly of the Church's members acquiesced without compunction in the nefarious bargain. By his *ipse dixit* he could banish the bishop[2] of bishops, the head of Christendom; he could starve a council[3] into submission, or roundly declare to recalcitrant orthodox bishops that he had determined to take the law into his own hands, and establish peace in the Church without their aid. His infallibility was more infallible than the Pope's own, for his decision was valid even when pronounced anything but *ex cathedra*. At the Council of Milan, having summoned the conclave from their proper place of meeting to his own imperial palace, he burst in upon the assembled bishops with the words[4], 'The doctrine you are combating is mine; if it is false, how comes it that all nations have been made subject to my power?' And once again, as the discussion waxed hot, he cried, 'Have I chosen you to be my counsellors, and shall my will be thwarted still?'

Such were the leaders who swayed the destinies of Church and State; such the court and such the Christianity beneath whose aegis Julian was nursed.

[1] De Broglie, *L'Église etc.* III. p. 363: 'Se croyant maître de l'Église, il lui convenait que l'Église, à son tour, fût maîtresse de tout. Il lui promettait la domination pour la consoler de la servitude.'
[2] Liberius.   [3] Sc. the Council at Ariminum.
[4] Luc. Cal. *pro Athan.* I. p. 834 D.

CHAPTER II.

JULIAN'S BOYHOOD, YOUTH, EDUCATION, AND CAESARSHIP.

> "This should have been a noble creature—he
> Hath all the energy which should have made
> A goodly frame of glorious elements
> Had they been wisely mingled."

It is not too much to say that Julian's personal motives, qualities and aims, all-decisive as they were in determining the character of the great reaction which history must always couple with his name, would remain a riddle, had no notices of his early years survived. The thoughts, training and experiences of Julian's boyhood and youth shed floods of light upon his subsequent career: they convert a historical surprise and crux into a consequent and little complicated narrative.

Among the earliest events indelibly impressed upon the memory of the imaginative child of six must have been those days of horror when he and his brother Gallus, hidden away in the obscure recesses of a church, listened in hushed terror to the tramp of soldiers and cries of bloodshed, watched the anxious faces of their protectors, the good Mark of Arethusa and his servants, and heard the whispered news passed from mouth to mouth of the death of those nearest and dearest to them. The sun of the sons of Constantine rose blood-red with the slaughter of their kin. Two uncles and four[1] cousins were the first-fruits of dominion offered up by

Julian's childhood.

---

[1] 'Seven,' writes M. Talbot in his *Étude sur Julien* p. v., misunderstanding (as appears in his subsequent translation), the passage in *Ep. ad Ath.* 270 c. The ἐξ ἀνεψιοί there spoken of *include* the two uncles and

him, whom the orphaned survivor might well call the butcher of his family[1]. These things remained to Julian the unutterable horrors of a tragedy which he shuddered to recall. In this indiscriminate and most unnatural carnage fell Julius Constantius, younger brother of the great Constantine and father to Julian. Alone of indirect branches of the Imperial house, his two sons survived the hideous massacre. If Constantius blamed fortune for having thus preserved them, he yet shrank from forthwith imbruing his hands yet more deeply in innocent blood. The oversight might be forgiven: the danger was not imminent. An emperor might spare awhile a child of six, and a boy of thirteen already, it was said, smitten with a deadly disease[2]. Thus Julian was saved. A mother's care he had never known, for the accomplished[3]

Julian's older brother; the Greek clearly runs ἐξ μὲν ἀνεψιούς......, ἐμὲ δὲ... Moreover there were not seven *cousins* of the Imperial stock left to murder.

The six ἀνεψιοί are:

(1) πατὴρ ἐμὸς, ἑαυτοῦ δὲ θεῖος, sc. Julius Constantius, father of Julian, and uncle to Constantius.

(2) ὁ πρὸς πατρὸς θεῖος not Dalmatius, but a second brother of Jul. Constantius, apparently named Constantine.

(3) ὁ πρεσβύτατος ἀδελφός of Julian, sc. an older son of Jul. Constantius and Galla: brother to Gallus, and half-brother to Julian. We do not elsewhere hear of him.

(4) (5) Dalmatius and Annibalianus, cousins alike to Constantius and to Julian.

The sixth remains uncertain. ? Constantine jun., son of the Constantine who was brother to Jul. Constantius. It was *not* Nepotianus, as Talbot says, for he survived till 350 A.D., when his feeble rivalry with Magnentius for the purple ended in his death. See *Appendix* A.

[1] Constantius' personal incrimination in these murders is habitually assumed, without very convincing proof. The chief witnesses against him are Athan. *Hist. Ar. ad Monach.* c. 69, p. 776 B, Jer. *Chron.*, Zos. II. 40, p. 106, as well as Julian himself *ad Ath.* 270. Sokr. III. 1, Eutrop. x. 9 and Aur. Victor imply a minor degree of guilt, allowing but not inciting to murder. Greg. Naz. *Or.* IV. xxi. p. 550 B, makes Constantius Julian's Saviour. For the sequence of events cf. de Brog. *L'Église &c.* III. p. 10 n. as against Tillemont, *Hist. des Emp.* IV. 313 pp.; see infr. p. 43 note.

[2] Soz. v. ii. 9.

[3] Of Basilina we know but little. Amm. Marc. xxv. iii. 23 mentions her noble lineage. Julianus, the praetorian prefect, was her father. According to Amm. M. xxii. ix. 4 she was distantly connected with Eusebius, the Arian Bishop of Nikomedia. Of her brother Julianus, *Comes Orientis* under

Basilina had survived but a few months the birth of her first-born. But the child promised to inherit something of his mother's fondness for the poems and masterpieces of ancient Greece. At least he drank in with avidity such Homeric or Hesiodic or philosophical lore as the family eunuch Mardonius, his precise and old-fashioned pedagogue, was pleased to instil. The child's eager teachableness must have often recalled even to the harsh eunuch reminiscences of the mother whom he had led along the same paths. To Eusebius, the Arian bishop of Nikomedia, it was entrusted to bring up the child, with whom on the mother's side he was distantly connected, in the way of the imperial religion[1]. About his religious education neither Julian himself nor his biographers enter into detail. He no doubt passed through the regular stages incident at that age to the Christian catechumen and neophyte—was counted among 'the purified,' 'the illuminated,' and 'the perfected' in orderly succession—received the seal of baptism—participated in the Eucharist—was instructed in the services of the Church, and initiated into the highest mysteries of faith and dogma[2]. The old culture and the new faith were each to mould his intellectual and moral growth: from the poison of Paganism he was to be guarded inviolate. For six years or more he was nurtured thus, in the society of tutors and grown-up folk alone. With no father's or mother's love to win his confidence, cut off from home affections, separate from other children, he enjoyed none of those bright sunny influences which are most essential to the free development of all child-nature. Mardonius, whatever his moral worth, was at least no congenial companion for a quick and susceptible child. He was Scythian-born, and rough in manner[3]. A eunuch moreover, well-advanced in years and

Julian under Mardonius.

Mis. 352 B

Mis. 352 A

Julian till his sudden death in 363, we know little good. For Basilina's study of the Classics and for her premature death, Julian himself is our witness, *Misop.* 352 B.

[1] Greg. Naz. *Or.* IV. 552 A.

[2] E. Lamé elaborates on this with almost fanciful minuteness. It is odd that Mücke, *Julian's Leben und Schriften* p. 70, should so vehemently and pertinaciously argue that Julian was never baptized.

[3] *Misop.* 352. Julian does not omit to notice significantly the corre-

not free, we may conjecture, from the repellent aspect, and the dwarfed moral nature that characterised his unhappy class[1]. His virtue, if such he possessed, was of a severe, forbidding type: he mistook distant surliness for dignity, harsh insensibility for wise reserve[2]. He was a precisian and a martinet, and made his pupil's life one monotonous round. In going to school he must perforce walk always by the same road and keep his eyes fixed upon the ground: he must regard with philosophical or puritanical aversion the pantomime, the dance, the horse-race, everything indeed that to a Roman boy savoured at all of fun or excitement. If ever, as happened twice or thrice, he went to the theatre, it was by order, as a part of educational training: if the child's heart longed for a dance or a romp about the garden, he was drearily referred to the dancing of the Phaeacian lads, the piping of Phemius or Demodokus, the bowery isle of Kalypso or the garden of Alkinous, as far more delicious than the living reality. He was properly steeped in philosophy from Sokrates to Theophrastus[3]. Thus at the most critical time of life all his spontaneity and natural affectionateness of disposition was chilled and nipped. A remarkably beautiful character was strangely marred. Not only, like all children who are thrown much or entirely with their elders, did he become precocious in habits and thoughts. He was by nature a wistful dreamy child, full of strange reveries; from his earliest years he would be possessed by a strange elation of soul as he gazed upon the splendour of the sun, and would strive to meet his

Mis. 351 A B, 352 C.

Mis. 351 C D

Mis. 353 B, 359 C.

spondence of name between his pedagogue and the general who urged Xerxes to the invasion of Hellas. We can hardly be sure how much of real esteem and gratitude towards Mardonius lurks under the satirical tone adopted in the *Misopogon*: the passing notice in *Or*. VIII. 241 C, which seems best referred to Mardonius, is affectionate in tone. Liban. *Epitaph*. p. 525 calls him βέλτιστος σωφροσύνης φύλαξ, but what else could he say of him who made Julian a 'Hellene'? Mücke p. 6—10 takes the more unfavourable view and is pulled to pieces for it by Rode, p. 23 note.

[1] Cf. Amm. Marc. XIV. vi. 17; XVI. vii. 4, 8; XVIII. iv. 5, and v. 4.
[2] Καλῶν σεμνότητα τὴν ἀγροικίαν καὶ σωφροσύνην τὴν ἀναισθησίαν.—*Mis*. 351 C.
[3] His young days may forcibly remind the reader of passages in John Stuart Mill's *Autobiography*, Ch. I.

rays with unblenching eyes; or again under the pure firmament, a child-worshipper, would meditate upon the wonder of the stars till all thought of self, all sense of surrounding sights or sounds were swallowed up in yearning contemplation of the Gods[1]. This rich emotional nature was all forced in upon itself: there was no one to encourage his child-confidences, or guide them into true channels. Hard experience made him day by day increasingly and sadly worldly-wise: reserve, distrust, dissimulation became a second nature to him[2]. The dullest reader may feel touched at the sad self-conscious irony of the *Misopogon*, as Julian with ill-concealed bitterness traces his rough ungraciousness of manner, his severe unsympathising view of life to the training of that loveless childhood: almost against his will he tells us how the iron had entered into his soul, and to his last day rankled there. From self-recorded traits of boyhood, nay even from the letters of his manhood, considering what a training he had endured, we see how full he by nature was of tender brimming lovingness. He possessed to a singular degree the twofold power of attaching others to himself, and not less himself to others. If he came out of the ordeal so frank and loyal a friend, so thoughtful and sympathising a master, so grateful and humble a disciple, so fervent and self-forgetful a worshipper of all that he believed good and true, what might not a happier training have made him?

But fate gave no amends for past unkindness. At thirteen years of age, when in years he had but just passed from the child into the boy, but in thought and premature discretion was almost full-grown, Julian was removed from Constantinople[3] to a new home. The jealous suspicions of Constantius could not suffer any prince of the blood royal so near the

Julian at Macellum.

---

[1] *Or.* iv. 130 c d. 'Emptier declamation was never written,' says the remorseless Schlosser (*Jena. Zeit.* p. 126), and denies all the nobler motives accentuated by Neander and Herwerden.

[2] ἔθος, φασί, δευτέρη φύσις, *Misop.* 353 A, says J., speaking of his own education.

[3] It is possible that the death of Eusebius, his relative and mentor, in 342 A.D. (according to other authorities 341 A.D.), contributed to this. See *App.* D, *Note* 3.

seat of power. Julian and Gallus[1], hitherto designedly kept separate, were now together banished to the wilds of Cappadocia. Not that the royal chateau of Macellum[2] was in itself unpleasing. True it was far from the haunts of men: yet placed on a spreading plain skirted by woods that climb towards the snowy peaks of the Argæan range, its natural situation was lovely and picturesque enough: without were gardens and fountains ever flowing, while within doors the appointments were admirable, the fare and service princely.

ad Ath. 271 B But to Julian it was in his own words an oriental stateprison. It was heaven's help, not man's kindness, that brought him safely through. His sole gain was the society of his step-brother Gallus, itself a questionable advantage. Not only was Gallus several years his senior: in character as in looks he was a complete contrast to Julian. His rough untutored mind, his strong natural passions were the very reverse of Julian's refined intellectual taste, and gentle selfcontrolled demeanour. A Titus was linked to a Domitian[3]. And Gallus' natural violence and savagery were aggravated, not subdued by the treatment to which the two brothers *ad Ath. 271* were in common subjected. Immured like very prisoners, *C D* kept under secret espionage as well as open surveillance, cut off from every play-mate, every teacher, every servant even in whom they could repose confidence, they were forced to consort with slaves ever on the watch for an unguarded word or look. Suspicion was the very air they breathed, repression of each natural sentiment the alphabet of their moral training. Under such auspices they 'sucked the milk of godly doctrine'[4] from paid agents of the tyrant. Stinted of

---

[1] Gallus had been educated at Ephesus, on his ancestral property. Sok. III. i.

[2] Macellum was in the immediate neighbourhood of Mons Argaeus, (the modern *Argi* or *Arjish Dagh*), at whose foot lay Caesarea, previously Mazaca (cf. Amm. M. xx. ix. 1), the capital of the district. For accounts see Soz. v. ii. and Greg. Naz. *Or.* IV. 550 c.

[3] Tantum a temperatis moribus Iuliani differens fratris, quantum inter Vespasiani filios fuit Domitianum et Titum.—Amm. M. XIV. xi. 28.

[4] Theod. *E. H.* III. ii., and cf. Jul. *ad Ath.* 271 c with Soz. *H. E.* v. ii. and Greg. Naz. *Or.* IV. 551 A.

more liberal culture, the youthful princes were taught the Christian evidences, were trained to give alms, to observe fasts, to venerate and with their own hands rear the shrines of martyrs, and even to officiate themselves in the services of the Church.

Such was Julian's life from thirteen to nineteen[1], such his preparation for the more active existence on which he next entered. What was the character of his sentiments at this time? Endowed by nature with intellectual capacities of a high order, he was yet by no means the mere student or recluse. The blood of Constantius Chlorus ran in his veins. The course of his life testifies to the full the practical vigour, the ardent courage, the restless indefatigable craving for action that animated him. It was because all other channels were closed to him that Julian plunged with characteristic vigour into literary pursuits. Though devoid, as his works testify, of originality or of actual genius, he was possessed of a quick active intellect, and of receptive powers of the very first order. The grace of style, the abounding readiness of allusion, the variety of knowledge he displays, show with what diligence and with how great success he steeped himself in the productions of the greatest writers of Greece. But his intellectual labours are for our immediate purpose less material; it is rather his religious standpoint at this juncture that we must seek clearly to realise. *Julian's disposition.*

That Julian was a professing Christian there is no doubt. Not only was he intimately acquainted with the Bible, and a practised theologian versed in patristic lore; but in his outward life he attended divine service, observed fasts, practised scrupulously the regimen of ecclesiastical discipline, built shrines to the holy martyr Mamas, and performed subordinate clerical functions. All this however, it is manifest, proves nothing whatever as to his private convictions. Theodoret[2] states explicitly that '*fear of Constantius*' instigated these outward exhibitions of Christianity. Christian or no Christian, he must regulate his outward conduct as such. It was *Julian's religion.*

---

[1] See *App*, B. *Note* 3.
[2] Theod. III. ii. Cf. Jul. *Ep.* 42, 423 c.

a part of the yoke laid upon him. Christianity was one of the accomplishments he was to acquire. To demur, to object, to rebel might have cost him his life. He was too subjugated now, and what is more, too discreet to think for an instant of anything but passive submission. By this time too he had become too practised a dissimulant to betray himself by unguarded words or acts. Years later, even when joint-emperor, in an outlying province, surrounded by trusty legions, while in private practice and conviction he was a complete Pagan, to all outward seeming he remained a Christian. How much more then as a solitary, defenceless youth! Not that he had become as yet even at heart an open dissident, a pronounced unbeliever[1]; but rather that the religion, which he obediently accepted in externals, had laid no hold upon him inwardly, while his bias was to see and notice the objections and imperfections with which it was surrounded.

Feelings towards Constantius.
Such at least would seem *a priori* the probable state of the case, if we consider how Christianity presented itself to him. It came to him under royal stamp and warrant, as the religion of his oppressors. It was part of his discipline, a wise prison-rule, so to speak, that the most beneficent Constantius was pleased to lay upon him. His gentle cousin[2], who had made him an orphan, had butchered his kinsmen, had driven him into exile, had treated him as a slave, provided him now with a religion. Would Julian be very eager

---

[1] M. Lamé (*Julien l'Apostat*, p. 25, 26), who knows a vast deal of what Mardonius thought and said to his pupil, writes thus of Julian's *youth:* 'Julien sut que la création et la lutte primitive des éléments, qui ne sont qu'esquissés à grands traits dans la Genèse, se trouvent avec tous leurs détails dans Hésiode ; que le Dieu Éros, qui féconde le chaos et en fait sortir l'éther et le jour, est la parole de Dieu, disant que la lumière soit; que le règne de Cronos et l'invasion des maux par l'imprudence de Pandore correspondent à la chute de l'homme et à l'imprudence d'Ève ; que la mutilation d'Uranus et la naissance d'Aphrodite sont les détails du déluge &c. &c.' in the same style: but I see no traces of Julian having been so clever or 'advanced' as M. Lamé.

[2] ὁ φιλανθρωπότατος οὗτος βασιλεύς, writes Julian, in one of the bitterest passages of his manifesto to the Athenians. *Ep. ad Ath.* 270 c. Cf. ὁ καλὸς Κωνστάντιος, *ibid.* 273 B.

to accept it unquestioned? With his works before us it is no mere conjecture to say that the first instinct of Julian's youth was a terrifying awe and a shrinking abhorrence of Constantius[1]. He speaks of the λυκοφιλία he was forced to assume: says how he shunned the hated presence; and what efforts it cost him to lodge under the same roof with his father's murderer. It was well enough for courtier slaves to palaver of Constantius' past innocence, of his present regrets, his wish to make amends, his sense that his childlessness was a deserved judgment from on high[2], but Julian had facts to speak to him as well as servile mouths. The Emperor had first spoiled him of his kin, then stripped him anew of every friend, then robbed him of liberty itself, and should he in return accept without demur the boon of the religion that he offered? Fear, suspicion, resentment, hate, passions not less potent because assiduously masked, were all enlisted against, not for the religion of the tyrant. *Ep. 68.*

Nor could the religion commend itself by its own virtue. Christianity, it must never be forgotten, was set before Julian in the mangled imperfect form of Arianism. From his later writings, from the contemptuous scorn with which he almost invariably treats the teaching and even the name of Christ, it may safely be affirmed that the moral beauty of Christ's character and work had never captivated the imagination of the Apostate; and there is little wonder in this, considering how violently Arian was his training, and also how that heresy neglects and tends therefore to mar and deface the true personality of Christ. *Imperfect view of Christianity.*

But not only was this mutilated distortion of Christianity the aspect of it displayed to Julian; even this was propounded *Insincere Teachers.*

---

[1] Cf. the narrative in Zonar. XIII. x. p. 21.
[2] *Ep. ad Ath.* 271 A. B. As the passage is important in respect to Constantius' *direct* implication (cf. p. 36) in the murders of 337 A. D., it shall be quoted in full. μετεμέλησε γὰρ αὐτῷ, φασί, καὶ ἐδήχθη δεινῶς, ἀπαιδίαν τε ἐντεῦθεν νομίζει δυστυχεῖν, τά τε ἐς τοὺς πολεμίους τοὺς Πέρσας οὐκ εὐτυχῶς πράττειν ἐκ τούτων ὑπολαμβάνει.......ἔλεγον τοσαῦτα καὶ δὴ καὶ ἔπειθον ἡμᾶς, ὅτι τὰ μὲν ἀπατηθεὶς εἰργάσατο, τὰ δὲ βίᾳ καὶ ταραχαῖς εἴξας ἀτάκτου καὶ ταραχώδους στρατεύματος. Similarly in the First Panegyric of Constantius (*Or.* 1. 17 A), the blame is transferred to the agents, who transgressed the wishes or orders of Constantius.

by most unworthy advocates. There is no positive evidence that *one* sincere Christian was numbered among the young prince's tutors: such were not readily found, nor greatly patronised among the dependents of Constantius: certain it is that most of his teachers were either wholly careless, or else Pagans in disguise, as they openly became so soon as the court breezes blew that way. Julian is hardly to be blamed if he regarded with indifference or even concealed dislike an enforced religion propounded so imperfectly, and commended so disadvantageously.

Pagan Literature. On the other hand, what were his relations towards Paganism? Besides his day-dreams, his yearning reveries, his communings with a felt but unknown Deity, his foremost pleasure was his books. They distracted him from the miserable present: in Homer he could revel by the hour, forgetful of frets and troubles and perils looming in the distance; Plato was already perhaps his darling author; Aristotle's keen dialectics were familiar ground[1]. And in all these authors whom he loved the best, in the poets and historians, in the orators and philosophers of Greece there was one common property; they were believers in and teachers of a polytheistic creed. Compared with their garlands of everlasting flowers, the writings of divines and longdrawn discussions on dogma or Christian evidence seemed colourless and perfumeless indeed. Was it not a legitimate inference that the inspiration of each was drawn from the creed, and that the value of the creed might be in some measure determined by the efficacy of the inspiration? At this age, be it remembered, the Bible had not yet attained, the chosen Classics had not yet lost that common sanction of the wisest, which conferred on them something more than their inherent lustre. The critic and schoolman still handled the Bible with contempt. Like Mohammed claiming the Koran as his *true* miracle, Paganism could point to her Homeric scriptures, that 'Old Testament' which enlisted nay enforced the admiring reverence even of the disbeliever, and say 'These are the

---

[1] This literary appreciativeness was the prime difference, which made the identical training of the two brothers bear fruits so dissimilar.

seal of my Apostleship.' Julian must thus early have begun to feel, what in later life he continually reiterates, that the splendid afflatus of the old culture was the gift of the Gods whom it reverenced.

This growing bias towards Paganism could not but tend to develope. It was Julian's misfortune to be brought up on book-learning without the healthy corrective of practical observation. Cut off from his fellows, except a picked and unworthy few, he saw things from the student's point of view; he became what in great part he continued to be through life, a pedant. Defrauded of all opportunity of testing their practical influence upon men's lives, he judged creeds by their self-enuntiation or their literary results. No view of polytheism could have been more favourable. What he knew from personal observation of Christianity, what he witnessed of its moral power, was not encouraging: the man he most hated for his crimes was the man most loud in Christian profession; the paid satellites, who were his spies and tools, were one and all Christians. Of Paganism on the other hand he knew only, on the positive side, that it was the avowed creed of all those whose works he most cherished and admired, and still the living[1] faith of one-half the Roman Empire; on the negative, that it was the faith not only hated by those whom he hated, and suspected by those who suspected him, but also feared for its power by those who prohibited him contact with its more gifted exponents. Not that such thoughts as these were consciously present to Julian in a developed form: he had not yet formulated a theory; self-analysis and introspection had not proceeded thus far. Some Sokrates was needed with skilled

View of Paganism.

---

[1] The term may seem strong, but cf. Mücke, p. 33. 'Nicht lange nach Julian's Tode verschlangen die Hellenenverfolgungen nicht weniger Opfer als einst die der Christen und richteten sich sogar gegen das zarte weibliche Geschlecht. Gerade der Umstand, dass viele der edelsten Hellenen für ihre zwar falsche, aber doch aufrichtige Ueberzeugung den Märtyrertod starben, weil sie mit der väterlichen Religion nicht die einzige Grundlage ihres sittlichen Denkens und Handels verlieren wollten, beweist unwiderleglich, dass der Hellenismus, wenn auch unheilbar krank und dem sicheren Tod geweiht, doch noch *eine lebende*, wenn auch keine tröstende Macht war.' Such I imagine it appeared at this time to Julian.

maieutic art to bring them to the birth; but dormant they lay there, a self-sown seed ready to spring up under the first warmth of sympathy, or the dew of judicious instruction.

Bias towards Paganism.

That such was Julian's state of mind is quite confirmed[1] by such intimations as remain. 'From the first rudiments of boyhood,' writes Ammian[2], 'his bias was towards Paganism; little by little with growing years his devotion that way grew with him. In fear and trembling, yet as often as he was able, he meditated in secret on all that looked thitherward.' With his own lips he himself declares with what

Or. 4. 130 c d

strange fascination in those early days he gazed upon the sun and stars, so that wholly forsaken of earthly thoughts, he was possessed with the beauties of heaven, and, a beardless astrologer, entered into strange and sensible *rapport* with them, as he pondered then upon the Gods. There is yet another testimony, which though rejected by some as coming from hostile sources yet seems so natural as even to invite belief. In the training of catechumens it was an established practice to set the students rhetorical theses, which constantly took the form of apologetic defence or attack upon Christianity[3]. In such school-room exercises Julian[4], it is said, was prone to conduct the defence of Paganism with unseemly vigour and ingenuity against the less impartial Gallus. Here is a genuine representation in the concrete of exactly that state of mind which it has been the aim of these pages to depict, and in which he continued to hang balanced until the day came when he bade adieu to Macellum, and by Imperial permission repaired to Constantinople.

[1] The passage in *Ep.* 51 (to the Alexandrians) proves nothing as to the *sincerity* of Julian's Christianity. The statement does not amount to this, and is further made with a definite ulterior object in view. Remonstrating with the Alexandrians on their stupid and obstinate adherence to Christianity, and urging them to become Pagans, he says : 'Be sure you won't go wrong in taking my advice, seeing that for twenty years I was a follower of that sect, and have now for twelve years been a follower of the Gods.' οὐχ ἁμαρτήσεσθε τῆς ὀρθῆς ὁδοῦ πειθόμενοι τῷ πορευθέντι κἀκείνην τὴν ὁδὸν ἄχρις ἐτῶν εἴκοσι καὶ ταύτην ἤδη σὺν θεοῖς πορευομένῳ δωδέκατον ἔτος.

[2] Amm. M. xxii. v. 1.

[3] Compare J. H. Newman, *Arians of the Fourth Century*, p. 31, 32.

[4] Greg. Naz. *Or.* iv. 557 a.

The five years that followed the recall from Macellum were decisive of the part Julian was to play in life. They were passed in the prosecution of his studies, in the first instance at Constantinople. He received the training of an ordinary well-educated citizen: grammar he learnt of Nikokles[1]; his master in rhetoric was the sophist Hekebolius, a sort of Vicar of Bray of his times, who an Arian under Constantius, and a hot Pagan under Julian, pleaded abjectly in the succeeding reign for readmission into the Christian communion. In philosophical acquirements as in natural genius he had by this time outstripped his instructors[2]. Fairly beaten and baffled by the precocity of their pupil, his teachers had petitioned[3] Constantius, that their young charge might be permitted to attend others of the more famous seats of learning. More important than this was the fact that in the metropolis his merits were too much before the world. It was not safe to leave a prince of the blood, brother to a reigning Emperor, free to his own devices. He was imprudent enough to make friends amid fellow-students and teachers; unfortunate enough to attract the notice of citizens. Dangerous talk of his talents, his sociability, his fitness for Empire reached the Imperial ear. Constantius' suspicions took fire. He must leave Constantinople. Fondly hoping that literary zeal might foster political indifference and supplant dangerous aspirations, he ordered or permitted Julian to proceed to Nikomedia. There he was to remain under the eye of Hekebolius, and was solemnly pledged not to imperil his orthodoxy by attendance at the lecture-room of Libanius. Hekebolius cared little about the taint of Paganism[4]. Perhaps he imagined that it was the

Julian at Constantinople.

Æts. 351 A.

Julian at Nikomedia.

---

[1] Sok. III. 1.
[2] Eunapius, *Vit. Maximi*, p. 68.
[3] This story of Eusebius is fairly enough called in question by Rode, p. 29. It seems an unlikely enough display of generosity and humility on the part of J.'s teachers. Both Lib. *Epitaph*. and Sok. III. i. give only the second ground here alleged, viz. that of an imperial order, and that beyond a doubt was the deciding reason. Still Eunapius' account is just possible, and may remain in the text 'suspect.'
[4] Liban. *Epit*. p. 527, asserts that the oath was exacted really by Hekebolius,

personal influence of Libanius that alone need be feared. Be that as it may, Julian, though keeping the letter of his oath, was enabled day by day to peruse the lectures that he was forbidden in person to attend. He devoured them voraciously; he made them the model of his style. They fell in with his half-formed prepossessions. Predisposed to Hellenism alike by his philosophical and literary studies, and by the estimate of Christianity which personal experience had taught him, Julian responded to the advances made to him by the leaders of the Neo-Platonist movement. They had not only arguments, and scoffs, and polite contempt for the Christian 'superstition,' but were also men of real culture, and not less of insight into character. They showed him sympathy, such as he had never before received: treated him with a kindness and deferential courtesy hitherto unknown to him: stimulated his industry, praised his acquirements, flattered his genius, entered into his difficulties. Their hazy cloud castles of mystic yearning and promise and hope, fabrics wrapped in visionary splendours, fascinated wistful longings nursed by the Phaedrus and the Republic; they chimed with

Contact with Neo-Platonists.

> those obstinate questionings
> of sense and outward things,
> fallings from us, vanishings;
> blank misgivings of a Creature
> moving about in worlds not realised,

of which his religious sentiment rather than conviction had consisted. He drank in the new Gospel. He was soon a convert to its creed.

Julian's Apostasy.

For to this period beyond all cavil his definite perversion to Paganism must be referred. Whatever his previous misgivings or self-questionings, he had not definitely renounced Christianity before his arrival in Nikomedia in 351. Under more favourable auspices he might yet have been won for the Church. Had he for instance chosen Alexandria as his school,

---

who was jealously afraid of his rival's attractive powers. This is clearly inconsistent with the idea of his having magnanimously petitioned in Julian's favour. Probably he exacted the oath by imperial command.

and fallen under the influence of an Athanasius, it is curious to think what a transposition of his whole subsequent career might have resulted. The testimonies here are decisive. Not only does Sozomen single this out as the period of his conversion, and Libanius speak of him as at this time bridling his virulent hate against the gods, and, tamed by divinations, breaking loose like a lion from the chains which fastened him, but Julian himself designates his twentieth year as that in which he began first 'to walk with the gods[1].' For the young man of twenty—for Julian as for many another—the impressions now received, the emotions now awakened were to mould his entire future. To himself he seemed issuing out of darkness into day: 'let the time of that darkness be forgotten,' he writes, speaking of the years immediately preceding this period. Light was streaming in upon his soul, chasing away the shadows that had rested there and illuminating the heights that lay before him. He was not yet wholly satisfied: his soul still panted *Excelsior!*: the old cravings after a goal still unattained spurred him on. His shrewd teachers perceived them, and forged them into chains that bound him fast. By wise reticence, by suppressed allusions, by mystical hints and inuendoes, they taught the neophyte to believe that there were new glories, unknown ecstasies, more transcendent revelations awaiting the initiated believer. The fame of Aedesius attracted him to Pergamus. With all the gravity of age but all the enthusiasm of youth, Julian sat at the old man's feet drinking in breathless and open-mouthed the master's wisdom[2]. Pressed to reveal those higher esoteric mysteries[3] to which from time to time he would refer, the old man answered, 'Thou knowest all my heart, thou hast heard all my instruction; thou seest with thine eyes how feeble is this outward tenement of soul, and its frame nigh to dissolution. If thou wouldst do aught, loved child of wisdom, get thee to mine own true-born sons, and there take thy fill of the

Aedesius.

---

[1] Soz. v. 2; Liban. *Epit.* p. 528, *Prosphon.* 408; Jul. *Ep.* 51, 434 D.
[2] Eunap. *Vit. Maximi*, p. 86—90.
[3] Liban. *Prosph.* 409. *Epit.* 528 dwells on the impression first produced on Julian by oracles and the various arts of divination.

sweet juices of all wisdom and instruction: if thou participatest in those holy mysteries, thou wilt verily blush to have borne the nature and name of man. Would that Maximus or Priscus were here present! But of my friends, Eusebius and Chrysanthius alone are left here. Take heed unto them and have compassion on my age.' Thus he was transferred to the teaching of Eusebius and Chrysanthius. At the close of elaborate philosophical discourses, Eusebius would utter obscure warnings against impostures that delude and mock the senses, magicians' acts, cheating and materialising men's conceptions by pretended miracles. On one such occasion Julian took Chrysanthius aside, and asked him to expound the meaning of such epilogues. Affecting a profound gravity he sagely replied, 'You will do well not to learn of me, but of their author;' in accordance with which advice he consulted Eusebius directly. After some fencing Eusebius, pressed hard by Julian's pertinacious curiosity, and finding him at length fairly in the net, told him of one Maximus, among the oldest and most honoured of their teachers, who with the magnificent boldness of genius, despising sober logical demonstration, applied himself to these fool's manifestations. He then went on to say how Maximus had one day summoned them to the temple of Hecate; and how, after he had adored the goddess and burned incense and chanted a hymn, the statue of the goddess, as they sat there, smiled visibly upon him, and the torches in her hands took fire. At this recital, continues the narrator, the divine Julian bade him farewell and stick to his books; 'for you have shewn me the man I was looking for.' So saying, he kissed Chrysanthius and set off with speed for Ephesus[1].

Maximus. The story, even if its literal correctness is questioned[2], is full of instruction and significance. It is a true picture of

---

[1] According to Sok. III. 1, whom Niceph. x. 1 follows, Maximus came to Nikomedia to proselytize Julian; his statement arises perhaps from careless reading of Liban. *ad Jul. Hyp.* p. 376. In Liban. *Prosph.* p. 408, Ionia is given quite correctly. Teuffel p. 151 is hasty in imputing the opposite version merely to Eunapius' desire to flatter his sophist.

[2] As it is, forcibly enough, by Teuffel p. 151. Neander, *Church Hist.* III. p. 54 *note*, and Naville p. 53, use much the same language as the text.

the restless agitation, the yet unsatisfied cravings that were driving him forward at all hazards, the constant pursuit of a higher truth, a completer revelation than any as yet vouchsafed him. It betrays at once the ardour and the weakness that characterised him: he was full of excitable impetuosity, and not less of a wistful superstition. He possessed a temperament dissatisfied yet sanguine, a mind docilely receptive[1] yet ardently inquisitive, a nature emotional rather than strong, imaginative and sensuous rather than calmly philosophical or patiently devotional. Maximus was a teacher well suited to such a pupil. To a venerable hoary beard, a quick searching eye, a rich harmonious intonation worthy of an Athene or Apollo, he united a commanding eloquence and a prophetic earnestness, that seem to have enforced assent, enchaining his hearers with a kind of awe. 'The hidden spark of divination' of which Libanius[2] speaks, was quickly nursed into flame. Julian became, what he remained through life, his devoted adherent. After due probation he was solemnly initiated in the temple of Artemis[3]. To the accompaniment of weird chants and unholy rites, amid awful apparitions of demons and spirits of the departed, with every accessory suited to impress the imagination and stifle calm deliberation, Julian was admitted to the new faith. He was disinfected from the pollution of Christianity[4]: the taint of baptism was washed off with the warm blood of a slaughtered bull sprinkled on his head[5]. From this time forth his conversion to Paganism was complete. The hopes of the party centred in him. He was in active correspondence or personal contact with the leading Neo-Platonists of Greece and Asia. His change of creed was not of course outwardly professed.

Julian turns Neo-Platonist.

[1] Thus we do not find Julian originating one new fragment of philosophy, or even without hesitation propounding a new allegorical interpretation.
[2] *Prosphon.* p. 408.
[3] M. Lamé, *Jul. l'Apost.* c. III., has brilliantly but fancifully worked up the events of successive days with the preparations, the surroundings, the words, looks, gestures and feelings of the principal actors into an elaborate bit of historical romance.
[4] Lib. *Epitaph.* 528.
[5] De Broglie (*L'Église, &c.*, IV. p. 100) and others refer the event to the time of his pronounced apostasy in Gaul.

4—2

The lion was unshackled, but had yet a while, says Libanius[1], to wear the ass's skin. No sooner did whispers of his apostasy, of at least undue familiarity with Pagan teachers, begin to circulate[2], than Julian shaved close, wore the tonsure, observed saints' days, assiduously read the Scriptures in public, and adopted the outward demeanour of a monk[3]. But in private he indulged in Pagan practices and mystic rites.

Julian's conversion.

The rapidity and the completeness of Julian's conversion demand neither surprise nor blame. Christianity was presented to him for perfunctory acceptance, not only in a maimed, disfigured shape, not only as the religion of his enemies, but also by wretchedly unworthy exponents. With Paganism his fortune was just opposite. Hellenism, wooing him in its most finished and becoming dress, courted his spontaneous acceptance, not only as the religion of new-found friends, but also as introduced to him by most worthy advocates. Not an Aedesius merely or Maximus 'the soul-physician[4],' but Libanius greatest of the sophists, Iamblichus the most divine[5], Themistius prince of orators[6], Proaeresius king of eloquence[7], such were the men through whom Julian learned Paganism. In the fact of his conversion[8] there was nothing unnatural nor ignoble, rather the reverse: it calls

---

[1] *Epitaph.* p. 528, cf. Greg. Naz. *Or.* iv. c. 79, p. 605 A.

[2] Amm. M. xxii. v. 1. To this period is attributed the epistle of Gallus to Julian, which, alluding to the sinister rumours afloat, adjures Julian to hold fast the memory of the martyrs and not forsake the religion of his fathers. Its authenticity is doubtful. For Gallus' communications with Julian cf. Philost. *E. H.* iii. 27.

[3] Soz. v. 2. Sok. iii. 1. Gallus, *Ep. ad Jul.*

[4] Liban. *ad Jul. Hyp.* p. 376.

[5] This Iamblichus is not the well-known Neo-Platonist philosopher, author of *De Vit. Pythag.*, &c., for he died earlier in the century: but Julian applies to him, *Ep.* 27. 401 B, the θεῖος—indeed θειότατος—which, with δαιμόνιος, was the characteristic epithet of Iamblichus the elder. Cf. *Or.* 4. 157 C D, *Or.* 6. 188 B, *Or.* 7. 222 B, &c.

[6] Gregory of Nazianzus calls Themistius 'the prince of orators.'

[7] Cf. the inscription upon his commemorative statue at Athens, "THE QUEEN OF CITIES TO THE KING OF ELOQUENCE."

[8] Herwerden *De Jul. Imp.* 12 pp. summarises very well the influences internal and external brought to bear.

for pity, not for condemnation; it is the permanence of it rather, when but for prejudice and pride and bigotry a better judgment might have been formed, that awakes regret. It proved too late to retrace his steps, when superstition, and pride of consistency, and intellectual self-sufficiency, and long-protracted pain of enforced disingenuousness, all barred the way.

If anything was yet lacking to confirm Julian in his adherence to Paganism, and alienation from Christianity, Constantius was careful to supply the want. Julian had still one relative in the world, cousin at once and brother-in-law[1] to the Emperor. His hour was now come to be brought to 'The Butcher.' Gallus, who had hitherto disregarded Constantius' threats and evaded his orders, was now enticed by soft promises to leave his Eastern province and visit the Emperor in person. At first he journeyed with the state befitting a Caesar; one by one, as the toils closed faster round him, the marks of homage were withdrawn; from Constantinople he was hurried away by imperial order: at Petobio (Pettau) creatures of the Emperor put him under arrest, stripped him of the purple, dressed him in common clothes, bade him 'Get up at once,' and so drove him in a post-chaise to Pola. The place[2] was ominous: the blood of Crispus still cried from its prison walls. It was destined to witness yet another Caesar's death, falling victim to his kinsman's jealousy. Gallus was spared the mockery of a trial. His hands tied behind him, he was dragged like a common felon to the block. Even the decency of burial was denied to the mutilated trunk[3].

Death of Gallus.

---

[1] Gallus and Constantius were connected as brothers-in-law by a double tie. An elder sister of Gallus had been Constantius' first wife, previous to his marriage with Eusebia: while Gallus had espoused Constantina, sister to the Emperor, and relict of the murdered Annibalianus (cf. *Ep. ad Ath.* 272 D). See *Genealogical Tables*, Appendix A.

[2] 'Near Pola,' says Amm. M. xiv. xi. 20, while Sok. ii. xxxiv. 4 and Soz. iv. vii. 7 designate the site of the murder as Flanona or Flavona, an island of Dalmatia; it is at no great distance from Pola.

[3] In connexion with the murders that inaugurated the accession of the sons of Constantine, Dr Auer had already written (*Kaiser Jul. &c.* p. 4), "Gallus and Julian had one fault; they could not forget, though

Julian summoned to Court.

Scarcely had the news of his brother's murder reached Julian, when he too received the mandate to repair from the quiet retreats of Ionia 'to visit the Emperor in person.' There had risen in Constantius' mind a doubt whether the Imperial consent had been formally attached to his departure from Macellum[1]. It was an authenticated fact that only three years before the young prince-student had had an interview with his brother on his royal progress eastward *ad Ath. 273 A* through Nikomedia[2]. Letters had passed at intervals between them. Besides there was an *a priori* probability that he was a co-conspirator. It was certain at least that he was connected by blood with the Emperor himself, and was now the sole offender who had not expiated by death that crime. *Ep. 68.* 'The wolf' thought well to be his watch-dog.

Julian at Court.

ad Ath. 272 D

Treated like a prisoner, dragged backwards and forwards between Milan and Comum, in daily terror of his life, forced to guard every word and look, he learned bitterly enough that 'it was better for him to entrust the care of his life to the gods than to the word of Constantius[3].' Possessed with deep-seated hatred for the murderer, for whom he was forced to simulate affection and loyal respect, he transferred no doubt some portion of that hate to the religion he so loudly professed. 'How often,' says an eloquent writer[4], 'as he

---

Constantius would gladly have drawn a veil over the past:" but it required some impudence to add concerning the death of Gallus, (p. 38) "Julian had no call to complain." To an ordinary reader the grounds alleged in *Ep. ad Ath.* 272 are not wholly trivial or unreasonable.

[1] Rode, p. 85, adopting Sievers' suggestion, *Studien &c.*, p. 228, supposes Ammian to have confused the departure from Nikomedia with that from Macellum, thinking the charge as it stands too ridiculously unsubstantial. If however it was Gallus' entreaties had extorted a tacit assent, the Emperor may have scouted a plot in fraternal good feeling.

[2] Amm. M. xv. ii. 7 places the interview at Constantinople, but is clearly outweighed by the authority of Libanius (cf. *Epit.* p. 527), a resident at the place, whose statement Sok. III. 1 corroborates.

[3] The words actually occur at a later crisis, cf. Zosim. III. 9; but in *Ep. ad Ath.* 273 A, Julian attributes his preservation from Constantius' violence to the direct intervention of the gods. Significantly enough, in the letter referred to this is the first crisis of his life where he acknowledges their direct guidance.

[4] De Broglie, *L'Église &c.*, III. p. 281.

raised his eyes to heaven, must he have seen, rearing itself between him and the God of Constantius, the bloody image of a father he had never known, and a brother that he dared not mourn.' 'His Eternity' had just reached the climax of arrogant self-sufficiency. He had cashiered[1] a fourth Caesar. Persia for the nonce was quiet. Emperor of Emperors he aspired too to be counted Bishop of Bishops. With a brutal candour he asserted his lordship in Church as well as in State, in doctrine no less than in discipline[2]. His civil supremacy he regarded as the proof and the measure of his religious orthodoxy. Arianism was demonstrably orthodox, if Constantius was Arian. *L'église c'est moi* was the position to which he committed himself. To assert it he browbeat or bribed, menaced or cajoled, imprisoned or exiled, tortured or deposed refractory bishops, as seemed best. No prestige of office could protect Liberius from Thracian exile, no extremity of venerable age deliver Hosius from the rack.

But it was not only a personal antipathy to Constantius, not only Constantius' own unworthiness[3], or his supercilious domineering over the Christian commonwealth, that finally discredited Christianity in the eyes of Julian. These things only corroborated or accorded with results to which personal observation must have led him. The Christians with whom he chiefly came in contact during his residence at the court of Milan were beyond a doubt the Arian bishops who clung about the throne. They justified the bitter taunt of Liberius,

[1] sc. Gallus. The first three alluded to are Magnentius, Vetranion and Nepotianus. For the titles assumed by Constantius, see Amm. M. xv. i. 3.

[2] For Constantius' behaviour at the Council of Milan, see pp. 33, 34: cf. also De Broglie's graphic narrative in *L'Église &c.*, III. 258 pp.

[3] The colours in which this Emperor appears in these pages are undeniably dark. The apologist of Constantius must draw his materials from almost any quarter sooner than his connexion with Julian or his administration of Church matters. Throughout the two long elaborate panegyrics which Julian has left us, he was unable to record a single personal favour conferred on him by Constantius, with the exception of the elevation to the Caesarship. Even this solitary boon was accorded under pressure of imminent external dangers (Julian's irony in *Or.* I. 45 A B, as compared with *ad Ath.* 278 and the like is quite audaciously broad), and only after prolonged vacillation had finally persuaded Constantius that it would be *more politic* to robe Julian in the purple than to assassinate him.

by which he bade the Emperor remember that bishops were not created to avenge his wrongs[1]. It so chanced that the council of Milan synchronised with Julian's stay in the place. It is needless to dwell in detail on the scenes of quarrelsome turbulence, or on individual cases of duplicity that marked the hey-day of ascendant Arianism, when a Valens and Ursacius swayed the helm of council, when honest men turned cowards, and wise men traitors, when prelatical violence and rancour and self-seeking drowned or gagged the voices of the solitary spokesmen of truth, and the blindness or timidity of her less unworthy leaders jeoparded well-nigh the existence of the Church of Christ. With what disdainful scorn must Julian in his hours of privacy have cast aside that mask of religion[2] which he was forced to wear, and turned from the present to dream of Hellas, 'home of the Muses'! Almost at the very hour[3] that he was joyfully turning his back on the palace to journey towards his mother's hearth[4], another illustrious exile also set his face north-

---

[1] Theod. II. xvi. 22, with which compare Athan. *Hist. Ar. ad Mon.* c. 37 &c.

[2] In the First Panegyric on Constantius—which, though dating from a somewhat later period, viz. Nov. 355 A.D., represents to us Julian as still fettered at the court—we are surprised at the most meagre recognition accorded to Christianity. Of Constantius' religious policy there is not one syllable. The expressions used to designate the Deity are barely neutral. If historic truth prompted Julian to speak of Maximian Hercules and Constantine Chlorus as worshipping 'The Higher Nature' only (τὴν κρείττονα φύσιν, 7 B), he might have found some more decisively Christian phrase than ' the deity bringing to happy fulfilment his destined end' (τὴν εἱμαρμένην τελευτὴν τοῦ δαίμονος μάλα ὀλβίαν παρασχόντος, 16 c) to describe the death of Constantine the Great. The 'All-good Providence' is another paraphrase he employs for God: while Rome he describes (29 D) as ' the hill-top, where is enshrined the image of Jupiter.' The text seems to have undergone subsequent revision.

[3] Newman, *Arians &c.*, postpones the exile of Liberius till 356. But the council of Milan sat at the very beginning of 355, and the proceedings against Liberius followed immediately. The expression in the text is that used by De Broglie, III. p. 272.

[4] ὡς οὖν ἀποφυγὼν ἐκεῖθεν ἄσμενος ἐπορευόμην ἐπὶ τὴν τῆς μητρὸς ἑστίαν. *Ep. ad Ath.* 273 B. In *Or.* III. 118 B, Ionia seems designated by οἴκαδε, though Athens eventually became his destination. Cf. also *Ad Them.* 260 A, ἀπιὼν δὲ ἐπὶ τὴν Ἑλλάδα πάλιν......, οὐχ ὡς ἐν ἑορτῇ τῇ μεγίστῃ τὴν τύχην ἐπαινῶν

wards, Liberius, chief bishop of the west, wending his way to weary exile in Thrace, because he declined to condemn a brother bishop unheard!

Thus we may consider that on Julian's arrival at Athens in the year 355 his prior alienation from Christianity had changed into positive aversion. The death of Gallus, the private and public bearing of Constantius, and the condition of official Christianity had riveted irrevocably the sentiments which Julian had derived from Macellum, from Nikomedia, and from Ephesus. At Athens he appears to have been initiated[1] into the Eleusinian mysteries. Outward repression and self-constraint only made his inward excitement more uncontrollable. The strange excited manner[2], the restless gait, the twitching shoulders, the dilated rolling eye, the distended nostril, attracted the notice even of his masters and fellow-students. At times he would fall into reveries, and so with nodding head and swaying steps, pass through the streets half-distraught. Then with a sudden jerk, or a harsh peal of laughter, would turn upon his companion with some strangely abrupt interrogation. Never, not in the first moments of elevation to the Caesarship, not in the perils of his Gallic wars, not in the sole possession of sovereign power, can life have been more intense to him than now. In the immemorial courts of Athens those convictions were finally matured which have given its permanent significance to Julian's life. There he moved amid the most intellectual circles, and though of royal blood proved not unable to hold his own with the bravest in the peaceful combats of the schools. Amid students of no common calibre, such for instance as the young Cappadocians, Basil and Gregory, he shone by his own

Julian at Athens.

ἡδίστην ἔφην εἶναι τὴν ἀμοιβὴν ἐμοὶ καὶ τὸ δὴ λεγόμενον

χρύσεα χαλκείων, ἑκατόμβοι' ἐννεαβοίων

ἔφην ἀντηλλάχθαι; compare *App. B. note* 4.

[1] For initiation Eunap. *Vit. Max.*, Theod. III. 3, Greg. Naz. *Or.* IV. c. 55 576 D, cf. *Or.* VII. 231 D, Soz. V. 2. Here again, though the historicity of the bare fact might well be disputed, Lamé 80 pp. revels in romancing every detail.

[2] Greg. Naz. *Or.* V. c. 23, p. 692 D.

merit. Needless to say that by professors and rhetoricians of the Pagan interest—though indeed, as Libanius[1] assures us, he was to be counted among teachers rather than taught—he was at once instructed and caressed: but the true history of his University life survives solidified in the thoughts, the writings, and the policy of maturer manhood.

Julian's mission.

To this same period we must refer the rise of another feeling that laid strong hold upon Julian. He became impressed with the sense of a mission[2]. He began to regard himself as the special instrument of the gods to fulfil the predestined restoration of Hellenism. Vague prophecies were current pointing to the imminent fall of Christianity; 'Peter,' said one heathen oracle, 'had by magic secured worship to Christ for three hundred and sixty five years; but thereafter his kingdom should fall[3].' Dreams of a Pagan Messiah floated through men's minds. Already the fabric of Christianity, triumphant externally, began to crumble from within. A seeming renaissance of Hellenism had set in. Julian, suggested far-sighted philosophers, and with growing buoyancy his own heart whispered the same hopes, alike by position and by actual gifts was the elect of heaven to consummate the change[4]. Such half-formed aspirations chimed admirably with his imaginative nature. His mind, like Constantine the Great's, was so tempered, that while he yielded willingly to superstition, he found in it rather a strength than a weakness. Julian could believe in a fortunate star, could credulously attribute each happy chance, each trivial success, which was due clearly to his own foresight, to the direct interposition of the gods on his behalf; while at the same time he was never frightened by childish omens, or cowed by superstitious fears from boldly facing and resolutely carrying out enterprises that demanded all

---

[1] *Epitaph.* p. 532, cf. Zos. III. 2, p. 123.

[2] It is to this stage that Theod. III. 3 refers Julian's first aspirations after empire, his consultation of oracles, and evocation of devils. With this Liban. *Epit.* pp. 529, 565 fully agree.

[3] Cf. Augustin, *De Civ. Dei* XVIII. 53.

[4] Henrik Ibsen, in his elaborate, but in details very unhistorical drama, *The Emperor and the Galilean*, draws this out powerfully.

his hardihood and natural resource. It was at this time[1] that he began to recognise the divine hand in each incident of his career; to hear voices or dream dreams, which he reverenced as supernatural monitors: to see in himself the favoured knight of Hermes and Athene. In his own language, from the day that he left Athens, the goddess was everywhere his guide, and compassed him about with guardian angels, assigned to him from the Sun and Moon. These things were signs of a growing self-confidence[2], presages of powers that as yet lay undeveloped, and indeed unsuspected, under the gauche exterior of the unprincely student. *ad Ath. 275 B*

It does not fall within the scope of this essay to follow Julian on his return from Athens to court, to unravel the court cabals and the Imperial hopes and fears which resulted in Julian's solemn investiture with the Caesarship and his espousal of Helena, sister to the Emperor. Nor are we concerned with the marches and counter-marches, that in three brilliant campaigns reduced Gaul and the Rhine provinces to entire submission to the young Caesar, and left him free to devote his whole attention to administrative and economical reform in the provinces entrusted to him. He had set out under the ignoble espionage of his own officers[3], restricted in all his powers, thwarted at every turn by privy conspiracies and opposition, with a school-boy's manual[4] in his pocket regulating his powers, his money allowance, his very diet, a lay-figure dressed in purple to scare barbarians with the terror of a name, a sort of shadow apparition king, wearing 'on his brow the round and top of sovereignty' and nothing more[5]. In three short years his native force, his industry, *Julian as Caesar.*

---

[1] Cf. particularly *Ep. ad Ath.* 273 A, and the narrative *ibid.* 275 B sqq. The allegory of *Or.* VII., large selections from which are given later (Chap. VI.), corroborates the text.

[2] For his previous timorous self-distrust, see *ad Them.* 253 A D.

[3] *ad Ath.* 281 D sqq.   [4] Amm. M. XVI. v. 3.

[5] *Ep. ad Ath.* 278, ἐπιτρέπει μοι βαδίζειν εἰς τὰ στρατόπεδα τὸ σχῆμα καὶ τὴν εἰκόνα περιοίσοντι τὴν ἑαυτοῦ· καὶ γάρ τοι καὶ τοῦτο εἴρητο καὶ ἐγέγραπτο, ὅτι τοῖς Γάλλοις οὐ βασιλέα δίδωσιν, ἀλλὰ τὸν τὴν ἑαυτοῦ πρὸς ἐκείνους εἰκόνα κομιοῦντα.

and his tenacity of purpose, had secured him a commanding ascendancy. His state of mind remained such as has been already described, though growing years and a career of almost unchequered success deepened no doubt his previous religious convictions. In life and belief a Pagan, in outward act a somewhat unpronounced Christian[1], he adopted a policy consonant with his ambiguous position. With, or more probably without his consent, his name was appended by Constantius to a law declaring it a capital offence to adore or sacrifice to idols. He interfered as little as possible with religious parties or disputes of any kind. Political necessities required perhaps his formal acquiescence in the banishment of Hilary, the young Bishop of Poitiers, from Gaul[2]. But this was an isolated act, the omission of which must have alarmed the suspicions of Constantius and fanned his growing jealousy. Julian was too astute to provoke collision or give a handle to opponents by open professions of Paganism. He satisfied the requirements of imperial orthodoxy. Even after his army had by acclaim declared him worthy of the supreme dignity of empire, when open war was imminent, if not proclaimed, between him and Con-

---

[1] The second Panegyric on Constantius, generally assigned to the year 357 A.D., startles us by its unmistakeable renunciation of Christianity. The religious element introduced is Hellenistic to the core. Homer and Plato are the authoritative exponents of morality and of the relations existing between soul and body, God and man (cf. pp. 68—70, 79, 82—84, &c.). Heathen myths are parabolic representations of truth. The Emperor is said to be a kind of priest or prophet (68 B). Besides the more general teaching and tone, we find the distinctively Pagan expression 'the king of the gods' (τῶν θεῶν τὸν βασιλέα, 90 A, cf. sqq.), while the disappearance of the traitor Marcellinus at the battle of Mursa is accounted for as the work of some god or demon (ὑπό του θεῶν ἢ δαιμόνων κρυφθείς, 59 B). The ideal prince (Constantius) must be οὐκ ὀλίγωρος θεραπείας θεῶν (86 A). We are almost forced to infer that the original writing was recast by Julian or some editor's hand (De Brog. IV. 24 n.). Mücke p. 161 prefers to assign a later date to the original publication (see Chronol. Tables in App. B). The heathenism of Or. VIII. 'Consolatory Reflections on the departure of Sallust,' written early in 358 A.D., is more chastened—θεός for instance appears throughout in the singular—but there too the court of spiritual and theological appeal is Homer.

[2] De Broglie, L'Église, &c., III. 362.

stantius, the young Augustus was still to be found wearing the ass' skin, and participating in Christian rites at Epiphany-tide in the church of Vienne¹. It was on the march to meet Constantius that he publicly abjured Christianity, took the title of Pontifex², and conducted sacrifice in Pagan temples³. Even then deference to the feelings of not a few of his soldiers led him to temporise in some points⁴. But from Illyria he can write joyfully to his foster-father in philosophy: 'We worship the gods publicly; the whole army which is following my fortunes are devout believers: we openly sacrifice oxen: with many a hecatomb we render thank-offerings to the gods.' He issued to all true Greeks his Pagan manifesto⁵. Confident in his mission, fortified by assurance of divine favour and looking for 'great fruit of labour,' amid the plaudits of men and with heaven's smile, he set his face eastward to regenerate a misguided world and by the gods' behest 'to make all things pure.' *Ep. 38.*

ib.

ib.

---

¹ Amm. M. xxi. ii. 5. Zon. xiii. xi. p. 22 says Christmas. ² Sok. iii. 1.
³ *e. g.* to Bellona, Amm. M. xxi. v. 1. Cf. Jul. *ad Ath.* 286 D.
⁴ Zonar. xiii. xi. p. 22.
⁵ The so-called *Epistola ad S. P. Q. Atheniensem*, which Zos. iii. 10 informs us was despatched to the Lacedaemonians, Corinthians and Athenians.

CHAPTER III.

NEO-PLATONISM.

Religion under the Empire. So far as concerns pagan religion and philosophy, the centuries preceding Julian have been depicted in the Introduction to this Essay as a time of exposure and disintegration. Along with the gradual extinction of patriotism under the incubus of an enormous centralised despotism, they witnessed a decay of morals, a despairing surrender of primitive faiths, and throughout the most honoured schools a trepidation, a nerveless depression, and an impotence that presaged imminent extinction. The heartiest attempt at conservation was revived Platonism; that[1] acknowledged the great truth of the unity of God, and renounced the balder fallacies of idol-worship: but it lacked sound basis and inherent vitality; it clung to extinct myths, and to solemn forms, and to edifying survivals of ritual, out of which all virtue and meaning had departed for generations, and which had long since become 'rudimentary' appendages. In the hour of distress Mystery-worship with mischievous and ill-directed sympathy had tried to drown men's legitimate and reasonable cravings, and to intoxicate them out of consciousness of their despair. Christianity meanwhile had owed its strength and achieved its progress by recognising the misery, the helplessness, the degradation of the world, and by supplying it with a solution of its misery, and also with a hope of redemption from it.

Neo-Platonism. There was one other system which recognised the same unsatisfied aspirations and present discontent, and strove not

---

[1] Capes' *Age of the Antonines*, p. 180—1. By revived Platonism I mean here and throughout the School of Plutarch &c. as distinct from Neo-Platonism.

altogether ineffectively to prescribe an explanation and a remedy. This system was Neo-Platonism. Historically it was collateral rather than antagonistic to Christianity. Its genius was philosophical, not sectarian; it was the intellectual expression of that revulsion against scepticism and materialism, which distinguishes third century thought. Not only did Pyrrhonism and Epicureanism die completely out, but the intellectual revolt against them took a positive form. The craving after worship, after some sure ground of belief, after communion with the deity, in a word the spiritual element in man's nature reasserted itself, and evolved a philosophic system at once reverential, dogmatic, and spiritual. 'To scepticism the new philosophy opposed dogmatism, to materialism an ascetic idealism.' The astounding boldness of the attempt is one of its most striking features. Starting from no historical basis, and claiming no direct revelation, on the sole strength of intuitive belief, it assumed its fundamental truth, and thence passing from step to step, lost in excess of daring, framed a spacious and elaborate theology, by which it strove to solve or elucidate the inscrutable problems that on all sides confronted it. It reposed upon complete subjectivity: the soul turned inwards upon itself, and there read the nature of God and the riddle of existence. 'Perfect abstraction from all without, when the soul centres upon itself, beholds beauty past understanding is the realisation of the highest life and identification with the divine.' It remains, if nothing else, a standing witness to the permanent strength, the irresistible determination and the boundless daring of the spiritual instinct of man.

In its original and most worthy cast Neo-Platonism was a system of philosophy. The satisfaction it offered was primarily intellectual, though it did not neglect, but indeed gave a splendid primacy to the spiritual element in man. In religious precision and definiteness of aim it towered above previous tentative efforts. It threw its whole strength of abstract thought and exposition into the fundamental questions concerning the being and attributes of God, the origin and existence of evil, the constitution and government

A religious philosophy.

of the phenomenal world, the nature and powers of the human soul, and the relations connecting together matter, man and God. The foundation of the system was laid in a reconstruction or reinterpretation of Platonic teaching; but it claimed, and not unsuccessfully, to absorb into itself all previous philosophies, all at least that acknowledged any active or even potential communion between God and man. It reconciled them not by arbitrary identification as offshoots from a common Platonic or Socratic stock, but as varying expressions of a single truth, which truth was declared to be perfectly enshrined and secreted in Plato. It is this which gives to Neo-Platonism its markedly eclectic character. It assimilated mystic numerical formulae from Neo-Pythagoreanism; it accepted all that was truest in the syncretic liberalism of revived Platonism: it endorsed the austere morality of the Stoic, and by its emanation system appropriated his captivating Pantheism; so far as mere reason was concerned it admitted the contention of the sceptic; it practically borrowed from Aristotle his scientific methods and forms of thought; while its obligations to Plato require no mention. It went further afield than Greek philosophy. Its new and hazardous conception of God as above all quality and specification, and its metaphysical separation of the Divine Mind from the absolute God is found in germ if anywhere in the Judaeo-Alexandrine doctrines of Philo: its views of matter, its account of the communication of the Deity to phenomenal things through intermediate agencies and gradations of being, its transcendental conception of the Godhead itself exhibit striking analogies to Gnostic teaching, and at least a superficial resemblance to the most original results of Oriental speculation. But Neo-Platonism did not concoct an undigested conglomerate of rival ideas, and call it a philosophy. It gave organic unity to the elements it incorporated. If it assimilated the strength, it radically modified the principle of Stoic Pantheism; it gave up the hard mechanical notion of the literal transfusion of the Deity through all parts of the universe, for it justly appeared a profane and illogical materialising of God to suppose him

Relation to previous philosophies.

actually present as fire or air-current or animating soul in all phenomenal objects. It substituted for this the more elevated notion of a dynamic and not a mechanical inherence, of an inward sustainment and impulse, an ever-present effect of divine will constituting for each creature the law of its being and the condition of existence. It recognised an indestructible duality, where Stoics discerned an indissoluble unity. To Chrysippus God was in all things; to Plotinus all things were in God[1]. Again, Neo-Platonism, we have said, conceded, nay reaffirmed and emphasised the sceptic invalidation of reason; but it escaped the Nihilism, which appeared its logical corollary, by revealing and calling into play a new faculty transcending reason, superseding it both in scope and efficacy. Even to the dicta of Plato it yielded no servile obedience: it selected and developed at pleasure. Metaphysical hints from the Sophistes and Protagoras, enigmatic allusions or metaphors from the Republic, speculative imagery from the Timaeus equipped it with doctrines which so exceeded as almost to efface much of Plato's most essential teaching. Convinced of the untrustworthiness of phenomena and sense-knowledge, Plato had taken refuge in the Ideal theory. He had claimed objective reality for Thought and Knowledge. They alone were real; their embodied forms peopled a suprasensual world of pure being. But the Neo-Platonist improved upon this conception. To him the Ideas[2], the 'Intelligible Forms' as he called them, were not the highest and last grade. They retained indeed their exaltation above the world of sense, but became intermediary agents whereby the effects of the primal One, the First Principle of all things, were conveyed to that world. In a word, the Platonic dualism between Thought and Sense, Pure Being and Phenomena, was superseded and merged in

[1] Cf. Zeller, *Phil. Griech.* III. 2, pp. 376, 451, 497. Ueberweg, *Hist. Phil.* I. 247.

[2] Iamblichus placed the Ideas in the lower 'Intellectual' World, while archetypes of them had a place in the 'Intelligible' world—a characteristic expansion of Plotinus' doctrine that they are immanent in the Nous. Infr. p. 68, and cf. Ueberweg, *Hist. Phil.* I. 248.

a Unity transcending both. So far from asserting the truth and absolute existence of thought, this theory accomplished the reverse; for it represented the ground of thought as uncognisable[1].

Plotinus.

Some ninety years before the birth of Julian there had come to Rome a stranger whose worn but philosophic garb, whose bright though sunken eye denoted at once the genius and the ascetic. The wisdom of Zoroaster, and the secret lore of India exercised it was said a strange spell over his imagination, but his training had been in the Greek philosophy; he was an adoring pupil of the Alexandrian, Ammonius Sakkas, who as an apostate Christian, under colour of the faith he had abjured, gave catechetical instruction under a veil of Pythagorean secrecy in the new doctrines he professed. Plotinus, such was the stranger's name, opened a school at Rome, and became the Chrysippus[2] of the Neo-Platonic philosophy. Disciplined austerity of person combined with rare acuteness and intensity of mind, and a philosophic fervour of conviction that bordered upon inspiration attracted pupils of every grade and temperament: emperors and titled dames mingled in his saloon with trained philosophers or threadbare students. For many years his characteristic and esoteric doctrines remained a secret, uncommitted to writing and but obscurely hinted in oral discourse. At length the representations or feigned attacks of favourite pupils, Amelius and Porphyry, induced him to systematise his philosophy. The result was the Enneads.

Aim and System.

The central aim of Plotinus was to explain and establish the connexion between God, man and the world. To this he pertinaciously adhered. He disregarded Physics; he meddled but little with Logic; even his Ethics were rigidly subordinated to his metaphysical inquiries. Only the roughest outline of his system can be here attempted; that is a necessary preface to any understanding of Julian's philosophical position.

---

[1] Zeller, III. 2, pp. 377, 422.
[2] εἰ μὴ γὰρ ἦν Χρύσιππος οὐκ ἂν ἦν στοά.

Spirit and Matter stand at opposite poles. Man in his *Spirit and Matter.* twofold nature implies the existence of both, testifies to the connexion of the two, and craves after an explanation of that connexion. Its nature and its mode are the problems set before him. In the Spirit world, such is the answer of Plotinus, there exists a triad—the One, Intelligence, and Soul. These are not three persons or substances[1] of a co-equal Trinity, but denote three descending orders of Spiritual Being. At the summit of all, absolute, unconditioned, *The One.* ineffable and incomprehensible stands the One. Unlike the One or the Good of Plato, the One of Plotinus is not an Idea, but rather the principle of all Ideas, itself raised above the sphere of the Ideas, and transcending all determinations of existence, so that neither rest nor motion, not even Being or not-Being can be predicated of it. It transcends thought, for thought implies a duality; still less can it be the Good, for that admits of a multiplicity of determinations. Its imperfect name, the One, is but an approximate description, correct only so far as absolute Oneness excludes the attribution of any but negative predicates. The One is not all things, but before all things. Unapproachable by thought, it is known only in its effects. In what way all things, the Many, were evolved from the One, transcends human reason to conceive. It is the overflowing source of essential Being, but as such even in emitting energy experiences no change, nor is its pre-existent Oneness affected or impaired[2].

From this excess of radiated energy, related to the One, *Nous.* as the image to the original, the sun to light, proceeded *Nous* or Intelligence. Classed next to the One, towards which it constantly turns, it represents the smallest degree of departure from absolute Oneness and perfection. Thought[3] and

[1] J. Simon's contention that they are (adopted by Lewes in his *Hist. of Philos.* I. 388 pp.) seems rightly denounced by Zeller as 'eine auffallende Verkennung der Plotinischen Lehre.' Cf. note in his *Phil. der Griech.* III. 2, p. 450.

[2] The activity implied in this absolute and primary causality contains of necessity an idea of plurality. Plotinus strove to meet the difficulty by regarding it as describing a modification of us rather than of the first cause.

[3] But Thought, be it added, abstracted from all thinking; premiss and

Being, the latter being the posterior of the two and definable as Thought made stationary, are regarded as its fundamental determinations. It is pure spirit still, hampered by none of the limitations or imperfections that attend on matter, independent of space or time, enjoying a repose which consists in equable and unchanging motion, so that its whole being is absolute activity. Emanating from the One, this *Nous* becomes in its turn the basis of all existence, for it includes as immanent parts of itself all the Ideas. In fact the whole sum of Ideas, regarded as a unity, constitutes the Νοῦς, which thus becomes the determining source of all being and all thought. The spiritual order which it contains and pervades is called the κόσμος νοητός or Intelligible World. From this every element of phenomenal finiteness is absent, and it combines in itself the apparent contradictories of absolute plurality, as containing perfectly all forms of being, and yet of perfect unity, with which it is imbued by the primal One. Harmony with this Νοῦς is the highest goal to which the spiritual part of man can attain.

Soul. The third factor in the Trinity, Soul, stands in the same relation to *Nous*, as *Nous* to the One. It is the image or reflection of *Nous*, as the moon's light to the sun's. It too belongs still to the order of Spirit, but is as it were on the outer fringe of the circle illumined by the central One. *Nous* may be represented by an inner immovable sphere described about the great centre of all Being, Soul as an outer movable sphere turning about the interior *Nous*. Spirit has now by a series of acts of self-estrangement from its creative centre reached the lowest gradation of which it is capable. Light has reached the confines of darkness, and potential connexion with matter has been secured : by another metaphor Soul is spoken of as extended *Nous*, which, just as the point extended becomes a line, is now brought within touch of matter. Thus Soul is made the link between the Many and the One, Rest and Motion, Eternity and Time. Into

---

consequence being to *Nous* simultaneous without intervention of the thinking process.

the subtler minutiæ of the double World-Soul, Earth-Soul, and Separate Souls, it is needless to enter. The final contact with Matter is established by emanative action analogous to that by which the One passed into *Nous* and *Nous* into Soul. On the nature of this so-called emanation it behoves to speak shortly.

Emanation is only a clumsy mode, imposed by the limitations of human thought and expression, of representing a transcendental act or series of acts. It should be called rather eternal procession, for it must not be regarded as occurring *in time* at all. The divisions of the triad as just described are all alike co-eternal; so too is matter, and the interdependence and relations of all these to each other. Further in Neo-Platonic emanation there is no communication of being, passing into or calling into existence lower intermediary orders: herein it is quite distinct from the emanation of Oriental philosophies. The First Cause is in essence incommunicable: there is a communication of force or effect only, not of being. The One, *Nous* and Soul are in themselves absolutely unaffected by any emanation to which they give rise: it does not take place at their expense: they are occupied solely with that from which they emanated. Emanation is not even produced by any act of volition, still less of self-impartition: it takes place by an internal and natural necessity, which is a part of the nature of Spirit, no more consciously exercised than gravity by a particle. Lastly, each act of emanation represents a degradation: *Nous* is lower than the One, and the Soul than *Nous*, though in its proper sphere each is perfect. By such progressive stages of imperfection is it alone possible to bridge the illimitable gulf between Spirit and Matter.

Emanation.

With regard to Matter, some substratum appeared to Plotinus a necessary assumption involved by the existence of the phenomenal world. This substratum he regards as the absolute privation of all being or quality. As such it is wholly unthinkable, and can be described by negatives only, as formless, indeterminate, unqualified and the like. One positive attribute it does appear at first sight to possess. It

Matter.

is the cause and origin of all Evil, which cannot by possibility be derived from the spiritual nature of the emanative Soul. This is explained however by representing Evil as a negative quantity, a certain absence or deprivation of Good which belongs properly to Matter. Into Matter so conceived Soul entering by voluntary emanation produces the phenomenal world, almost every degree of intermixture or rather proportionate prevalence of the elements being provided for by gradations descending from angels, dæmons and heroes through men to animals and inanimate matter.

Ecstasy. Of Neo-Platonic anthropology or ethics no analysis need be given, but its most original and characteristic tenet demands an allusion. Intelligence ($νοῦς$) the highest rational faculty of man might, as in the Platonic scheme, be trained more and more to harmony with the supreme *Nous*. Yet by no conceivable perfection of mere reason could the finite attain to communion with the incomprehensible infinite. The nature of the two things forbade it. Reduced by rigorous metaphysical reasoning to this result, and yet intuitively assured that knowledge of the infinite was within the range of man, Plotinus fell back on the doctrine of Ecstasy. Above reason and above intelligence man, so he taught, possesses an energy kindred to the One whereby he may attain to direct communion with it. Leaving thought and spirit behind, divesting itself of personality and individual consciousness, the soul by an ecstatic elevation of being might enter into actual unification or contact ($ἅπλωσις, ἀφή$) with God, and become absorbed in the Infinite Intelligence from which it emanated. For that rapturous space 'reminiscence might be changed into intuition.' Weaned altogether from the flesh, disenthralled of desire and lust, trained to the sincere unalloyed contemplation of the divine Ideas, four times in a lifetime was Plotinus caught up to the seventh heaven and admitted to this transcending and ineffable communion: and once, when he was an old man of near seventy, the same exalted privilege was vouchsafed to Porphyry[1]. For this

---

[1] In records of Iamblichus the spiritual ecstasy becomes degraded to bodily levitation. His domestics alleged that during his orisons he would

supreme end, this final term of knowledge, the Neo-Platonist was invited to mortify the flesh, to pursue after virtue and to purify the soul. Such was his incentive and his reward.

As regards all forms of religion Plotinus himself had the intellectual strength to take a singularly independent attitude. The spirit of his system was doubtless antagonistic to Christianity: that reposed on objective historical facts by which it declared God was brought down to man; while Neo-Platonism from a purely subjective basis claimed to enable men to rise to God. The analogies that appear between the two are more verbal than real. On the other hand, Neo-Platonism lent itself readily to current Pagan beliefs: its final monotheism left abundant room for any amount of subordinate polytheism. This Plotinus admitted without turning aside to corroborate or refute details. To him Paganism was an amplified and not always trustworthy commentary, which fell short of deserving a place in his text. *Popular Religion.*

Such is a rough outline of Plotinus' solution of the great world-problem. It attained its purest and most masculine development in his hands. His successor Porphyrius did indeed add details and advance individual arguments a step or two further, but was little more than a skilful and trusty expositor: such real modification as he did introduce was in the direction of co-ordination of Pagan beliefs with Neo-Platonic philosophy, and the abandonment of the free position taken by Plotinus towards all extant forms of religion. But under Iamblichus[1] the school entered upon what is justly regarded as a new stage. Though overflowing with intellectual pretentiousness he added nothing of metaphysical or ethical value. To him the religious attitude of the philosophy became all in all. He caught at numerical formulae of the Pythagoreans, and though in that department he discovered nothing new and misunderstood much that was old, proclaimed that there lay deep secrets of religion and philosophy. *Plotinus' successors.*

be bodily raised to a height of 15 or 18 feet, his flesh and his robes assuming meanwhile a golden hue. Eunap. *Vit. Soph. Iambl.*

[1] Lewes, *Hist. Philos.* I. 383 seems hasty in writing, 'With *Porphyry and Iamblichus* Neo-Platonism becomes a sort of Church.'

He multiplied Gods *ad nauseam*: he accumulated insipid divisions and subdivisions of spiritual genera. In fact, he and the Syrian School used to fatal effect the mysticism which Plotinus' own intellect had not always kept in bounds. They employed Neo-Platonism as an engine against Christianity, as the new and last stronghold of Polytheism. They converted a school of inquirers into a church of believers. In order to this they recklessly degraded their philosophy. In attempting to popularise they also irremediably vulgarised: they depreciated the intellectual side, to expand the mystical or theurgic. They exalted Pythagoras and deposed Aristotle[1]. Iamblichus, foiled in a dialectical discussion, coolly replied that the intuitions of virtue were above logic. Julian fell into the hands of this school when he was referred by his first teachers to one who 'for the grandeur and power of his natural intellect could discard philosophical demonstration[2].' In spite of the protests of the aged Porphyry, magic or theurgy was made the highest branch of philosophy. 'The philosopher' while admitting a true art of augury and divination, in a series of sceptical questions and doubts partly practical and partly metaphysical, criticised many current manifestations of the art as interposing material obstacles between man and God, with whom the heart was the one true organ of communion and revealer of oracles, and did not conceal his perplexity concerning the modes, and causes, and tests of divination depending on the strange material mediums or adjuncts which were coming into vogue. Thus in his Epistle to Anebon, the *cygneus cantus* of the dying sage, he enters his final protest against the new-fangled hocus-pocus of priestcraft. But in vain: cabbalistic fatuity, fantastic ceremonies, bloody initiative rites, miracles, evocation of spirits, theophanies, sorceries, with their accompanying abominations came crowding in. Superstition and philosophy signed an adulterous compact, and were made one flesh. The intellectual ingenuity with which Iamblichus

---

[1] Cf. Iamblichus' *Life of Pythagoras*.
[2] Eunap. *Maximus*.

made necromancy and thaumaturgy the handmaids of philosophy only wakens a regret that his talents were not better employed than in stultifying the learned and imposing on the incredulous.

With the third stage of Neo-Platonism, the acute but sterile scholastic period of Proclus, an essay on Julian has no concern.

CHAPTER IV.

JULIAN'S THEOLOGY.

> "In the silent mind of One all-pure
> At first imagined lay
> The sacred world, and by procession sure
> From those still deeps, in form and colour drest,
> Seasons alternating and night and day,
> The long-nursed thought to north, south, east, and west,
> Took then its all-seen way."

Julian's Theology. THE ground is now cleared for examining Julian's scheme of religious revival. The first step in this will be to master its intellectual basis, in other words Julian's theology.

The One. Julian nowhere in his surviving works develops his doctrine concerning the One with any fulness or precision. In the incidental allusions which occur, he wavers as to the rightful title to be assigned; whether this highest original principle is to be regarded as ineffable and to be described

Or. 4. 132 c d simply as that which is beyond or transcending *Nous* (τὸ ἐπέκεινα τοῦ Νοῦ), or as the One, or in Platonic terminology as the Good, or lastly as the Idea of all Existences, by which he explains himself to mean the Intelligible (τὸ νοητόν) in its entirety. So far as he goes, he agrees with Plotinus in either assigning to it negative determinations only, or allowing it by courtesy the imperfect title of the Good, or finally treating it positively through the medium of its effects as absolute causality. On the exact relation of the One to *Nous* Julian is silent: in the above there seems a tendency to confuse the highest Deity with either the first or second members of the trinity of Plotinus. On the essential being *Or. 4. 139 B* of the One Julian is sufficiently orthodox. It transcends all human description or conception: it is from eternity pre-subsistent; it includes within itself all Being; its very essence is unity. Itself incomprehensible it is the sole unique incomposite cause of the whole universe. Julian most fre- *132 D, 133 B &c.* quently denominates it the Good. Itself the crown and source of every existence, it enters into transcendental relations with the subordinate orders of Being. These are three in number, and carefully differentiated by Julian. To distinguish them in English, recourse must be had to terms of formal philosophy. The first and highest order is styled the Intelligible (τὸ νοητόν); the second, the Intellectual (τὸ νοερόν); the third, the Cosmic. This strict trinitarian conception runs through the whole system: the triad involves a pantheistic belief, since the lowest member of the trinity includes the material world. It is with the first and most spiritual alone that the Good has direct communication. In that order, in other words in the Intelligible Gods[1], it becomes *133 B* the author of the beauty, the essential being, the perfectness and the unity which characterise them. Thus through them *132 D* it is said to originate in all existences their beauty and perfection, their unity and power inexplicable. These Intelligible Gods are not generally conceived to issue from the supreme One, though such language is in loose usage admissible. More strictly they cluster *round*[2] the One, being as it were with all creation a part of his ever-emitted radiance. 'He transcends all things, round him are all things, *136 D* and for his sake all things are.' The One is not so much a creator, as an everlasting well of existence: in the case of the Intelligible Gods, immediately, elsewhere mediately, by *Or. 5. 161 C* virtue of essence transmitted to the Intelligible Gods. To *Cyr. 58* such demiurgic functions committed to these last, and by

[1] See infr. p. 77.
[2] Cf. βασλέα, περὶ ὃν πάντα ἔστιν. Or. 4. 132 c. τῶν ἀΰλων καὶ νοητῶν θεῶν, οἳ περὶ τἀγαθόν εἰσιν. Or. 4. 138 D. The two phrases are combined in "Ἥλιος ὁ περὶ τὴν τἀγαθοῦ γόνιμον οὐσίαν ἐξ ἀϊδίου προελθών 156 c, showing emanation to be synonymous with eternal procession.

them in turn transmitted to the inferior grades of deities, all orders of being are due, until contact is finally attained with mortal perishable forms of matter.

Nature of the Gods. Or. 4. 145 A ff.

142 D, 143 A.

The Gods, those at any rate of the two higher orders, the Intelligible and the Intellectual, are unsubstantial (ἄϋλοι) and immaterial (ἀσώματοι). Goodness, and that which is good, is an inseparable part of their essence, and remains ever inherent in their very nature. No duality of nature, corresponding to the spiritual and carnal elements in man, is conceivable in the Gods. They are not to be regarded as non-natural magnified men: for in truth the divine nature is radically different from the human. It is indivisible, and does not admit the analysis or the modifications to which man's nature is liable. The kind of personality which they possessed in Julian's eyes is a difficult matter to settle. They combined strangely the impersonal nature of the Platonic Ideas with the personality attributed to the polytheistic deities[1]. There is a confusion of their persons one with another, and a necessitarianism attributed to their whole mode of being and acting, that converts them into forces rather than living wills. Both the limitations and the powers of strict personality seem not seldom denied to them. But, on the other hand, they are habitually feared, addressed, adored and propitiated as though gifted with personal will, and the power to put it into effect. With the Gods, will, power, action, are one and the same thing, a part of their essence

142 C D and inseparable. 'Whatsoever a God wills, that he is and can and does: he neither wills what he is not, nor is thwarted in what he wills, nor is of the mind to do what he cannot.'

Frag. Ep. 301 A

Good being a constant element of their essence, or rather actually constituting their essence, they are in action, whether towards one another or towards man, entirely and invariably beneficent. This description, though vouchsafed primarily of the higher orders of Gods, is applicable also to the lower Cosmic Gods—the visible and sensible as contrasted with the invisible and spiritual Gods—whose functions will be

---

[1] Naville, *Jul. l'Apost.* pp. 72, 133 sq.

considered in due course. For to depict their true relations, it is essential to treat of the Gods according to their proper grades.

The highest sphere is, as has been repeated, the Intelligible[1]. The Intelligible World is characterised by what Julian speaks of as an exuberant superabundance of life-producing fecundity. As the superfluous energy of the One produced the Intelligible World round about the One, so too does it in its turn manifest a like exuberance. All that belongs to it enjoys pure, uncontaminated immaterial being; nothing of alien nature inheres in it, nor ever has or can approach it from without. In attributes of beauty, eternity, absoluteness, spirituality, or, if the term be allowed, intellectuality, it corresponds to the Platonic world of Ideas; it is full of its own proper untainted purity. It is peopled by the Intelligible Gods, and by them alone.

Intelligible Gods. Or. 4. 140 A

140 c

Essentially the Intelligible Gods exist around the Good, by eternal emanation from him. From the Good they inherit direct all their gifts and powers; he supplies them ungrudgingly with beauty, with being, with perfection, with unity, in Neo-Platonic language he 'contains' them all, and illuminates them with that ἀγαθοειδὴς δύναμις, that inherited element or faculty of the archetypal Good, in which their majesty consists, and which they transmit in measure to subordinate orders of being. Among these Intelligible Gods, and highest of them all, is ranked Helios, King Sun.

139 A

133 B

At this point a digression becomes necessary. One of Julian's surviving works is a kind of devotional rhapsody— addressed to Salustius—in honour of King Sun. The address is manifestly an effort of rhetoric rather than a spontaneous effusion of devotion[2]. Hastily[3], often confusedly put together, and too pretentiously embellished, it yet remains the most

Julian's Fourth Oration.

---

[1] This particular triple arrangement, quite unrecognised by Plotinus, was one of the elaborations of Iamblichus.

[2] 'Partly plagiarised, partly parodied from Iamblichus,' says Schlosser bluntly. *Jenaische allg.*, p. 126.

[3] It was the work of three evenings only (157 c), and covers nearly forty pages.

fruitful quarry from which to extract Julian's dogmatic beliefs. No doubt it exaggerates the functions and pre-eminence of Sun, or rather throws them out of just proportion as compared with those of other deities. Sun, his position and his work, are in the foreground; the rest are aside or in the background, jumbled, slurred, and out of focus. But from sources quite independent of this elogium, it is plain that Julian did elevate King Sun, under one representation or another, to the first place among Gods. Neo-Platonism hailed from the East, and most grew and flourished there; it became deeply tinged with influences of the Mithras cult and various forms of fire-worship, every one of which sprang *Cyr. 69 D C* from, while most still acknowledged, Sun adoration as the groundwork of religion[1]. Julian espoused the worship with devotion: it appeared to him instinctive; it dovetailed with his philosophy, no less than it charmed his imagination. King Sun was the supreme deity, whom under many various names all peoples of the world combined to worship. He was the most tangible link by which Neo-Platonism gave unity to Paganism, rendered Polytheism philosophical, and by aid of which, minds like Julian's became reconciled to the incongruous superstitions or bizarre confusions of popular beliefs. Julian regarded him moreover as in a special sense his patron; and delights to call himself his follower, his liegeman, or his devotee[2].

Its mysticism. Exaggeration or displacement of relations it will be easy in the main to rectify. More misleading than either is a lack of lucidity and inconsistency, the inevitable result of a pervading mysticism of tone. If the writer himself was mystified, it became his penalty, or perhaps duty, to mystify his reader. The action of King Sun in the Intelligible and Intellectual spheres has to be spiritually derived from the analogous action of the phenomenal Sun in the world of

[1] From the very beginning of the Empire this influence made itself felt. Augustus professed peculiar devotion for Apollo. Aurelian and Heliogabalus gave Sun pre-eminence in the Pantheon. Constantine's Solar coins are familiar to all.

[2] *Or.* 4. 130 D C, 131 D, 157 A, &c. &c., *Or.* 7. 229 PP. (see *Chapter VI.*), *Caes.* 336 C, *Ep.* 13, 38, 51, &c. &c.

sense. Julian is at great pains to work out these analogies, and contributes both knowledge and ingenuity to the task: but he is for ever confounding metaphor with fact, and converting analogies into modes of action; much in the same spirit as when to the Alexandrians he insists upon the alter- *Ep.* 51 nations of summer and winter, the blessings of sunlight and growth of plants, as evidences of the existence of Serapis (the Sun God), constituting in his behalf a claim to adoration. At times he seems purposely to confuse phenomenal action with its spiritual counterpart, and throughout leaves a vast deal to be interpreted by the spiritual intuitions of the reader. Happily, a large residuum of solid information is left.

King Sun himself, most frequently entitled 'King of the *King Sun.* Universe¹,' is himself primarily one of the Intelligible Gods, and chiefest among them all. He is the immediate and *Or.* 4. 132 c, trueborn offspring of the Good, emanating by eternal proces- 144 B. sion from the One, or as it is elsewhere phrased, 'around the 156 c fruitful essence of the Good.' 'By virtue of its abiding and initiative essence the Good produced from its own being and 132 D in all things like itself Sun the most high God.' This emanative production must not be looked upon as an act of creation, or as realised *in time.* To every Neo-Platonic deity, and to Sun if any, belongs eternal procession: he 'subsisted 133 B from Eternity around the abiding essence of the Good,' and thus is legitimately spoken of more than once as self-subsis- 139 D tent (αὐθυπόστατος).

Among the Intelligible Gods, or as they are sometimes *Sun and* styled, Intelligible Ideas (εἴδη), he not only himself shines *the Intelligible* with pure uncontaminated radiance, but *primus inter pares, Gods.* as incapable of admixture or impurity as light in the sensi- 140 D ble world, holds predominance. He is the centre of the Intelligible system; he almost usurps functions which are elsewhere attributed to the One; at any rate, his action begins at the point where the direct activity of the One ceases; to his centrality is imputed the emanative multi- 139 A

¹ ὁ βασιλεὺς τῶν ὅλων. Cf. e.g. *Or.* 1. 145 c, 146 A, 149 D, 154 D, 156 c, 158 B.

plication of the divine Intelligible essence, which without thereby receiving diminution or increase or any kind of affection gives rise to the Intellectual order of existences.

His position among Gods.

It is not a little curious that in more than one passage[1] Julian speaks of Sun apparently as one of the Intellectual Gods. His language, taken alone, hardly admits another interpretation. Yet that Sun's position is such as has been just described is undeniable. The fact is, that Julian has three separate Suns, or phases of Sun in his mind, and is not sufficiently precise in distinguishing them. In the actual passage where he alludes to this tripleness, he makes it perfectly clear that the third Sun is the phenomenal Sun: as for the two others, he leaves the reader in obscurity[2]. Both from the immediate context however and from the whole oration the obvious interpretation is, that the first Sun is King Sun himself, the Intelligible Deity, whose harmonizing office in his own sphere almost intrudes upon that of the Good itself; while the second Sun is the Sun regarded in his action on the Intellectual sphere. This forms the subject of whole pages of the treatise, and it is his sovereignty and most intimate action among the Intellectual Gods of which Julian is thinking, when he loosely classes Sun as one of them rather than one above them.

Or. 4. 133 c

Unity of the Spiritual Orders.
139 B C
Intelligible World.

Each of the three orders, Intelligible, Intellectual and Cosmic, enjoys perfection after its own kind. In the Intelligible World there is a pervading unity, the gift of the One, which contains, conjoins or confederates the whole into a One or perfect harmony. This unifying principle in the Intelligible World is analogous to that Quintessence or Fifth Substance, which, in constant motion round and round the heaven, by virtue of such periphery contains and welds together all the

---

[1] Cf. *Or.* 4. 132 D, 141 D—142 A. Zeller, III. 2, p. 629, admitting the uncertainty, speaks of Sun as belonging *relatively* to the first order, but positively (comparing hints from Iamblichus) to the second triad of Intellectual Gods.

[2] Obscurity such that I suspect a lacuna or misreading of some kind in the preceding lines. I have not been able to consult M. Tourlet's unsuccessful elucidation of the matter, to which De Broglie refers *L'Église*, IV. p. 129 n. Semisch, pp. 29, 30, stops short where the difficulties begin.

parts of the Cosmic order, and forbids separation or dissolution. The corresponding harmony that rules the Intellectual World, is the immediate work of Sun, whose energies in that sphere are as all-important as those of the Good in the higher sphere, or of the visible Sun in the lower. This is the place to examine these in detail.

First then the Intellectual Gods were derived from Sun essentially. To Neo-Platonist thought the one mode of origination was eternal emanation. But emanation was carried on by successive stages. At the head of all being, the one original Demiurge, from whom every entity and essence is primarily derived, stands the One or the Good. He becomes immediately the principle or first cause of the whole Intelligible order. From that point his demiurgic work is carried on mediately. Later refinements of Neo-Platonic theology subtilised the demiurgic succession into a series of triads, each issuing from a monad. Phanes was selected in the Intelligible triad[1] as the term from which emanated the Intellectual triad, Kronos Rhea and Zeus[2]. From Zeus issues the supramundane triad: at the extremity of which comes Apollo, who produces a triad of so-called liberated gods (θεοὶ ἀπόλυτοι). Their extreme becomes the generative monad of a triad of mundane gods. Julian nowhere endorses in detail these refinements; he retails, by his own confession, but 'few out of many' of the inventions of the divine Iamblichus: in his classification of Gods there are marked divergencies; but the general principle is strongly asseverated.

Grades of Gods.

Or. 4. 140 a

150 c, 157 d.

King Sun, the arch-demiurge in the Intelligible World, plays towards the Intellectual the same part that in the

Sun and the Intellectual Gods.

---

[1] In a different terminology Iamblichus denotes the highest Intelligible triad, as Father, Power, and Mind (Νοῦς). His most symmetrical arrangement provided three trinities for the Intelligible, and three for the Intellectual order, and he appears to have extended a like classification to a lower psychical order. The twelve superior Gods are thus tripled into thirty-six, which are in turn multiplied to 360, and also by duplication branch into the seventy-two orders of lower Gods. Cf. Jul. *Or.* 4. 148 c, and specific references in Prokl. on *Tim.* 299 D E. Theodorus of Asine had the courage to enlarge still further. For this and like flimsy theosophy, see Zeller, *Phil. der Griech.* III. 2. 620 pp.

[2] Cf. Taylor's Pref. to Iamblichus *On Mysteries*, p. vii.

higher sphere is played by the Good, who there causes and directs all things aright in accordance with presiding intelligence or Νοῦς. Thus, though metaphysically the Intellectual Gods share original co-procession and co-subsistence with Sun, they are yet said to owe their being to him. This means that without his agency their being would never be realised. He supplies them, and in constant unfailing measure, with what to the Intellectual God is the very condition of being, viz. τὸ νοεῖν and νοεῖσθαι. Without this active and apprehended intelligence, their existence is but potential; they are as eye-sight without light. Nor does his task end here with this creation, or more strictly actualisation of their essential being and attributes. Having received from the Good dominion among the Intellectual Gods, he actively and incessantly exercises it: they are as subordinate and inferior to him as the stars are to the natural sun; their whole being is directed by his providing guidance. It is Sun that imparts its unity to all Intellectual being throughout the universe. In technical phraseology he 'contains them intellectually' in himself, fills all heaven with them, and himself becomes a unifying centre about which their action is harmonised. He may be called a harmonic mean or centre (μέσον); not (Julian is careful to explain) as a mean between extremes, but as a central principle everywhere infusing unity of action, perfecting and harmonising diverse energies, and combining otherwise conflicting extremes into a single identity. Like the phenomenal Sun he controls, adjusts and regulates the centrifugal forces of the system.

In addition to his originative and regulative functions, he exercises distributive powers on a royal scale. He is directly commissioned to dispense to all Intellectual forms of being the rich endowments of perfectness and beauty, which the Good originates and imparts among the Intelligible Gods. Being, unity, illimitable beauty, productive fecundity, perfected intelligence, all the divine attributes proceed from great Sun. His counterpart or image (εἰκών) in the visible world acts imitatively as a revealing medium

whereby men may adore and understand the analogous work of sovereign Sun in the Intellectual order. Just as the phenomenal Sun imprints harmony upon the visible universe, of which he forms the centre, as he regulates the concentric motions of the spheres, guides the circling orbits of the planets at measured distances, and no less the changeful phases of the moon, as with creative energy he ministers to earth her unbroken power of being, as he gives the beauty of day for work, and in turn the terror of night wherein men rest from their labours, as he brings to pass storm and wind and cloud and all atmospheric changes, so does the royal Sun act in the Intellectual world. The sincere uncontaminated radiance of light, which Sun ever sheds abroad in this world, which gives sight to the eyes as the artist gives form to the marble, is but the counterpart of that undefiled illuminating Truth in which he bathes the Intellectual forms of being. Light is to the visible as Truth to the Intelligible.
Or. 4. 139 D
133 C
146 C D
135 A B
152 C
133 A
134 D—135 A
153 C
151 D– 152 A
133 D, 140 D.
134 C D
133 A

Thus King Sun originates, impels and harmoniously adjusts, endows and equips with appropriate excellences and energies. He continues too to exercise a providing control. But he is often mythologically represented as performing this by deputy. Thus he is said, having controlled the gods to a single unity, to hand them over as a mighty army to *Athene Pronoia* to do at her bidding their appointed work. She acts as his subordinate consort. Elsewhere his guiding control finds a different personification as *Prometheia*[1], identified with the Mother of the Gods, and constantly in concert with the higher deity assuming preservative direction of the Intellectual Gods.
Sun's ministers.
135 A B
149 A B

Sun's influence does not end with the Intellectual sphere, and pass from thence by transmitted emanation only into the Cosmic order. He exercises a direct palpable influence over the Kosmos. His demiurgic power is active there. He is said to have called the Kosmos into being, reserving for his representative the central place, so as to secure ready and equal distribution of goods and ordering of the heavenly
The Cosmic order.
138 B
146 C

[1] With *Or.* 4. 135 A B, cf. *Or.* 5. 166 B, 170 D.

bodies, the subordinate co-proceeding Gods. His demiurgic action in the Kosmos occupies a central place between that of the primal demiurge and the numerous lower demiurgic deities: but no delimitation is attempted of the provinces in which each acts. Relatively to the Kosmos these inferior creative agencies exhibit themselves in diverse and multiplied activities; relatively to Sun they are uniform, 'crowning the uncontaminated essence of the deity.' In regard to the origination of the Kosmos one warning deserves repetition. Its creation is not a chronological event. It might appear such in the bold representations of Plato and Iamblichus. It is convenient to describe it so; indeed hardly possible to do otherwise. But the strict theological conception is that things proceeded or rather were produced from eternity. Sun procreated things visible from the invisible in the infinite present, by the ineffable celerity and unsurpassed power of the divine will.

King Sun and Cosmic Sun.

Beyond this point it is hard to push with precision any account of the functions of King Sun. They mingle inextricably with those of his mundane representative. Julian is so busy with tracing affinities, with extorting spiritual correspondences from scientific analyses of the nature and uses of light, with wresting astronomical arrangements and speculations into allegorical representations of higher truth[1], and so often veils the transition from the sign to the thing signified under an ambiguous 'Sun,' that it is impossible without arbitrariness to decide whether the agency of the higher or the lower deity is intended. Sun, for instance, is described as being with man the joint and universal begetter of men: he gathers souls from himself and from other Gods, and sows them on earth: in life he ministers to them every good, he judges, he directs, he purges them; finally, he liberates them from their bodily tenement, reunites them to the kindred and divine essences, converting the ethereal

---

[1] From Porphyrius onwards Neo-Platonists strangely mixed physical and metaphysical speculations. According to Porphyrius Soul before its entrance on earthly existence inhabited the sphere of the fixed stars, and made its descent to earth *viâ* that of the seven planets.

activity of his divine rays into a vehicle for their conveyance. These might seem duties worthily ascribed to the sovereign Sun; yet are almost unmistakeably transferred to his lower representative. Can any other interpretation be placed on these words: 'Just as Sun is author of day and *Ep. 77.* night, and of winter or summer by his approach or retrocession, so is he most venerable of the Gods; to him are all things and of him are all things; he appoints us rulers during life, and after death apportions us governors'? Julian is either enhancing the dignity of the cosmic Sun, or purposely giving him the advantage of his name and confounding him with his better.

It would be tedious to rehearse all Julian's praises of the *Phenomenal Sun.* Sun apparent. He is leader and lord in the sensible world. *Or. 4. 151 b* He is the originative cause of heaven and the stars, and upholds them with sustaining force. His vast productive, *141 c, 142 b.* fertilising power is dwelt upon persistently. He supplies *140 b, Or. 5. 172 b.* a never-ceasing stimulus of life to the earth by alternate *Or. 4. 137 d— 138 A* approach and retirement. He enriches men with equable unceasing distribution of blessings, material and spiritual. *141 A* The simplicity of his motion betokens the excellence and *138 A B* superiority of his power beyond that of all planets and stars and heavenly bodies. His appearance, his position, his work, his action upon natural phenomena proclaim his majesty.

This is the barest outline of Sun's specific work: but it *Cosmology.* will be more instructive to view the Kosmos as a whole, and range its different parts according to their proper dignity. 'The divine and all lovely universe from the highest arc of *132 c, 145 d.* heaven to the utmost ends of earth is from everlasting to everlasting.' 'It is a single animate whole, everywhere instinct with Soul[1] and Intellect, perfect and of perfect parts.' *139 b* It is not the immediate work of the great First Cause, but *Cyr. 58*

---

[1] This Neo-Platonic *anima mundi* differs materially from the Stoic conception, as has been noticed p. 65. The soul does not physically or mechanically inhere in the body it animates, but dynamically, supplying a certain force or effect, in the same kind of way as warm air feels the dynamic effect of fire without any inherence of the heat-producing agent. Cf. Zeller, III. 2. 519 pp. It is according to Plotinus an innate inclination of the inferior generated product towards the generative power. Zeller, 585 pp.

of those Intelligible Gods to whom he has committed his Demiurgic Functions. Its origin is emanative, and it subsists *around* the supreme God Helios or Sun. It is ruled directly by the so-called visible or apparent Gods, of whom phenomenal Sun is the chief. Moon, planets, stars are all such apparent Gods, emanating from primal Sun, and counterparts in the Cosmic sphere of the Intelligible Gods corresponding to them in the higher order. Between the supramundane and mundane Gods Julian draws no plain line of demarcation.

Or. 4. 145 D

Cyr. 65 B
Or. 4. 146 D

Immediately beneath the Gods come the so-called 'divine kinds' of being. These ubiquitous spirits exercise superhuman agencies, and are distributed in various classes, Angels, Dæmons, Heroes and Separate Souls. The precise differentia of dæmons, heroes and souls respectively had been one of Porphyry's[1] perplexities, and Julian does not emulate the extravagances of Iamblichus by any scientific analysis. He teaches in general terms that all alike owe their innate energy to Sun. Of Angels there are various classes; the highest are Solar Angels (ἡλιακοὶ ἄγγελοι), who are the first creation of Sun about the Kosmos: there are also Lunar Angels. One at least of their functions is to act as guardian spirits[2]. The Dæmons too are active agents of the Gods. Porphyry[3] had assigned to them superintendence over distinct animal or vegetable or meteorological departments of nature; had honoured them as patrons of particular arts, and commissioned ambassadors between Gods and men. But they are of uncertain character: exceptional dæmons may be altogether beneficent, but as a rule the dæmon is not

Demonology.
141 B, 145 C.
Or. 5. 168 A
Or. 7. 233 D

Or. 4. 141 B,
142 A, 145 C.

ad Ath. 275 B.

---

[1] *Ad Aneb.* with which cf. the answer as touching these points in the tract περὶ μυστηρίων, I. 5—7, 20, II. 1—3, 5, &c.

[2] The doctrine of guardian spirits was hard pressed by some Neo-Platonists, who believed in separate dæmons presiding over the different parts and functions of the body, though in subordination to a central controlling dæmon.

[3] *Ad Aneb.* 10. 16. According to Plotinus they combined divine and material attributes. Their body was composed of 'Intelligible Matter' (Zeller, 604 pp.); they could also manifest themselves as luminous bodies; they possessed affections, sensibility, memory and even language. For further peculiarities, cf. Zeller, pp. 510, 511.

absolutely pure or perfectly good, like the Gods, but participates in some alloy of evil: some are no better than imps or bogies. Dæmons of distinct characters preside over nations, acting under the superintendence of the patron God, and helping to mould and perpetuate their national characteristics. Conversely there is an appointed tribe of malicious dæmons[1] who, guarding the honour of the eternal and saving Gods, delude the apostate Christians with dreams of heaven after death, or drive them out as anchorites into the wildernesses far from their fellow-men. The μεριϲταὶ ψυχαί or Separate Souls[2] are products or effects of the great central Soul, which pervades the All. Though in contact with matter temporarily individualised, they are yet one and the same, just as Knowledge or Light though divisible into parts remain nevertheless essentially wholes. So the Soul of the Universe remains indivisible, though each individual soul derives from it its proper complement, when it accepts the self-imposed limitations of time, space, and quasi-personality involved in the combination with matter. *Ep. 59. 415 B*

At this stage the world of matter is reached. Matter, in Julian's belief, is eternal, subsisting beside the procreative essence of the Gods, and generated by eternal co-procession with the Gods, by virtue of that superfluous energy of procreative and constructive powers, with which the Gods, no less than the First Cause himself, are endowed. Matter in its raw form consists only of negations; it is the substratum void of all attributes and incomprehensible to sense: it is utterly lifeless and sterile, the filth, the refuse, the dregs of existence; no language can be too strong to express its demerits. Potential determination of being is the sole attribute allowed to what is in itself 'the absolutely non-existent.' It requires to be animated by divine essence before it is raised to that degree of possible being, in which we apprehend it by sense. It then becomes materialised form (ἔνυλον *Material World. Or. 5. 170 C D Or. 5. 161 D pp.*

---

[1] *Frag. Ep.* 288 A B, with which the views of Porph. *De Abst.* II. 40—42 may be compared. Cf. Aug. *Civ. Dei*, x. 9.

[2] *Or.* 4. 151 c. Compare Zeller, *Phil. der Griech.* III. 2. 481, 484 pp. and 509, which set forth the correspondence between the views of Plotinus and Porphyry.

εἶδος). Thus the material world consists of so many junctions of matter with immaterial cause, which confers on it sensible being. Matter and spirit alike are primary and necessary assumptions; the union of the two is inexplicable; neither the mode nor agent of the combination is discoverable: we only see the result. Some cause of the union there must of course have been. That it was not blind chance we *Or. 5. 162 A* may rest satisfied. Any Epicurean theory of fortuitousness may be dismissed at the bare mention. Peripatetics attribute the conjunction to the action of the *Quintum Genus* or Fifth element. But this merely pushes the difficulty a step back, not solving it. The earth is supported on the elephant, the elephant on the tortoise, and the tortoise—on what? It remains a final fact that soul is united with various forms of material being. The mode or cause of union transcends reason. It is best regarded not as an act of free-will on the part of animating soul, but as necessarily arising from the natural constitution of things[1]. Soul in a figure lying on the outskirts of the supra-sensual world could not but illuminate the darkness on which it bordered, formless matter, and thereby brought into being before all time the phenomenal world. The only reasonable explanation of the final dualism that everywhere meets the philosopher is offered by the Neo-Platonic scheme of eternally existent spirit and eternally existent matter connected by emanative processes. The union *Or. 5. 171 B* is brought about solely for the improvement and elevation of matter. Much as it may have to endure in the union, soul *Or. 2. 69 B, 70 B.* the superior nature, akin to God, can take no hurt or hindrance from contact with its baser companion. If cause and *Or. 4. 141 A* effect be traced so far back it is thanks to Sun that the ideas enter into combination with the ὕλη: it is his co-operating energy alone that prevents the dissipation of the Ideas when they have ventured on the contact. The coherence of the combination is due to his unifying power.

Cybele and Attis Myth. But a nearer insight into the stage, so to speak, at which the connexion was divinely consummated is granted to us in the myth of Attis[2]. Therein it is recounted how Attis ex-

---

[1] Zeller, *Phil. der Griech.* III. 2. 491 pp., 513 pp.
[2] Jul. *Or.* 5. 165 B ff. Cf. Ovid *Fast.* IV. 221 vv.

posed beside the eddies of the Gallus grew to the perfect flower of beauty; how the mother of the Gods conceived a passion for him, loaded him with gifts and crowned him with stars; how afterwards false to that love he went down into the cave and had intercourse with the nymph; whereupon followed his mutilation, and the visitation with madness. In this pregnant myth the initiated will discern the true account of the union between spirit and matter, and the origination of the material world.

The Mother of the Gods is the faithful handmaid of King Helios. She personifies his providing control. As such she directs and preserves the lower orders of Gods. She dispenses to them Sun's gifts, among others the prime gift of demiurgic power, which she at once stimulates and guides. Of this there are various grades corresponding to the grades of Gods. Attis represents the lowest stage of demiurgic productiveness, that namely at which the divine comes in contact with the material. He is the last link in the chain which unites earth with the superabundant fertility of the productive principle. The Gallus beside which Attis lay blooming is the γαλαξίας or Milky Way, which is confessedly the junction of passible substance with the impassible Quintessence. The Mother's love, her gifts, the crown of stars show her at her proper work, elevating, stimulating, etherealising the demiurgic force and desire of the lower God, so as to win it and wean it from its perilous inclination towards matter. Spite of that preserving love Attis goes down into the cave, forsaking heaven for earth, and impregnates the nymph, who typifies the immaterial cause which converts matter into material being. Such declension from divine continence might argue Attis less than divine. He has been called a demigod. But in reality it was a gracious, generous condescension, a sacrifice for the sake of outcast matter. His end achieved he returns to heaven. His emasculation has a most real meaning. It signifies the restraint of his infinite productive power, in other words the fact that in the material world generation is limited by the demiurgic Providence to definite forms. So too has his ensuing madness. The gene-

Its Interpretation.
Or. 5. 166 A B

161 D, 162 A.

165 c, 171 A.

166 c

165 D, 171 A.

168 A

171 D

167 D, 171 D, 173 B.

rative cause at the last stage, where the divine is brought into contact with matter, loses self-control: that is to say, the material world is not self-subsistent, but subject to never-ceasing change and decay.

Conservation of the Material World.

Or. 5. 167 D

Or. 4. 137 D

Such, temporally depicted, is the origination of the material world. The combination remains ever active : otherwise every organism ($\sigma\hat{\omega}\mu\alpha$)[1], matter that is to say informed with spirit, being neither uncreate nor self-subsistent, would revert to abstract indeterminate matter ($\H{u}\lambda\eta$). Its whole Being is but Becoming; in other words life depends on constant change of conditions, the means towards which is supplied from without. There is need of constant, outward sustainment, or as the Neo-Platonists prefer to say containment, by divine power. Primarily this must be conferred by the action of the sovereign One, secondarily by the Intelligible order, but immediately the world is preserved or contained by nothing else than that 'fifth substance' or Quintessence, of which the principal component is the sun's ray. This pericosmic Quintessence, not seldom spoken of as the cyclic substance, is incessantly busy at the borders of the universe coercing and welding together all the naturally dispersive elements. It belongs to the divine impassible portion of being, being that part of it which comes in contact with lower passible existences. The Milky Way marks the border line, where the creative reign of the higher Gods ends, and that of Attis commences.

132 c, 137 c.

130 c

Or. 5. 170 c

171 A

The Quintessence conserves being : it is not said to originate it. This function is constantly attributed to Sun. The necessary influx and efflux of Being, which is essential to an active existence, is provided by his ordered approach and retirement. To take a specific instance man is, as Aristotle[2] says, the offspring of man and of Sun, the former transmitting the mortal material element, the latter providing for the indwelling presence of Soul. The procreative Gods produced man, having from the beginning received souls from the

Or. 4. 137 D. 138 A.

131 c, 151 D.

Frag. Ep. 292 D

---

[1] To the Neo-Platonist all *phenomenal* matter consists necessarily of σώματα: for use of word cf. *Or.* 6. 182 D.

[2] Ar. *Phys.* II. 2, p. 194 b.

prime Demiurge. As to the act of creation, while admitting as an alternative the Scripture account, he prefers to believe that numerous couples and not one merely were created. It would have been as easy to create many as one, and the distinctive characteristics of race, features, laws, customs, and the like, no less than the vast numbers existing, point decidedly to the former as the true hypothesis. And not the nobler parts of the Universe alone, not man or the celestial bodies only, but every stick or stone is animate with its proper complement of soul, without which it would be mere formless undetermined matter. At the same time the nature of the soul animating man, living creatures, plants and inanimate matter differs[1] with the respective differences of the body animated. Inanimate objects possess qualities only, plants a living organism, animals soul, man a reasonable soul: though it is a grave question whether the superiority is not one of energy rather than of essential kind.

Frag. Ep. 291 D

291 D—292 C.

300 A

Or. 6. 182 D, 194 C.

As a brief summary of what may be called Julian's doctrinal theology, the grand ascription of praise which closes his Hymn to the Sun deserves quotation. There he addresses him as 'before all Gods Sun himself, monarch of the Universe, Who proceedeth from everlasting around the procreative essence of The Good, midmost and in the midst of the Intellectual Gods, Who before time was fulfilleth them with cohesion[2] and infinite beauty and procreative abundance and perfect intellect and all good gifts together, Who in time present radiateth light from everlasting into His visible and proper seat that hath its course in the midst of the whole heaven, Who imparteth of the intelligible beauty to all the Universe, Who fulfilleth the whole heaven with all those Gods whom He Himself intellectually containeth within Himself, multiplying around Him in indivisible fellowship and joined to Him in single unity, Who not less containeth also the sublunar space by perpetual generation and the good gifts ministered from His cyclic frame, Who careth for the

Doctrinal Theology.

Or. 4. 156 C sq.

---

[1] *Or.* 6. 182 D, to which Plot. *Sent.* 10 gives a useful parallel. Cf. also Zeller, III. 2, p. 590.

[2] συνοχή.

whole common race of men and for Rome our city in peculiar wise, even as He hath supplied[1] the substance of my soul that is from everlasting, and hath made me His own devotee.'

View of Hellenic Mythology.

It will now become plain at once that Julian did not decompose the Hellenic mythology into representations of nature worship, detecting in its tales so many transformed and fossilised solar myths. For this he had not the materials with which Sanskrit and Zend mythology have supplied moderns. An extract from Cyril's work will furnish the most compact summary of Julian's doctrine concerning the popular divinities. 'The Demiurge is common father and king of all, but he hath moreover assigned all peoples to Gods presiding over peoples and caring for commonwealths, each of whom governs his allotment conformably to his own nature. For seeing that in the Father all things are perfect and all one, while in the separate deities one or another quality predominates, therefore is it that Ares presides over the bellicose, Athene over them that combine wisdom with war, Hermes over them that are shrewd rather than adventurous, and the nations over which they preside follow each the several natures of their proper Gods.' The language here is plain; a fuller personality than usual is accorded, and in itself the passage seems clear of ambiguities. But one question remains. Into what part of this theology were the current Pagan Gods fitted?

Cyr. 115 D E

How far the Gods themselves, like the stories of Homer concerning them, are mythical, and do but adumbrate the Divine essences with which popular theology confounds them, it is difficult to determine. The question indeed at this point becomes one of terms: in short are the names assigned true names or misnomers? The answer is that the names are of human invention, the beings denoted are real. With very few exceptions they take rank among the Intellectual Gods[2] as subordinate helpers of King Sun. But

---

[1] ὑπέστησεν.

[2] Thus the real object of adoration becomes the second member—person

it would be a vain hope to search Julian's pages for a consistent account of their respective relations, functions and priority. He is too enamoured of arbitrary allegorising from Homeric genealogies, of subtle inferences from oracular verses, and of mystic interpretations of popular myths, to adhere to any plain uniform classification of deities. Their relations to King Sun are as determinate as anything, and offer the best standard of comparison.

Zeus is the highest God. In order to accommodate Hellenic beliefs and revelations[1] to the Neo-Platonic theology, he is placed usually on an exact equality with Sun, though here and there slight traces of inferiority are permitted to appear. It is only in casual adjuration that great Sun is allowed to stand second. Most commonly the two are identified as sharing single coequal sovereignty over the whole tribe of Intellectual Gods. The identification is actually justified by a Homeric genealogy[2]. To both alike is given the title 'Father of the Gods.' Incidentally Serapis is identified with Zeus or Sun, mainly on the strength of an oracular verse; he is elsewhere spoken of as the brother of Zeus. The only other God elevated to such rank is Hades. He too must thank the oracle for his representation as the gentle propitious deity[3] whose kindly hand dissolves that

The Hellenic Gods.

Or. 7. 232 c
Ep. 38. 415 A
Or. 4. 136 A, 143 D, 144 A C, 149 B C, &c.
Or. 7. 228 – 9, 231 A B.
Or. 4. 136 A
Ep. 51.

Caes. 310 D

---

we cannot say—of Julian's main triad. But I cannot follow Lamé, 235 pp., and Naville (cf. p. 104) in supposing any intentional imitation of Christian theology, or a desire to provide popular adoration with an object of worship analogous to the Son, or the Word proceeding from the Father. The analogy is far too latent and obscured to have had that practical aim, though subsequently the Manichean exponents of Magianism, in their futile endeavour to engraft their own creed on Christianity, identified Christ, regarded as the Logos, with the vivifying power of Sun. (Cf. Aug. *contra Faust.* xx. 2.) The subject is touched and Baur quoted in Hilgenfeld's *Zeitsch. für wiss. Theol.* 1861, p. 411. Herwerden's theory (p. 76), adopted by Naville, p. 114, of a comparison between Asklepius—engendered by God, and made manifest on earth as the universal Saviour of men (cf. *Or.* 4. 144 c, 153 B, Cyril, 200 A B) —and Jesus, appears to me no less fallacious. Lamé preceded Naville with like elaborated analogies: the task proved comparatively easy, after that 'pour la théologie hellénique, nous avons montré qu'elle était identique à la théologie chrétienne.'

[1] Through Homer and others.   [2] See infr. p. 97.
[3] *Or.* 4. 136 A, 152 B. Cf. Plat. *Cratyl.* xx. p. 403.

union between soul and matter, which it is the reciprocal work of Sun to bring to pass. The Muses follow him as the leader of their choir, while Dionysus is the son and consort to whom Sun appoints his proper work. Horus and Mithras are other names for Sun rather than coequal deities. None other can claim a place among Intelligible Gods unless it be Apollo. His identification with Sun can be only of a popular character, but as consort with him he takes unsurpassed rank, partaking of the same simplicity of intelligence, the same stability of being, the same immutability of energy as Sun himself. It is he who in joint ascendancy instructs men by oracles, inspires them with wisdom, and adorns societies with religions, constitutions, laws and civilisation. The other Gods are definitely inferior to Sun, and assist in special departments of his wide range of activities, personifying as it were those activities. None transcend in dignity Athene and the Mother of the Gods, between whom there is a clear affinity. Each represents Sun's controlling Providence: each may be spoken of as his consort, and acts in full communion with the Intelligible Gods[1]. The Athene myth stereotypes anthropomorphically the direct emanation of Athene from Sun or Zeus, and does not conceal her inferiority. Justice has been already done to their controlling, preservative custodianship of forces imparted to the Intellectual Gods. Athene is moreover the wisest of goddesses, and virtue and wisdom and contrivance and statesmanship are among her bounties to men. Aphrodite too consorts with Sun, as a busy handmaid in his service. Among the heavenly Gods she acts as a combining principle; she is the concord and unity of their harmony, and goes everywhere with Sun tempering his creative work. On earth she sheds forth rays of purest loveliness, brighter than very gold, melting men's souls with delight, and becoming to all living things the principle of generation and the source of self-renewing life. Dionysus represents and shares the disseminative productive power of Sun, and is a loyal fellow-worker and ruler, whom

---

[1] *Or.* 4. 145 c, *Or.* 5. 170 d, 179 d, with which cf. *Or.* 6. 182 c, *Or.* 7. 220 a.

Sun regards with paternal love. Asklepius is begotten of Sun in the Kosmos, to preserve the life and harmony of which he is the author and sustainer. Though enjoying with Sun a premundane existence, he was made incarnate on earth by the vivifying power of Sun, and endowed with human form to heal both bodies and souls of men, with which beneficent purpose he wandered—whether allegorically or no it is hard to decide—through all the great towns of earth. The Muses and the Graces are the offspring of Sun and serve him as their lord. The lower demigods, such as Korybants, Satyrs, Fauns, Bacchants take rank as dæmons.

Or. 4. 144 B, 153 B.

Cyr. 200 A

Or. 4. 152 D Or. 6. 199 D

Or. 5. 168 B, Or. 7. 220 D.

These shadowy identities are gleaned submissively from the preserves of Iamblichus. Both in spirit and form Plotinus' identifications had been more philosophic and rational, though open to a charge of tameness from the monotonous recurrence of personifications of the World-soul as manifested in higher or lower spheres[1]. The obvious vagueness of this survey, which minimises not exaggerates Julian's own lack of precision, shows how shadowy and unreal his assumed personifications are. They are of a random, caleidoscopic character. The picturesque stir and life of the old Hellenic Olympus is all gone. It has nothing in common with the new-fangled mysticism but some borrowed names and metaphors[2]. The Gods are no longer living, breathing men and women, active in love and in hate, girded with poetry, ravishing to the sense. All individuality is lost. There is no form and no colour left. The vivid lines and outlines are smeared into a neutral expressionless smudge. Personal Gods have been metamorphosed into scientific and theological conceptions or mathematical ideas; mythology has become 'a philosopho-cosmical and physico-astronomical system[3].' One

Homeric Olympus contrasted.

---

[1] Zeus, Aphrodite (in twofold manifestation), Here, Demeter, Hestia all represent one or other phase of this. Cf. Zeller, III. 2, p. 561.

[2] Schlosser, *Jen. allg. Literat.-Ztg.* p. 127.

[3] Strauss, *Der Romant.* p. 190; and from the same work compare p. 192. "In diesem Neuplatonischen Himmel dagegen ist nichts mehr fest, Alles taumelt durcheinander, in einer Götterdämmerung gleichsam zerfliessen alle scharfen Umrisse der Gestalten: Zeus ist Helios, ist auch Hades und Serapis; Prometheus ist die über alles sterbliche waltende Vorsehung;

effect of this is to invest the entire religion with a frigid and laboured artificiality that must have chilled piety and lamed all devout enthusiasm, even if it did not suggest a self-conscious insincerity. It showed the very opposite of the free Hellenic spirit; it was forced instead of natural, exaggerated instead of true, constrained instead of free. Amid this misty confounding of deities one positive idea of some interest is discernible. For the old republican constitution of the Homeric Olympus with its independent and often mutually antagonistic powers, with its jealousies and favouritisms and animosities, there has been substituted a strict and ordered hierarchy of graded deities, centering their aspirations and even merging their personality in the supreme divinity, whose sway represented in ideal perfection that absolute dominion to which the Emperor of Rome only in theory attained [1].

Relation to popular theology.

To discover hard and fast identities, or even principles of arrangement in this cloudland, is impossible. But it is easy to define the general position taken up towards the popular theology. This was contained primarily in Homer, Hesiod, and various collections of Hymns of the Gods. These the new religion accepted as of divine authority, and written by direct inspiration. Homer is habitually quoted in Julian's works with the weight of an inspired authority. How keenly the defectiveness of these as Sacred Books was felt by the Neo-Platonists is shown by Porphyrius' endeavour to supply the lacuna by a collection of the utterances of the Oracles. Such as they were, however, Julian and his confederates accepted them, and adapted them to their purpose by an elastic system of allegorical interpretation. It was in the myths more than anywhere else that the popular religious concep-

Frag. Ep. 301 B, 302 A.

aber dasselbe ist auch Athene; welche in diesem Systeme Tochter des Helios heisst;" and p. 193, "Die Götter bilden (das hatte man der christlichen Trinitäts-Terminologie abgehört) eine Vielheit ohne Theilung und eine Einheit ohne Vermischung; zu der absoluten Wirksamkeit des obersten Gottes verhalten sich alle übrigen nur noch als unselbstständige Durchgangspunkte." Compare Or. 4. 149 D, 153 D, 156 C—157 A. Also Semisch, p. 33.

[1] Strauss, *Der Rcm.* p. 191, Semisch, p. 32.

tions were really enshrined. Julian's treatment of these is bold and instructive: so bold that at times he seems almost to stand on his defence against a charge of irreverence. He freely admits that many of the ancient myths were as they stood grossly immoral and impious. But this very fact goes to prove that they cannot be actually and nakedly true. Venerable with the dust of antiquity, but stamped with the brand of inspiration, they are handed down to us as apocalyptic glimpses into those truths which the flagging intellect of man can neither accurately grasp nor formulate. They are sign-posts, not termini; their function is to excite the intellectual powers, not satisfy. Myths then, such is his theory, stand to the intellectual sense much in the same relation as images to the spiritual. They are but emblematic representations of the truth, not literal statements of fact. Wrongly regarded they infallibly obscure and misrepresent the inner truth they allegorise. They are so to say concrete mental projections into time and place of that which happened out of all temporary or local relations. The very contradictions or incongruities with which they abound are meant expressly to stimulate men to look behind the veil and decipher the hidden mystery. From the necessity of the case they are in every particular anthropomorphic in conception, whereas the truths and processes they adumbrate are wholly spiritual[1]. The mythical birth of *Helios* from *Hyperion* and *Theia* is not meant as an account of marriage and processes of generation among the Gods, ideas which are wholly incongruous with their very nature: its real signification is that Helios, first among the Intelligible Gods, sprang by emanation from a Cause yet higher still, that Cause to wit which is of all most divine ($\theta\epsilon\iota\acute{o}\tau\alpha\tau\text{ov}$), and which wholly transcends ($\Upsilon\pi\epsilon\rho\iota\omega\nu$ going beyond, above) all comprehension, for Whom and round Whom are all things create or uncreate. So again the procession of Athene from the head of Zeus, which materially conceived becomes meaningless blasphemy, sets forth in a figure the spiritual truth that she came forth entire by imme-

Myths, their interpretation
Cses. 306 c
Cyr. 44 A B

Or. 5. 170 A B

Or. 7. 206 c

Or. 5. 170 A—c

Or. 7. 220

Or. 4. 136 C D

Or. 4. 149 B
Or. 7. 220 A

---
[1] Julian of course is simply adopting the regular Neo-Platonic teaching on Myths; cf. e.g. Sallust, *De diis et mundo*, c. XIV. XVIII.

diate emanation from the highest God. The interpretation of the myth of Cybele and Attis, which runs through so much of Julian's Fifth Oration, is a more elaborate and ambitious effort in the same direction. Under Julian's handling it becomes in part a 'solar myth,' but primarily a more transcendental revelation.

and rationale.
Or. 7. 206 A

Myths thus regarded are a testimony to something of a progressive revelation of God to man. As birds fly and fish swim by instinct, with none to teach or guide the way, so man too has his nobler instinct, that will not be denied its satisfaction. The Gods have given him a soul, and that soul, even in man's infancy, could not but flutter and try its wings. Imbued with godlike affinities it tugged at the chain that held it, soaring toward truth. Shadowy images, visions of unknown glories floated before it. As the feathers[1] sprouted upon the infant soul, a strange tingling, half of pleasure half of pain, thrilled it through and through. The soul itching with intolerable desire found relief in myths. They were like nurses rubbing the infant's gums at teeth-cutting, relieving the irritation and quickening the growth. The itching was but the herald of growing powers, myths but the foreshadowing of coming revelations. The full-grown philosopher, while recognising that they may serve the infant still, knows that they were presages of more solid supervening

Or. 7. 207 A– 208 A

abilities. They are of use still maybe to spice moral teaching distasteful in its severe simplicity, and so to sweeten nauseous truths. But the perfect man has no need of sweets. He seeks rather the strong meat and medicine, which the sweet but obscured or rendered ineffective.

Popular adaptation of Neo-Platonic theory.

Such was Julian's abstract dogmatic theology. It is no disparagement of his creed to say that it was impossible to present its loftier truths to the capacities of popular intelligence. If theology is a science at all, it follows at once that its deeper mysteries will be accessible to those only who are versed in the science. The popular creed will remain a rough and imperfect representation of the truths it but dimly per-

---

[1] Julian here (*Or.* 7. 206) is almost quoting the *Phaedrus*.

ceives. By what modifications then or adaptations were these religious conceptions commended to the public?

In the first place, the purely intellectual side was perforce left in the background. The doctrine of a trinity, the relation of emanating Deities to the incomprehensible First Cause, the interdependence of Intelligible and Intellectual Gods on each other and on the primal One were left to the philosophers. But a far more vital modification than this was adopted. Monotheism, which was in a sense the creed of the Neo-Platonist, and the language of which Julian constantly employs in intercourse with his philosophic friends, was in its popular representation wholly abandoned. It is metamorphosed into polytheism, pure and simple. Nor does Julian attempt to conceal it. In temple-worship, lustrations, sacrifices, indeed in everything, he says, the Jews are in exact accord with the Pagans, *except in the peculiarity of a monotheistic belief.* 'Their sole error is in doing a displeasure to the other Gods by reserving their worship for the God whom they with barbarian pride and stupidity regard as their special property, relegating the rest to the Gentiles alone.' Monotheism is positively denounced as 'a calumniation of the Deity.' The transformation was as simple as it was necessary to win the popular ear. It merely involved a certain ignoring or rather reticence concerning higher esoteric mysteries, which is not even chargeable with insincerity. Philosophers themselves believed in the Gods as emanating agents of the One God: nay more believed that through them alone contact with the One was possible for anything short of the highest philosophic intuition.

Intellectual simplification.

Monotheism disguised.
e.g. Ep. 44.

Cyr. 306 A B

Ep. 63. 454 A

Cyr. 155 C

The whole genius of Neo-Platonism was essentially polytheistic. The Monotheistic element was subsidiary, a satisfaction and a secret for the philosopher, but for the multitude at most a tenet never a belief, a theory not a motive power. The One was incomprehensible, incommunicable, unapproachable by man; the Gods who governed the universe about him, who ruled him and his destiny, who heard his petitions, who shielded him from evil, were subordinate, many in number, diverse in form and desires and powers. This concep-

Polytheistic cast.

tion had firmly embedded itself in the religion of mankind. 'Throughout the whole world you find one single concurrent law and testimony, that there is one God, king and father of all, and Gods many, sons of God and joint rulers with God. This Greek declares and this Barbarian, this the dweller on the mainland and the dweller by the sea, this the wise man and the fool¹.' In Julian's own language, 'The Demiurge of the universe is one; the demiurgic deities, the denizens of heaven, are many.' It was a belief requiring the concentrated forces of Christianity to extirpate it: within the Church, in its last subtle phase of Arianism, it only not prevailed; without, it was seized by Neo-Platonism, coordinated with the highest reason and conscience of mankind, systematised, sanctioned, and wielded in all its versatile applications.

Or. 4. 140 A. cf. Cyr. 65.

Adaptivity of beliefs.

From this standpoint Julian was able to exhibit a ready and generous sympathy with whatever form of cult had commended itself to the people with whom he might be concerned². He assiduously emphasizes the value he attaches to the preservation of local rites or beliefs. Each is in itself a revelation: to surrender an ancestral rite is to fling away a fragment of revealed truth. Hence a scrupulous reverence for all traditional sanctities. Nations by a curious inversion of facts are regarded as representing, or as moulded by, the character of their tutelar Gods. To Heliopolis must be given back its Aphrodite-worship, to the Jews their temple, to the shrine of Serapis the cubit of the Nile. 'In things holy we do well to preserve whatsoever ancestral custom prescribes: we must neither add thereto nor diminish a whit therefrom; for that which is of the Gods is everlasting.' High priests were directed to follow the same rule in their visitations, never to extemporise new rites or improve upon old, but to shun innovation above all things³. In precisely the same spirit Julian systematically endeavours

Cyr. 116 A, 131 B C, 138.

Frag. Ep. 302 D

Ep. 63. 453 B

---

¹ Maxim. Tyrius, *Diss.* I.

² His teaching here is in complete accord with Porphyry's. For passages see Zeller, III. 2, pp. 610, 611.

³ At the deification of Emperors, partly as unspiritual, but much more as an innovation, Julian launches a bitter sarcasm, *Caes.* 332 D.

appropriately to localise his references to the Gods. If he writes to the Romans, he dwells on the special connexion of Helios with Rome, reminding them how the great God by his connexion with Venus and Mars becomes through Aeneas and Romulus respectively the immediate patron of Rome: how further the tale of the miraculous assumption of Quirinus, and not less Numa's ordinance concerning the sacred fire recognises him still as tutelar divinity of their favoured town; and how they are even reminded of the fact by the measurement of months and the season of the opening of the new year. If it is to the Athenians he addresses himself, it is to Athene, the most wise Goddess, that he appeals. If he takes up his pen to the Alexandrians, he exhorts them to a better mind by the reverence that they owe their patron-saint and founder Alexander, or adjures them by the name of Serapis their city-holding King and his maiden-consort Isis. To the Jews, to take a yet more interesting sample of the same spirit, he adopts their own monotheistic language. Their God, he says, is the same all-powerful and beneficent ruler of the universe whom we Greeks worship, though under varying names. After commending their faith and sympathising with the maltreatment they had endured, he entreats them to offer up prayers for him and for the Empire, 'to the most high God and Creator, who has deigned to crown me with his undefiled right hand'; in his treatise against the Christians he says in so many words, 'I adore always the God of Abraham, Isaac and Jacob.' It is droll to watch with what scrupulous consistency Julian carries out the same principle even in playful and familiar correspondence. If he writes to a philosopher, Hermes of reason, or the Muses will be the Deity selected; unless indeed he be in poor health, when wishes for his convalescence will be fortified by the name of Asklepius: while in a letter to an Egyptian official the name of Serapis naturally becomes the appropriate vehicle for indignation. The changes in adjuration that are rung remind the reader of Acres' device for adding point and relevance to the formulæ of oath[1].

[1] Cf. Sheridan, *The Rivals*.

Exoteric Teaching.

Caes. 314 c

Ep. 51

In his exoteric teaching Julian is perfectly content to put forward the lower and more popular motive or explanation, where he does not think an appeal to the higher will wake a responsive echo. The appeal he thought must be accommodated to the audience. In the Caesars he gently censures the stern uncompromising Probus for not thus adapting himself to the people. Wise doctors mix bitter draughts with honey to suit the unaccustomed palate: like cows or horses, men are easiest led by what they like. A good instance of this occurs in one of his letters to the Alexandrians: there in exhorting them to the worship of Helios, he says no word of the theological position or relations of that divinity, but appeals simply to the natural power of the visible sun, and bids them as they look on the changing seasons, on the processes of birth and growth, and on the ordered phases of the Moon, fall down and worship the manifested and all-powerful Deity.

His popular as contra-distinguished from his philosophical teaching on the nature and attributes of these Gods, and the manner in which he desired they should be regarded, leads naturally to a consideration of Julian's idea of personal religion.

CHAPTER V.

JULIAN'S IDEA OF RELIGION.

τὸ κεφάλαιον εὐδαιμονίας ἡ τῶν θεῶν γνῶσις.
μέγιστον τῶν καλῶν ἡ θεοσέβεια.
JULIAN.

IN his religious teaching Julian does not commence with evidences of the existence of God. God with him was a primary assumption; the knowledge of God is intuitive in man. 'By our souls,' he writes, 'we are all intuitively per- Or. 7. 209 c suaded of the existence of a Deity[1].' Thus assuming the religious sense, he deduces from it the true relations of man to God, and to his fellow creatures.

Julian's idea of personal religion is undeniably lofty: its Inward re- elevation of tone again and again betrays the Christian ligion. sources from which it was in large measure—and not seldom confessedly—drawn. If Christian shortcomings inevitably paved the way for a Pagan reaction, at least Christian virtues determined the cast which that reaction must take. Soaring Duty to beyond a utilitarian morality it recognised a duty to God as God. well as a duty to man. Religion is the highest concern of Ep. 52. 438 c
Frag. Ep.
300 man, the most essential factor of happiness. Knowledge of the Or. 5. 180 B
Or. 7. 222 c Gods is more desirable than the Empire of Rome; likeness to Or. 6. 183 A
Or. 7. 225 D the Gods the crown of philosophy; devoutness and diligence Cyr. 171 D in the service of the Gods are the primary requisites for due Or. 2. 80 A discharge of duty. Our souls—it is a noble Neo-Platonic thought—are *not our own*, but rather lent by God for a Frag. Ep.
302 c

---

[1] So too very explicitly the author of *De Myst.* I. 3. 'Knowledge of the Gods is an inherent impression inseparably implanted in us, co-operating with the essential inclination of the soul towards the good, superseding every judgment or deliberation, and antecedent to thought or argumentation upon the subject.'

season. They are given to each man as genii or spiritual powers, located as it were on the highest surface of the body, so as to raise men from earth to the proper kinship that belongs to them in heaven. The soul is 'the God within us': it is of heavenly birth, a colonist for a little space upon earth, imprisoned in the human body as a sanctifying and elevating power. And with this godlike element, waging unintermitting warfare with the dark and murky powers of the flesh[1], we must make it our endeavour to attain to absolute devotion of heart to God. 'When the soul surrenders itself entire unto the Gods, committing itself and all it hath to them that are greater than itself; then if purification follows under the guidance of the ordinances of the Gods, so that there is thenceforth nought to let or hinder—for all things are in the Gods, around them do all things consist, and of the Gods all things are full—forthwith there shineth in such souls the divine light; instinct with God they brace and enable the kindred spirit, which thereby steeled as it were by them and waxing strong is made salvation unto the whole body.' This knowledge or spiritual recognition of God is not merely worthy of a monarch or general, but lifts man almost to the level of divinity itself. Imitation of the Gods, as evinced by the suppression of human wants and weaknesses, and by constant enlargement of virtuous activity must be the aim of the believer. True holiness (εἰσέβεια) is to live ever in the practice of the presence of God. Unseen though they be, the Gods are ever near, watching our every action: so that in the words of the inspired oracle

> Everywhere the ray of Phœbus darts its all-pervading light;
> Through the flint rocks unimpeded it pursues its nimble flight;
> Through the azure depths it courses; not the circling starry throng
> Ranging heaven under sway of laws inexorably strong
> Can escape it; nor the toiling denizens of nether gloom
> Whom dim Tartarus inmureth, each according to his doom—
> But in godly souls unto virtue given
> I have joy that passeth the joys of heaven.

---

[1] For conflict in man between body and soul, cf. *Or.* 4. 142 D, διττὴ γὰρ ἐστὶ μαχομένη φύσις εἰς ἓν κεκραμένη ψυχῆς καὶ σώματος, τῆς μὲν θείας, τοῦ δὲ σκοτεινοῦ τε καὶ ζοφώδους· ἔοικέ τε εἶναι μάχη τις καὶ στάσις. Cf. *Frag. Ep.* 299 A, *Or.* 2. 70 A B, *Or.* 6. 184 A.

Thus God himself of his great kindness declares that he takes delight in the thoughts of the holy, which are dear to him as heaven's self. This holiness or godly reverence must declare itself in all our actions. Zeal in the small duties of life, in whatsoever is given us to do, is the surest test of true holiness. Among other parts of men's duty to God are enjoined piety, chastity, solemn meditation on divine things, and honour paid to God by holy worship. Prayer too is the duty of every believer, and no less his privilege, for so ready is the divine ear that 'the Gods prevent our prayers[1].' No precise rule for laymen is laid down, beyond that prayer should be conducted reverently and in silence; by his own example[2] Julian would bid them pray at least in all great emergencies and crises of life; but priests are expressly bidden to pray *often*, both in private and in public, certainly thrice a day, or at least twice, at daybreak and at nightfall, for it is not seemly that any priest should spend day or night without a sacrifice.

Frag. Ep. 300 B
293 D
293 A, 300 C.
Mis. 341 D
Frag. Ep. 302 A

In his conception of duty to man, Julian takes no less high a tone. 'Ye are all,' he says, 'brothers one of another. God is the common father of us all.' From this fundamental truth of the universal brotherhood of man follows by logical deduction the obligation of charity to all. 'I maintain,' writes Julian, 'though I speak a paradox, that it is a sacred duty to impart raiment and food even to our enemies; for the bond of humanity, not the disposition of individuals, regulates our giving.' The duty of kindness, of almsgiving in the widest sense, he emphasizes again and again. It is the homily put in the mouth of every priest to every Gentile; the good customs of first-fruits and contributions to the service of the sanctuaries had fallen into a shameful desuetude: Believers had forgotten the undying precept of Homer, that

Duty to Man.
291 D, 292 B.
290 D
Ep. 49. 429 D—431 B

---

[1] φθάνουσι οἱ θεοὶ τὰς εὐχάς, *Or.* 2. 92 D. As regards the rationale of prayer, its efficacy according to the Neo-Platonist scheme was bound up with the sympathetic though unconscious coherence of all nature by virtue of the one pervading soul. Doctrinally it stands on the same footing as magic in its widest sense. See Zeller, *Phil. der Gr.* III. 2, p. 564, and *De Myst.* I. 15, v. 26.

[2] Sc. before his exaltation; for of course as Emperor, Julian was priest as well.

> Zeus unfolds our hospitable door,
> 'Tis Zeus that sends the stranger and the poor[1].

Frag. Ep. 289 D—290 A

Each beggar that goes about the street is, says Julian, an insult upon the Gods. It is our greed, not the unkindness of the Gods, that leaves him in such a plight; and in passing him by unaided we make ourselves the authors of untrue conceptions and unjust reproaches against the Deity. 'No

290 C

man,' he continues, 'ever became poor from giving alms to his neighbours. Often have I given to the needy and received back mine own from them a hundredfold, and never do I repent of having given aught.' We must give according to the measure of our means, for the virtue lies in the disposition of the giver rather than in the amount of the gift. As Julian borrowing almost the language of the New Testament again and again bids the believer 'above all things practise charity[2], for in its train come many other goods,' there rings in the reader's ears the familiar 'the greatest of these is charity.'

Moral Virtues. Frag. Ep. 293 A Mis. 343 B C Or. 6. 198 C

Personal chastity[3] is another moral obligation on which he strongly insists. All criminal or even unseemly self-indulgence is prohibited to the moral man, who will abstain from the exciting and often licentious spectacles to be witnessed at the theatres or other places of public resort. To be in bond-

Or. 6. 198 c

age to the grosser appetites or passions is to create for ourselves a very hell upon earth. Sins of temper, hatred,

Mis. 343 D

passion, abusiveness, are to be guarded against; patience, forbearance and gentleness to be practised. Another remarkable characteristic of Julian's religious code is the very close connexion into which he brings observance of law with

Or. 2. 89 A

religion. 'The law is the daughter of justice, a hallowed and divinely consecrated treasure of the most high God, which no

---

[1] Hom. *Od.* 14. 56, Pope's version. The same quotation recurs in a similar context in *Frag. Ep.* 291 D.

[2] φιλανθρωπία, love of the neighbour, in its fullest sense. *Frag. Ep.* 289 A.

[3] This obligation formed part of the Neo-Platonic view of ἄσκησις: see infr. p. 118, 133. Porphyrius denounced all sexual indulgence, first as directly prejudicial to the soul and subjecting it to the dominion of sense, secondly indirectly, as producing new forms of life in which spirit was tied to matter. Zeller, III. 2, p. 598.

sensible man will undervalue or dishonour.' It is distinctly a part of a man's duty to his neighbour to be submissive, respectful to the authorities, observant of law. 'The true prince must be a prophet and minister of the king of the Gods,' for 'the laws are holy unto the Gods:' 'the guardians of the laws are in a manner priests unto the Gods.' Service of the Gods and the laws are coupled together as equally essential to true morality ($\sigma\omega\phi\rho\sigma\acute{v}\nu\eta$). *Mis.* 343 A, 356 B. *Or.* 2. 90 A *Frag. Ep.* 289 A 295 C *Mis.* 343 A

Such then were Julian's ideas regarding religion as an inward moral power, and such the rules of conduct he laid down. By way of sanction and confirmation these were to be supplemented by ceremonial observances. The Pagan convert was to be admitted—or readmitted—into his new religion by rites of purification analogous to baptism, and by prayer to the averting[1] Deities. Julian himself was duly initiated into the Eleusinian rites at Athens, and then or on some other occasion washed off the taint of Christian baptism with the blood of slain sacrifices; as the Christian father puts it, 'he purged off the laver with unholy blood, matching our initiation with the initiation of defilement[2].' He declined to admit to Pagan worship any Christian, who had not first been purged in soul by solemn litanies, and in body by set lustral rites. From thenceforth he was to become a regular attendant at divine service, to revere the temples, groves and images of the Gods, to the maintenance of which, as a pious believer, he would naturally contribute. Indeed he was in all respects to invest with its proper dignity and use that elaborate ceremonialism and public ritual which Julian laboured so energetically to restore. *Outward religion.*

For Julian, here palpably and confessedly plagiarising from Christianity, endeavoured to fortify his religious revival by a restored and purified ceremonialism. He came forward with a carefully prepared system of sacerdotalism. The priesthood was no longer to be a kind of hereditary property, transmitted as a social prerogative from father to son, irre- *The Priesthood. Ep.* 62. 450 C

---

[1] *Ep.* 52. 436 C, ἀποτρόπαιοι θεοί.

[2] Greg. Naz. *Or.* 4. 576 D, with which cf. Soz. 5. 2, and Jul. *Or.* 7. 231 D. V. supr. p. 51.

spective of the qualifications of the possessor. It was no more to be confined to favoured families. Distinctions of poverty or wealth, high birth or low, were obliterated. The qualifications required were henceforth to be moral not social: the sole tests of fitness love of God and love of man : love of God first, as displayed in the religion and godly bringing up of a man's own household ; love of man second, as tested by a ready and liberal charity in proportion to the means at command. The most religious and best of the citizens being thus selected, were to be carefully trained in a manner suitable to their high calling. A guard was to be set on their thoughts, no less than upon their tongues. For their intellectual training, they were to avoid scrupulously not only indecent and lascivious writings, the sarcasms of Archilochus and the snarls of Hipponax, not only profane and sceptical philosophies, but also all that was trivial and frivolous, such as the Old Comedy, or love-tales, or works of fiction. They should study history, and for their philosophical training be reared on the pure milk of Pythagoras and Plato, and on the sound meat of Aristotle, to which should be added judicious selections from the religious teaching of Chrysippus and Zeno. But no word of Epicurus or of Pyrrho must enter their ears. For devotional training, besides private exercises of prayer and attendance at public worship, they were to commit to heart and meditate upon the Sacred Hymns, the direct revelations of the Gods. When thus duly trained they were doubtless consecrated for their high functions by a solemn ordination service. No positive directions have chanced to survive, for Julian composed no formal Priest's Manual, but left only a variety of pastoral letters, called out by special occasions, and treating therefore of special points, from which his complete system may be fairly gleaned. But taking into account the common practice of Pagans and Christians alike, together with the analogy of the lustral rites of admission to the Church, it may fairly be assumed that provisions for priestly consecration were not omitted in the code of ritual elaborated by Julian.

The duties of the priest are carefully prescribed. To take

first his distinctly religious duties. Twice or thrice a day must he sacrifice, not without prayer: when his turn for duty in the public celebration of temple-worship arrives, he must purify himself night and day: he must continually be at his post within the temple for his term of office, which according to the Roman custom at least extends over thirty[1] days: during that space he should neither visit the market nor go to his own dwelling, but occupy himself wholly with divine worship and philosophic meditations. For his private bearing similarly strict injunctions are laid down. Among the first duties of a priest is that charity, on which Julian so strenuously insists: it is an attribute of the Deity[2], and therefore precious in his eyes: it will exercise itself in liberal almsgiving and ready hospitality. For active practical virtue is the highest religion, and holiness the child of righteous dealing. Habitual chastity, not only of person but in thought and word[3], holiness, which is to say the constant realised sense of God's presence, modesty, forbearance and gentleness of demeanour, and what is more vaguely termed goodness, are among the duties specially inculcated. Further, there must be always that gravity of demeanour, that sanctity, the habitual assumption of which by the Christian priests has tended so effectively to promote their religion. In order to this the priest will abstain rigidly from attendance at the theatres: he will eschew all public games, horse-races, and the like: he will never frequent the wine-taverns, nor engage in any kind of business that could bring contempt upon his profession. Nay more, not content with these negative protests against dissolute or careless living, he will be very choice as to the society he keeps. Actors, jockeys and

Frag. Ep. 302 A—303 A

Priests' daily life.

305 B Or. 2. 70 D

Frag. Ep. 299 D, 300 B C.

Ep 63. 453 A

Ep. 49. 429 D

Frag. Ep. 304 B—D Ep. 49. 430 B

Frag. Ep. 304 B

---

[1] La Bleterie in his note observes that the minimum of residence enjoined by local statutes to the prebendaries in most cathedrals is exactly the same amount. The terms or rather duties of residence are certainly far less arduous.

[2] φιλανθρωπία is Julian's word thrice repeated in *Frag. Ep.* 289 A D, cf. also *Frag. Ep.* 300 D, *Ep.* 49. 429 D. With it is conjoined χρηστότης in *Ep.* 63. 453 A. There can be little doubt that Tit. iii. 4 was present to Julian's mind, ἡ χρηστότης καὶ ἡ φιλανθρωπία τοῦ σωτῆρος ἡμῶν Θεοῦ.

[3] *Frag. Ep.* 300 C D, 302 D, cf. Niceph. x. 4.

dancers he will absolutely avoid; and while permitted to resort freely to the houses and entertainments of his friends, to enhance his priestly dignity he will but rarely frequent the market; and will moreover seldom visit or meet municipal dignitaries or officers, except in temples and places where his sacerdotal position gives him acknowledged precedence: as a general rule he will communicate with them by letter alone. Above all he will bring up his own family in sobriety and the fear of God: the women, children, and domestics of his household will attend regularly the public services: a priest failing in this deserves to be dismissed from his priestly office.

Priestly orders.

Among the priests there is to be a regular discipline and various orders. Below the priest came the inferior orders of clergy, acolytes, and the like, who will be drawn from the poorer classes, and as paid subordinates of the priests will 'serve' at the celebrations of temple-worship. While above the priests, administering set districts or dioceses as overseers, will be the 'high priests' or 'bishops.' These Julian frequently chose from among the philosophers, who were his personal friends and guides. Chrysanthius, for instance, was named high priest of Lydia. It was their duty to conduct regular visitations of their dioceses, to promote meritorious priests; and, on the other hand, to exhort, rebuke, chastise, or even dismiss the unworthy: at the same time he was bound rigorously to abstain from personal violence; 'a bishop must be no striker.' Moderation and appreciative kindness are the primary requisites. In one of his 'pastoral' letters Julian promotes the high priest Theodorus to such a position in Asia: another he addresses to Arsakius, who holds a similar place in the district of Galatia; while in a third, he himself, in virtue of his high priestly authority, suspends an unworthy priest for a term of three calendar months. In this instance, as habitually in sacrifice and temple-worship, Julian asserts very plainly his own sacerdotal prerogative: it is as sovereign pontiff of the national Church, and as mouthpiece of the Didymaean oracle that he pronounces sentence.

His treatment of this question of unworthy priests is full *Discipline of priests.* of interest, and shows how strongly he was impressed with the need and value of that ecclesiastical discipline which was theoretically maintained in the Christian Church, though among his own contemporaries it so often fell into abeyance before the consuming blight of heresy and its attendant spirit of faction. In his surviving Pontifical 'Charge' he *Frag. Ep. 295 D* dwells upon it at length. The unworthiness of a priest or a prophet cannot indeed cast any reflection upon the perfectness of the God he unworthily serves, nor can any personal demerit degrade the majesty of his office. So long as he *297 A—C* bears the name of priest and ministers before the altar, he must be regarded with a submissive and reverential piety as the authorised representative of God, to strike or insult *Ep. 62. 451 D / Ep. 62. 450 B* whom is sacrilege. He is no less consecrate to God than the inanimate stones of which the image or altar is fashioned, and like them is to be reverenced for his consecration's sake. But if he is a notorious or open sinner, then the high priest *Ep.49.130 A B / Ep. 63. 453 A* should first openly admonish and rebuke him, and if he still persist, should chastise him heavily, and at the last strip him *Frag. Ep. 297 A* of his priesthood as a reprobate. For the solemn anathema with which the ancients accompanied such degradation Julian finds no divine, or as we may say Scriptural, authority. *Ep.62. 451 C D*

Thus it is in our power to gather very fully Julian's conception of the priestly office. It is a calling more exalted *Dignity of the Priest. Frag. Ep. 289 A. 297 C, 298 B. Ep. 62. 450 C* than that of any citizen, for the lustre of the divine dignity is reflected upon it. As the immediate servants and ministers of the Gods, priests are in the truest sense their vicars or representatives. They pray, they sacrifice, on behalf of the *Frag. Ep. 296 B C 295 D* congregation and in its stead. And no personal unworthiness can derogate from their high office. It follows immediately that corresponding honour must be paid them. In the temple they are supreme, and take rank before all *296 C D* earthly potentates: the highest officer of state is but a private individual, and lower than the priest so soon as he *Ep.49. 431 C D* passes the threshold of the shrine. This inalienable dignity it is the bounden duty of the priest on all occasions to assert; no pious believer will contest it, be he an officer of army, of city, or of State, unless he is puffed up with self-conceit and vain-glory.

Priestesses.

It will be sufficient merely to mention the fact that priestesses as well as priests found a place, as always, in the ranks of the Pagan ministry. A brief but interesting letter survives from Julian to the priestess Callixene; all men, he writes, sing the praises of Penelope for the constancy of her love to man[1], sc. Ulysses. Not less praise could be due to Callixene for her love to God; and the constancy of her devotion had stood the test of not ten but twenty years. As a fitting acknowledgment of merit, Julian nominates her priestess of Cybele at the famous shrine of Pessinus, in addition to the previous dignity she held as priestess of Demeter—a proof by the way that pluralists were tolerated in the Pagan Church.

Ep. 21.

Temple Restoration.

With a sound polytheistic basis thus firmly laid, a moral law annexed, depending for vitality on its purity and elevation, and an elaborate sacerdotal structure superadded, Julian attempted to reanimate the decaying reverence for the temples, to revive the beauties of neglected precincts and the splendour of the ancient festivals, to attract and awe the public imagination by a more gorgeous ritual, to which the genius of Hellenism so freely lent itself. The prophecy of the blind hag who met him on his entry to Vienne[2], and hearing that it was Julian Caesar passing by, cried out that he should be the restorer of the temples of the Gods, found a very literal fulfilment. He did the work in part directly, in part indirectly. In some cases he gave state subsidies, or set apart local imposts, or contributed from the fiscal purse to promote these objects, while at other places he encouraged the people to restore the fallen fabric, or duly celebrate the time-honoured festivals, by promises of his favour and patronage, which not seldom took, as at Pessinus, the very substantial form of remission of taxation, if they satisfied his wishes in this respect. Among the most famous of these attempts at Church restoration was the proposed rebuilding of the

Ep. 49. 431 D

Rebuilding of the Temple.

---

[1] φιλανδρία, not φιλανθρωπία.
[2] Amm. M. xv. viii. 22.

Jewish Temple[1]. Partly from a desire to signalise his reign by lasting architectural memorials, partly from his habitual partiality to the Jews, partly perhaps in the hope of giving prophecy the lie, he took in hand the enterprise in compliance with the petition of the Jews. The strange issue of the undertaking, and the controversies that have raged around it, have imparted a fictitious importance to this particular attempt. In itself it was but one item in a long list, and one too to which Julian himself has left but one or two passing allusions[2]. Everywhere throughout the realm, at Heliopolis, at Pessinus, at Alexandria, at Antioch, at Cyzicus, he stimulated like efforts[3]. Besides rebuilding the temples, Julian tried everywhere to restore[4] to something of their ancient splendour the solemn festivals, that had everywhere fallen into disrepute. To forward this object he not only expressed special delight, when such celebrations formed part of the programme of his reception, but used himself to contribute largely to the maintenance of their becoming magnificence. At Batnæ, a small Pagan town east of the Euphrates, not very far from Carrhæ in Mesopotamia, he was overjoyed at the excellent preservation in which he found the temples and groves, and with unfeigned satisfaction contrasted their well-to-do appearance with the simple structure of mud and wood that served him there for a palace. As Emperor, careless of the offence he might give to a giddy population like that of Antioch, he declined to give any of those frivolous or immodest exhibitions that most gratified the popular taste, and confined his bounty to religious celebrations of various kinds, the magnificence of which entailed a lavish outlay. The Apostle of Paganism employed the imperial prerogative to preach as well as practice. He made bold to go down in person to the Council of Antioch, and deliver an indignant remonstrance at the scandalous neglect shown in the conduct

Festivals, &c.

Ep. 27. 400 c sq.

Mis. 346 A

Mis. 362 B sq.

---

[1] For accounts cf. Amm. M. xxiii. 1, Greg. Naz. *Or.* 5, p. 668 sq., Chrys. in Iud., Sok. iii. 20, Soz. v. 22, Theod. iii. 20, Philost. vii. 9, Theoph. i. p. 80, Kedr. i. p. 537, Glyk. iv. p. 470, Nikeph. x. 23. Warburton's *Julian* is a volume 300 pages long on this topic.

[2] *Frag. Ep.* 295 c, *Ep.* 25, and perhaps *Ep.* 30. [3] Soz. v. 3.

[4] Lib. περὶ τιμ. Ἰουλ. p. 57.

of the yearly festivals. In their dinners and banquets, he bitterly said, there was no stint of lavish expenditure: while the poverty and meanness of their temple ceremonial would have disgraced the remotest hamlet in Pontus. Nor was it only to the conduct of special festivals that he devoted himself.

Ritual. The ordinary temple-service was to be rendered at once more attractive and more imposing by an improved ritual. His taste for music, and that general æsthetic susceptibility which characterised him as a true Hellene, made him specially alive to the advantage of such accessories to worship. In the *Ep. 56* great towns choir-boys were to be selected and carefully trained in sacred music, their maintenance being provided for at the public cost. These Ephebi, or choristers, were to *Mis. 362 A* be habited in white, richly set off by ornamental appendages. *Ep. 27. 400 c* Thus the charm of surplices, the steam of incense, the lines of initiated hierophants and bearers of the sacred basket[1] would match or outvie the nascent pomp of Christian ritual; nor in allurements for the æsthetic were the tastes of the religious overlooked. However undevotional was the spirit of fourth century Paganism, Julian hoped it might become less so. Pulpits, with all the charm of novelty, swelled the furniture of the sanctuary; lectures were held and addresses delivered by trained expositors of Hellenic dogma. The *Frag. Ep.* officiating priest was to be robed very sumptuously, though *303 B– 304 A* when not acting officially he was to wear the modest garments that befitted his humility, imitating the retiring modesty of Amphiaraus, who when he went to the battle bore no crest or blazon upon his shield. The holy vestments were not to be made a public spectacle or gazingstock about the streets: to do so were dishonour to the symbolised majesty of the Gods: they must be seen and worn only in the holy place, where none but the pure in heart drew nigh.

Temple Services. By example and precept alike Julian did his utmost to encourage, at times almost to enforce, regular attendance at *Mis. 344 c* religious services[2]. Worship he looked upon not as necessary

---

[1] Nikeph. x. 4.

[2] So, immediately on his perversion, Soz. v. 1, cf. Amm. M. XXII. v. 2, Sok. III. 11.

to the Gods, as though in any carnal sense they fed on the smoke and reck of sacrifice: nor again as positively necessary to man, for indeed the highest natures might rise above it; but rather as the natural outward correlative of inward reverence and virtue, a due to the Gods, and not less a benefit and delight to godfearing men. Their abandonment of sacrificial practices is one of the allegations brought against the Christians, while the Jews are praised aloud for adherence to the old rites[1]. Accordingly fixed days and hours were set apart for public sacrifice and prayer[2]. No less important in his eyes than regularity was reverential demeanour on the part of those present: he longed to see the service conducted with decency and quiet gravity: it was real pain to him to find a disorderly crowd rushing to the temples to catch a good sight of the Emperor, and receiving him it may be with vivas and plaudits that honoured the sovereign to the dishonour of the sovereign's God. He went so far as to deliver a public harangue against such desecration. The shortest and pithiest of his surviving letters is the order addressed to the populace who cheered in the temple of Fortune: 'If I enter the theatre unexpectedly, cheer; but if the temple, then keep silence, giving cheer to the Gods alone—nay, but the Gods have no need of cheers[3].'

Caes. 333 D

Or. 2. 70 D

Frag. Ep. 296 B
Mis. 365 D

Mis. 344 C

The whole rationale of reverence paid to temples, altars and images, he expounds very clearly. Between his view of the case and that of an enlightened Romanist at the present day, there is little sensible difference[4]. He scornfully and indignantly rejects the supposition that the worshippers confound the sticks or stones they reverence with the God whom these symbolise. Such a notion could emanate only from the addled prejudice of a Christian. Jewish denunciations of idols arise from pure misconception. Their prophets are

Idol worship.

Frag. Ep. 293 B, 294 B C.

---

[1] Cyr. 299, 305—306, 351 D; cf. Sokr. III. 20.
[2] Soz. v. 16.
[3] *Ep.* 64. The play on εὐφήμιαι cannot be satisfactorily reproduced.
[4] Mr J. Duncombe translating large portions of Julian in the last century, omits in his rendering of this Epistle those very pages of 'arguments equally futile and jesuitical,' which alone Mr W. Nevins, the more recent Roman Catholic translator, selects as having the first claim upon his labours.

in reality like men who gaze through a cloud of mist upon a light perfectly serene and pure: then in their short-sightedness not discerning the purity of the light beyond, but beholding only the illuminated mist, they mistake the mist itself for fire, and screaming out Fire! Murder! Sudden Death! and such alarmist cries, set to work to extinguish what they suppose to be the devouring element. The true and reasonable use of images is very different. They are but human handiwork; they are not the Gods themselves, but symbolic representations of the Gods: material images of deities who themselves are immaterial. Nay, they are acknowledged to be an accommodation to man's creature limitations; it is man's bodily nature alone that makes them useful adjuncts of worship. Of the highest supreme Being no physical representation has ever been attempted. Even in the case of the second grade of deities emanating immediately from the first, all corporeal embodiment and service proved impossible; for they are by nature unindigent of such, and can be approached only by more exalted spiritual communion. It is the third order of Gods alone that the service of images can propitiate, and thus in this third grade of worship only do they become effectual[1]. But in their proper sphere they are to be commended and to receive due honour: they become evidences of alacrity in worship: like other rites they have the sanction of antiquity: our fathers delighted thus to do honour to the Gods, in precisely the same way as we delight to do honour to kings or princes by rearing statues or images to represent them. Thus images are not to be regarded as mere bits of wood or stone, any more than they are to be confounded with the Gods. What they really are is simply what they set up to be, wood or stones representing, symbolising the Gods. As such they are entitled to reverence. A fond parent will take delight in the likeness of his child; why? because it is stone? or because it

---

[1] Cf. Porph. *De Abst.* II. 34. 37, who says that to the highest God, man must offer pure contemplation, to the intelligible Gods words combined with contemplation, to the Universe and the other Gods bloodless sacrifice and gifts as well as prayers.

is bronze? or because it is his child? No, but because it is stone or bronze representing and recalling the likeness of his child. A loyal subject will honour the statue of his sovereign for precisely the same reason. Just as the parent loves the likeness of his child, or the subject honours the statue of his prince, so will the worshipper revere the image of his God, and in its presence realise in trembling awe the unseen pre- *Frag. Ep.* 299 B sence in whose gaze he at that moment stands. True of course the Gods have no need of images; neither have they 294 A any need of prayers. The need lies with the worshipper. It would be as reasonable to deny the Gods the service of the lips, that is prayer, as that service of the hands which comes to us with the sanction of thrice a thousand years and the 294 A consent of all known races. It is needless Julian thinks to refute the sorry argument of those who would discredit images by acts of wanton insult or destruction. It is they, not the image-worshippers, who are discredited by such exhibitions of folly and crime. A wicked brutal man can easily 295 A enough destroy the handiwork of a wise good man: that is all that is done. Even then there remain the living uneffaceable images of the unseen essence of the Gods, even the im- *Frag. Ep.* 295 A perishable stars which from everlasting to everlasting run their courses in the heavens.

This survey of Julian's position with regard to the exter- *Absti-* *nence, and* nal expression of the religious sense would be incomplete *selection* without a reference to his leaning towards observances which *of meats.* are apt to be regarded as even more formal ceremonialism than any yet alluded to. He approved and justified ceremonial abstinence at stated seasons from certain kinds of food. This was a genuine part of his Neo-Platonic creed, in more than one branch of which Orphic influences[1] are clearly traceable. Plotinus had abstained almost entirely from meat, and seldom touched even bread: subsisted indeed on the scantiest diet that sufficed to support life, and recommended similar self-denial to his disciples[2]. One explanation of the name

---

[1] So again in the interpretation of myths: cf. Naville, p. 128.
[2] Cf. the story of Rogatianus in Porphyry's *Vita Plotini*, c. VII.

Βατανεώτης¹ applied to Porphyry is that he was a vegetarian. Following in the same track, Julian, not content with himself adopting sparse², if not vegetarian fare and fasting at appointed religious seasons, recommends to others the observance of traditional rules about diet, and sees in them a genuine and permanent symbolical significance. He takes a devout pride in the insight vouchsafed to him in these matters: but does not press his theories intolerantly. The rules are for set times and certain persons, where the means, the physical condition, and the individual's will are favourably disposed. The benefit to be derived is primarily moral, and only indirectly physical. 'Purification'³ was a catch-word of Neo-Platonic Ethics: and soul being in itself perfectly pure, and every contamination derived from man's corporeal part, mortification, asceticism and fasting availed naturally for personal holiness. In his Oration to the Mother of the Gods Julian vents his opinions at length, prescribing minute dietary rules for the religious observance of the Cybelean ceremonial. With regard to vegetables, while cabbages, sprouts and the like were permissible articles of food, seeds and all roots such as turnips, were forbidden; while in the case of fruit, figs received the preference over apples, pomegranates or dates. Fish was prohibited, while birds of almost every kind were approved. Among four-footed beasts the swine attained an enviable monopoly of uncleanness. Julian proceeds to point out the underlying significance of these at first sight arbitrary restrictions. Seeds (except indeed the pods of leguminous plants whose manner of growth secured them exemption) and roots, no less than creeping plants, are forbidden as symbolising a grovelling earthward tendency, while vegetable shoots typify the opposite heavenward desire, always looking upward to the pure æther. The apple or rather probably the orange is too holy for consumption; it recals the golden

---

¹ More probably as born at Batanea in Syria.   ² Liban. *Epit.* p. 579.
³ πᾶσα ἀρετὴ κάθαρσις. Plot. *Enn.* I. vi. 6, cf. III. vi. 5, p. 308 A, and Zeller III. 2, p. 538, on Plotinus. Porphyrius (cf. Zeller 596 pp.) went even farther than his master, as may be read in his *De Abstinentia*, and Iamblichus follows in his wake in the fragment περὶ ψυχῆς, for which cf. Stob. *Ekl.* I. 1065 ff.

apples of the Hesperides, and has served as the guerdon and symbol of mystic quests and triumphs. The pomegranate is interdicted as a ground plant[1]; the sanctity of the date is perhaps a survival from Phrygia, birthplace of the Phrygian Mother's rites, where the palm grows not. But Julian rather descries in it the fruit sacred to the sun, and which never grows old. Fish are spared, first, in compliance with the general rule that that which is not sacrificed to the Gods is not to be eaten of men; and secondly, because they too diving down into the depths signify those lower grovelling desires which have been already attributed to the root-plants. Birds, on the contrary, who constantly soar, seeking the mountain-tops or the expanse of heaven, are fit food (except such as be sacrosanct to the Gods) for the soul that would aspire upwards. No wonder that the leprous pig is tabooed. He is pursy of habit, fleshly, gross: he cannot, if he would, turn his eyes heavenwards: he is fit only to be the victim offered to the nether Gods. The seriousness and manifest earnestness of the writer in tracing these rather droll symbolisms[2] remind the reader of works like the Epistle of Barnabas, or later writers of the allegorical school with whom Julian had little enough of common ground. Quite consistently with this expression of his views, he lauds the rigidity of Jewish abstinence in the matter of meats clean or unclean, Cyr. 314 c and denounces Christian laxity in this respect. It is to this apparently as much as to anything that he refers, when he charges the Christians with having abandoned the purer portion of the law, and retained all that was less edifying. Cyr. 202 A

[1] χθόνιον φύτον. I do not understand χθόνιον. He alludes apparently to the fact of the pomegranate growing comparatively low, though to call it distinctly *ground* plant seems absurd. The other sense of χθόνιος, 'infernal,' is no more satisfactory, and the expression would moreover be extremely bald if taken to mean a plant sacred to the infernal Gods. The pig is treated to the same epithet; but it is *not* connected with the fact stated immediately after that he is used in sacrifices to the χθονίοις θεοῖς.

Apples and pomegranates had an amorous signification, and their avoidance was perhaps emblematic of chastity, though Julian gives more strained interpretations.

[2] In one or two Julian has probably the Jewish law in mind, which the Christians are sharply reprimanded for ignoring. Cyril 314 c d, 343 c.

Ep. 63. 453 D

Elsewhere drawing a nobler contrast, he says that Pagan coldness and unbelief is put to shame by those who display the burning zeal that would choose death rather than violate the law of holiness, and that would suffer hunger and starvation rather than eat of the flesh of swine, or of meat that had been choked or strangled.

Outward and inward religion.

Or. 7. 214 A
Or. 6. 199 B C,
201 D.
Or. 7. 239 B C

Yet while thus insisting on the consistent and prominent recognition of the value of externals in religion, Julian taught that these were after all secondary to that inner life and spirit of which they were but the outward expression. Without holiness, he says, the hecatomb, aye and chiliomb as well, are waste only and nothing else. Sanctification of the soul was the first supreme necessity, the alpha and omega of true philosophy. So completely did he recognise this, that he explains and defends the avowed contempt expressed by Diogenes the Cynic for the outward paraphernalia of worship.

Or. 6. 199 B

'If any detect atheism in his not drawing near nor ministering to temples or statues or altars, they are mistaken; none such did he use, neither frankincense, nor libation, nor silver wherewith to buy them. But if his heart was right toward the Gods, that and that only sufficed; for with his true and very soul he worshipped, giving them I ween the most precious of all things he had, the sanctification of his own soul by the thoughts of his heart.' Thus he obeyed the voice of the oracle within and wisdom was justified of her child. The mysteries as then conducted were one of those shams of custom against which his whole life was a protest. It was his very reverence for the universal Gods and his desire for communion with them, that made him revolt against that narrow exclusive ritualistic temper, that religious quackery which limited participation in the mysteries to citizens of Athens. This is a spirit so free and noble that only a chosen few can attain to it: for the mass it is safer and more laudable to follow obediently on the lines of religion laid down for them.

Or. 6. 202 sq.

Or. 7. 238 B C

Theurgy.

Neo-Platonism sought also to catch converts by more questionable attractions, stored in the theurgic or supernatural department. These were more effective than unintelligible mysticism, doomed to elicit from the masses nothing but impatience or blank bewilderment. On Julian's own mind they laid fast hold. Not only was belief in oracles, dreams, prophecies, augury and divination a constituent part of his faith, but the sorceries of the necromancer or spiritualist[1] enchained him with their spell. But he never[2] thrusts these forward as evidences of Paganism, nor in any single passage of his works adduces them either as corroborative of the existence of the Gods, or as inducements to convert the unbeliever. He appears to have felt the dangers of popular superstitions in these respects, to have endeavoured to extirpate quackery in divination, and reduced the practice of it to a science, governed by revealed and rigid laws, and administered only by trained exponents.

His dogmas and rules of conduct were further enforced by a doctrine of future retribution, not however very loudly or prominently put forward. Holding fast in person the hope of immortality, allowing that hope as a motive to effort, and confronting with a resolute denial those who believed that the soul's life was as frail or frailer than that of the body, he acknowledges that the life to come is veiled in mystery, known to the Gods but unrevealed to man: 'men do well to conjecture, the Gods *must* know.' The retributive punishment of vice commences in this life; for if not all, at any rate most, and those the most virulent, diseases are the result of spiritual aberrations or delinquencies[3]. The childlessness of Constantius Julian regards as a distinct dispen- *Future Existence.* Or. 7. 234 c Ep. 63. 452 c d Or. 5. 178 c Or. 7. 229 A. Cf. ad Ath. 271 A

---

[1] Amm. M. xxix. i. 29 minutely describes processes that furnish a singularly close parallel to some forms of modern table-turning. Neo-Platonist references to levitation, materialised apparitions, &c. are constant. Iamblichus, for example (Eunap. *Vit.*), is credited with eliciting from the springs at Gadara a living Eros and Anteros, incarnate in boyish forms. The effect on his followers was striking: 'they believed everything' (πᾶσιν ἐπίστευον).

[2] His arguments on the Mysteries and temple-worship generally in *Or.* 6. 199 and *Or.* 7. 238 are purely defensive, and in these places he does not touch on secret magic arts.

[3] In the fragment of the letter to Photinus (preserved from Facundus of Hermiane and numbered 79 in Hertlein) Julian attributes to divine retribution the bodily emaciation, the pallor and the sunken features which Diodorus the Bishop of Tarsus owed in part to prolonged asceticism, and in part to advanced consumption.

sation of Divine displeasure. After death sinful souls will be imprisoned in the darkness of Tartarus; but 'the pit itself does not lie outside the omnipotence of God, for God knoweth even them that are fast shut up in Tartarus,' and them that draw nigh to him with godliness he will deliver. But Julian loves far more to dwell upon the brighter side, to hail death as the entering into rest[1], and the cessation of the long conflict, as the separation of body from spirit, which will then be remitted to the Gods from whom it came, and fare trustfully forth under guidance of its tutelar deity; or he will picture the heaven which is reserved for the souls of the righteous, or tell of Hades the gentle beneficent God, who sets souls free for the communion for which they pine. When the conflict is all ended, he writes impressively, and the immortal soul set free, when the dead body is turned to dust, then will the Gods be potent to make good all their promises to men; and we know of a surety, that great are the rewards which the Gods give unto their priests for a possession. The immortality to which he taught men to aspire was not a continuance, but rather an entire change of being to a new and more perfect state which can at present be only spiritually imagined. Indeed, notwithstanding fugitive expressions of an opposite character, Julian did not believe in *personal* immortality. He rejected the Christian doctrine, in favour of the Neo-Platonic supposition of pre-existent emanation before life, and subsequent re-absorption into the ocean of divinity. He held no doctrine of the resurrection of the body, an idea absolutely alien to the Neo-Platonist. His conviction of life after death was resolute; but the individual life was merged in a higher life, assimilated by kindred and divine essence: the emanative soul was once more absorbed in the spiritual order determined by its own choice and bias in mundane life; unless it passed by self-determination into other congenial phases of material connexion[2]. The one

---

[1] ἡσυχία ὁ θάνατός ἐστιν. Ep. 77.

[2] Transmigration of souls was a genuine Neo-Platonic tenet. Iamblichus, following Porphyrius, denied the transmigration of human souls into brutes or lower orders, though Plotinus imposed no such disabilities.

Tartarus of physical suffering on which Julian dwells is of *Or. 5. 178 c, Or. 6. 198 c.* this earth: the horrors of alarmist myths are flatly discarded: when the souls of the righteous are translated to the presence of Serapis the unseen[1], Hades the mild and placable absolves them absolutely from the bonds of created being, and *Or. 4. 136 B* at their enfranchisement does not fasten them to other material forms, as vehicles for chastisement and retribution, but conducts and elevates them to the sphere from which they were derived. There the separated soul[2] is affiliated to the inseparate essence with which it is most homogeneous.

Towards alien philosophies Julian adopted the normal *Attitude towards Philosophies.* attitude of the Neo-Platonist. First of all with some characteristic inexactness of thought he strove to identify them all, all at least which he approved. Herein later Neo-Platonism followed the same bent which it displayed in identifying all the shifting forms of Paganism, and evolving theoretic monotheism from a ferment of active Polytheism. Here is Julian's superficial generalisation: 'Truth is one and philosophy is *Or. 6. 184 c D, 185 c.* one;...all philosophers had one single end, which they reached *186 A* by different paths:...the tasks of Plato and Diogenes were not *188 c* different, but one and the same;...why should we erect partition walls, and separate men conjoined by love of truth, *189 A* disdain for popular prejudice, and aspiration after virtue?' By this route Stoicism is but a form of Cynicism, and both *185 c—186 A* of Platonism. At the same time minuter differences were partially recognised, and two philosophies at least were denied a place in the goodly company. The Neo-Platonist estimate of philosophies corresponds very closely to the appreciativeness displayed by them towards current religion[3]. Epicureanism was the most open and bitter foe of Paganism, Scepticism a less violent but as insidious an opponent, Stoic-

---

[1] ἀιδῆ: punning on the name Hades (Ἀιδης) with whom by oracle Serapis is identified. *Or. 4. 136 A.*

[2] μεριστὴ ψυχή is the normal term employed of the individualised souls or portions of soul, which animate matter, and are the second essential element in the compound nature of man. Supr. p. 87.

[3] As traced in the Introduction to this Essay, § 2.

ism a friendly neutral, Platonism and Pythagoreanism bold and ardent supporters. To Epicureanism accordingly Julian never gives one kind word. To refer the creation or generation of the material world to the impulse of blind uncaused forces in accordance with the Epicurean theory, he accounts the *reductio ad absurdum* of a philosophic system. Epicurean morality likewise with its scientific selfishness and apathetic indifference he condemns most strongly; while as for the dogmatic teaching of Epicureanism and Pyrrhonism alike, he thanks God that nearly all the treatises of these schools have perished. Stoics on the contrary he treats with modified approval. While criticising their doctrine of happiness, he admires their stern self-control and self-denying virtue; this he could to the full appreciate, and regarded with no less admiration the deeply religious sentiment which pervades their greatest masters' teaching on the Gods. He even recommends extracts from Zeno and Chrysippus as useful devotional manuals for priests, notwithstanding that some of their professed opinions were dangerously heterodox or immoral. In the satirical *Cæsars* Zeno finds admission and patronage in heaven, where no Epicurus or Pyrrho may enter. Octavian there makes his appearance, his colour changeful as the chameleon's, now pale, now red, now black and dark and lowering. Silenus jocosely suspects that there is mischief in the beast, but Apollo rebukes him with these words, 'Hush! nonsense, Silenus! I will consign him to Zeno's charge and will forthwith make of him pure gold. Come, Zeno,' said the God, 'take my child in charge.' Then Zeno hearkened to his bidding, and sang over him catches from the dogmas, like the incantations of Zamolxis, and made him a wise good man.

Epicureanism and Scepticism.
Or. 5. 162 A

ad Them.
255 B C

Frag. Ep.
301 C
Stoicism.
ad Them.
256 B C

Frag. Ep.
300 D

Cæs. 309

Cynicism.
Much that attracted Julian in Stoicism was present also in Cynicism[1]. The sixth and seventh Orations are a full exposition of Julian's views on Cynicism true and Cynicism false. As a rebound from the utilitarianism and insincerity of those about him, its self-abnegation and reality laid hold of him

---

[1] Their close affinity he dwells upon in *Or.* 6. 185 C—186 A.

with peculiar force. With all its defects and one-sidedness, *Or.* 6. 194, 195.
its mistakes as to the true nature of happiness, and its
failure to acknowledge the real claims and needs of soul as
opposed to body, it yet remained a worthy monument of
genuine philosophic zeal. For the poor self-deceptions and
the low worldliness of his own day, no better physic could be
prescribed than the old Cynic maxims of self-knowledge and
war against all shams. Γνῶθι σεαυτόν—παραχάραττε τὰ *Or.* 6. 188
νομίσματα—Know thyself—Down with convention—let men *Or.* 7. 211
guide their lives by that twin rule, and brighter days would
dawn for all. In true Cynicism, though least of all in that
base counterfeit of the original which did but ape the outward ugliness of the Silenus mask and contained no God, *Or.* 6. 187 B
Julian recognised a stalwart protest for the truth, more
articulate than speech. Such Cynicism was an acted creed,
a sermon written in the life. Julian reaches the very bounds
of praise when he declares the genuine Cynic to be a kind of
incarnate Platonism. Indeed Julian was himself, if the term *Mis.* 338, 339.
may pass, a rationalising Cynic; latitudinarian enough to
reject its eccentricities and indecencies, though viewing them
not without tenderness, but faithfully following the principles *Or.* 6. 187 D,
of the school as adapted to his own times and position, and 189 A.
repudiating the extravagance which disparaged all book-
learning as compared with the practice of virtue.

The Peripatetic philosophy is rated higher than any of *Aristotle.*
the preceding. On the moral side Julian considers that it
has hardly received full justice as compared with Stoicism.
In one of his letters, after quoting an Aristotelian adage,
'Better a brief span of right, than a life-time of wrong,' he *Ep.* 17. 366 A
adds, 'Whatever people may say the Peripatetic teaching is
as high-souled as the Stoic. The only difference is that
Peripateticism is less habitually cool and prudential, while
Stoicism commends itself permanently to the intelligence of
its disciples.' But intellectually, if not morally or theologi-
cally, Aristotle stands side by side with Plato; in a brief *Ep.* 55
note to two fellow-students Julian urges them to concentrate
their efforts on the doctrines of Aristotle and Plato, to make
them 'the base, the foundation, the walls and the roof' of

Or. 5. 162 B

Plato.

all knowledge. But with all this exalted respect for Aristotle he dares criticise and at times reject Peripatetic teaching, as well as compare it eclectically with other systems. For Plato such criticism or comparison, even by way of commendation, were an insult: far better strain an interpretation or distort an argument, than correct an error, or acknowledge a defect. Plato is an infallible guide. He is quoted, lauded, imitated in almost every treatise Julian wrote. His *ipse dixit* is absolute. He is the perfect seer, standing on the pinnacle of truth, the sure guide for this world and the next. Iamblichus himself cannot soar higher than to be an *alter* Plato.

CHAPTER VI.

JULIAN'S PERSONAL RELIGION.

Οὗτός ἐστιν ὁ μερίσας αὑτοῦ τὸν βίον εἴς τε τὰς ὑπὲρ τῶν ὅλων
βουλὰς εἴς τε τὰς περὶ τοὺς βωμοὺς διατριβάς.
LIBANIUS.

IT will be useful to supplement the last chapter by some *Julian's* details of Julian's own personal religion. This will serve in *personal religion.* some measure as a test of the sincerity and efficacy of his teaching, and also exemplify its working. In the main he strove conscientiously to carry out the ideal which he set before others. Recognising the grand truth that increased opportunities imply increased responsibilities, he endeavoured in imperial measure to perform the duties of a private individual. As a citizen he had been liberal to the destitute; when, *Frag. Ep.* in days of comparative poverty, his grandmother's estate, long *290 D* forcibly withheld, was at length secured to him, of his little fortune he gave ungrudgingly to those in greater need than himself: raised later to princely power, his alms must be princely. It is almost with despair that he contemplates the accumulated responsibilities of an emperor. He numbers up the virtues that are required of the man, whose highest func- *Mis. 343 C D* tion it is to be the servant not the ruler of his subjects: *Ad Them.* modesty and sobriety, gentleness and goodness, humility and *251 A,* patience, impartiality and conscientiousness, unswerving jus- *262 A–C,* tice and philosophic foresight; these and a thousand others, *Ep. 63. 453 A* and coupled to them all, an entire self-abnegation ready to forego every indulgence, to shake off all sloth, and to make the whole life a sacrifice to others' welfare: and then as he thinks of the mountainous heaps of abuses everywhere rife, he cries out in half-despair that it is verily a Herculean task thus throughly to purge earth and sea of prevalent vice, and that the true king must in sober reality, as Plato has fabled and Aristotle reasoned, be no man but a demi-god. Yet tremblingly conscious of the magnitude of his task, he faced it bravely. Not, it may safely be said, without stern effort. Early and late, in 363 A.D. no less than in 356 or 361 A.D., he confesses the shrinking reluctance with which he entered upon power. His lonely frostbitten boyhood produced an acute, not to say morbid sense of personal deficiencies. This was only partially removed by his collegiate education: it continued to paralyse energies as yet untested and therefore undeveloped. He shrunk instinctively from active life; he mapped out for himself the student's career, singing Attic tales to solace the ennui of existence[1]. The Epicurean maxim 'Live and let live[2]' seemed life's best motto. There were moments when suicide appeared the readiest solution of unhappiness. On leaving Athens for the Caesarship he wept 'fountains of tears.' One letter of that epoch or earlier is preserved. It is addressed to the philosopher Iamblichus and closes thus dejectedly:—'Do thou remain at home, and fare thou well, and never forfeit the peace thou now enjoyest; we for our part, we will bear with fortitude whatever God may dispense; for good men ought, they say, to cherish hopefulness, and do their duty while they follow destiny.' The last phrase is eminently true to his frame of mind at the time. He seemed fortune's toy; she for good or for evil was mistress of man's acts and destinies. He accepted provisionally a Stoic idea of duty, but accepted it perfunctorily: for Stoicism with its summons to action, perseverance, fortitude for their own sake, with its arbitrary definitions of happiness, with its reversal of all ordinary standards of success looked to him a bleak disappointing creed invented to disguise the failures of its best exemplars. Had not Cato failed, and Dion failed? At the moment when the insignia of pomp were conferred, there rose to his lips the

---

[1] *Ad Them.* 253 B, 262 D. Cf. Liban. *Epit.* p. 527.
[2] βιώσαντα λαθεῖν, *ad Them.* 255 B.

line of Homer[1], that on its prey 'purple death lays hold and mastering fate.' The burden of his constant presentiment was that now 'he should die busier[2].'

But no sooner was power in his hands, and he by short trial made conscious of his real aptitudes for command and influence, than these nightmares passed away. Now or never was the time to justify his old boast, to give the lie to those who assumed that good philosophers must be indifferent citizens, and to show that even a student might be cast in a 'princely and courageous' mould. It would be travelling too far aside to depict the young Cæsar as soldier, combining dash with prudence, shaming cowardice, regenerating discipline, inspiring devotion in his friends and terror in his foes; or to review with any fulness his exploits or mistakes as legislator, as administrator, as economist, as judge, as orator or as student; but the moral gist of his whole bearing as Cæsar and as Augustus claims some summary. *Energy rous^{ed}.* *Ep. 35. 410 c* *Or. 2. 86 a*

No stress need be laid on his easier excellences, manliness, courage, generosity, fidelity to friends, and such like: they belonged to the man, and were little affected by his creed.—Of his more strictly moral virtues the most striking is his unselfish, untiring devotion to work. At the close of his first year of power he pictured the virtuous prince as one 'laborious and of capacious mind, allotting their proper tasks to all, reserving for himself the largest share, but without reserve distributing the rewards of peril among the workers.' Five years later his panegyrist[3] speaks thus:—'Our most virtuous emperor spares nothing to make us live as our station demands, abounding in all things needful, leading chaste but cheerful lives. Other emperors have been either chafed by hard work or enervated by sloth. The strenuous have failed in graciousness, the gracious in earnestness.......Our emperor spares himself no trouble and no fatigue; but exacts neither from his friends. His toil secures others' leisure. He is the dispenser of wealth, the eager recipient of cares, *Self-forgetful industry.* *Or. 2. 86 c*

---

[1] ἑλλαδε πορφύρεος θάνατος καὶ μοῖρα κραταιή. Hom. *Il.* v. 83 in Amm. M. xv. viii. 17.

[2] Amm. M. xv. viii. 20.   [3] Mamert. 12.

readier always to discharge the most irksome offices in person rather than impose them upon others.' But testimonies[1] to his indefatigable self-denying industry are too common to multiply; the more as it will appear abundantly in the sequel. Physical weakness[2] renders this elastic energy the more admirable.

Julian's Motives.
Or. 2. 87 c
Mis. 354 b

The motive which impelled him was partly a high Neo-Platonic sense of duty and religion; partly a deep conviction of the power of his example, as it is written in Plato, 'Rulers and elders must practise modesty and temperance, that the people may see and be beautified:' partly too, it is just to add, an intense love of applause, degenerating at times to vanity, wilfulness and egoism[3]. Another characteristic of Julian was kindliness: it is prominent both in public and private relations. One striking instance of leniency was his treatment of Constantius' adherents, who were about him when proclaimed Augustus: at that critical hour he neither committed nor allowed a single execution, though more than one declared personal enemy was in his grasp[4]. Few usurpers of the Empire could say the same. It is hardly less rare to find an autocrat pleading for clemency of treatment to prisoners in gaol previously to sentence being declared: to the innocent it is a due; to the guilty it will do no harm. Most victors would agree with Julian in the policy of relentlessly pushing and harrying a foe till he acknowledges defeat, but not all, of his age not many, would have seriously called it 'a pollution' to strike or slay the enemy who asks for quarter. But his gentleness appears not only in lenient treatment of enemies, nor only in the general indulgence of his rule, and his affectionate solicitude for the welfare of his subjects[5], but quite as prominently in more personal relations: in courtly

Kindliness.

Frag. Ep. 291 a

Or. 2. 86 b c

---

[1] For instance Amm. M. xvi. v. 4—6: and in war even more than in peace.

[2] In his private letters it is by no means uncommon to find Julian suffering from severe indisposition. Cf. *Ep.* 44, 48, 60. 446 d—447 b. Cf. *Ad Them.* 259 d.

[3] See Semisch, p. 19. who well quotes Amm. M. xxii. vii. 3, xxv. iv. 18.

[4] Schlosser, a hard critic, selects this for special praise. *Uebersicht der Gesch.,* &c. iii. ii. p. 337.

[5] Cf. *Mis.* 345—6, *Or.* ii. 86, Eutrop. x. 16.

deference towards officials[1]; in affability towards councillors, with frank acceptance of wise rebukes; in devotion to teachers, such as Maximus, Libanius, Iamblichus; in gratitude to benefactors, such as Eusebia; in private life, as for instance in the kindly letter, by which he hopes to console the bereaved Amerius for the loss of a young wife: the news had 'filled his eyes with tears.' But natural lenity did not shove justice aside. Julian was just, yet not afraid on occasion to temper justice[2]. Rigidly exacting of proof, he presumed innocence till guilt was substantiated. When an angry advocate, baffled in his indictment, cried impatiently, 'Can any one be found guilty, if denial is to clear him?' Julian promptly responded, 'Can any one be found innocent, if assertion is to convict him[3]?' He aimed at being 'slow to condemn, but slower still to relax a sentence once given[4].' Moreover an habitual earnestness armed him with great power of righteous indignation at acts of unjust oppression. At no small risk he manfully shielded the provincials from the exactions of Florentius, a prefect appointed in Gaul by Constantius. Hear his own words[5] to his private friend and physician:

Ep. 37

Justice.

Ep. 6

'He thought to implicate me in his own infamy, by sending me his knavish infamous memorials for signature. What was I to do? hold my peace or show fight? The first was a feeble, cringing, debasing course; the second was honest, manly, and free, though circumstances made it inconvenient....... Was I to abandon an unfortunate population to the mercy of thieves, or to the best of my ability defend them, reduced as they are to the last gasp by the villainous machinations of rogues like him? To me it appears cruel injustice to put military tribunes on trial for

[1] Mamert. 28, 30, with which cf. Amm. M. xxii. vii. 1, 2.
[2] For instances, cf. Amm. M. xvi. v. 12, 13.
[3] Amm. M. xviii. i. 4.
[4] Amm. M. xxii. ix. 9. ille iudicibus Cassiis tristior et Lycurgis, causarum momenta aequo iure perpendens, suum cuique tribuebat. In xxii. ix. 9—12, xxii. x. and other passages referred to on p. 186, *notes* 1, 2, 3, may be found corroborating testimony.
[5] *Ep.* 17. The official is not named; Heyler and others following Petau, insisting on a particular term of abuse (τοῦ μιαροῦ ἀνδρογύνου), suppose the eunuch Eusebius is alluded to, but La Bleterie seems more right in referring the account to Florentius, concerning whom cf. *Ep. ad Ath.* 280 A, 282 c sq., as well as Amm. Marc.

leaving their post, to punish them with immediate death, and refuse them burial; and then myself to desert my post as champion of the unfortunate, when called on to fight against thieves like these, and that too with God, who gave me my commission, contending on my side.—Well, if it should turn out ill, it is no small consolation to have a good conscience for a companion.'

The Virtuous Prince. Or. 2. 86 D

Thus as a ruler he sought to be a faithful shepherd of the flock entrusted to him. He regarded σωφροσύνη as essential to the true monarch, and he gave to the term a daunting comprehensiveness. By his definition it included 'conscious active subjection to the Gods and the laws[1], frank recognition of the claims of equals, courteous acknowledgment of superior merit, watchful precautions against class oppression, with constant readiness to brave prejudice, passion and abuse; all this moreover with unruffled resolute composure, disciplining and controlling every passionate impulse.' It included too 'abstinence from questionable pleasures of all kinds, even from those tolerated by an elastic public opinion, in the conviction that private personal indulgence is the sure outcome of public laxity and frivolity.'

Mis. 343 A B

Chastity.

It is time now to inquire into his more inward practice of virtue and beliefs. First then his personal chastity stands above reproach. No Christian writer[2] has impugned it,

[1] This is well illustrated by Amm. M. xxii. vii. 2.

[2] Contemporary or ancient writer I mean, for moderns have been found less charitable. The best, La Bleterie, Gibbon, Lardner, De Broglie (with some qualification), as of course Mücke, Semisch, Mangold, Röde, &c., clear Julian of all incontinence. Tillemont it should be said takes an opposite view. Auer's more vicious attempt to blacken Julian into a false husband and a treacherous assassin by ransacking the fathers, by adopting everywhere the unkindest construction of passages, and by adding hypotheses of his own as prurient as they are baseless, deserves no detailed refutation. Not content with hinting that Julian was the author of Constantius' death, and asserting that he was the father of bastard children, he does not even spare the reputation of Eusebia, and wantonly asperses the pure and (to both) most creditable relations that existed between the gentle empress and Julian. Cf. Auer, *Kaiser Julian*, II. §§ 4, 5, 6. Lamé, be it said by the way, makes quite sure (p. 69) that the gifted Eusebia designedly 'set her cap' at the taking and gifted young student, in preparation for the eventuality of Constantius' death. Nothing can be added to the data discussed by La Bleterie on *Misop.* 345 c, and De Broglie, IV. p. 51 n. Briefly, if the most unfavourable interpretation be put on ὡς ἐπίπαν of *Mis.* 345 c, the broad

while Pagans with one mouth extol even if in some cases almost deprecating it. 'Purer than a Vestal' is the description of Mamertinus, while Libanius and Ammian[1] are to modern reserve indelicately precise in their emphatic acquittals of Julian from all frailty: to Zonaras he seemed unnaturally fastidious. In Julian's own eyes personal purity was a part of that entire subdual of the flesh, which his philosophic creed inculcated. When first introduced to the highest mysteries of Neo-Platonism, he was told that such were the ecstatic revelations reserved for the initiated, that he would shortly blush to own the nature and name of man. He should be like Plotinus, who would neither hear nor make mention of his parents, his country or his birth; who replied to the disciple who desired his portrait, that it was enough to bear the image in which nature had veiled us, without perpetuating it for posterity. Julian was a humble follower in the same track. Not only did he practise strict continence, and abstain from the frivolities of the theatre and the exciting or bloody spectacles of the amphitheatre with resolute determination, but in his private life practised a strict asceticism. Abstemious in diet, stinting himself of sleep, rejecting downy coverlets for the coarse carpet rug and palliasse, he guarded against the first approaches of effeminacy[2]; in the hardest winter he went

Personal morality.

---

irony of the whole piece disarms it of strict evidential value. As to the curious notice of 'his children's nurse' or 'attendant' (ὁ τροφεύς) in *Ep.* 40, 417 c and *Ep.* 67, it is probably a pleasantry to which the clue has been lost. Some, e.g. Lardner, have supposed the παῖδες or παιδία to mean slaves, or to refer to certain children adopted or at least cared for by Julian. This is more plausible than the impossible supposition that they were bastard children elsewhere unmentioned and unknown. At the same time it can hardly be right. The τροφεύς is on both occasions engaged in the irrelevant occupation of travelling about the empire: and on both occasions has letters in charge: in fact he turns out to be a confidential courier or postman. The children whom he 'nursed' were an Athene offspring of Julian's own head, his epistles to philosophers. This gives a tangible force to the ἐμαυτοῦ both times repeated (τῶν ἐμαυτοῦ παιδίων—τῶν ἐμαυτοῦ παίδων) which the other alternative denies it. [La Bleterie's idea that the τροφεύς was husband to the midwife who attended at Helena's unhappy confinement some six years previously is desperately far-fetched.]

[1] Amm. M. xvi. v, xxiv. iv. 27, xxv. iv. 2, 3.
[2] *Mis.* 340 B c, Liban. *Epit.* p. 579, Amm. M. xvi. v. 4, 5, &c.

Mis. 341 B c — without fires: striving in every way by constant discipline of the flesh to follow out those precepts of Plato and Aristotle which from childhood he had imbibed.

Belief in Providence. — His religious life demands a closer scrutiny. The first most noticeable trait is his ever-present belief in an overruling Providence. 'For it is against all reason,' he writes, 'that a man who commits himself wholly to the Almighty should be dis-

Or. 8. 249 A — regarded of him and left utterly desolate: rather, God shelters him with his own arm, endues him with courage, inspires him with strength, teaches him all he ought to do, and deters him from all he ought not to do.' Like professions recur again and again in the pages of his writings. They appear in

ad Ath. 276 A — his state manifesto to the Athenians. Human wisdom, he tells them, is powerless to change the past or foretell the future: even for the present it is not infallible, and may be content with a comparative exemption from error. But the far-reaching wisdom of the Gods, with its omniscient gaze, knows and does always what is best; for the Gods themselves are the authors of the future no less than of the present. To their guidance men may entrust themselves without reserve. The same belief is reiterated till it becomes a common

Mis. 352 D, 354 B, &c. &c. — place in his devotional works. It meets us in his Satires. And perhaps no religious thought recurs more frequently in his private correspondence. Writing immediately after the

Ep. 13 — death of Constantius to his uncle Julian, he says that all his actions had been prompted by an immediate impulse from the Gods: he had been but a passive agent in their hands: had the issue been put to the stake of a battle-field, he should have trusted all to fortune and the Gods, awaiting such issue as might seem good to their love. To the provi-

Ep. 44 — dence of the all-seeing God he attributes his falling into sick-
Ep. 66 — ness, no less than his recovery from it. From Him comes all
Ep. 27. 399 D, 68. — success and all disaster. The saying 'Deo volente' glides as naturally into Julian's correspondence as into the letters of a modern Christian.

Fatalism.
Or. 7. 232 D — Not unfrequently indeed this present sense of an overruling Providence is exaggerated into a kind of semi-Fatalism, from excesses of which however Julian's masculine good sense

preserved him. He speaks of conduct 'regulated not by vir- *ad Them.* tue only nor resolute free choice, but far rather controlled by *255 D* an ever-ruling fate constraining the bent of action to its will.' Once again dwelling on the active power of fate, he quotes with approval the dictum of Plato, which in his own experi- *257 D* ence he has found true—'God is all things, and with God's help fate and circumstance control all human action.' In this connexion, for the sake of the insight it gives into Julian's religious life, it will be useful to cite long extracts from the allegory[1] in which Julian has described the phases or crises of belief which he passed through. Nothing could show more vividly how completely Julian regarded himself as an instrument in the hands of the Gods, from whom he had derived an altogether special mission.

Having portrayed Constantine under the image of an *Autobio-* unscrupulous rich man[2], and described the scenes of disorder *graphical Allegory.* and crime that ensued upon the distribution of his vast wealth to his unworthy heirs, he represents Zeus and Helios taking counsel together to counteract the mischief and impiety that had resulted from the insolent pride of these heirs. A consultation with the Fates results in the weaving of a new thread of life for Julian.

"Then Zeus addressing himself to Helios says, 'Behold this *Or. 7.* young child; kinsman though he is, nephew of the rich man of *229 c sqq.* whom we spake and cousin to his heirs, he is just flung aside in utter neglect; yet is this child thy offspring. Swear then by my sceptre and thine, that thou wilt take him in special charge, wilt tend him and heal him of his sickness. Thou seest how he has been as it were begrimed with smoke and filth and soot[3]; and that the flame which thou hast sown in him is in danger of being quenched, unless *thou* gird him with strength. To thy charge I and the Fates do commit him. Take him hence and nurture him.' Thereat King Helios was glad and took pleasure in the babe, seeing yet alive in him a tiny spark of his own fire, and

---

[1] It forms a part of *Orat.* VII, levelled against the Cynic Heraklius as his penalty for *mis*-allegorising.

[2] The opening 'A rich man had many flocks and herds and droves of goats' looks like a direct imitation of 2 Sam. xii. 2.

[3] The reference is to Julian's Christian training.

from that day forth he nurtured the young child, and withdrew him

> From blood and the war-din and slaughter of men.

And father Zeus bade Athene too, born without mother and ever-virgin goddess, aid Helios in the nurturing up of the tender child. Now as soon as he was nurtured and come to youth's estate

> With the down on his chin, and in youth's fresh bloom,

when he surveyed the multitude of wrongs that had been wrought upon his kinsmen and his cousins, his impulse was to fling himself down to Tartarus in horror at the magnitude of those wrongs. But of his good grace Helios and Athene of Providence cast him into the slumber of a deep sleep and banished that design; then when he had awaked he went into a wilderness. Now it came to pass he lighted there upon a stone, where he rested for a space and considered with himself how he might escape the throng of all his woes: for so far everything looked to him untoward, and there was no good thing anywhere. Then Hermes, whose heart was wholly towards him, appeared to him in the form of a young man as one of his associates, and accosted him affectionately and said, 'Come hither, and I will guide you along a smooth and more level track, as soon as you have surmounted this little space of crooked broken ground, where every one, as you see, stumbles and then makes his way back again.' Then the young man turned and set forward very warily. Now he had with him a sword and a shield and a lance, but his head was still quite bare. Trusting to his guide he pushed forward by a smooth unbroken path, beautifully clean and teeming with fruits, and many goodly blossoms, such as the Gods love, and with shrubs of ivy and bay and myrtle.

So he led him to a great and tall mountain, and said, 'Upon the crest of this mountain sits the father of all the Gods. Take heed therefore: here is your great peril: first worship him with all reverence, then ask from him whatever you desire; mayest thou choose, my son, that which is best.' When he had said these words, Hermes hid himself again. Now he would fain have inquired of Hermes what thing he ought to ask of the father of the Gods; but when he did not see him near, he said, His counsel was good, though incomplete. Let me therefore with good success make entreaty for the best gifts, though I do not clearly behold as yet the father of the Gods. 'O father Zeus, or by whatsoever name thou delightest to be called, point me the way that leadeth upwards to thee. For yonder regions where thou dwellest are incomparably beautiful, if I may divine their beauty that is at thy side from the pleasantness of the path which I have already travelled.' When he had prayed thus, there fell upon him a kind of sleep or trance. And the God showed him Helios himself. Then the young man, astonished out of measure at the sight, exclaimed, 'To thee, O father of the Gods, in return for these and all thy other gifts, I offer and consecrate myself.' Then casting his hands about the knees of Helios, he laid hold of him and besought him to be his saviour. Then Helios called Athene, and bade her first examine the arms that he carried. Now when she saw the shield and the sword and the spear, she said, 'But where, my son, is your ægis and your helmet?' Then he made answer, 'Even these I had work to procure; for in my kinsmen's house I was despised and flung aside, and there was no man to be my helper.' 'Know therefore,' said great Helios, 'that thou must assuredly return thither.' Then the youth entreated him not to send him thither again, but rather keep him; otherwise he should certainly never return again, but perish of the ills he suffered there. And as he besought him importunately with tears, the God said to him, 'Nay, you are young and uninitiated. Get you therefore to your own folk, that you may be initiated and dwell there in safety: for you must go hence and purge away all those iniquities, praying for aid to me and to Athene and to the other Gods.' As soon as the young man heard that, he stood still in silence.

Then great Helios led him to a certain eminence, whose top was full of light, but the lower parts of fold on fold of mist, through which the light of the brightness of King Helios pierced dimly as through water. 'Do you see,' asked the God, 'your cousin who hath the inheritance?' 'Yea,' said he. 'And yonder herdsmen too and shepherds?' Once more the young man answered in the affirmative. 'What like, pray, is he that hath the inheritance? and what like are the shepherds and herdsmen?' The young man made answer, 'Methinks he is sodden with sleep, and keeps himself close and is given over to pleasure: and the dutiful Shepherds methinks are few, for the most are bad and brutal. For they both devour and sell the sheep, and so do double wrong to their master. For they destroy his flocks and bring in small returns from ample means, and grumble for wages and make complaint. And yet it were better to secure their wages in full than to destroy the flock.' 'Suppose that I and Athene, at the behest of Zeus,' said Helios, 'were to make you steward of all these in the room of him that hath the inheritance?' Then the young man clung to him once more, and besought him greatly that he might remain there. But he said, 'Be not very rebellious,

Lest the excess of my love be turned to the fierceness of hatred.'

So the young man answered, 'Most mighty Helios, and thee Athene, and Zeus himself, I do adjure, do with me what ye will.'

After this Hermes, suddenly re-appearing, filled him with new courage, for now he thought he had found a guide for his return journey, and his sojourn on earth. And Athene said, 'Listen, most goodly child of mine and of this good sire divine! This heir, you see, finds no pleasure in the best of his shepherds, while the flatterers and rogues have made him their subject and slave. Consequently the good love him not, while his supposed friends wrong and injure him most fatally. Take heed therefore when you return, not to put the flatterer before the friend. Give ear, my son, to yet a second admonition. Yon sleeper is habitually deceived; do you therefore be sober and watch, that the flatterer may never deceive and cheat you by a show of friendly candour, just as some sooty and grimy smith by dressing in white and plastering his cheeks with enamel might finally induce you to give him one of your daughters to wife. List now to a third admonition. Set a strong watch upon yourself: reverence us and us alone, and of men him that is like us and none other. You see what tricks self-consciousness and dumb-foundering faint-heartedness have played with yonder idiot.' Great Helios here took up the discourse and said, 'Choose your friends, then treat them as friends; do not regard them like slaves or servants, but associate with them frankly and simply and generously; not saying one thing of them and thinking something else. See how distrust towards friends has damaged yonder heritor. Love your subjects as we love you. Let respect toward us take precedence of all goods: for we are your benefactors and friends and saviours.'

At these words the young man's heart was full, and he made ready there and then to obey the Gods implicitly always. 'Away, then,' said Helios, 'and good hope go with you. For we shall be with you everywhere, I and Athene and Hermes here, and with us all the Gods that are in Olympus, and Gods of the air and of the earth, and all manner of deities everywhere, so long as you are holy toward us, loyal to your friends, kindly to your subjects, ruling and guiding them for their good. Never yield yourself a slave to your own desires or theirs. And now, besides the armour, in which you came hither, take this torch from me for your journey, that even on earth its light may shine mightily before you, so that you will desire nothing upon earth; and as fair Athene's gift take this ægis and helmet, for she has many another gift, you see, and she gives to whom she will. Hermes likewise will give you a golden wand. Go therefore furnished with this armour, over land and over sea, stedfastly obeying our laws; and let none, neither man nor woman, nor friend, nor stranger, persuade you to neglect our precepts. So long as you cleave to them, you will be dear and precious to us, reverenced by our good servants, and the terror of miscreants and evil-doers. Know that your poor body hath been bestowed on you for this service; for from respect to your fathers we will cleanse you your father's house. Remember therefore that your soul is immortal and born of us, and that if you follow us you shall be a god, and with us shall behold our father.'"

The last words of the extract emphasize Julian's belief in *Immor-*
immortality. This has already been discussed, but it will be *tality.*
pertinent to remark that his personal belief was more than a
dim transient hope, useful to grace a philosophic period, and
remained with him unshaken, his solace in the hour of death.
When the fatal wound had been received, and Julian faint
with loss of blood and conscious of approaching death, lay in
the tent amid the sorrowing throng of friends and comrades
who surrounded the bedside, he addressed them all. The
time of departure he said was at hand: like an honest debtor
he must render back to nature the life that she had lent.
Death he could face with joy rather than sorrow, remembering that it was the most precious gift of the celestial Gods to
pious souls. He had nothing to repent of, and no wilful
wrong to regret: alike in the obscurity of youth and in the
exercise of sovereign power he had striven to keep his hands
unspotted with crime. The tranquillity for which he had
long yearned would now be his; that thought filled him with
an almost exultant joy. He had long foreseen his end: none
could be more happy or more glorious. As he had been
ready to live, so he did not fear to die. His strength was
ebbing fast. His latest prayer was that a virtuous ruler
might be found to succeed him. During the brief span of
life that yet remained, he discoursed with Maximus and
Priscus on the exalted nature of the soul, till at midnight the
gush of blood came which painlessly set him at rest. In spite
of philosophic affectation, and a characteristically Pagan self-
complacence, it is hardly gross exaggeration to say that his
death was 'not only, like that of Sokrates or Marcus Aurelius,
resigned and dignified, but full also of faith and hope and
spiritual exaltation and passionate yearnings for his celestial
abode[1].'

Throughout the whole of the above extract stands promi- *Commu-*
nently forward Julian's pervading sense of intimate personal *nion with God.*
communion with God. 'Though I tremble before the Gods,' *Or. 7. 212 B*

---

[1] Lamé, *Jul. l'Apost.* p. 193. The *unchristian* aspect of it is admirably
given in a passage well worth perusal in Newman's *Idea of a Univ.* p. 194.
Amm. M. xxv. iii. 15—23 is the one prime authority.

he elsewhere writes, 'and love and worship and hold them in awe, yet alway and in all things do they deal with me as gentle masters, as teachers, as fathers, as my own kin, yea, in all things it is always so.' The same trait manifests itself in his earnestness and regularity in prayer, which reappears often quite incidentally at most of the great crises of his life. When summoned from Athens, to the throne or the scaffold, *ad Ath. 275 A* he scarce knew which, he relates how he lifted up his hands to Athene's consecrated mount in passionate entreaty that she would not desert nor betray her suppliant, but suffer him if it might be even to die in Athens. Once more, in Gaul when the sound fell upon his ears of the voices of soldiers *ad Ath. 284 c* proclaiming him Augustus, there in the upper chamber he fell upon his knees in prayer to Zeus, and called upon the God not unavailingly to guide him by a sign. And it was so in the small crises no less than in the great. He would constantly rise at midnight and in secret pray to Hermes, the God of sound judgment, as the best preparation for his official duties on the coming day[1].

Julian's prayer. As a specimen of Julian's prayers, it cannot be wrong to quote the supplication with which he concludes his address to the Mother of the Gods:—

Or. 5. 179–180. 'Mother of Gods and men, consort and partner in the throne of mighty Zeus, Source of the Intellectual Gods, thou who farest ever with the undefiled essences of the Intelligible Gods, who receivest from them all the common source of being and dost transmit it to the Intellectual Deities, life-bearing Mother, thou Wisdom and Providence and Creatress of our Souls, thou who lovest great Dionysus, who didst succour Attis when exposed, and didst raise him again after his descent into earth's cavern, thou who dost minister all blessings to the Intellectual Gods, and satisfiest with all things the sensible Universe, who givest to us all things alway good, vouchsafe to all men happiness, whereof the chiefest element is knowledge of the Gods: grant unto the Roman people at large, first and foremost to wipe off the stain of atheism, and next thereto grant also that favouring fortune may guide the helm of state for many thousands of years; and to mine own self vouchsafe as the fruit of my service toward thee, truth in my views about the Gods, perfectness in theurgic art, and in all things, to whatsoever tasks of peace or war I lay my hand, virtue

---

[1] Amm. M. xvi. v. 5, and cf. Liban. *Epitaph.* i. 564.

and happy fortune, and to the end of this life peace within and a fair name without, with a good hope for the journey that shall bring me to the Gods.'

One letter is interesting as showing Julian's belief in intercessory prayer: it is that to the Jewish Council, where remarking that in the press and worry of business princes had but brief leisure to pray, he begs that public supplications may be offered in his behalf for God's blessing and guidance in the affairs of state. *Intercessory prayer. Ep. 25*

His punctilious regularity at public worship[1] is so characteristic a trait of his life as to deserve renewed emphasis. It was a part of that scrupulousness in all religious matters which is stamped on every portion of the religious revival which he led. It provoked the amusement of friends and the derision of enemies. He is at pains to justify it more than once in his own writings. But he does not make it sufficiently clear, how far it was as a devout layman, and how far in his imperial character as high priest that he admitted and fulfilled obligations of worship. It was his custom to offer public sacrifice morning and evening[2]. He erected a shrine to the sun within the palace walls: he 'initiated and was initiated.' When he and his little philosophers' clique of seven came to Antioch, they went nowhere at all, ironically writes the ringleader, but to the temples, and just now and then by detachments to the theatres. 'He divided his life between political occupations and service about the altars[3].' So prodigal were his sacrifices that the people of Antioch nicknamed him 'the Slaughterer[4].' During his campaigns he endeavoured to secure the attendance of the soldiers at these celebrations. Such a practice, on the authority of a trustworthy historian, was not without its abuses: the multitude of oxen and smaller cattle, not to mention birds, offered almost daily by Julian was such, that according to Ammian *Attendance at worship, &c.*

Mis. 345 c

Ep. 38. 415 c

---

[1] Soz. v. iii. 2, Liban. *Ad Iul. Hyp.* 394, 395, *Monod.* 509, &c.

[2] *Ep.* 27. 401 D, corroborated by Liban. *Epit.* i. p. 564, *Ad. Iul. Hyp.* p. 394.

[3] Lib. περὶ τιμ. Ἰουλ. § 22, p. 56.

[4] Amm. M. xxii. xiv. 3, Zonar. xiii. 12.

his troops, *more particularly the Petulantes and the Celts*[1], gourmandized so freely on the victuals and drink thus liberally furnished, that many of them had to be carried home to their quarters on the shoulders of bystanders. The supply of animals threatened to run short: the witty epigram composed against another philosopher emperor could not but recur to the minds of the spectators:

> We the white bulls bid Marcus Cæsar hail!
> Win but one victory more, our kind will fail[2]!

Mis. 346 B

Perhaps it was no wonder that Julian found his soldiers very religiously disposed! Here is the ironical description of his conduct, put in his own mouth in the *Misopogon*: 'The Emperor, to be sure, offered sacrifice once in the temple of Zeus, again in that of Fortune, and then marched off thrice running to Demeter's. For I have lost count of the number of times I resorted to the shrine of Daphne, that august fabric which the negligence of its warders betrayed, and the presumption of the atheists demolished. The Syrian kalends are here, and the Emperor is off again to Zeus *Philios;* then comes the state festival, and with it the Emperor on his way to Fortune's precincts: and no sooner is the one fast-day over than he is once more paying his vows to Zeus *Philios.*'

Ep. 27

His letter to Libanius descriptive of his doings during the opening days of the Persian expedition reads like the account of a religious rather than a military campaign. So great was his conscientious, but dispiriting waste of energy! It amounted to a nervous excited assiduity ill calculated to express contained and restful piety, induced it has seemed to some[3] by misgivings rather than fulness of conviction.

---

[1] Amm. M. XXII. xii. 6. The touch is graphic, and may be looked upon as an '*undesigned coincidence*' confirming the general statement. Ammian here writes as an eye-witness.

[2] οἱ βόες οἱ λευκοὶ Μάρκῳ τῷ Καίσαρι χαίρειν.
ἂν πάλι νικήσῃς, ἄμμες ἀπωλόμεθα.

Quoted Amm. M. xxv. iv. 17. The *white bull* is the particular sacrifice specified in *Ep.* 27. 399 D as offered to Zeus at Bercœa: it was the recognised triumphal sacrifice.

[3] Mangold, *Jul. der Abtr.* 21.

His religious activity found another vent in proselytizing *Julian's* efforts. He employed not merely example, nor only the ob- *proselytis-* vious indefinable methods, which thickly strew a monarch's *ing.* path, of making new converts, but active preaching and argument as well[1], and not less, if occasion served, ridicule or sarcasm, or even hard cash. Perhaps the most sterling witness is his elaborate work against the Christians, which occupied so many of his long winter nights, and remained to the death of Greek Paganism the text-book of Pagan evidences; but the tale of his relations with Cæsarius will illustrate it more graphically[2]. Success had smiled upon the accomplished Cæsarius from early youth. He was the brother of Gregory of Nazianzus, and seems to have shared his talents. Medicine was the profession he had chosen. Of a brilliant address, and a singularly ready kindness, the young physician was soon the darling of Constantinopolitan society. He was well known at court, and on Julian's accession, like other Christians, received a share of his favours. In spite of the apprehensions and adjurations of his brother Gregory, the young doctor, stout Christian as he was, did not decline the Emperor's advances. Anxious to gain such a convert, Julian one day, before the assembled court, held a set conference lasting several hours. Not till all arguments were exhausted on either side, and Cæsarius still declared, 'I have been, I am, I will be a Christian,' did the Emperor desist with a good grace from his self-imposed task. In like manner he harangued the leading men of Antioch on their remissness, *Mis.* 363 and delivered a religious address to the Council at Berœa; *Ep.* 27. 399 D but on neither occasion apparently with much happier effect than in the case of Cæsarius. Of less generous proselytizing attempts, if such they were, notice will be taken presently. Finally, what has been happily called his 'pastoral' correspondence, a unique phenomenon amid the despatches of Roman emperors, shows the living interest and force he spent in the effort to inoculate others with his own beliefs

---

[1] Liban. *Epit.* pp. 562, 578.

[2] The story may be gathered in the main from Greg. Naz.'s Seventh Oration, which is a funeral panegyric on Cæsarius. Cf. too Greg. *Ep.* 7.

and aspirations. Borrowed as it was from Christianity, the idea of thus grafting a fruitful Church life on the stock of Paganism, is Julian's best claim to originality, if not to greatness. In the close union he assumes between religion and politics, he becomes the precursor of a Louis IX. or a Cromwell. He persuades us almost against ourselves that he quite believed, and believed in, his own creed.

One last noticeable trait is Julian's faith in the various sources of communication between God and man. It serves to show the weaker and more superstitious side of his character and his religion. He was a genuine disciple of Iamblichus' credulity[1], which is only the more debased by its veneer of philosophy. His admirer Ammian, himself far from a complete rationalist in these matters, numbers it among his *faults*, and compares him in this respect to the Emperor Hadrian[2].

Oracles.
Or. 4. 152 D

Oracles he regarded with implicit reverence[3] as due to the direct agency of Apollo. In his works their utterances are quoted with credulous respect, as decisive in most questions of philosophy or theology. One instance of his curiosity and pertinacity in consulting oracles was his attempt to disinter the sources of the Castalian fount near Antioch. The power of these waters had first communicated to Hadrian his future accession to the throne. To prevent any repetition of the prophecy to other applicants, Hadrian choked the fountain mouth with masses of stone; the subsequent interment of Christian martyrs hard by had further hallowed, or desecrated, the spot. Julian's solemn exhumation of these with purificatory rites led to issues anything but oracular. Prophecies again he reverently accepted: nor did he regard them as a lost privilege of former ages[4]. By his own account he

Prophecies.

---

[1] Zeller, III. 2. 630 *pp.*

[2] Amm. M. xxv. iv. 17. No better comment on the gist of this allusion could be given than Julian's own description of Hadrian in the *Cæsars*. There he is introduced (a little sarcastically of course) 'with a flowing beard and a confident mien, an expert in music and all the arts, ever and anon gazing on the heaven and preoccupied with strange secrets.' *Cæsars*, 311 D.

[3] Theod. III. x. 1.   [4] Amm. M. xxi. i.

received distinct predictions both of Constantius'[1] death and his own[2]. As soon as he heard that the place where he lay wounded was named Phrygia, he knew that the wound would be to death; for an oracle (as usual true in letter, and misleading in spirit) had predicted he should die there. Such soothsaying power he attributed to denizens of the spirit world, over whom Themis presided[3]. But both prophecies and oracles were rather irregular and intermittent than ordinary channels of Divine communications. Inspiration had spoken most clearly in the past, and the day of seers was wellnigh gone. Oracles yielded so to say at periods of time, lying fallow in the interim. Their place was supplied by omens and sacred arts, skill in which was derived from divine illumination. To these, whether given by divination or by augury, or by other means, he yielded willing credence[4], seeing in them a merciful gift of the Gods. The philosophical basis on which to his mind the art of divination[5] rested, was that adopted by the Platonists of the preceding century. Auspices[6] are not gathered from the will of silly birds; but the kindness of the deity governs their motions and their cries in such a way as to make them significant to those who can read the sign: ultimately they depend upon the sympathetic unity of the whole universe which is secured by the all-pervading activity of the central world-soul. Divination obtained a new lease of popularity, and the emperor was constantly attended by soothsayers, augurs, and interpreters of dreams[7]. At the same time he did not suffer himself to be weakly dismayed by superstitious fears; he was unfeignedly pleased if Zeus favoured him with gracious signs[8], or if by happy omen the garland from some triumphal arch fell and rested on his

Cyr. 198 c

Omens.

---

[1] *Ep.* 17. 384 D c. Cf. Lib. *Epitaph.* p. 561. Amm. xxi. ii. 2. Soz. v. 1.
[2] Amm. M. xxv. iii. 9 and 19, xxiii. iii. 2, 3.
[3] Amm. M. xxi. i. 8.   [4] Liban. *Epit.* p. 582.
[5] In his work against the Christians he defends the propriety of divination and preferences of method by Scriptural quotations and arguments. Cyril 343 E, 347, 356 c, 358 c—E.
[6] Cf. Amm. M. xxi. i. 9, 10.
[7] Amm. M. xxi. ii. 4, xxii. i. 1, xii. 7, xxiii. iii. 3 and v. 10, xxv. ii. 7, 8.
[8] *Ep.* 27. 399 D, and cf. the stories in Amm. M. xxiii. iii. 6, v. 8.

head[1], but gaily discarded less auspicious presages, or showed a felicitous readiness in construing favourably omens which at first sight might seem adverse. When, after his proclamation as Augustus, during martial exercises at Paris his shield of a sudden broke leaving nothing but the handle in his grasp, he reassured the dismayed bystanders with the prompt interpretation, 'Let no one fear: I hold fast what I held before[2].' He would boldly defy auguries when in conflict with his better judgment: as Ammian[3] phrases it, 'he thought it unadvised to put faith in forecasts, that events might falsify.' In the Persian war, when the Etruscan diviners were for ever seeing stars and discovering unpropitious portents, 'the emperor fairly struck against the whole science of vaticination[4].' On the eve of his expected conflict with Constantius, as Julian was mounting his horse, the soldier who was helping him to the saddle suddenly slipped and fell. 'See,' cried the Emperor, 'he has fallen who raised me to my present elevation[5].' As his army marched through Illyria, though vintage time was past, unripe grapes hung still upon the trees. Boding hearts prognosticated for Julian marred hopes and premature death; but to him the unswelled clusters spoke only of fortunes still to ripen[6]. If in the prepared entrails a cross appeared surrounded by a ring[7], Julian interpreted it not as the circle of eternity, but the emblem of circumscription that enwreathed the symbol of Christianity. Here too consciously or unconsciously he adopted the teaching of Maximus. That gentleman, when Julian's invitation to court reached him, at once consulted the auspices: on these turning out villainously unfavourable Maximus observed to his fellow, the alarmed and chagrined Chrysanthius, that it was the lesson of a life-time 'not to succumb to the first repulse, but if need were to take the kingdom of heaven by

---

[1] Sok. III. i. 29, Nikeph. x. 1, &c.
[2] Amm. M. xxi. ii. 2.   [3] Ib. xxii. i. 2.
[4] Ib. xxiii. v. 10, 13, xxv. ii. 8.
[5] Amm. M. xxii. i. 2. The story of the fall of Julian's horse 'Babylon' Amm. M. xxiii. iii. 6 is in spirit exactly similar.
[6] Soz. v. 1.
[7] Ib. v. 2, Greg. Naz. Or. iv. liv. p. 577 B.

violence[1].' Perseverance triumphed: Maximus' persistent efforts were rewarded with success; and presently to court he went. Is it something of this sort that Libanius means, when he speaks of Julian in the Persian war being 'his own Pythia'? His boldness in this respect is credible enough when we read of the rebuff he laid upon an unconciliatory God. Outside Ktesiphon[2] one of ten bulls offered to Mars the Avenger had the independence to break his bonds, resist his sacrificers, and finally after death display most unfavourable omens; therefore Julian swore to let Mars go without victims for the future, and faithfully kept his word[3].

Magic rites and the paraphernalia of Neo-Platonic theurgy *Theurgy.* exercised from the outset a strange spell of fascination over Julian's mind. Christian theology of the fourth century probably enough familiarised him with belief in the existence of angels and a hierarchy of demoniacal powers[4]. His teachers laid hold of these conceptions. 'The nature of dæmons and of the beings who formed and preserved this universe' was his introductory lesson in Neo-Platonism[5], mystic intercourse with familiar spirits his constant occupation and delight[6]. Maximus was the representative of this charlatan department of philosophy, and to his dying breath Maximus remained his most trusted friend. Apparitions, coming as mysterious visitants from the spirit world, thrilled and attracted him with a vague irresistible awe. We read[7] how he went down to subterranean caverns to face the summoned spectres; yet how when they stood before him, the sign of the cross involuntarily made scared them away. Such tales may well have a foundation in truth. It is as likely that shrewd sorcerers

---

[1] μὴ πάντως εἴκειν τοῖς πρώτοις ἀπαντήμασιν, ἀλλ' ἐμβιάζεσθαι τὴν τοῦ θείου φύσιν. Eunap. *Vit. Max.*   [2] Amm. M. xxiv. vi. 16.

[3] Lamé, *Jul. l'Apost.* p. 195, in the fictitious death-bed discourse with which he has supplied Julian, explains this as a patient acquiescence in the will of the Deity. The God was not to be pestered with inquiries to which he had already vouchsafed a plain response.

[4] Cyril 224 E, cf. Naville, pp. 80—82.

[5] Lib. *Epit.* 528.   [6] Lib. περὶ τιμ. Ἰουλ. § 22 p. 56, *Presb.* p. 460.

[7] Greg. Naz. *Or.* iv. lv. p. 577. Soz. v. 2. Idle rumour no doubt propagated secrets which assuredly neither Julian nor Maximus would have confided to Christian ears. But rumour does not always largely err from truth.

contrived the show as that Christian historians invented it. In Julian's remains the direct allusions to mystery worship and theurgic practices are rare. He treats the matter with reverent reserve, as unsuited to popular exposition. Whenever he does mention it, it is with a worshipful approval that speaks volumes. Without theurgic instruction God's prophets and spokesmen cannot attain to excellence. Theurgy makes man divine; it is the way of perfectness, which in prayers for divine guidance comes prior to every kind of outward gifts or successes.

Dreams. In the numerous references to direct communications from the deities to himself, dreams appear to have been the ordinary channel. What the sign ($\tau\epsilon\rho\alpha\varsigma$) was[1], by which, at a sudden crisis and in open day, the Gods in answer to prayer directed his conduct, on his soldiers proclaiming him Augustus, we cannot tell; but it was by a dream that heaven warned him against sending an imprudent letter which he had composed to the Empress Eusebia: and in a dream that the shining figure communicated the warning which foretold the death of Constantius. In one letter where he expresses a strong belief in revelations by dreams, he recounts to his friend Oribasius a vision foreshowing his own rise and the imminent death of Constantius. We are not surprised to find this particular prediction recurring more than once in various forms[2]. The final and most detailed version of it occurred at Vienne, on the eve of Julian's final march against Constantius. He was in a state of grievous indecision, sorely troubled at the thought of civil war, when in the night watches a form of superhuman splendour stood before him and pointed to the stars, and recited in Greek hexameters these verses[3]:

[1] Lamé, *Jul. l'Apost.* pp. 108–117, alone is in the secret, and describes with every minutia the room, the preparations and the prayers of Julian, together with the appearance and utterances of the Gods. De Broglie, *L'Église, &c.*, IV. p. 81, treats it as the waking vision of an ecstatic enthusiast; cf. *Ep. ad Ath.* 284 c, 285 A with Amm. M. xx. v. 10. In *Epitaph.* p. 579, Libanius talks of his beholding Zeus visibly at midday (cf. *Presb.* p. 460), and this Ioan. Mal. *Chron.* xiii. p. 327 embellishes appropriately.

[2] Amm. M. xx. v. 10, xxi. i. 6, cf. xxii. i. 2.

[3] The dream is given in full, with unimportant differences, by Zos. III. 9, Zonar. xiii. 11, Amm. M. xxi. ii. 2.

> When Zeus the Waterer's broad domain invades,
> And Kronos thrice eight tracks across the Maid's
> Hath drawn, lo Asia's land shall mourn her king
> Sweet life to churlish death surrendering.

A not less famous dream[1] is that which intimated his own approaching death. Julian dreamed that a young man, dressed in consular attire, met him in a tent near Ktesiphon, in a place called Rhasia, and wounded him with a spear. When he received his fatal wound, Julian asked those about him 'What is the name of the place where my tent is set up?' On receiving the answer 'Rhasia[2],' he exclaimed, 'Sun, thou hast undone Julian!'

[1] *Chron. Pasch.* I. p. 581.

[2] 'Asia' in Magnus and Entychian and cf. Ioan. Mal. *Chron.* p. 327, while Amm. M. xxv. iii. 9, supported by Zon. xiii. 13, gives Phrygia as the name. In xxv. ii. 3, 4 he recounts other portents which warned Julian of impending death.

CHAPTER VII.

JULIAN'S ADMINISTRATION.

> "ductor fortissimus armis,
> conditor et legum, celeberrimus ore manuque,
> consultor patriae, sed non consultor habendae
> relligionis, amans tercentum milia divom,
> perfidus ille Deo, quamvis non perfidus Urbi."
> PRUDENTIUS.

Julian's Apostasy. WHEN Julian on his march from Gaul first publicly announced his apostasy, and took the title of *Pontifex Maximus*[1], men paid small heed to the avowal. Technically he was but Cæsar still, and not Augustus: and at least he had a Christian colleague and superior to hold his zeal in check. The declaration was assumed to be a political stratagem, and nothing more. Men's politics in those days made them Arians or Eusebians or Anomœans, and by the same token Pagans as well. Even as a political move its dexterity was questionable. Licinius forty years previously had done the same thing. In his final rupture with the Christian emperor, he had used the name of the 'Gods of our fathers' as an effective war-cry. Licinius' discomfiture before the father was a poor presage for Julian's success against the son. But when *Julian sole Emperor.* Julian's proclaimed apostasy and march into Illyria was followed by Constantius' sudden death[2] at Mopsukrenae, and the young pretender stood alone at the head of Empire, Christians must have watched anxiously, and bethought them

---

[1] Sok. III. 1.

[2] Apart from ingenious combinations and inferences, and that 'reading between the lines' which he recommends to the student, Dr Auer's elaborate attempt to fasten the guilt of Constantius' death on Julian rests solely on the *on dit* to which Gregory of Nazianzus is pleased to give his approval.

of the days¹ when they groaned beneath a Galerius or a Maximin. In spite of Constantius' cunning suppressions, and free fabrication of lying despatches, the sound of Julian's exploits, and the praises of his troops had ere now traversed East and West alike. The cause which had seemed forlorn² was, without one blow, triumphant. People might be excused for ascribing his triumph to the direct intervention of God, or—the Gods.

His earliest care was the funeral of his illustrious predecessor. It was conducted with becoming pomp of royal and Christian ritual³. The entire army joined in the procession, and multitudes of citizens thronged without the gates of Constantinople to meet the imperial cortege. The emperor himself as chief mourner took part in the procession, wearing the purple, but with the diadem reverently removed from his head. So with night-long chants, amid the blaze of torches and the homage of multitudes, the corpse was brought to its own chosen resting-place in the Church of the Holy Apostles. The death of Constantius took place on Nov. 3, 362⁴; the obsequies were completed in the same month. The latest recorded law of Julian belongs to the middle of March 363 A.D., when he was already moving eastward on his Persian campaign. Thus the period of his legislative and administrative activity as sole Emperor is confined within narrow limits of less than a year and a half. And though, according to La Bleterie, no Emperor made so many laws in so short a reign, his legislation is not alarming in bulk. It is our business in the present chapter to examine it, more particularly in its bearing on Julian's attitude towards the religions of his day.

Constantius' obsequies.

Duration of Julian's reign.

The earliest acts of the young Emperor were reassuring. A religious amnesty was proclaimed⁵. Bishops, orthodox or heterodox, were recalled from banishment, and no doubt

Religious amnesty.

---

¹ Liban. *Epit.* p. 562.   ² Amm. M. xxi. vii. 3, xxii. ii. 3.

³ Philost. vi. vi, Greg. Naz. *Or.* v. 16, 17, pp. 158—9, whom Liban. *Epitaph.* pp. 561, 562 corroborates.

⁴ See *Appendix* B, *Note 5.*

⁵ Rufin. i. 27, Amm. M. xxii. v, cf. Sokr. ii. xxxviii. 23, iii. i, xi. 3, Soz. v. 5, Theod. iii. 4, Philost. vi. 7, vii. 4.

reinstated in their sees if vacant; heretics of all shades were invited to return from exile. The breadth of his toleration has been manufactured into an accusation: he has been abused for recalling not only the orthodox bishops, but also suffering Arians, Semi-Arians, and Novatians to flock back unhindered, and even rehabilitating Donatists[1] and Circumcellions in the political rights of which preceding Emperors had deprived them. For such a course it is easy to impute sinister motives[2], but it would have been a breach of principle to penalise opinions, and most certainly a hard matter to draw the line between their civil and their dogmatic offences; restitution of their rights was the most equitable course, leaving it perfectly open to any one to prosecute the heretics for any criminal misdemeanour. Julian, no doubt, had the political sagacity to leave Arians and Catholics and Sects to fight out their own quarrels, but it is unfair to make that the motive of his policy of toleration. Invitations to court were addressed not only to Neo-Platonists and Pagans, but to Procœresius the Christian professor, to Basil[3], whose piety and learning already marked him out as bishop designate of Cæsarea, and to Aetius[4] the Arian, subsequently bishop of Constantinople. Nothing could be fairer than the monarch's professions of tolerance: nothing warmer than his letters of invitation. Basil is to come 'as friend to friend[5]'; to stay as long as he pleases, and as soon as tired to be sent on his way,

Ep. 12

---

[1] Aug. *Contr. Petil.* II. c. 83 and 92, Optat. II. 16.

[2] Cf. Ruf., Philost., Sok., Soz., Theod. as just cited, and Amm. M. XXII. 5. De Broglie's remark (*L'Église, &c.* IV. 133 pp.) that Julian always took the side of the sectaries against the Catholics is plausible, and, if only we had the sectaries' side of the question as well, would be weighty.

[3] Basil had as early as 358 adopted the life of a recluse on the Neo-Cæsarean hills. Called to deacons' orders in 360, in protest or sorrow at the heresy of Dianius he once more retired to his sequestered monastery, where Julian's invitation must have reached his hands. La Bleterie denies on grounds of style the genuineness of all the reputed letters from Julian to Basil, or *vice versa*. In the case of *Ep.* 12, no particular objections are intimated, and none are patent. It is generally regarded as the *one* genuine letter surviving from Julian to Basil, the Great Basil. De Broglie, IV. p. 205, Rode, p. 62.

[4] *Ep.* 31, Soz. V. v. 9, Nikeph. x. 5, &c.

[5] Julian quotes playfully from Plat. *Menex.* 247 c.

where he will: both he and Aetius are allowed to travel at the state's expense. In fact Julian's court was to be of an entirely new model. Wise councillors and skilled administrators should be his courtiers. Titles of servile respect were to disappear[1]: hypocrisy, envy and sloth to be replaced by the candour of outspoken friendship and the energy of beneficent co-operation[2].

Ep. 12

But in his desire for peace Julian did not weakly overlook criminal offences. He appointed a commission[3] to investigate and chastise the official misdemeanours and crimes of the late reign. It was composed of Mamertinus and Nevitta, consuls for 362, of Arbitio an ex-consul of known severity, of Agilo, and of Julian's own master of the horse Jovinus. Over these presided Salustius prætorian prefect, and in the ensuing year Julian's colleague in the consulship. Cases of spoliation were investigated, prompt restoration enforced, and where reparation was impossible, severe penalties inflicted. No elevation of rank secured immunity. The infamous favourites of Constantius, the tribes of informers who had thronged his court, were among the earliest victims[4]. Eusebius, the Chamberlain, as prime instigator[5] of the murder of Gallus, expiated his crimes on the scaffold. Apodemius, the vile agent who had concerted the death both of Silvanus and Gallus, was burned alive; Paul, the infamous notary, surnamed 'the Chain,' a kind of Titus Oates, shared the same cruel fate. More innocent victims also fell, or suffered banish-

Chalcedon Commission.

---

[1] *Mis.* 343 δεσπότης, sc. *dominus*, on which La Bleterie's note *in loc.* is interesting.

[2] *Or.* VII. 233 A c. Cf. Liban. *Epit.* p. 585, *Presb.* p. 455. Not that Julian was by any means unsusceptible to flattery when rightly couched. Far from it!

[3] Amm. M. XXII. 3 gives the fullest accounts of its proceedings: cf. Liban. *Epit.* p. 572.

[4] In *Ep.* 25. 397 B, Julian dwells more savagely than is his wont on having 'taken with his hands and thrust into the pit the barbarians in mind and atheists in heart, who had sat at the table of Constantius.' De Broglie, IV. 331 *n.*, follows earlier Edd. in rejecting this letter on the strength of this sentence, but Teuffel's defence in Schmidt's *Zeitsch. für Gesch.*, 1845, Vol. IV. 156 *pp.*, appears quite adequate. Hertlein inserts without comment.

[5] Cf. Jul. *Ep. ad Ath.* 272 D, Sok. III. i. 49, Soz. v. v. 8, Philost. IV. 1, Zonar. XIII. 12.

ment[1]. Information once invited is hard to curb or control perfectly; the guillotine once set in motion *ne va pas mal;* in that active discouragement of Christianity which the Emperor approved, his agents probably transgressed the strict observance of justice which he enjoined in the same breath; but it is fair to say that the Commission if not happily selected[2], was honestly required, honourably intended, and removed only too punctiliously from the immediate sphere and influence of court, that there might be no suspicion[3] of Julian's personal sentiments unfairly prejudicing his enemies. Years before attaining to the supreme power he had laid it down as a theory of government[4], that the wise prince, while taking strict personal cognisance of minor 'remediable' crimes, ought rigorously to abstain from sitting in judgment on capital offences. These should be tried by proved impartial judges, whose verdict could neither be warped by prejudice, nor impaired by unjudicial haste. In this edict then he carried out in practice a principle which had approved itself to his calm judgment, and may be acquitted without reserve from the odium of wilful persecution.

Palace Retrenchment.

Justice satisfied, or at least a way to its satisfaction duly prepared, Julian devoted himself to reform. His charity began at home. The severest retrenchments were enforced in the palace expenditure[5]. On his accession Julian found in occupation a thousand cooks and barbers, butlers and serving-men innumerable, and eunuchs 'thicker than summer flies[6].' At a blow he dismissed them all, and turned the palace into a

---

[1] Amm. M. xxii. 3. Greg. Naz. *Or.* iv. 64, p. 106.

[2] The writer in Hilg.'s *Zeitschr. für wiss. Theologie,* 1861, notices (p. 409) the undue predominance of the military element in the Commission. Gibbon shows how unimpeachable was Salustius, how self-satisfied Mamertinus, and how violent the remaining four.

[3] This was the object of their holding their sittings across the water at Chalcedon. Cf. Jul. *Ep.* 23.

[4] *Or.* ii. 89 c d. The monarch, he adds, should be like the queen bee who carries no sting.

[5] Amm. M. xxii. 4, Sok. iii. 1, Zonar. xiii. 12, Mamert. 11, Liban. *Epit.* p. 565. Schlosser, *Uebers. der Gesch.* iii. ii. 342 (cf. also iii. 15 *pp.*), condemns this policy, and so too Robertson, *Hist. Christ. Church,* Bk. ii. c. iii. p. 341.

[6] Liban. *Epit.* p. 565.

desert. For the cooks, he wanted, he said, but simple fare, and the preparers of it to dress like cooks, not senators: for barbers, one was enough for many (which was all the more true, no doubt, in days when the Emperor wore the philosopher's beard, and the courtiers followed suit): for eunuchs, he wanted not one, for his first wife was dead, and he had no mind to marry a second[1]. So a general cataclysm swept away the whole army of domestics, retainers, official detectives and spies (the so-called *Curiosi*), and other parasites who had previously clung about the person of the monarch. That the bulk of the servants of Constantius were Christians is no mere conjecture[2]. Doubtless that royal barber who[3] waited on Julian so daintily apparelled, and in addition to his handsome salary and perquisites received daily rations for twenty squires and as many horses, was a pronounced Christian. Whether this be so or no, the abuse was flagrant, the reformation just, and no blame attaches to the reformer if Christians were the principal sufferers. The sole ground for complaint is that their places were refilled in great measure by that 'conflux of so-called philosophers,' for which Sokrates[4] denounces the Emperor. Sophists, litterati, quacks and soothsayers, they came pricking in hungry swarms from three continents, thirsting for a share of the spoil[5]. Each had his special claim on the new monarch, his special sufferings for the good cause to recount, or his special qualifications for useful work in the future. The philosophic maxims of their obscurity were forgotten or abjured with a marvellous readiness. Ascetics turned Sybarites, and Neo-Platonists Epicureans. Maximus himself, dropping the Cynic's cloak and stick[6], appeared attired in silk and gold; was attended by his train of slaves; feasted luxuriously; received sumptuously, and in all respects affected Asiatic pomp. Nor

Sophists, &c.

---

[1] Zonar. XIII. 12, Sok. III. i. 50, cf. *Misop.* 349 c.
[2] Cf. Greg. Naz. *Or.* IV. p. 586.
[3] Amm. M. XXII. iv. 9.
[4] Sok. III. xiii. 11.
[5] τοὺς πανταχῇ ἦγεν ἡ φήμη βρυάζοντας ἐπὶ τὰ βασίλεια, Sok. III. i. 56, cf. Jul. *Or.* VII. 224.
[6] *Ep.* 37. 111 D.

were imitators slow to follow where the master led. Others, by a more refined flattery, adopted the coarse dress and the shaggy beard of the Cynic, but at that point ceased to be the followers of Diogenes. They neither bridled the appetites, nor kept under the sensual passions, nor subdued covetousness and self-seeking. Their exterior was Cynic, but their heart Cyrenaic. Julian's worst foes were of his own household. Personally he did what he could: by word and look and act he protested. He wrote an indignant tirade[1] against false Cynics; his dress and appearance grew more and more severe; above all he strove by example of active self-denial to shame these courtier-philosophers into worthier ways[2]. His diet became more spare; his devotion to business more unremitting; his reforms and edicts more rigorous. No man could say that he spared himself[3]. 'Always abstemious, and never oppressed by food, he applied himself to business with the activity of a bird, and despatched it with infinite ease[4].' He would write, dictate, and give audience at the same time[5]. His ministers came to him by relays; as soon as one retired to rest or sleep, another was admitted, and then the next, till perhaps the circle began again. When the rest of the palace was wrapped in sleep the Emperor[6] sat alone in his library despatching correspondence, composing orations, framing decrees, or composing elaborate philosophic lucubrations. Yet in the grey of morning he might be found receiving complimentary calls, hearing petitions, or giving audience to his consuls[7]. 'He multiplied time by subtracting from leisure[8].'

---

[1] *Orat.* 6 Εἰς τοὺς ἀπαιδεύτους κύνας belongs to the spring of 362: cf. 181 A.

[2] On his fastidious self-restraint of a physical kind Zonar. XIII. xiii. p. 1156 has this curious notice; ἦν περὶ τὴν δίαιταν ἐγκρατὴς ὥστε καὶ τὰ φυσικὰ ταῦτα (αὐτὰ?) διαφυγγάνειν, ὡς μάλιστα ἐρυγὰς καὶ τὰς ἐκκρίσεις τὰς διὰ στόματος.

[3] 'Nihil somno, nihil epulis, nihil otio tribuit; ipsa se naturalium necessariarumque rerum usurpatione defraudat, totus commodis publicis vacat.' Mamert. 14, and cf. 12, with which cf. Amm. M. xxv. iv. 4, and *Mis.* 338 c, 340 B.

[4] Duncombe's version, I. p. 232 note. Cf. Liban. *Epit.* p. 580.

[5] Liban. *Epit.* p. 580.   [6] Sok. III. i. 54.

[7] Mamert. 28.   [8] Ibid. 14.

The few hours that he doled out to sleep, were passed often *Mis.* 340 B upon the hard ground[1]. Under such circumstances censure will be lenient if the prince was able to bridle only, not eradicate the rapacity of his followers. Numbers of these impostors, on an enemy's testimony[2], went disappointed away, cursing their own folly, and the deceit, as they were pleased to call it, of the Emperor, in not following up his invitation with more substantial rewards. While recognising his liberality, impartial historians[3] add that towards unworthy recipients he was less indulgent in favours than his position was supposed to demand.

But Julian's projects of retrenchment were not limited to the palace of Constantinople: nor again to mere sumptuary laws[4], feeble attempts to cure only and not prevent. They took a much wider sweep. His legislation testifies to unceasing activity in this department. His Gallic administration had yielded him varied large experience; if in his first years he spent 'summer in the camp, winter in the tribunal[5],' during his last year in that country financial and judicial reform had engrossed his whole attention. In nothing had he been more successful than in reducing the burdens[6] of the overtaxed provincials, and reinvigorating industrial enterprise: during his brief sojourn at or near Sirmium he had engaged in the same good work for the Illyrian and Dalmatian districts[7]: from Hadria to Nikopolis his life-giving hand had touched decaying industries. Now sole Emperor he extended like efforts[8] through the realm. The two great principles that guided his legislation were the withdrawal of immunities from favoured classes or individuals, and the prevention of corrupt exactions or returns by the official collectors of *Collection of taxes.*

Financial Reforms.

---

[1] Amm. M. xvi. v. 5, xxv. iv. 5, Liban. *Epit.* p. 613, *In Iul. Hyp.* 400 sq.
[2] Greg. Naz. *Or.* v. xx. p. 689.
[3] Eutrop. x. 16. Schlosser, *Uebers. der Gesch.* iii. ii., 'rightly notices that none but Maximus and Priscus ranked among his councillors.
[4] Such as *Cod. Just.* viii. x. 7.
[5] Mamert. 4, 8.
[6] Amm. M. xvi. v. 14, xxv. iv. 15.   [7] Mamert. 9.
[8] So at Antioch, cf. *Misop.* 365 B, 367 A D, Zos. iii. 11, and Thrace, cf. *Ep.* 47.

taxes. To this last end his earliest and his latest edict[1] are alike directed, and others reinforce them in the interval. The principal provisions are for the transmission of exact and speedy returns[2] to the provincial governors, who in turn forwarded the reports to the emperor: unpunctuality is made punishable by a considerable fine. Falsification of the returns by the official collectors (*rationales*) is visited with bodily pains and penalties[3]: and without the imperial leave no new impost may be introduced, nor existing one modified[4]. Further, a quinquennial tenure of office is prescribed, after which is intercalated a non-official year, to the express end that complainants may appeal unawed by the terror of official persecution and revenge[5]. Other regulations are directed against official bribery and corruption[6], and against abuses of judicial procedure in the case of public functionaries[7]. While adopting these precautions against official extortion, Julian displayed still greater energy in the direct relief of the provincials, chiefly by rigid limitation of diverse forms of immunities. Constantius, following but exaggerating his father's method, had accorded exemptions on the largest scale to the Christian clergy. Not only monks, not only religious communities of virgins and widows, not only the higher clergy, but even the lower orders in the Church were wholly or in great part exempted from the ordinary burdens of the subject. Indeed, if the letter of Julian's decree may be pressed, the conclusion would be that the bare profession of Christianity in some cases bestowed pecuniary advantages. Not seldom too, besides special endowments of churches and the like, the clergy received fixed allowances of the public corn without payment. The system was unmistakeably pernicious. It crippled the State and burdened

Exemptions.

---

[1] *Theod. Cod.* VIII. i. 6, issued at Constantinople in Jan. 362. *Theod. Cod.* XI. xxx. 31, issued Mar. 13, 363, a week after Julian's departure from Antioch on his expedition against Persia.

[2] *Theod. Cod.* XI. xxx. 31, 1. xv. 4.

[3] *Theod. Cod.* VIII. i. 6, cf. Greg. Naz. *Or.* IV. 75, p. 113.

[4] *Theod. Cod.* XI. xvi. 10.

[5] *Theod. Cod.* VIII. i. 6, 7, 8.

[6] *Theod. Cod.* II. xxix. 1.   [7] *Theod. Cod.* IX. ii. 1.

industry; it pauperised and not less corrupted the Church by making Christianity a form of money investment. Julian at a stroke did away with this large class of immunities. He decreed, not indeed of any conscious kindness to the Church, that all decurions who as Christians claimed exemption from public burdens, should be restored to the tax-roll[1]. Though a few more vehement advocates decried the enactment as persecuting, its substantial justice is tacitly admitted by soberer ecclesiastical writers. No other edict preserved in the Theodosian Code mentions the Christians by name; obviously these need no defence, as they merit no reproach. When Julian went beyond this[2], and conferred immunities and allowances of corn on Pagan priests, he swerved from strict justice and sound economy, though merely adopting, be it remembered, the practice of all his predecessors. In the one case where details are furnished the corn and wine dues are not granted to the priests for their own support, but for distribution among the sick and needy, the alleged motive being that Jews and Christians may not have all the good almsgiving to themselves. Nor was it Christians alone whom he robbed of their exemptions. Their due share of taxes is exacted from all hereditary holders of estates[3] and from all landowners, all private arrangements between vendors and lessees and tax-collectors being strictly prohibited[4]. On the other hand certain exemptions are accorded. One edict of the kind guaranteeing large vested immunities to privileged persons[5] appears wide in scope. Another secures the cus-

---

[1] *Theod. Cod.* xii. i. 50, xiii. i. 4, and Jul. *Ep.* 11 : cf. Soz. v. v. 2, Philost. vii. 4, Nikeph. x. 5.

[2] Soz. v. iii. 2 makes the charge, which Cassiod. vi. 4 transcribes and Nikeph. x. iv. 13 rehearses. So too Philost. vii. 4. *Ep.* 49. 430 c grants 30,000 *modii* of corn and 60,000 pints (ξέσται) of wine yearly to Arsakius highpriest of Galatia.

[3] *Theod. Cod.* xi. xix. 2. So in particular at Antioch : *Misop.* 367 D.

[4] *Theod. Cod.* xi. iii. 3, xi. iii. 4.

[5] It extends to all without exception, *quicumque capitationis indulgentiam immunitatemque meruerunt. Theod. Cod.* xi. xii. 2. I do not know how large a class the provision included, or by what extraordinary services the privilege had been acquired. The ensuing sentences teach us the requirements of Julian.

tomary privileges of physicians of the highest grade[1]. New exemptions are accorded only to limited classes and in acknowledgment of special services to the state. Military service would seem to take precedence. Three years of military service exonerate all *agentes in palatio* from subsequent curial functions[2], while ten years suffice to do the same for all of curial descent[3]. There are but two other exempting enactments preserved in the Theodosian Code. The first is characteristic and runs thus: "First of all things comes war; second, letters the adornment of peace. Therefore on all engaged in the service of our *scrinia*, we bestow the second place in privilege: all who have served for 15 years in the office of records and in the due custody of despatches and charters shall be, every liability notwithstanding, excused from curial obligations[4]." The one remaining immunity granted is very complete; for it absolves even from assessment as a decurion; its attainment in the fourth century must have been indeed exceptional, and perhaps not ill-deserved; it was the guerdon reserved for *fathers of thirteen children*[5]*!*

In his imperial progresses Julian was used to confer privileges on special towns. But these took most generally the form of increased municipal privileges—for Julian did his utmost to foster a healthy spirit of independence and self-government[6]—or of special rights or freedoms for the promotion of trade or the encouragement of religion. No instance is reported of the remission of the ordinary taxes. Church

---

[1] *Theod. Cod.* XIII. iii. 4, and Jul. *Ep.* 25 *b*, which does not limit the exemption from curial services to ἀρχιατροί alone.

[2] *Theod. Cod.* VI. xxvii. 2. An additional clause, the motive of which is unexplained, bestows the same privilege on the *agentes* gaining their discharge from the services during Julian's fourth consulship, sc. 363 A.D.

[3] *Theod. Cod.* XII. i. 56, by an obvious error assigned to 363 instead of 362.

[4] *Theod. Cod.* VI. xxvi. 1. There were four departments of the *Sacra Scrinia* or Record Office—*memoriae, epistolarum, libellorum, epistolarum Graecarum*.

[5] *Theod. Cod.* XII. i. 55.

[6] Cf. Mamert. 24, *Misop.* 365 A with many indications in the same piece of liberties vested in the Curia of Antioch: also his reconstruction of the Senate of Constantinople, and other benefits conferred on the town: Zos. III. 11, Himer. *Or.* 7. See further Gibbon, ch. XXII.

writers¹ complain, and not improbably with some truth, of partiality displayed towards Pagan cities, but as specific instances² are not alleged, and the murmurs are withal rare, this can hardly have been very aggravated, and would probably, could the truth be discovered, resolve itself into indirect favours conferred on cities possessed of famous sanctuaries³. That he did not confine his favours to Pagan cities is certain from his treatment of Constantinople and Antioch. By origin and tradition Constantinople was Christian to the backbone. At Julian's accession alone among great cities it had not even one temple: yet he showered benefits upon it. Than Antioch there was no more 'protestant' city in the Empire, nor any more defiant against Julian personally. Yet he by no means withheld from it wise favours, and was able to make there large abatements of taxation⁴. It is observable that while Julian thus carefully restricted immunities, and exacted their due quota impartially from all holders of property, and while he constantly bore in mind the needs and welfare of his poorer subjects, he did not rush into the opposite extreme of grinding down the wealthy. In the absence of much indirect taxation there was a dangerous tendency to this in Imperial finance. No class in the state were so heavily taxed in proportion to their means as the *curiales:* accordingly Julian while fining severely all evasion of their duties was careful in the same edict to protect them from undue exactions⁵. In the same way he declined to levy either from senators or others forced contributions to the so-called 'Crown Gold,' declaring it by edict voluntary in fact and not in pretence alone.

If it was to general principles, to annulling exemptions and enforcing honest punctual collection of the taxes that Julian devoted his fullest energies, he did not neglect surveillance over minor matters and removed at least one burdensome abuse with a very firm hand. Throughout the empire

Public post.

¹ Soz. v. iii. 2, with Nikeph. x. 4.
² Cf. however, Julian's award between Maiuma and Gaza, *inf.* p. 185, and his answer to Pessinus (see p. 112) in *Ep.* 49. 431 D.
³ Cf. Lib. *Epit.* p. 565.
⁴ Zos. iii. 11, *Misop.* 365 B, 367 A D.
⁵ *Theod. Cod.* xii. i. 50, cf. xiii. i. 4.

one of the normal demands made upon the subject was the repair of roads and the provision of horses for the public service of the district. Rising from small beginnings, the charge had reached formidable dimensions: it had become the fashion for not merely the highest functionaries, but for all provincial magnates or petty officers of state to travel hither and thither at the public expense. Not content with the modest one-horse vehicle, they required their two and their three horses as the case might be, or perhaps a train of carriages to transport their wives, children and baggage to boot. To such a pass had things come, that even the transport of bulky wares, the conveyance of blocks of marble for the enrichment of private edifices, and suchlike gratifications of luxury were charged upon the suffering provincials[1]. The system had become a crying scandal: the poor were sinking under the burdens it involved: the whole administration of the public post threatened to break down under its own weight. More than one vigorous decree[2] copes with this evil. The privilege is restricted to certain defined officials; none but the governor is permitted to use it at discretion: on all others very definite limitations are imposed both as to the character of the vehicle and the frequency of use: no extension of these is allowed except under the Imperial hand. Bishops, it appears, had under the regime of Constantius been among the most hardened offenders. Ammian[3] singles them out as the chief culprits, and if so they would be among the sufferers, or rather the losers by Julian's decree. But so far as the edict itself particularises, it is 'the inordinate requirements and restless peregrinations' of 'prefects, magistrates and consulars' that are assailed: nothing but prejudice can expound this legislation by religious sympathies or antipathies.

Financial legislation.

On the whole, though Julian—as his Antioch Corn Laws testify—was not infallible enough to escape every economical error, it cannot be gainsaid, what even his vilifiers[4] admit, that

[1] Theod. Cod. VIII. v. 15.
[2] Theod. Cod. VIII. v. 12, 13, 14. Cf. Sok. III. 1.
[3] Amm. M. XXI. xvi. 18.
[4] φορῶν ἄνεσις and κλοπῶν ἐπιτίμησις are both accorded to him by Greg. Naz. Or. IV. c. 75, p. 113.

he relieved the overtaxed provincial, that he checked official avarice, that he diminished pauperism, and gave honest industry its rightful due, in fact, that to the extent of his powers and knowledge he laboured, without fear and without favour, to protect without pampering the poor, to toll without plundering the rich, to economise yet not stint imperial expenditure[1].

Over Julian's judicial legislation, apart from the already recorded Chalcedon Commission, there is no call to linger. It aims at improving the procedure of courts[2], at preventing partialities[3], at mitigating the position of debtors[4], at protecting minors and amending the marriage laws, but can nowhere be twisted to a suspicion of religious partisanship, unless indeed the abolition of the irregular Church jurisdiction[5] that had already sprung up for the settlement of wills, the appropriation of property, and the arbitration of suits, by episcopal courts can be included in that category. *Judiciary laws. Ep. 52. 437 A*

With regard to administration the case stands differently. Statements diverge concerning Julian's choice of his subordinates. Rufinus[6] declares that Julian debarred Christians from becoming governors of provinces, on the ground that their law forbade them to inflict capital punishment; others dilate on the rapacity, arrogance and inhumanity of his prefects and officers. It is true that in parting spite he inflicted a rough governor on the recalcitrant Antiochenes. But the fellow seems to have frightened his troublesome vassals into order without any great enormities[7]. On the other hand even Gregory of Nazianzus[8], though maligning Julian's creatures, and averring that apostasy was the royal road to office, seems elsewhere to admit some sort of justifi- *Governors.*

---

[1] Eutrop. x. 16, in provinciales iustissimus: et tributorum, quatenus fieri posset, repressor. civilis in cunctos ; mediocrem habens aerarii curam.
[2] Theod. Cod. I. xvi. 8; II. v. 1, xii. 1; v. xii. 1; xi. xxx. 29, 30; xv. i. 8, 9.
[3] Theod. Cod. IX. ii. 1. [4] Theod. Cod. XI. xxviii. 1.
[5] Theod. Cod. III. i. 3, xiii. 2.
[6] Ruf. I. 32, and so Sok. III. xiii. 2, Soz. v. 18, Nikeph. x. 21.
[7] Amm. M. XXIII. ii. 3. with which cf. Liban. *Epist.* 722.
[8] Or. IV. 75, p. 113.

cation for the pride Julian took in his selection of agents, and Mamertinus[1] avers that in selecting governors he looked not to intimacy of friendship, but to blamelessness of character. The most natural conclusion is that, as might *prima facie* be expected, Julian's appointments were for the most part or perhaps altogether confined to Pagans, but that in making his choice he used all possible discrimination[2]. In theory, if not in act, he certainly laid much stress on the duty of careful selection of his ministers by the monarch. What diligence he displayed in providing against preventible abuses of power has been already shown. This very diligence exposed him to misrepresentations: he enacted a salutary decree[3] that any one of whatsoever rank or order who had attained to public functions of any kind whatsoever by irregular or underhand methods should forthwith forfeit all emolument therefrom derived. As a matter of course the officials, who were nominated by Constantius, were by profession Christians to a man. And Christian writers were too apt to regard as martyrs for their faith men whose degradation was really due to far less honourable causes. Artemius[4] secured a decent or even honourable niche in ecclesiastical records; even Bp. George himself was supposed to have been transfigured into the titular saint and patron of English chivalry.

Cf. Or. 2. 91.

Funerals, &c.

There is in the Theodosian Code one Statute which may fairly be traced to religious differences. It is a sort of police regulation against trespass and desecration of grave plots[5],

---

[1] Mamert. 25. Cf. Amm. M. xxii. vii. 6, 7.

[2] It is just to say that Amm. M. xxi. x. 8, gives a very poor character to Nevitta, one of Julian's most favoured nominees. Cf. *Or.* ii. 87 c.

[3] The decree is worth quoting in full, for its decision and thoroughness. Quicumque cuiuslibet ordinis, dignitatis, aliquod opus publicum, quoquo genere, obscura interpretatione meruerit, fructu talis beneficii sine aliqua dubitatione privetur. Non solum enim revocamus, quod factum est, verum etiam in futurum cavemus, ne qua fraude tentetur. *Theod. Cod.* xv. i. 10.

[4] Artemius, *infr.* p. 184. About George, Gibbon there can be no doubt blundered: the saint's pedigree is better traced in Baring Gould's *Curious Myths of the Middle Ages.*

[5] Rifling of graves became at this time a common practice. Muratori (*Anecdota Graeca*) collected eighty short copies of verses by Greg. Naz. against the violators of tombs. Cf. De Bleterie on this decree.

accompanied by a clause prohibiting funerals by day, as inauspicious and unpleasant to the living, without any gain to the dead. Though the philosophy of the decree is explained and justified in a lengthy rescript[1] quite in Julian's own manner, in which he expounds the natural affinities between Darkness and the Grave, Sleep and Death, and the probable diversities between the Gods Celestial and the Gods Infernal, with some enlargement on the dissonance of funerals with the market, the law-court, the daily round of town life, and above all the worship of the Gods, the date of the decree, Feb. 12, and the place, Antioch, irresistibly compel us to connect it with the famous removal of the bones of Babylas, and the impulse thereby given to converting public funerals into Christian demonstrations. So viewed the decree remains legitimate enough, rather a wise safeguard against irritating disorders than in any sense persecution.

Julian's legislation on property touched the Church on one of its tenderest sides. The age of endowments, of magnificent buildings, of landed estates and propertied communities had commenced. The fervour of acquisition, which late emperors had so fostered, received from Julian a rude slap. He decreed[2] in general terms that municipal property which during late troubles had passed into private hands should be restored to the townships, to be leased out at a just valuation. Equitable as was the spirit of the decree, its practical execution involved many hardships and aroused fierce resentment. Much of the property in question, probably by far the greater portion, had passed into the hands of Christians, not seldom for directly religious purposes[3]. During the later years of Constantius, when fortune had sunned him into a full-blown tyrant, capricious, arrogant and intolerant, Pagans had everywhere felt the weight of the displeasure of their most Christian king. Never perhaps was monarch served by more unscrupulous ministers: his organised system of espionage drove

Restoration of property.

---

[1] *Ep.* 77 in Hertlein, disinterred by him from a MS. [366] in S. Mark's library, Venice, and first edited in Hermes, Vol. VIII. pp. 167—172.
[2] *Theod. Cod.* x. iii. 1.
[3] Liban. *Epit.* p. 564, Soz. v. 5.

every true man from his court and his service: if such a one held to his post, he soon became, like Silvanus, the victim of the plots of the wretched underlings whose interests he thwarted. Men of the Eusebian stamp were everywhere busy at their work of spoliation and embezzlement. Independently of these private depredations, an almost official pillage[1] of temples was carried on. Some were rifled, some closed, some completely demolished[2]. Now the edict decreed the restoration of all these. It was enforced upon Christian Bishops, like Eleusius of Kyzikus, no less than upon unprincipled speculators. Injustice once committed, nothing is harder than to repair it. Reparation too often involves injustice hardly less grievous than that which it attempts to cure. Of this the present edict is an instance. That the original owners should receive compensation was fair and reasonable: that the existing owners should give the compensation by no means followed. In many cases the property in question had been put up to open sale, and the title of the owner was perfectly legitimate. The real defaulter had long ago disappeared, or wasted the proceeds, or perhaps met his proper doom. A case in point is that of Theodulus, a Christian gentleman of Antioch. He had the misfortune to buy (at its full price) a plot of ground fraudulently come by: he had beautified it by a palatial residence, which formed a new ornament to the town. The site had now to be restored to the city authorities, and all that was upon it mercilessly confiscated or destroyed. Another Christian, Basiliskus by name, who in their darker days had befriended Pagan fellow-townsmen, found himself on similar grounds called upon for an enormous compensation; nothing but the leniency of his creditors stood between him and absolute penury. These are instances furnished by Pagan evidence: they serve to

[1] The *closing* of temples is actually decreed in a law (Just. Cod. 1. xi. 1) supposed to date from 353. But the absence of date as well as a (perhaps clerical) mistake in the Consular names appended, casts some doubt on the actual publication of the edict.

[2] For the systematic spoliation and demolition of temples by the state authorities, cf. Liban. Pro Templ. pp. 163, 185, &c. and *Epp.* 607, 673, 1080. Christian writers, e.g. Soz. III. 17, quite bear out the statements.

show the incompleteness of a decree in its main tenor perfectly equitable.

There is one class of cases, in which the complications were greater still. There was no commoner destination of the sites, materials or embellishments of heathen temples than their conversion to the use of Christian sanctuaries. Often enough the holders had no real vested right of ownership: some unprincipled patron had perhaps handed over to the church, by way of atonement for his sins, a rich site or a handsome edifice torn from the rightful proprietors. One ordinary sample will illustrate the action of the edict. At Tarsus, on his way to the Persian war, Artemius, priest of the temple of Æsculapius at Ægæ, represented to Julian that the chief Christian minister of the place had taken away the temple columns and employed them in rearing a Christian Church. The emperor forthwith ordered restoration of the stolen property at the expense of the bishop[1]. In this and analogous cases a real grievance, not the less real because it may be dubbed sentimental, was involved. However faulty the title, the place had now become holy, set apart by episcopal benediction, sanctified by the feet of worshippers, consecrated maybe by the tombs of martyrs. The rare marble that held the holy water or formed the altar slab had been torn perchance from Pagan shrines, yet had not the sacramental water rested there and the holy elements reposed upon it? The gold of the chalices and the jewels that sparkled round them had graced the thankoffering to some heathen God, yet now had not the blood of Christ made them for ever sacred? It is easy to imagine the strength of passions stirred by such associations, and the bitterness of disputes into which they entered. In some cases a compromise might be effected by pecuniary compensation; in others this was impossible; in others refused. No better illustration could be found than the story of Mark of Arethusa[2]. He had taken advantage of *Mark of Arethusa.* Constantius' proclivities to demolish an ancient and much

---

[1] Zonar. XIII. xii. 25. After Julian's death the disputed column (one only had been as yet removed) returned to the Christian sanctuary.
[2] Greg. Naz. Or. IV. c. 88, 122 pp. Soz. v. 10. Theod. III. 7.

revered temple, and on its site had reared his metropolitan
church. The order came that he should restore the site and
rebuild the shrine; or as an alternative provide the equiva-
lent sum according to fair valuation. He refused to do either.
Avoiding the fury of the rabble, at first he fled. The mob
then turned upon his followers. Hearing of the danger to
which he had exposed his flock, the old man returned to
brave their rage. His grey hairs won him no reverence, nor
his stately bearing. There were magistrates and philosophers
and ladies there; but none raised a hand in his defence. He
was stripped naked and dragged through the filth. Wanton
women jeered him; schoolboys pricked him with their pens,
or leaped upon him. When abuse and insult had exhausted
themselves, the holy man, bruised, bleeding, torn, but still
alive, was smeared with honey and treacle, and hung up as
the prey of bees and wasps. But his spirit rose at every
affront; his tone grew higher each moment. Suspended
there he told them scornfully that he was higher than they.
He rejected every overture[1]. Not one penny, he said, could
a Christian bishop contribute to the cost of a Pagan shrine.
He would as soon pay the whole as a single penny. Nothing
could move him, or extort one word of compromise. His
stubborn patience turned the laugh, says Sozomen, against
his persecutors; and even among the highest officers of state
new souls that day were added to the Church.

This may serve as a sample of the working of this famous
edict. Though his stedfastness of faith, and his courage
under torture may condone his fault, clearly Mark was in the
wrong. The original aggressor he was bound to make full
reparation. Cases analogous to these and few in number
hardly merit the name of persecution. Yet during the opening months at any rate of his reign it is difficult to adduce
others against Julian. In the enactment of this edict an
impartial judgment will acquit him of bigotry or wilful persecution. The worst charge that can be brought is that of
haste and indiscretion, a serious but more venial allegation.

[1] By Gregory's admission the Pagans abridged their demands to a charge
little short of nominal. Greg. Naz. Or. IV. 90. So Theod. III. vii. 10.

No bare edict could meet the case. A permanent commission could alone have examined and adjusted conflicting claims, for which Julian's own enactment rightly laid down the general rule. In places doubtless acting magistrates exceeded their commission, but this must not be laid entirely at Julian's door. It was the fear of Julian's displeasure which more than anything else restrained the mob of Arethusa from the worst extremities of violence. Mark was the bishop who had saved[1] him when a child of six from the clutch of the murderers. From respect for Julian's wrath even the infuriated mob dared not put him to death: nor did the emperor subsequently withdraw his sheltering ægis[2]. Thus even this horrible tale becomes a testimony to Julian's personal tolerance rather than his violence.

It is time to pass to Julian's directly religious legislation. *Religious legislation.* In that department his policy was, it need hardly be said, reactionary. Historians[3] impute to him an eagerness to undo the work of Constantius. If Constantius had exiled Christians, Julian recalled them: clerical immunities which Constantius had granted Julian rescinded; his favours are said to have been more marked towards the sects or the individuals, who had been visited by his predecessor with the severest tokens of displeasure. If there is partial truth in the charge that Constantius' adoption of one policy was in itself a recommendation of the opposite to Julian, he certainly did not hamper his action by this petty negative conception. His idea of the true relations of Church and State was too large, too positive, it might almost be said too dogmatic for such a procedure. He may justly be called the Constantine of Paganism. Not merely because in his religious legislation *Church and State.*

---

[1] On this the silence of the historians casts some doubt; Valesius to satisfy a chronological difficulty as to the death of the first Mark (cf. note on Soz. v. x. 10) assumes a second Mark to have succeeded to the same see. Greg. Naz. *Or.* iv. 91 identifies the two without misgiving. The orator questions whether Mark's sufferings were not a just, though imperfect, retribution for his misplaced act of humanity.

[2] Liban. *Ep.* 730. Theoph.'s romance (1. p. 73) of Mark's entrails being torn out is a useful warning.

[3] E.g. Soz. v. 5.

he returned to the lines laid down by the edict of Milan, with this difference, that while free toleration was accorded to all, the weight of State favour and material support was transferred from the Christians to the Pagans: but also because he did endeavour in some sort to realise a Pagan Church[1], to create a mutually helpful union between the State and the new Church, at once imparting religious sanctions to services undertaken for the state, and conversely conferring recognised civic rank on the ministers of religion, in a word to establish Paganism. But though *prima facie* the Constantine of Paganism, he was actuated by a more religious spirit than the Christian Constantine. Both hoped to effect a spiritual as well as temporal unity in the Roman Empire. But with Constantine the union of Church with State was attempted primarily in the interests of the latter. Julian conceived religious unity to be no less important than political. The achievement of the former was of the two the higher task. The priest took precedence of the magistrate; Julian as *Pontifex Maximus*, Pope Julian as one writer calls him, was a more exalted personage than Julian *Imperator*: the suppression of Germany, the overthrow of Persia were preliminaries to the reconstruction of Hellenism. This reconstruction aimed at nothing less than a federation of all existing cults into a Pagan Church Catholic, realising its intellectual unity in the doctrines of Neo-Platonism, its administrative in the person of the Emperor its head.

Paganism established. His conception of this Pagan Church will be presently examined: at this point its relation to the body politic alone comes under discussion. All persecution of Paganism was as a matter of course forbidden: the destruction of Pagan temples became a criminal offence, an attack upon the property of the State. The official observance of Sunday and Christian feasts was at once discontinued. But much more positive steps were taken. The world-stage witnessed a veritable

---

[1] It is odd enough to find Neander's translator (*The Emp. Julian*, p. 107) shrinking from the collocation which Neander had correctly supplied, and devoting a naive note "*Kirche* in the German; but I cannot render it *Church*...T." to an avowal of shyness.

transformation scene. It was one of Julian's first acts to ensure the re-opening of the temples[1]; he did not confine himself to exhortation or example: charges were laid upon the Christian destroyers, grants were made from the Imperial treasury, in aid of restoration[2]; worshippers, in the army if not elsewhere, were officially remunerated[3]; immunities were granted to priests, or at least privileges conferred upon them. The great festivals of heathendom, the *Ludi Saeculares* for instance, were reinaugurated with historic pomp. The Emperor, as Pontifex Maximus, became in virtue of his office head of the Church, Defender of the Faith: he turned the palace into a temple: at sunrise and sunset he offered libations[4]: he appointed priests; established grades and orders; distributed provinces into dioceses; visited or deprived unworthy priests; *Ep.* 62 prescribed rules of Church Discipline; regulated vestments, precedence civil and ecclesiastical, celebration of festivals, indeed everything short of doctrine, which was left to national or congregational predilections.

Nor was it within the Church alone, as distinct from *Paganism* State, that he manifested this activity. The Church was to *and the Army.* be a definitely recognised factor in the State, almost another aspect of the State itself. Now the first duty of the State, almost its *raison d'être*, was war[5]; from a Roman point of view that function took undisputed precedence of all arts of peace. In so far, the Emperor himself excepted, the army was the truest as well as the most tangible representative of the State. It was there that Julian made the most consistent efforts to revive Paganism, and that his efforts were most rewarded with success[6]. Religion with the army had always been in the main a matter of discipline; Constantine had made services a part of drill. Re-conversion was easy. Soldiers rendered very unquestioning adhesion to the creed of a suc-

---

[1] Amm. M. xxii. v. 2, Sok. iii. i. 18, xi. 4, Soz. v. 1. Lib. *Epit.* p. 564, Περὶ τῇμ. Ἰουλ. p. 57. In this paragraph I restate in its legal connexion what has been already treated in its religious aspects.

[2] Soz. v. iii. 1. Nikeph. x. 5. [3] Liban. *Epit.* lxxxi. p. 578.

[4] Liban. *Epit.* lx. p. 564, *Ad Iul. Hyp.* p. 394.

[5] Cf. Theod. Cod. vi. xxvi. 1, *supra*, p. 160.

[6] Greg. Naz. *Or.* iv. 64, p. 106.

cessful and thoroughly popular commander: and a little pious adjustment of decorations and promotions would produce a most rapid and sensible effect. When Christianity was publicly adopted as the state religion, such religious requirements as army discipline recognised were modified suitably to the emergency. Now that Christianity yielded in turn to Paganism, the reverse process ensued as a matter of course. The religious observance of Sunday was officially ignored. The *Labarum*[1] was in turn supplanted. The genius of Rome replaced the figure of the Cross. Statues of the Emperor were surrounded with Pagan emblems[2]; he was represented as receiving from Jupiter the purple and the diadem, or going to battle with the approving smile of Mars. Christian writers, new and old, have combined to interpret this as a cunning plot, worthy of the Apostate, to catch men unawares and render them unconscious perverts. In reality it was nothing of the kind; it was the most obvious and the only consistent carrying out of Julian's first principles. Rather, it would have been duplicity to do otherwise. Julian did not conceal his Paganism: he paraded it. To have played the Pagan as an individual, as legislator, and as Pontifex Maximus, and then to have flinched from the part as Imperator would have been sheer childishness. He claimed the right, which in Roman law and public opinion he indubitably possessed, of regulating the religious ceremonial of the State. The view that such representations as those just alluded to were crafty traps to contrive that men, in doing obeisance to their Emperor, should in the act pay homage to the heathen Gods, is a clumsy aspersion, far less consonant with the character or the political position of Julian. It is on a line with that reading of history, which can only explain Julian's abstinence from persecution, by assuming that he grudged Christians the honour of martyrdom.

The Donative Mutiny.

There is one occasion[3] at least, which has been somewhat coloured by Gregory's rhetoric, on which state ritual evoked

---

[1] Cf. Ruinart, *Passio Bonosi et Maximiliani*, Soz. v. xvii. 2, Greg. Naz. *Or.* iv. c. 66, p. 107.

[2] Greg. Naz. *Or.* iv. 80, 81, pp. 116, 117. Soz. v. 17.

[3] Greg. Naz. *Or.* iv. 83, p. 118 sqq., Soz. v. 17, Theod. iii. 16, 17.

rebellion. It was usual to celebrate great festivals on the Emperor's natal day by a donative to the prætorian troops. It had been the immemorial custom, in loyal acknowledgment of the gift, to sprinkle frankincense upon the altar prepared in readiness. When Julian's day of distribution came, the antique custom was adhered to. The ceremony was made easy even to the scrupulous. No Pagan image was there, no Pagan God invoked. There was mere compliance with a piece of military etiquette. So those that hesitated were assured, and so the judicious reader may still be ready to believe. At the time not a man seems to have demurred. Afterwards, however, when they had returned to quarters, as they sat at mess[1], significant inuendoes were flung out, whether by the zeal of indiscreet Pagans or the malice of renegade Christians. Over the cups words ran high: consternation and uproar ensued. Some of the more vehement Christians, carried away by excitement, rushed to the palace, loudly proclaiming their loyalty to Christ. It was an act of mutiny; and Julian was too wise and strict a disciplinarian to allow such military insubordination to pass unnoticed. Christianity was the last pretext that he was likely to accept as an excuse for license. He ordered the ringleaders to be flogged. But this sentence, in deference we are given to understand to popular feeling, he subsequently commuted for exchange to a less favoured military post[2].

An analogous policy was pursued in the empire at large— *Coinage.* Pagan emblems were re-adopted in the Imperial mint; in the

---

[1] Johnson, *Answer to Jovian*, p. 202, shrewdly observes, 'This terrible Legion...consists of a dozen or fourteen Men at the most, for they all rose up from one Table.' The 'Theban Legion' became a byword in these seventeenth century controversies on Passive Obedience.

[2] Theodoret embellishes his account with more romantic details. By his reading the offenders were led out to *execution*. The eldest generously besought the executioner to begin with the youngest, for fear the death of his elder comrades might sap his courage. The sword was bared, the youngest of the number, Romanus by name, was kneeling to the blow, when the reprieve came. 'So Romanus then,' said the intrepid youth, 'is not worthy to be called Christ's martyr.' Theod. III. 17. Rode, p. 63, points out with perfect justice that the whole proceeding affected only the prætorian troops, and not the army at large.

strictly Roman coinage impersonations of the Glory, the Valour, or the Safety of Rome predominate; but on the Alexandrian the commonest of impressions is the Serapis head, with some personification of Nilus, Anubis, or Isis, on the reverse; the latter very variously figured, sometimes crowned with the lotus or holding the sistrum, now standing on her galley, or drawn in her hippopotamus car, or once again mounted on wolf or dog, or suckling the infant Horus. On the few surviving specimens of Antiochene coinage occurs more than once the veiled Genius of Antioch with her turreted crown and at her feet a river God, while Apollo is portrayed on the reverse. Even more distinctively Pagan than these is the die representing the sacrificial bull[1] with twin stars above the victim's head. Strangely enough no single coin with the impress of a heathen God bears Julian's name[2].

Public edifices, &c.

Public buildings received a similar treatment. The great public fountain at Antioch for instance was dedicated to heathen Gods. Theodoret[3] scents a plot to incriminate Christians in the guilt of eating meats or drinking from vessels that had been sprinkled with the lustral water of a heathen deity. A less unfavourable construction is more in accordance with the facts. Julian did but reassert the right assumed by Constantine, the right namely of the Emperor to share that religious liberty which was the privilege of his subjects. But the Emperor was in many respects the individual representative of the State. He was so in religion as in other things. The State religion was in other terms the religion of the Emperor, not the religion of the majority, or of any representative body. With a change in the Emperor's

---

[1] On this cf. Sok. III. 17, Soz. v. 19, *Mis.* 355 D, and notes on *Mis.* 360 D in Duncombe's translation (p. 278). I have figured this interesting historical coin as frontispiece. The two stars are unexplained; as symbols of the Dioskuri they would here seem irrelevant; Mr King suggests to me that they *may* have reference to the notion (still prevalent in the East) of the world resting on a bull's horns, and being tossed at times from one to the other. The specimen engraved is in Trinity College Library, Cambridge, and in respect of the full legend HERACLA seems unique.

[2] He and his wife are more than once represented as Serapis and Isis.

[3] Theod. III. 15, repeated in the *Acta of Iuventinus and Maximinus.* (Ruinart, p. 523.)

religion came necessarily a change in the State ceremonial, wherever religion came into play. It was a matter of course that at Julian's accession the State religious ceremonial should change. He had as perfect a right to restore Pagan ensigns as had Constantine to introduce the Labarum. It was no more mean of Julian to set Jupiter over the head of his statues than of Constantine to be portrayed with the Cross. It was as natural for him to dedicate public buildings to heathen Gods as for Constantine to dedicate them to martyrs.

CHAPTER VIII.

PERSECUTION UNDER JULIAN.

ὅσοι τ' ἐγένοντο διῶκται
πρόσθεν καὶ μετέπειτα καὶ ὑστατίοισι χρόνοισι,
ὧν πύματον πρῶτόν τε, κακὸν Βελίαο βέρεθρον,
δεινὸν Ἰουλιανοῖο κράτος, ψυχῶν ὀλετῆρος.
Greg. Naz.

πείθειν μὲν ἐπιχειρῶν βιάζεσθαι δὲ οὐκ ἀξιῶν αὐτὸς οὐδὲν
ὄφελος εὕρισκε τῆς ἀνάγκης. Libanius.

Section I.
Acts of Persecution.

Division of reign into periods.

THE quotations that head this chapter show that no slight discrepancies must be faced in considering the question whether and how far Julian deserves the title of persecutor. The Christian historians appear, if but roughly, to recognise two distinct periods in Julian's reign, or at least a change of policy, which though it cannot be assigned definitely to a very precise time or place, yet stamped the beginning and close of his reign with distinguishable characters. *At the outset of his reign*, writes Sokrates[1], 'the emperor Julian was indulgent to all alike, but *as time went on* he began to display partialities.' And Theodoret[2] is hardly less explicit. True the materials have been so ill labelled and sorted, that only approximate correctness can be attained[3]: but something

---

[1] Sok. III. 11.   [2] Theod. III. 15.

[3] Sozomen, after rehearsing the main instances of martyrdom which had come to his knowledge, says candidly, v. xi. 'For the sake of clearness I have recounted all together, even where the various occasions differed from each other.'

will be gained in precision if we refer to the period of the residence at Antioch such incidents as demonstrably fall within it, grouping the rest together even at the risk of sometimes unduly anticipating. Further, in considering charges of persecution during the earlier part of Julian's reign, it will be well to discriminate various classes into which the alleged instances naturally fall. First, instances of local outbreaks of popular violence[1]: secondly, official acts of persecution by local governors: thirdly, cases in which the emperor was directly implicated. Under our first head might fall the sufferings of Mark of Arethusa, which have already been recited. A more notorious instance is the fate of the virgins of Heliopolis[2]. In this town had flourished a famous temple of Venus, in connexion with which the inhabitants used to drive a vile but lucrative trade in their daughters' virtue. Constantine had closed, and apparently destroyed the shrine on the score of the licentiousness of the rites there practised. A church was erected in its place: a community of holy virgins replaced the 'priestesses' of Venus. This Christian travesty of what had been, bitterly galled the Pagan patrons of the shrine. For years they brooded revengefully, but impotently. On the accession of Julian, leave was given to reopen the temple. The elated Pagans were wild with joy. The time for retaliation had come. Cyril the deacon who 'in the reign of Constantine, fired with godly zeal, had broken in pieces many of the sacred idols[3],' was seized, killed and disembowelled by the savage mob. Fitly to inaugurate old forms of Venus-worship, the holy virgins were stripped naked, publicly exposed, and after every indignity ripped up, and

Classification of cases.

1. *Local outbreaks.*

Heliopolis.

---

[1] Soz. v. xv. 13 marks the distinction. 'Even in such outbreaks,' he adds, 'one must ascribe the blame to the Emperor; for he did not put the laws in execution upon such offenders: from aversion to Christianity, while pretending to rebuke, he really encouraged the wrong doers.' Persecutions at Bostra are cited by way of example.

[2] No precise mark of time is given, but perhaps there is a reasonable probability that the Heliopolitans did not wait for more than six months of the new régime before restoring their temple. Authorities are Greg. Naz. Or. iv. 87, p. 616 n, Soz. v. 10, Theod. iii. 7, Theoph. i. p. 73, *Chron. Pasch.* i. p. 546, Ruinart, p. 507, Kedren. i. p. 533.

[3] Theod. iii. vii. 3.

their entrails flung to the pigs. Such is the account of Sozomen, and we do not hear of condign punishment being inflicted on the offenders.

Ascalon and Gaza. Theodoret[1] gives a very similar story of outrage on Christian priests and virgins at Ascalon and Gaza. In case of the latter we have a more particular account of the martyrdom of the brothers Eusebius, Nestabus and Zeno[2]. In the dark days of Paganism the three had been conspicuous for the insults and injuries they heaped on the temples and images of the Gods. At the time of the reaction they were imprisoned and then scourged. Their taunts and mutual exhortations enraged the bystanders to such heat, that women with their bodkins, cooks with boiling water, and roughs with sheer force of hauling and tossing and bruising worried to death their helpless victims. What is important to notice is that the whole affair was an unpremeditated outburst of passion, not any systematised persecution: and further, that 'the perpetrators, as soon as sober reflection revealed the true nature of their excesses, seriously dreaded sharp chastisement from the imperial justice: reports of Julian's vexation went abroad, and that he even thought of decimating the mob who were implicated[3].' The sequel, as Sozomen gives it, must in fairness be added. The rumour of the Emperor's anger turned out mere gossip. So far from even blaming the populace, Julian deposed the governor of the district of his office, giving him to understand that his previous leniency [presumably towards Christians] looked suspicious, and that he had exceeded his rights in putting the ringleaders of the riot under arrest. 'What need to arrest the fellows,' he said,

---

[1] Theod. III. vii. 1. It is clear that borrowing from Greg. Naz. he has referred to Gaza the incidents which Sozomen localises at Heliopolis. Gregory's account is open to either rendering.

[2] Soz. v. 9, Theoph. I. p. 73, Nikeph. x. 8. Their Acts are found in Ruinart. Here once more chronological precision is unattainable. There seems quite as much probability that the outrage was the sequel of the Maiuma and Gaza award, recounted later, p. 185. The anxiety however of those implicated suggests perhaps an earlier date, so—to be sure of not treating Julian too handsomely—I have placed it here. Mücke takes advantage of Soz.'s 'so it is said' to reject the tale.

[3] Soz. v. 9.

'for retaliating on a few Galileans for all the wrongs they had done to them and the Gods?' Here therefore, if Sozomen's tale be true[1], we have an *ex post facto* implication of Julian in a passionate outburst of persecution.

The records of acts of desecration are curiously scanty; perhaps from their very commonness[2] they became so much a matter of course, that to enumerate them was beneath the dignity of history. Samples however are not wanting. Independently of the confiscation of church vessels, as at Antioch or Cæsarea, accompanied by acts of grossest profanation, Sebaste[3] was stripped of her treasured relics, the reputed bones of Elisha and of John the Baptist, while at Emesa[4] the Pagans burnt the martyrs' shrines and rededicated the church to Dionysus Gynnis (γύννις), setting up withal a grotesque image of the androgynous deity; some similar profanation took place at Epiphania[5] in Syria, and Ambrose[6] speaks of two Christian basilicas being fired by the Jews. At Paneas[7] (Cæsarea Philippi), the miracle-working statue of Jesus was thrown from its pedestal in the sacristy of the Church, and ruthlessly broken in fragments. *Desecration.*

Under our present head no other instances of persecution with bloodshed are alleged with any pretence to exactitude, in the earlier months of Julian's reign. To summarise then the results so far obtained. First, the instances are surprisingly few, three *at most:* secondly, individuals only were assailed, not classes: thirdly, each case is of the nature of an outburst of passion, nothing approaching methodical persecution *Summary.*

---

[1] The story, coming on Sozomen's sole authority, reads curiously enough: he appears to be thinking of an anecdote of Greg. Naz. against Julian, which belongs to a different time and occasion, viz. the destruction of the Temple of Fortune at Cæsarea (cf. Greg. Naz. *Or.* IV. 92, 93). We are not told who formed the deputation, or in what dress the facts were brought before the Emperor.

[2] Greg. Naz. *Or.* IV. 86, 613 c.

[3] Philost. VII. 4, Theod. III. vii. 2, *Chron. Pasch.* I. p. 546, Glykas, IV. p. 470. Elisha (cf. Nikeph.) appears to be a later addition, and is probably a mere mistake for 'the second Elisha.'

[4] Theod. III. vii. 5, *Chron. Pasch.* I. p. 547. This was the work of the townsmen, not officials. *Misop.* 357 c, 361 A.

[5] *Chron. Pasch.* I. p. 517.   [6] Amb. *Ep.* 40, p. 949 sq.

[7] Philost. VII. 3, Soz. v. 21, Glykas, IV. p. 470, Kedr. I. p. 534.

occurs: finally, every instance is distinctly retaliative, and the provocation given was considerable[1]. On the whole we infer that during Julian's earlier months there were quite remarkably few cases of intolerance proceeding to bloodshed: and that the Emperor's influence must have been, as more than once we have proof that it was, strongly exerted on the side of peace and toleration.

2. Official Persecution. S. Æmilian of Dorostolus.

We have next to handle the reported instances of official persecution, and to consider how far they reflect upon Julian.

The first case for notice is that of S. Æmilian. He was a young soldier, resident at Dorostolus, a town in Thrace. Pagan worship, for some time in abeyance, having been reinaugurated there under the impulse of court favour, Æmilian, indignant at what he deemed a sacrilegious insult, made his way into the temple, overturned the altars, and flung sacrifices and libations right and left. For this offence he was brought to the bar of Capitolinus, scourged, and put to a cruel death by burning. His punishment calls for two remarks. First, by medieval and more modern use death by burning became more or less the monopoly of religious misdemeanours, but Roman law appears to have recognised it still as a penalty for purely political offences[2]. Secondly, as to the severity of the punishment. The Church has canonised S. Æmilian, we are told[3], owing to the disproportion between

---

[1] It may also be noticed that all the instances are drawn from the East. To insist on this too strongly would be unwarrantable. The fact is, writers themselves as a rule have repeated for the most part the charges of Gregory of Nazianzus, whose sources of information were confined to the East. Ruinart, *Acta Mart.* p. 507, alludes to martyrs at Rome, mentioning the names of the brothers John and Paul, but all evidence is wanting. A mass is appropriated to them in the Gelasian Missal, but their pretended *Acts* are apocryphal. Tillemont, *Hist. Eccl.* VII. 350 pp., more than exhausts the subject. De Broglie (*L'Église, &c.* IV. p. 294 note) is probably right in concluding that there was little or no persecution in the Western Empire.

[2] Cf. Amm. M. XXII. iii. 11. From Jul. *Ep.* 74, where there is an allusion to the burning of Paul 'the Chain,' the Emperor might appear to have disapproved and even abrogated death by burning. But the old barbarian αἰθοῦντα must give way to ἀνθοῦντα, and the reference consequently becomes obscured if not obliterated.

[3] Cf. De Broglie, IV. p. 182, where the narrative is as usual somewhat richly coloured. Sokr. and Soz. do not mention, while Theod. III. 7 devotes

his offence and its chastisement. Now sacrilege by the Roman code was by no means a venial peccadillo: still more, at a time when public feeling was perilously tense, when a taunt or a prank might have proved the signal for a general riot, exploits like that of Æmilian could not but become dangerously incendiary in character, and merit corresponding severity of treatment.

Another cardinal instance of savage zeal against Christian sacrilege is that of the prefect Amachius[1]. At Merus in Phrygia the decaying temple had been by official order restored, and the statues belonging to it cleaned and replaced. Such proceedings incensed the Christians, and one morning the guardian of the temple woke to find the cherished statues shivered in pieces. The prefect was not unnaturally enraged: to shelter the innocent from his anger, the real perpetrators, three young Phrygians named Macedonius, Theodulus, and Tatian, generously surrendered to justice. They were granted the option of offering sacrifice, but scornfully refused thus to redeem their guilt. They suffered torture with great constancy, and as the terrible penalty of their sacrilege were slowly roasted to death.

Amachius.

Ankyra was another place at which the strife of parties appears to have been both violent and confused. Perhaps the prospect or the realisation of the Emperor's presence in the town stimulated zeal into fanaticism. We read[2] of a certain Busiris, of the sect of the Encratites, who for insults against the Pagans was arrested by order of the Governor, tortured and imprisoned, and only released on the news of Julian's death. Genellus, we are briefly told, was crucified[3]. But in the case of S. Basil of Ankyra we have far more pungent particularities[4]. This fiery young presbyter[5] had been put

Ankyra and S. Basil.

---

only two lines to Æmilian. S. Jer. in *Euseb. Chron.*, *Chron. Pasch.* 1. p. 549, Nikeph. x. 9.

[1] Sok. III. 15, Soz. v. xi. 1—3, Nikeph. x. 10.
[2] Soz. v. xi. 4—6.   [3] Ruinart, *Acta Mart.* 507.
[4] Ruinart, *Acta Mart.* 510 pp., Nikeph. x. 10.
[5] He had aspired to the see of Ankyra, and the recent elevation of Eudoxius to the office proved a considerable mortification to him. Philost. *E. H.* IV. 6. See Soz. v. xi. 10, 11.

under arrest for insults publicly offered to persons engaged in sacrifice, and for seditious preaching in the streets. Brought before the bar of Saturninus the Proconsul, and exhibiting nothing but the most uncompromising defiance, he was flogged and imprisoned. There he was visited by a special imperial commissioner Pegasius, whom he taunted with apostasy. After a second hearing before the Proconsul, Basil was remanded until the arrival of the Emperor[1]. Julian summoned the saint before his tribune. His efforts to convince him of the foolishness of Christianity were met with reproaches and anathemas. 'Misguided man,' said the Emperor at last, 'I wished to set you free; as you do but reiterate insult, and spurn my advice, and treat me to one affront after another, the dignity of Empire requires that seven strips be flayed from your body every day.' In the sequel we are told how the confessor cast one of the ordained strips in the Emperor's face, saying, "Take, Julian, the food you relish.' His indignant warder forthwith made the daily flaying more severe, and on Julian's departure for Antioch ended his slow torture by execution. When brought to the block all traces of the martyr's scars had miraculously[2] disappeared, so that his body was presented to the executioner pure and whole as his soul was to the Saviour! As the irons heated white hot were plunged into his entrails, he fell into a sweet sleep and died! The Acts intimate, what Sozomen's more sober account states explicitly, that his death was contrary to the Emperor's will.

Summary. The evidence[3] is now duly ranged and marshalled, which will enable the reader to distinguish equitably between Julian and his subordinates. In times of great religious excitement embittered partisans invariably outrun their orders. It was so at Ankyra: it was so later at Alexandria, where fines and corporal punishments were inflicted,

---

[1] This fixes the date to June 362, when Julian was journeying from Constantinople to Antioch.

[2] The miracle might cause temporary uneasiness to the most credulous.

[3] It will be observed that there is no recorded instance of official persecution of the Christians on the score of religion, without aggressive provocation on their part.

we read, 'beyond the Imperial instructions[1].' In such cases their party is made responsible for their excesses, and not altogether unjustly. But an individual leader of a party is morally innocent, if he has neither inflamed nor approved such outrageous exhibitions of zeal. By this standard, no man can rate Julian's culpability very high. On the whole, whether we regard the dealings of citizens with one another or of governors with their subordinates, we may fairly congratulate all parties concerned on the general restraint put upon actions in an age when sectarian animosities, alike in feeling and in word, ran very strong. Since the promulgation of the Edict of Milan principles of tolerance had made enormous strides. Christians as a body, whatever may have been the conduct of a Constantius or of not a few scheming prelates, had not yet renounced tenets which during three centuries of oppression they had urged importunately. It had come to the turn of the Pagans to advocate like principles in their own interest—and this was done now as before not only by Julian, but by most leading Hellenists, eminently by the most representative of all, Libanius. Hence it came about that only a few individual, and it may almost be added pardonable, instances of persecution resulted from the spasmodic reintroduction of an abandoned State-religion, in defiance of the sentiments of the subjects at large. For these stories of persecution entirely corroborate what is certain from other sources, namely, that Christianity was at this time consciously the winning religion. They prove that the bureaucratic machinery of a perfectly centralised despotism was impotent seriously to check Christianity, nay had a struggle even to vindicate its proper rights and secure respect for its established ceremonial. Where persecution did occur, it was provoked, if not necessitated, by Christians: Christians took the initiative in intolerance. Nor need this surprise. There is a noble intolerance which Christianity has always avowed; *Christian* laying claim to be universal, she has never patiently acqui- *intolerance.* esced in the triumph or coexistence of a rival: never, except when palsied by corruption or indifference. It is theoretically

[1] Sok. III. 14.

impossible for any universal religion to make truce with rival systems. To do so were an abdication of right, a confession of falseness. But Christianity has too often forgotten the sphere to which alone this noble intolerance may extend. She has confounded with it a bastard intolerance, unchristian in aim and action, intruding itself beyond the proper sphere of religion into outer spheres of thought, or science, or law, or policy, or even brute violence. Such was the case with Christianity at this epoch. No sooner had it attained legal equality with other religions than it claimed superiority; no sooner had superiority been granted, than elate with success it claimed autocracy and summoned State police to its assistance. A Pagan reaction, a reassertion of trampled superstitions, was a startling surprise. Astonished Christians used illegitimate means of resistance; not only breach of courtesy or breach of charity, but stubborn breach of law, was accounted a fair weapon for the fight. Nay even offensive tactics were adopted: Pagans had to seek protection from the law. Christianity had mistaken her right sphere of intolerance, and needed to be taught her error. For this end severe punishments were often necessary. And persecution is no right name for the assertion of the paramount majesty of law over the freaks of unruly citizens.

Cf. Ep. 52. 436 b c

Julian's implication.

Finally, confining ourselves still to the earlier months of the reign, we consider Julian's personal implication in acts of persecution. The tenor of his laws, and to some extent his idea of the relations between Church and State are already before us. The simple remembrance of the principles therein embodied will explain many damaging charges. Oct. 20 was consecrated by the Greek and Latin Churches to the memory of Artemius, military prefect in Egypt, whom Theodoret[1] represents as stripped of his goods and beheaded by 'the most humane' Emperor for his zeal against idols in the days of Constantius[2]. In reality, a worthy successor to Sebastian, he

Artemius.

---

[1] Theod. III. 18.

[2] *Chron Pasch.* similarly records his death, which Nikeph. x. xi. further imputes partly to his having conveyed the bones of S. Andrew, S. Luke and S. Timothy from Patrae, Achaia, and Ephesus to Constantinople. It did not take place till after Julian's arrival at Antioch. Amm. M. xxii. xi. 2.

was the detested abettor of the infamous Bp. George, whose iniquities and exactions[1] he upheld by military violence, and was put to death for civil not religious offences, one main allegation being complicity in the death of Gallus.

At Kyzikus the Novatian Church had been destroyed by Eleusius the orthodox bishop of the town[2]. He was peremptorily required to rebuild it, and at a subsequent period was apparently banished by the Emperor from his see. At the same time Sozomen[3], who gives us the information, does not conceal that the assigned cause was political agitation. The offences named are desecration, and damage inflicted on Pagan shrines; institution of widows' houses, and establishments for sisterhoods; proselytism; introduction of bodies of Christian partisans into the town; organisation of anti-Pagan demonstrations, more particularly among the important guilds of the wool-workers and coin-casters. *Kyzikus.*

Julian was naturally brought into constant contact with Christianity in his judicial functions. In one instance a whole town is said to have been prejudiced by the unjudicial religious animosities of the judge. Maiuma, the Piræus[4] of Gaza, for its devotion to Christianity, was elevated by Constantine to the rank of an independent city, and was christened Constantia after its benefactor's son. The Pagans of Gaza were violently jealous of their upstart dependents. The story of Eusebius and Nestabus has shown what extremes religious feuds reached. The independence of Maiuma was an injury as well as an insult, and one too ever present in a galling form. On Julian's accession the Gazæans laid a plea before the Emperor. Be it that, as Christian historians say, he *Maiuma.*

---

[1] George appears to have levied arbitrary dues on baptism, burial, and other church rites, besides enjoying profitable monopolies in saltpetre, salt and paper. De Broglie, *L'Eglise, &c.* IV. 75. Mr Johnson, p. 47, summarising Artemius' virtues, writes, 'The whole business amounts to no more than this, that he was a Good, Godly, Lawful, Wicked, Profane, Sacrilegious Image-breaker!' Cf. Amm. M. XXII. xi. 2, Nikeph. x. xi. p. 30.

[2] Sok. III. 11, Soz. v. 5.

[3] Soz. v. 15 supported, or rather quoted, by Nikeph. x. v. p. 17, x. xx. p. 44.

[4] Soz. v. 3, Nikeph. x. 4. The harbour suburb stood some two and a half miles from the main town. This piece of arbitration is usually, and I do not doubt rightly, referred to Julian's residence at Antioch, but I know of no evidence absolutely defining the exact date: see however, p. 178, n. 2.

took especial delight in undoing the work of Constantine and Constantius, or rather that in pursuance of his avowed policy he desired to disconnect political and material advantages from religious creed, Julian rescinded the privileges and immunities conferred by Constantius. At the same time while unifying the municipal organisation, he retained the twofold episcopal jurisdiction initiated by Constantine. The decision does not bear the stamp of a very violent *odium theologicum*, and taken alone cannot substantiate a charge of persecution against Julian.

Julian on the bench. In his personal demeanour as a judge Julian aimed at preserving rigorous impartiality. He was too loquacious and argumentative, too fussy[1] and inquisitive, perhaps even too sensitive and too anxious after certainty, to be a really powerful judge. But he spared no pains and prided himself on his strict fairness. It was characteristic of the man to inquire[2] of each pleader what religion he professed, if only to certify to himself as well as to others his superiority to all prejudice. Anecdotes even like that of S. Basil of Ankyra, stripped of their sensational appendages, fairly bear out Ammian's verdict that 'neither religion nor anything else made him swerve from the path of equity[3].'

Maris, Bp. of Chalcedon. As an individual moreover, even when most nearly touched, he seems to have exercised the same self-control as in his official guise. Considering the impetuosity of his character, and not less the vanity which again and again peeps through the philosopher's mask, the following incident[4] does Julian no small credit. The scene is laid at Constantinople, the imperial city. There the Emperor before assembled multitudes was doing public sacrifice to the Genius of the City. An old blind man is led in, Maris, the bishop of Chalcedon. Interrupting the solemn service, he brands the Emperor aloud with the title of Heathen and Apostate. Julian with characteristic[5] want of dignity, taunted him with his blindness.

---

[1] 'In disceptando aliquotiens erat intempestivus,' says Amm. M. XXII. x. 2, criticising him as a judge, but cf. p. 131, *n.* 4. [2] Amm. M. XXII. x. 2.
[3] Amm. M. XXII. x. 2; cf. XVIII. i. 2—4; XXII. ix. 9—12, x. 1—7; XXV. iv. 7—9, 19.
[4] Sok. III. 12, Soz. v. 4, Theoph. I. p. 74, Zonar. XIII. 12, Kedr. I. p. 535.
[5] At the same time the story we must remember has passed through the

'Be sure,' he said, 'your Galilean God will never heal you.' 'Nay,' answered Maris, 'I thank God for my blindness, that has spared me the sight of an apostate!' The Emperor had by this time recovered his composure, and without a word passed quietly out of the building. Of these earlier months better words could hardly be found than the terse summary of the Christian chronicler, who describes Julian's policy as 'a gentle violence that strove to win not drive[1].'

But as months went by Julian, we are told, grew embittered. In the words of Theodoret, 'Then did Julian begin more openly or rather more shamelessly to wage war upon the faith. Wearing a mask of clemency, he set snares and pitfalls to catch the unwary and bring them to everlasting perdition.' There was much to tempt it. In his policy of persistent toleration he stood almost solitary. It proved neither so easy nor so triumphant as he had anticipated. It was too often interpreted as conscious weakness by enemies, as a stupid scrupulosity by friends. Pagans besieged him with importunities; Christians nettled him by ingratitude. As fear subsided, sectarian animosities swelled more turbulently. Julian set out for the East bent on maintaining the same policy he had hitherto pursued. In his progress through Asia he was met constantly by indifference, not seldom by open derision. He was compelled to avoid or hurry by the more Christian towns. Arrived at Antioch, his tone assumes a sterner type. Writings and acts alike betray his mortification. It is this period we must now examine more minutely. His changed temper is evident in his correspondence. He chafes more irritably under opposition; he condescends to pettier expedients. Vexation sours his generosity: irritation distorts his sense of justice. His imperial acts faithfully reflect the personal asperities into which he was galled.

Julian goes to Antioch.

An instance of this is furnished by Julian's letter to the people of Bostra[2], dating from the earliest part of his residence

Julian and the Bostrenians.

mint of Sozomen. Perhaps Julian alluded to his physical infirmity as a fair emblem of the moral or intellectual darkness that encompassed him.

[1] 'Blanda persecutio illiciens magis quam impellens ad sacrificandum.' S. Jer. Euseb. Chron. pp. 503, 504.

[2] Ep. 52. Little is added by Soz. v. 15, Theoph. i. p. 74, &c.

at Antioch. It can hardly be omitted in the present connexion, though strictly it involves meanness, rather than violence, in the endeavour to put down Christianity. At Bostra[1] much party rancour had been displayed. The rival religious factions were numerically well balanced, and the clergy seem to have incited the mob to various misdemeanours. Titus, however, the bishop, had at any rate done his utmost to appease irritation, and, the storm having abated, wrote to Julian to say that the Christians, though a fair match for the Pagans, had been restrained by his exhortations from any excesses. Thereupon Julian, trumping up a paltry charge against Titus of stigmatising the citizens to belaud himself, advises the Bostrenians to drive out their bishop as a slanderer. So petty a piece of backbiting was received, it may be hoped, with the contempt it merited. In such conduct the Pagans found an incentive to persecution, outweighing many maxims of toleration[2].

Julian and Edessa. Ep. 43. Referring at a venture to this same period[3] the letter that deals with the Christians of Edessa, we have in it another display of signally bad taste, if no worse charge is involved. Constantius[4] had handed over the great basilica of the place, dedicated to S. Thomas the Apostle, to the Arian faction. The Valentinians however formed a considerable party in the town. Internecine war raged between the two sects; till the weaker were suppressed by a series of atrocities, disgraceful to any civilised community. Hereupon Julian made the wealthy Arians feel the weight of imperial displeasure, by handing over the ecclesiastical funds to the resident military, and confiscating the church domain to fiscal uses. The punishment may have been deserved[5], but whether that be

---

[1] Tourlet, whom Talbot follows, supposes the Bostra in Arabia (cf. Amm. M. xiv. viii. 13) is the town addressed.

[2] Soz. v. xv. 13.

[3] There appears no satisfactory evidence as to the exact date of the letter. On the way to his Persian expedition Julian hurried past Edessa, in displeasure at the Christianity of the townsmen (Soz. vi. i. 1), a more reasonable prejudice perhaps than Soz. or Theod. (iii. 26) would lead us to suspect.

[4] Sok. iv. xviii.

[5] There are good reasons for interpreting Julian's conduct thus favour-

so or not, Julian had no right to add the scornful remark that such a deprivation of goods would minister for them a readier entrance into that kingdom of heaven for which they looked. It is just such a pettish unjudicial remark as reflects doubt on the justice of the sentence itself.

Julian's treatment of Cæsarea, in time[1] probably as in kind, belongs to this period. This town[2], the metropolis of Cappadocia, had in years gone by been adorned with three handsome temples, two of which, those namely of Jupiter and Apollo, had been razed during the reign of Constantius. When Julian's policy of toleration became known, the town-council proceeded to demolish the surviving shrine sacred to the Genius of the State. Julian, indignant at this open defiance of his known sentiments, avenged the breach of state-law by penalties similar to but severer than those inflicted at Edessa. Not only were orders given for the immediate restoration of the temples, the confiscation of the ecclesiasti-

Julian and Cæsarea.

---

ably. The fanaticism of parties at Edessa is exemplified by the stubborn zeal of Christians there in the reign of Valens. The basilica of S. Thomas, as well as the other churches, being in the hands of the Arians, the orthodox Catholics used to muster in a plain immediately outside the walls (Soz. vi. 18, Sok. iv. 18). Valens, with the concurrence it may be assumed of the Arians, ordered a general massacre: whereupon women and children hurried to the spot, that they might not miss the glory of expected martyrdom. Further, none of the Church historians adduce Julian's treatment of Edessa as an instance of persecution: this would be decisive, were it not that heretics were the people affected.

[1] Soz. v. 4, dates these occurrences vaguely as about synchronous with Julian's arbitration between Gaza and Maiuma (see p. 185), but implies that they did not long precede Julian's death. The spurious letter announcing to Basil the penalties inflicted on the town may be correct in its assumption of being written on the eve of the Persian campaign. The letter in question (*Ep.* 75) is derived only from the collection of letters of Basil (the Great), and is rejected by the best editors. It is not the least in Julian's style: it is filled with the strangest bombast: it introduces tribes unknown to geographies, and words unknown to lexicons: it contains more than one grammatical solecism, and closes with a well-known *jeu d'esprit* of Julian, which in the context is absolutely deprived not merely of point, but of bare sense. Neither Gregory nor the Church Historians were cognisant of its contents. Teuffel in Schmidt's *Zeitsch. für Gesch.* 1845, Vol. iv. 160 pp. refers it on the internal evidence of language to a Christian hand.

[2] Soz. v. 4, Nikeph. x. 4, Theoph. i. p. 73.

cal estates, and the imposition of a fine of 300 lbs. of gold[1], but a capitation-tax was levied on all Christians, the prefect was deposed and banished, and the ecclesiastics degraded to the most costly and humiliating kind of military service[2]. We are told[3] conjecturally that a certain noble, Eupsychius, was put to death with others of his co-religionists, but against the will of the Emperor. If Sozomen is correct in his facts, the penalty decreed was certainly severe[4], though hardly exceeding the provocation.

Julian and Alexandria.
George of Alexandria.

To turn from Asia to Africa, Alexandrian politics[5] engaged a considerable share of Julian's attention. At his accession the see was occupied by the unscrupulous George. Armed violence of Constantius' agent had banished the lawful bishop Athanasius, and replaced him after horrible scenes of outrage and desecration by this infamous successor. The adherents of Athanasius, numbering all the better Christians of the town, had perforce tolerated the bishop whom in their hearts they hated: meanwhile in secret they were guided by the councils, and looked longingly for the return, of the fugitive Athanasius himself. George's real support was derived first from the Arian Court which had nominated him, afterwards from the rude soldiery who obeyed the governor's beck. No sooner had this governor Artemius, and some of his most guilty accomplices in crime expiated their past misdeeds before the bar of Julian's special tribunal, than George was left at the mercy of the citizens. For indeed Bishop George was yet more execrated by Pagans than by orthodox Christians. He violated their sanctuaries alike in word and act; he forbade their worship, openly threatening to set light to 'the death-vault,' as he contemptuously designated the prin-

---

[1] *Ep.* 75 converts 300 into 1000, and threatens to raze the entire town, building temples and shrines from the ruins of the principal edifices.

[2] Commentators are at a loss to explain this. The lowest form of military service, sc. the *cohortalis*, was the least expensive. Doubtless Gregory (*Or.* iv. p. 92 A) means the worst remunerated.

[3] Soz. v. xi. 7, 8, Nikeph. x. 10.

[4] How much of the decree was executed and how much 'prevented by Julian's death' is not left very clear by Soz.

[5] Amm. M. xxii. xi, Greg. Naz. *Or.* iv. 86 and xxi., Philost. vii. 2, Sok. iii. 2—4, Soz. v. 7, Theoph. i. p. 72, Nikeph. x. vi--vii.

cipal temple[1] of the place. A certain plot of land too, the site of the ancient Mithrium or temple of Mithras, had been made over to him for the erection of a church. In clearing the foundations a subterranean vault was found, in which numerous skulls were discovered, and a variety of grotesque implements were found, employed formerly for the inspection of livers, and for various bloody and obscene rites that characterised the Mithras cult. The bishop wantonly and mortally exasperated the heathen population by parading these through the streets amid the jeers and hoots of assembled crowds[2]. Riots followed, resulting in the incarceration of the bishop: subsequently watching their opportunity, the Pagans stormed the prison, dragged out the bishop, and kicked or trampled him to death. The disfigured remains they paraded through the streets on a camel, finally burning them and casting the ashes into the sea. Two imperial officers[3], who had abetted his crimes, shared his fate. The Christians, little caring to defend so unworthy a chief, remained as a body passive spectators, certain of the more violent partisans of Athanasius actually compromising themselves among the Pagan rioters[4]. To complete the tale, Julian, while acknowledging and denouncing the criminality of the detestable George, rebuked the Alexandrians for their precipitate violence in anticipating the hand of justice, and warns them that by their inhuman atrocity they had forfeited the good opinion of them he had but so lately expressed. He purposed at first sharp punishment, but eventually, beyond this rather faint reprimand, took no steps to bring the conspicuous culprits to justice, from respect, he says, to the God Serapis, and

---

[1] A temple consecrated to the Genius of the town. Amm. M. xxii. xi. 7. It was a common gibe, first invented by the Christians, but after the days of martyrs effectively retorted upon them by Pagans, to call places of worship τάφους.

[2] Rode, p. 90 *note*, rather arbitrarily rejects all this as a fiction of Sokrates. On the chronology see Note 6 in *Appendix* B.

[3] One, Dracontius, had pulled down the altar of Moneta, while the other, a zealous church builder, had forced the tonsure upon ungrown boys. Amm. M. xxii. xi. 9.

[4] Proved by Greg. Naz. *Or.* xxi. 26, while Amm. M. mentions Pagans only as actively concerned.

to their late governor Julian his uncle. In discerning Pagan partialities, which indeed are not far to seek, in this behaviour, we must remember that it would have been an extremely delicate task to single out the ringleaders and to apportion punishments rightly, and further that Roman emperors from Cæsar downwards had learnt to recognise and, if possible, conciliate, the passions of the Alexandrian mob. Julian therefore contented himself with providing for the restoration and due conservation of George's valuable books to swell his private library.

Athanasius.

Up to this point Athanasius had remained in concealment. Not even Julian's edict in favour of banished bishops had tempted him out of the deserts of the Thebais: his advent could but have embroiled matters and initiated new disturbances and schisms. No sooner however was George murdered, than Athanasius re-appeared. His return to the city was an ovation. A Christian father[1] daringly compares his entry into Alexandria to that of the Lord Christ into Jerusalem. He came riding on the foal of an ass; before him people cast flowers and branches and rich tapestries, and shouted in acclaim. He soon showed that he had lost none of his old vigour; and yet had added to it increased forbearance and discretion. As peacemaker, as pastor, as evangelist, he carried all before him. Chagrined at the deadness of Pagans, Julian was exasperated at the vitality of 'the Galileans.' The impotence of his own revival was a dark contrast to the triumphs of Athanasius. He contracted a jealous hatred against that great man. He seldom speaks of him without some opprobrious epithet. Scoundrel, knave, adventurer, intriguer, accursed—such are the habitual terms of description[2]. He formally charged Athanasius with insulting and contumelious defiance of law

Julian and Athanasius.

Ep. 26.
398 c d

---

[1] Greg. Naz. *Or.* xxi. 29.

[2] ὁ τολμηρότατος ὑπὸ τοῦ συνήθους ἐπαρθεὶς θράσους, Ep. 26—ὁ θεοῖς ἐχθρός, ὁ μιαρός, Ep. 6—δυσσεβής, πανοῦργος, πολυπράγμων, οὐδὲ ἀνὴρ ἀλλ' ἀνθρωπίσκος εὐτελής, Ep. 51—are the epithets by which Julian, even in state documents, describes the great bishop, in whom he discerned only μοχθηρίαν and ἐντρέχειαν (Ep. 51).

in thus returning to his see. The edict in favour of exiled bishops, he said, contemplated only return to their countries, not reinstatement in their sees[1]. It was an instance of his habitual lawlessness thus to re-usurp his so-called episcopal throne without express permission from the Emperor[2]. Doubtless his conduct was displeasing to all God-fearing[3] citizens, and he was to depart forthwith from the city, the very day, says Julian, on which the letters of our clemency come to hand. Disregard of the order would entail a severe punishment. A more frank and no less imperious missive was at the same time[4] addressed to Ekdikius the prefect. The impious Athanasius, it said, had actually dared to baptize Pagan ladies of illustrious rank, and that while Julian was on the throne. He must forthwith be chased not from Alexandria merely, but beyond the confines of Egypt. In default of this a fine of 100 lbs. of gold should be levied on the prefect's division. The emperor added with his own hand a violent postscript closing with the curt fierce malediction, διωκέσθω—'persecute him[5].' But the 'God-fearing' citizens of Alexandria, so far from being displeased with their prelate, sent a deputation to the Emperor expressly to appeal for the revocation of the edict. It was in reply to this deputation that Julian wrote the well-known despatch in which, contrasting the fatuity of the words of Jesus with the splendour of the deeds of Alexander of Macedon and the Ptolemies, he cries shame on the Alexandrians for their degenerate declension to that sect, whose spiritual ancestors (nobler far than their progeny) had been slaves to the very people whom

Ep. 6.

Alexandrians take his part, and are chid.

Ep. 51.

---

[1] Soz. v. xv. 2.

[2] Julian in his pragmatical way urges that Athanasius might at least have waited for *one* edict of recall to annul the *many* edicts of banishment.

[3] θεοσεβεῖs, sc. Pagans, as always in Julian's vocabulary.

[4] By previous writers *Ep.* 6 is supposed to have been evoked by Athanasius' contemptuous disregard of *Ep.* 26: but Rode, p. 80 *note*, cleverly urges that the contents of *Ep.* 6 do not bear this out, and that evidence of Athanasius' passive disobedience is wanting. He suggests that both letters belong to the same time, the first being a despatch to the Alexandrians, the second a private memorandum to the governor.

[5] The old reading διώκεσθαι, which Gibbon retained, gives impossible Greek and feeble sense. Apparently some MSS. omit the word.

the Alexandrians had subjugated. As for the scheming Athanasius, the villain, with whose shifty wiles and teaching they were so enchanted, the order for his expulsion[1] not from Alexandria only but from all Egypt was emphatically repeated. Athanasius once more left his see an exile[2], with the prophetic words that it was a little cloud which would soon blow over. Julian's death put a stop to further proceedings; but in this case undeniably Julian's antipathies led him first to sophistry, which set forced interpretations on plain decrees, and then to bitterness which found vent in ill-mannered and undignified abuse, and which practically pledged Julian to open persecution. In fact no sooner had the bishop been chased away, than government officials proceeded to enrich themselves at the expense of Christians by exactions[3], which though unauthorised by Julian and indeed unconstitutional, were, if not connived at, at least unpunished by the Emperor.

Julian and Antioch.

If such was Julian's temper in dealing with outlying towns and provinces, what treatment did he accord to the disputatious townsmen of Christian Antioch? His residence there was an unbroken series of petty mortifications: they came to a head in what may be called the Babylas riot, which is significant enough to merit detailed description. At the hamlet of Daphne adjoining[4] Antioch was the famous oracular spring of Castalia, which since the days of Hadrian had remained sealed from the eyes of men[5]. The prophecy that he should one day be Emperor was the last it had been suffered to announce. Julian, with the morbid curiosity and superstition that characterised him, desired to consult the

The Babylas Demonstration.

---

[1] According to Theod. III. ix. 2, Julian ordered the execution of Athanasius. No other historian corroborates the charge—(the *Narrat. ad Ammon.* in Athan. *Op.* p. 979 speaks only of his expecting a sentence of death)—while Julian's own despatches contradict it. Even if they are incomplete, Greg. Naz. (cf. *Or.* XXI. xxxii. p. 407) would certainly not have passed over the decree, had it been historical. Theoph. I. p. 74 expressly attributes the sentence of banishment to pressure exercised on Julian by Hellenes.

[2] Ruf. I. xxxiv. p. 259, Theod. III. ix. 2, Soz. v. xv. 3, Sok. III. xiv. 1, Kedr. I. p. 536. [3] Sok. III. xiv. 7.

[4] The grove was some five miles from the centre of the city, Soz. v. xix. 17: according to Rufinus I. 35, nearly six.

[5] Amm. M. XXII. xii. 8, Soz. v. xix. 11.

sacred fount. He ordered the stones to be removed. The oracular voice was dumb; from the pollution, 'twas said, of bodies that lay within the holy precincts. Sacrifices and libations could only extract a muffled reiteration, 'The dead! The dead!' Among the bones that lay there, were those of the holy Babylas of Antioch, martyr and bishop[1]. In their presence demons could find no voice to speak. By the Emperor's order, the spot was to be disenchanted of the spell by the most approved propitiatory rites. The removal of the honoured bones gave occasion for a mass demonstration on the part of the Christians of Antioch. Men, women, and children gathered in organised procession, and as they wound along the streets, behind the bier, sang aloud in chorus of antiphonal chanting, 'Confounded be all they that worship graven images, and that delight in vain gods.' Again and again the triumphant denunciation of the Psalmist rang along the streets, as in the old time when Israel welcomed the ark to the hill of Sion. But the monarch was not now among the dancers or singers. As he listened to that chorus of menace he rued bitterly the ill-judged order he had given; he issued an edict[2] prohibiting funerals in the day-time: they were, said the decree, inauspicious, inconvenient, and to bystanders distasteful: henceforth obsequies were to take place at night, and to be occasions for mourning, not for parade or ostentation. This was not all: he pondered schemes of counter demonstrations, or revenge. While he thus brooded, a still more stinging injury trod close upon the last[3].

The magnificent shrine of Apollo stood sequestered amid deep groves of cypress, myrtle and bay, commemorating the metamorphosis of Daphne. Within, at the very spot where the kind earth had sheltered the nymph from her amorous pursuer, towered a colossal figure of the god overlaid with gold, and bending earthward with the golden libation cup; the statues and fountains had been renovated; the gardens

Temple of Daphne burnt.

---

[1] Sok. III. 18, Theod. III. x. 2, Euseb. *H. E.* VI. 29. They had been transferred to the spot by Julian's brother Gallus, on purpose to confound the demons and their worshippers. For following details cf. also Ruf. I. 35, Philost. VII. 8, Soz. v. 19, Theod. III. 10—11, Amm. M. XXII. 13.

[2] *Theod. Cod.* IX. xvii. 5.   [3] Amm. M. XXII. xiii. 1.

smiled with choice exotics; all had been done to charm back the tutelar deity to his consecrated haunt. One night[1] the city was roused by the glare of a conflagration; at daybreak nothing of the great temple remained but charred walls and blackened columns standing amid a heap of ashes. How the fire arose was never ascertained: one probable account[2] asserts that a Pagan philosopher had left a burning taper on the altar where he had placed his offerings. Whatever the true cause[3], accident, malice, or as the Christians said the descent of fire from heaven, Julian at least had no doubt it was the handiwork of 'the atheists.' The principal church of Antioch was closed[4], and the sacred vessels removed: at least one young Christian hero[5] was placed on the rack. For the livelong day, from dawn till the tenth hour, hung Theodore upon the cruel horse, bearing the stinging torture of the harrowing hooks and the smart of the branding iron. Again and again he chanted the triumphant refrain, 'Confounded be all they that worship carved images;' and in after times would tell[6] how there had seemed to stand beside him in those hours of trial a young man who wiped away the sweat of agony with a fine linen cloth, and sprinkled over him cool water, so that the rapture of the vision took from him all sense of pain. From such a sufferer as this no information could be gained;

Mis. 346 B, 361 C.

---

[1] I have found the statement repeated that the fire took place on the night preceding the grand feast of inauguration, but have not come across it in ancient writers. Nor again do I know Gibbon's authority for saying the fire took place on the night following the Babylas demonstration, but I suspect the less precise '*eodem tempore*' of Amm. M. xxii. xiii. 1.

[2] Amm. M. xxii. xiii. 3.

[3] Cf. Philost. vii. 8, Theod. iii. xi. 5, Soz. v. xx. 5. Libanius in his 'Monody on the temple at Daphne' adds no facts, and hardly an opinion; and this though he was resident at Antioch at the time.

[4] Theod. iii. xii. 1.

[5] The *Acta* in Ruinart are derived from Rufinus i. 36, from whom Sok. iii. 19, Soz. v. 20, Theod. iii. 11, Aug. *de Civ. Dei* xviii. 52 and others take their accounts.

[6] Rufinus, the historian, heard the tale from the lips of the aged confessor. Ruf. i. 36. The most impartial Rode, p. 74 *note*, accepts only the arrest and flogging of Theodorus as historical, and supposes that Theodorus' pride over his Confessorship was rather too much for his exact veracity, so that lengthened memory magnified facts.

he was released by imperial command, nor do we hear of other Christians[1] being imprisoned or tortured.

If the purification and the burning of the temple of Daphne were the affronts on the largest scale that Julian had to bear, pettier aggravations were not lacking. In a principal street of the city lived Publia[2], one of the most prominent Christians in the town: she was mother of John, chief of the presbyters, who had more than once declined elevation to the Apostolic see of Antioch: herself a widow, she had founded a seminary for holy virgins, and superintended their training in person. Chanting was one of their accomplishments: and whenever the Emperor passed, they were bidden to sing at the top of their voices: *Publia.*

> "The idols of the heathen are silver and gold,
> The work of men's hands.
> They that make them are like unto them:
> So is every one that trusteth in them."

The Emperor ordered the singing to stop when he was passing by. Publia, disregarding the injunction, on the next occasion incited her choir to strike up,

> "Let God arise, and let his enemies be scattered;"

and succeeded in eliciting from the Emperor a public reprimand.

John Malalas and the Paschal Chronicle[3] yield an uncorroborated account of the death of the hermit St Dometius. The holy man had taken up his abode in a certain cave in the district of Cyrestica. Crowds resorted thither, to be healed of diseases. Julian told him to adhere to his self-imposed life of solitude: but the monk responded that he could not hinder them that came to him in faith. Then the Emperor ordered the cave to be walled up: and the saint remaining within died there. *S. Dometius.*

---

[1] The Pagan *aeditui* were subjected to the question, and also the presbyter Theodoritus if indeed he be a real historical personage. I discuss this point in a *Note* at the end of this Section. Zonar. XIII. 12, p. 26 and Kedr. I. p. 537 speak of the presbyters Eugenius and Makarius reaping the crown of martyrdom, but whether in immediate connexion with the burning of the temple is not clear. [2] Theod. III. 19.
[3] Ioan. Malalas, *Chronog.* XIII. p. 328, *Chron. Pasch.* p. 550.

Persecution in the Army.

It remains to consider a certain class of acts of persecution: those, namely, directed against military offenders. The standard instance, that of the soldiers at Constantinople[1], has been already commented on. It has been shown that the punishment inflicted was exacted by the laws of military discipline, just as the original ground of offence was a natural outcome of the existing relations between Church and State. But though neither the punishment of the Constantinopolitan troops, nor kindred instances, deserve to be classed as persecutions, it will at least be fair to set them before the reader.

Valentinianus.

Valentinianus, the future Emperor, was, say the historians, Captain of the Jovians[2], the 'crack corps' of the Imperial Guards. As such he would walk immediately behind the Emperor on public occasions. One festival-tide he was thus in attendance on the Emperor, as he visited the temple of Fortune. At the entrance the sacristan sprinkled him with the lustral water. Like a good protestant, but a bad soldier, he ostentatiously shook off the drops, and rent away the polluted portion of his uniform, by one account actually abusing and striking the keeper of the shrine. Julian subsequently relegated him to the provinces for a military offence, but without degrading him from the army[3].

[1] Supr. p. 173.

[2] He appears really not to have filled this post till later. Philost. vii. 7 styles him Tribune of the Cornuti. So too *Chron. Pasch.* p. 549, 555. For authorities see also Ruf. ii. 2, Aug. *De Civ. Dei.* xviii. 52, Theod. iii. 16, Sok. iv. 1, Soz. vi. vi. 4—6, Glykas iv. p. 473.

[3] Theod. dramatically makes the exile the immediate punishment of this particular act of insubordination. If, as Soz. precisely affirms, the scene of the incident was Gaul and Valentinian was banished to Armenia, we have a certain and undesigned proof that the offence and the supposed punishment were *not* immediately connected, for Julian would not at the crisis of his fortunes have driven one of his ablest officers to the camp of Constantius. Philost. makes Thebes in Egypt the scene of his exile, and speaks of his banishment to Mesopotamia as inflicted by Constantius. But Egypt no less than Armenia was under Constantius' jurisdiction. Mücke, p. 249, 282, discredits the whole tale as neither Ammian (in spite of his full accounts), nor Greg. Naz., nor Sokrates corroborate it. It seems clear that from 357 (cf. Amm. M. xvi. xi. 6) until Jovian's accession, when Valentinian reappears as a tribune, he was not serving near Julian's person: and this turned out a handy peg for the above good story.

The names of Juventinus and Maximinus are[1] enshrined in a homily of Chrysostom. They were legionaries and Christians. At some drinking bout, their hearts and tongues were enlarged to cry out against the abominations of the heathen reaction: quoting Scripture[2] they said, 'Thou didst deliver us into the hands of an unjust king, and the most wicked in all the world.' The mutinous words were reported. They were arrested and put upon their trial, at which they stiffly maintained the spirit of their previous utterances. Finally, on the charge of being drunk and disorderly, and having been guilty of treasonable language, they were put to death. Jan. 25 was kept holy as their day at Antioch[3], the scene of their martyrdom.

Juventinus and Maximinus.

Many others are said to have resigned rank[4] or left the service, rather than deny the faith. The names of three future Emperors, Jovian, Valentinian, and Valens are given. Valentinian's case has been discussed. Jovian held one of the highest commands[5] in Julian's own army at the time of the Emperor's death in the Persian campaign. About Valens corroborative evidence is lacking. To these names Paulinus adds that of a certain Victricius[6]. How easily charges of persecution might falsely intrude in such cases is

Military Confessors.

---

[1] Chrys. *in Iuv. et Maxim. Mart.*; cf. *Acta* in Ruinart drawn from Theod. III. xv. 4—9. Cf. Ioan. Mal. *Chron.* XIII. p. 327.

[2] *Song of Three Children*, v. 8. Theod.'s version (βασιλεῖ παρανόμῳ ἀποστάτῃ παρὰ πάντα τὰ ἔθνη τὰ ὄντα ἐπὶ τῆς γῆς) is more pointed than the LXX or E. V. If they could talk to such edification in a tavern, is the comment of Chrys., what manner of men must they have been in domestic privacy!

[3] This would be the place to insert the sufferings of the soldiers Bonosus and Maximilian, said to have been tortured before *Count* Julian (not the Emperor) for declining to remove the Christian emblems of the *labarum*. But the Acts, derived from a solitary MS. belonging to the monastery of Silvamaior, and unsupported from any other quarter, seem, with their hotchpotch of horror, miracle and prediction, wholly unworthy of credence. Prof. to Homily in Migne. Cf..Ioan. Mal.

[4] Sok. III. xiii. 3. Cf. Ruinart, *Acta Mart.* The expression ζώνην ἀποτίθεσθαι, sc. *cingulum deponere*, though normally used of retirement from the service, might mean only some form of degradation, cf. Zos. III. 19. Sokrates, if we compare his comments in III. xiii. 2, 3, perhaps only means that men professed themselves *ready* to retire rather than seem to apostatise.

[5] He was 'domesticorum ordinis primus.'

[6] Ap. Ruinart, *Acta*, p. 506.

clear from the story of S. Martin. Enlisted at the age of fifteen, as a young man of twenty he was serving as a private in Julian's army. On the eve of an engagement conviction smote him of the wrongfulness of the soldier's calling. Thereupon he declined the donative distributed by the Caesar to encourage his troops, and announced his resolution to be God's soldier alone. To rebut an undeserved taunt of cowardice, the Saint professed his readiness to take his usual place in the ranks unarmed, relying for safety on the sign of the Cross alone. The danger blew over, and Martin renounced the service. How easily might this incident, which belongs to the period of Julian's Caesarship[1] when he still professed the faith, be twisted into a charge of persecution! As it is he by no means escapes hard names from the pious narrator.

Alleged acts of persecution.

Julian's educational policy is so important as to demand a section to itself. The compliance with set forms of the State religion exacted from the imperial troops admits obviously a different interpretation to that assigned to it in this work. With these, no doubt important, exceptions, the category of charges brought to affix on Julian the name of persecutor is complete; for we cannot seriously notice tales of the inspection of human livers, more particularly of ungrown boys and girls, sacrificed for the purpose[2]. Nor again shall we give credence to Theodoret's statement that the Emperor, having summoned Publia into the streets of Antioch, *ordered one of his body-guard to box her ears and scratch her cheeks*[3]: or his still wilder figments that, after the Emperor's death, chests filled with heads were found at Antioch, and in a

---

[1] The story is drawn from Sulpic. Severus' Life of S. Martin. It is very likely fictitious in all details. The scene is localised at Worms (*apud Vangionum civitatem*, c. IV), and it seems impossible to fit in the narrative of the impending engagement with any surviving account of Julian's campaigns. The argument in the text remains sound, if inapplicable to this particular instance.

[2] Sok. III. xiii. 11 accepted and quoted by Nikeph. x. 24. The traditional sites of these atrocities, Alexandria and Athens, would exculpate Julian personally.

[3] Theod. III. xix. 5. It is possible of course that in resisting the soldiers she received some slight external injury.

temple at Carrhæ, last visited by the Emperor and sealed till his return, the corpse of a woman suspended by the hair and ripped up to expose the fatidical reading of her liver[1]. Some vague[2] charges have been left unrehearsed, besides those considered in the account of Julian's legislation. Theodoret[3], for instance, says that all Christians were expelled from the army, while others modify the statement to expulsion from the household troops, the most privileged branch that is of the service[4]. The history of the Persian campaign renders both charges demonstrably untrue. That to secure funds for the Persian campaign fines were levied on all who refused to sacrifice is highly improbable[5], though we can readily believe[6] that Pagan tax-collectors did not abate their legal claims in assessing Christian contributors. Sozomen[7] informs us that Julian replied to the ambassadors of beleaguered Nisibis, that if they wanted help they must first revert to Paganism: but answering this unproved imputation stands the solid fact that in his Persian campaign Julian did despatch aid to Nisibis.

With the above reservations no single allegation of real weight[8] has been consciously omitted or underrated. The collection of so many scattered charges into a single focus necessarily tends to intensify their real magnitude[9]. But on judicial survey of the whole evidence in array it is just to conclude—

Conclusions.

---

[1] Greg. Naz. *Or.* IV. 92 hints at similar atrocities, but without attempting to specify or substantiate his charges. Kedrenus I. p. 525, and also Glykas IV. p. 472, improve on these tales at pleasure.

[2] Greg. Naz. *Or.* xxv. ix. p. 461, Philost. *E. H.* VII. 1.

[3] Theod. III. viii., supported by Chrys. *In Iuv. et Maxim. Mart.* p. 573, § 1, Ioan. Antioch. *Frag.* 179.

[4] Sok. III. xiii. 1 (cf. III. xxii. 2). Julian probably to some extent purged the troops about his person of Christians. Motives of personal security would prompt the step.

[5] The charge appears in Sok. III. xiii. 9, xvii. 1, Nikeph. x. 24, Theoph. I. p. 81.

[6] Sok. III. xiii. 9.   [7] Soz. V. 3.

[8] I cannot retail quite all the gossip of later centuries. For instance though Theoph. I. p. 74 *murders* Bp. Dorotheus of Tyre at 107 years of age, I allow him to die a natural death.

[9] Justice plainly demands some deduction from the representations of the various Church historians. For, apart from all conscious insincerity,

1. That no organised or widespread persecution prevailed during Julian's reign.

2. That the sporadic instances which occurred were in almost every case provoked, and in part excused, by aggressive acts of Christians.

3. That, while culpably condoning some Pagan excesses, the Emperor steadily set his face against persecution[1].

4. That he never authorised any execution on the ground of religion; that, where his conduct amounted to persecution, he did not abjure but set a strained interpretation on the laws of toleration which he professed.

NOTE.

On the torturing of Theodore, &c.

Independently of conflicting accounts of the whole matter, a curious question of identity arises. Not only Julian was implicated in these events, but also his uncle and namesake, who was resident at the time in Antioch as *Comes Orientis*. If Julian gave the order for closing the Church of Antioch, to his uncle alone is imputed desecration of the holy vessels, defilement of the sanctuary, and brutality to the presbyter in charge, conduct censured by Julian himself, *Mis.* 365 c. Theod. and Soz. expatiate on the revolting details of the malady with which Divine retribution compassed his death. It seems *possible* that he too was responsible for the torture of Theodorus (v. infr.). Rufinus, Sokrates, Sozomen and Theodoret agree in representing Theodorus as arrested for his share in the Babylas demonstration, and the Emperor as authorising the arrest, which was executed against his own judgment by Salustius

they wrote at a time when the persecutions they record had become matter of history or hearsay, not of autoptic testimony, and were environed and magnified by the glamour of fading Paganism; they were credulous and uncritical in sifting evidence; they accepted as literal truth the declamation of Gregory of Nazianzus, from whom they largely quote; and they commenced with strong bias against the Apostate. On the other hand, to regard with Mücke the *silence* of Rufinus (or Ammianus Marcellinus) as disproof of the charges of Sokrates and Sozomen is to give up writing history. (Mücke p. 333.)

[1] There is no place where Julian more plainly insists on abstinence from persecution and violence, than that very letter to the people of Bostra, which has been quoted already as a signal instance of Julian's meanness.

the prætorian prefect. According to Theod., only Salustius' representations prevented additional arrests and violence. Torture was inflicted by Salustius. The order for release came from the Emperor. Both Theod. III. xi. 4 and Soz. v. xx. 5 make these events prior to the burning of the temple. I have ventured to adopt a slightly different sequence of events.

There seems reason for thinking that it was really in connexion with the fire that Theodorus was put to torture. For (1) Amm. M. XXII. xiii. 1 (and so Theod. and Philost.) connects the Babylas demonstration very closely with the fire. '*At the same time*,' he writes, '*on the twenty-second day of October* there was a sudden conflagration, &c. ;' (2) on that occasion torture was employed to discover the truth ; (3) the custodians of the temple and others (A. M. XXII. xiii. 2, Theod. III. xi. 5) were put to the torture *by Julian, the uncle of the Emperor* (Theod. III. xi. 5): while *the only* presbyter mentioned (Soz. v. viii.) as maltreated by the said Julian, was named Theodoritus, or by another reading Theodorus: this certainly suggests confused identity. In Ruinart, Theodoritus is credited with a separate *Passio*, professing to come from the hand of one who lived in the palace at Antioch, and took part in the Persian campaign. Of the three (anonymous) MSS. from which it is derived I know nothing, but Mabillon, the earliest compiler, seems half to suspect them; the *Acta Martyrum* are not highly trustworthy documents: in this particular *Passio* various confusions of dates and persons occur: the whole reads like an insipid compilation from the notices of the historians, interspersed with appropriate conversations and portents. To Julian personally, though at the expense of his uncle, the *Passio* is favourable.

Section II.

Educational Policy.

Libanius. This princely youth is dangerous to the cause of knowledge.
Basilius. Prince Julian is dangerous to many things.
      Cæsar the Apostate, Act II. HENRIK IBSEN (trans. by C. Ray).

But of all Julian's proceedings levelled directly or indirectly against Christianity, none is more noteworthy than his educational policy. Paganism and the old culture were to Julian's mind inseparably bound up together. The venerable

Roman Education.

mother who had produced so choice an offspring must now lean on her child as her chief support. It was through the sophists and in the schools, not less than by the priests and in the shrines, that the great polytheistic revival was to be achieved. The conversion of one sophist was in Julian's eyes worth that of a hundred unlearned folk. Nor in so thinking did he exaggerate the truth. The power of the sophists must have been almost incalculable; the whole higher education of the Roman Empire was in their hands; the moral charge and training of students no less than the intellectual was their province. Every great city, nay every country town, had its schools or school. At the head of the school was the sophist who frequently held the position of state official, appointed sometimes by the crown direct, sometimes by the municipality, sometimes by informal *plébiscite* among the citizens themselves. In the large towns teachers could set up on their own account, but it needed unusual brilliance[1] to compete successfully with the prestige and assured emolument of a Regius Professor. The curriculum of teaching was strictly 'classical'; the main staple of education being rhetoric and philosophy. Homer and Virgil, Demosthenes and Cicero, Plato and Aristotle were then as now the models proposed for imitation[2]. Thus the text-books of education were entirely Pagan: the object of the schools was secular not religious: they aimed at training young gentlemen to exact thought and facile expression, combined with some intelligent knowledge of law and history. When that was achieved, their work was done. No 'religious difficulty' had as yet been raised to complicate educational arrangements: the moral and doctrinal training of its members was left to the discretion of the church to which they belonged. Yet to many Christians educational work had seemed an honourable

[1] Libanius at Constantinople successfully emptying the class-room of Nikokles is one notorious instance.
[2] Cf. Capes' *University Life in Ancient Athens*, 81 pp. At Athens attention was confined to Greek only, to the contempt of Latin (*ibid.* p. 82), but in the Western Empire, especially the schools of Gaul, this was not the case.

calling. It was no more distinctively Christian than the bar or the army, but certainly it was not less so: men of so lofty and uncompromising a type of Christianity as Basil of Caesarea and Gregory of Nazianzus were among the chief ornaments of the profession[1]. When Basil was appointed to the chair of rhetoric at Caesarea, the great Libanius himself had written congratulating the Cappadocians on having such a master and himself such a colleague.

Julian shrewdly perceived that here was a most powerful engine ready to his hand. Each school might become an active centre of Pagan propagandism. Paganism should no longer fall a victim to arrows winged from her own feathers[2]. In an evil hour for his own reputation he conceived a belief, that by cutting off Christians from the higher culture of the day, he might effectually if gradually checkmate Christianity. Apparently it was in his power to do so, provided that the Christians made no forcible resistance. It would be difficult to name a law prohibiting Christian professors from keeping open schools upon their own account; but both from the terms of Julian's edicts and from the resignation of their chairs by Christian occupants, the inference seems clear that it was at the Emperor's discretion that each professor held his seat, or might keep open lecture-rooms. His first educational edict[3], issued May 12, 362 A.D., merely confirmed the existing privileges of all doctors of medicine and professors, and their immunity from public burdens. So far the new Emperor's educational policy was conservative. Shortly however it shewed a reforming tendency of the paternal government type. The new edict, five weeks[4] later in date, runs thus:— *Julian and the Professors.*

First Edict.

"Seeing that it is expedient that all masters and teachers be patterns not less of morality than of eloquence, and seeing that I cannot be present in person in each individual township, be it enacted that whoever desires the work of a teacher, do not intrude into the office suddenly or rashly, but that after orderly examination held his appointment be sanctioned by decree of the *curiales*, *Second Edict.*

---

[1] In Sozomen's language v. xviii., they 'cast all others into the shade.'
[2] Theod. III. 8, 9.
[3] Theod. Cod. XIII. iii. 4.
[4] Issued June 17, shortly before his arrival at Antioch. Theod. Cod. XIII. iii. 5.

with consent and confirmation of the *optimi*. Such decree shall be transmitted to me for endorsement, that under our sanction teachers may with more exalted honour conduct the studies of the townships."

Its effect. Due allowance being made for the bureaucratic system of the Empire, for the personal prerogative of the Emperor, and for Julian's own activity of supervision in all departments of state, the enactment is unobjectionable. At the same time the preliminary clause concerning morals (*mores*) might arouse suspicion. For religion was at least an admissible interpretation of the word, and thus the preamble might cover and portend an assault upon Christian teachers in the Schools. However as the election of professors was left in the hands of the municipal authorities, subject only to the Imperial veto, the Christians might still hope, where in a majority upon the Council, to secure such teachers as they desired. Doubtless court influences would be strong, but Christian unanimity might counteract them; for the present at any rate, there was no open grievance on which to ground an agitation. The decree proved far less, or less speedily, effectual than Julian hoped. It was too timid and tentative to do much. It was quite clear that no conciliar resolution would dismiss the aged Marius Victorinus, on whose lips for more than forty years the youth of Rome had hung: yet no Christian sophist was of greater mark. It must have been the talk of every drawing-room, as well as the joy of every Christian, when the venerable professor, in the white robe of the catechumen, made in open church the baptismal profession and was marked with the sacramental sign of allegiance to Christ[1]. The edict indeed contains no provision for dismissal. Christians in possession remained untouched. Even if they did not outlive the law itself, their disappearance would be provokingly slow. It might be difficult too, if not engender serious troubles, for the imperial veto continually to exercise itself on Christian nominations. It would be better, so at least it seemed to Julian, to show his hand, trusting to the weakness of the adversary for victory. Julian

[1] Augustine narrates the story in his Confessions, vIII. ii. and v.

possessed that impatient, restless, nervous temperament which can never be content to play the waiting game. Hardly any trait in his character is more marked. In war, in religion, in the conduct of public business it is always there: it betrayed itself in the glance of his eye, nay in his very gait. He had none of that calm, still reliance, that serene intrepidity, that imperturbable nonchalance, that characterised no one more vividly than his great contemporary Athanasius. Julian could never stand long on the defensive, or fight from behind lines: better, if need were, to burn his ships and at all risks go forward. Accordingly the following remarkable rescript[1] shortly appeared, on this occasion radical enough in tone:—

"Right education[2] we take to consist not in outward polish of phrase and expression, but in a sound disposition of intelligent thought and in just notions touching virtue and vice, honour and shame. Whoever thinks one thing, but teaches his scholars another, falls short from an educational, no less than from a moral point of view. If the difference between the mind and the tongue of the teacher extended only to trifles, his dishonesty, though objectionable, might yet be tolerated. But where the subject is all-important and the teacher instils the exact contrary of his own convictions, it becomes nothing less than intellectual huck-

[1] *Ep.* 42. It is matter for regret that the date of this rescript is uncertain. De Broglie, iv. 210, in his rather rhetorical manner speaks of it being posted upon the walls of Constantinople, and hesitatingly assigns it a date very shortly succeeding that of the May (*sic*) edict. Alike in charity and judgment I assign it (with M. Desjardins) to Julian's later Antioch legislation. For, first, the June edict (De Broglie errs in saying May) falls outside the close of Julian's residence at Constantinople; he left Constantinople in May; at the end of July he was already legislating at Antioch. Secondly, notwithstanding De Broglie's argument from the natural correlation of the two, surely some interval is required, if only to suggest the afterthought or to give trial to the previous experiment, between the June edict and this. Thirdly, its contents relegate it to the latter part of Julian's reign when he was growing embittered against Christianity. Fourthly, Amm. Marc., whose arrangement is throughout chronological, does not allude to it till after Julian's arrival at Antioch. One indirect piece of chronological evidence supports this view. Eunapius (born 347) went to Athens we know at the age of sixteen, that is in the year 363, with the intention of studying under Prœresius. On his arrival Prœresius had but just been suspended from his functions as professor. This seems to point conclusively to 363, or the very end of 362 as the date of the edict.

[2] I find one more version of this notorious edict appended to G. A. Denison's *Notes of my Life*.

stering, the immoral and shameful trade of men who teach most energetically what they contemn most completely, to cajole and inveigle by sham commendations those to whom they wish to dispose of their own—I can give it no better name—bad stuff.

'All would-be educators must be moral, and must sincerely hold opinions not antagonistic to current beliefs; more especially those who are engaged in the education of the young, as expounders of the old classical authors, whether as rhetoricians, or grammarians, or, above all, as sophists. For sophists, apart from other claims, affect to be teachers of morals as well as language, and claim social philosophy as their proper province. How far this is true or untrue we need not stay to inquire. But in commending the lofty aim of their professions, I could commend them more highly if they spoke the truth, and did not stand self-convicted of believing one thing and teaching their hearers another. And in this way:—Homer, Hesiod, Demosthenes, Herodotus, Thukydides, Isokrates, Lysias, found in the Gods the source of all learning. Some esteemed themselves priests of Hermes, others of the Muses. I hold it absurd and improper for those who undertake to expound these authors to dishonour the Gods whom they honoured. I do not say—it would be absurd to do so—that they are bound to reform their opinions and remain instructors of the young. I leave them the option of not teaching what they consider vicious, or else, if anxious to continue teaching, of primarily and *bonâ fide* impressing upon their scholars that neither Homer nor Hesiod nor any other author, whom in their teaching they have charged with irreligion and theological folly and error, is such as they have represented. Otherwise in drawing the fees for their support from the works of such authors they own to a mean sordidness, that for the sake of a few pence will go all lengths.

'Hitherto there have been many reasons for not attending at temple worship: the prevailing terrorism furnished some excuse for disguising the truest religious convictions. But now that the Gods have granted us liberty, it is monstrous for men any longer to teach what they do not believe sound. If they acknowledge the wisdom of those whose writings they interpret, and whose prophets as it were they are, let them first of all imitate their piety towards the Gods. But if they feel that they have gone astray concerning the Gods, the most adorable, then let them go to the churches of the Galilæans to expound Matthew and Luke, in obedience to whom ye are bidden to abstain from holy rites. And may your ears[1], as ye would say, and your tongue be born again to those doctrines, to which I pray that I and all that love me in thought or deed may ever cleave.

'To guides and instructors of youth this is the law that I

---

[1] Julian uses scoffingly the Hellenistic or Hebraistic ἀκοάς. The ὡς ἂν ὑμεῖς εἴποιτε clearly cannot be levelled at the ἐξαναγεννηθῆναι.

ordain for all. None that desire to attend lectures are debarred. For it is as unreasonable to debar from the right path children ignorant as yet whither they should turn, as to drive them by fear and by force to the religion of their fathers. Indeed it would be right to treat them like imbeciles and head them against their will, only that allowance has to be made for all afflicted with this kind of malady. Fools are better taught than punished.'

The form in which this remarkable production has been preserved deserves notice. It is numbered among the letters. It finds no place, even in an abbreviated form, in the Theodosian Code. In other words it is a Greek rescript, in some sort of private or special application[1], not an Imperial law promulgated in Latin, and circulated throughout the realm. To pass from the form to the matter; the preamble, having indulged in some very proper philosophic moralising on the function of the teacher, next assumes that all sound education must take for its basis the old classical authors. The preliminary fencing testifies to some sense of constraint in the writer, to an awkward misgiving with regard to the next step in the argument. However the plunge is made. By a reckless leap it is asserted, with the complacent pretentiousness of an axiom, that it is absurd, that it is improper, to teach the classics yet reject their theological beliefs. To make money by such a course is the depth of meanness and duplicity. The ensuing flourish about toleration and liberty of belief forms an odd preface to the undignified taunts that follow. Argument degenerates into sneers, and they to profanity, till the document gracelessly concludes with concessions couched in the form of insults. Altogether the performance is as little creditable a one as Julian ever penned. It is as clear as manner can make it that Julian was at heart dissatisfied at the part he was playing, even if he afterwards flattered or argued himself into self-approval. Persecuting

The Rescript criticised

as illogical,

[1] The documents with which in form it is to be compared are the despatches to the Alexandrians (*Epp.* 10. 26. 51. 58), to the Jews (*Ep.* 25), to the Bostrenians (*Ep.* 52), or to public functionaries (e.g. *Epp.* 6. 9. 50. 56). To treat it (cf. Rode 64) as Julian's interpretation of his June decree, for the benefit of some particular officer or township, does not appear to me justifiable. Schröckh assumes a second edict corresponding to *Ep.* 42, and to the statements of Christian historians.

enactments of this kind are never bettered by shallow attempts at self-justification: which merely go to prove the conscious weakness and embarrassment of the author. Julian's brief was really hopeless, whatever special pleading he might adopt. To impute hypocrisy to Christian teachers was ridiculous. The real grievance against them was that they discredited the classics. Whatever admiration they expressed for their eloquence or their poetry, they never for one instant canonised their creed. In their eyes the futility of their religious teaching hardly merited exposure. Thus Julian has to invest them with his own beliefs (which they loudly disavowed) by way of peg for the imputation to hang upon. From an earnest if narrow Christian point of view much might have been said, as to the propriety of making these heathen authors the staple of education. Much might have been urged, as Tertullian had urged, as to the demoralising tendency of the obscenities and vulgarities with which they abound; much too, in the days when Paganism was still a living power, against the *unsettling* influence of the polytheistic teaching[1]. And among contemporary Christians there were not wanting warm advocates of such views. But this whole field of argument was cut off from Julian. He could not in consistency say one word against the fables of Homer or the morals of Hesiod. Nay, with one breath he asserted that these were the sole possible staple of a sound education whether moral or intellectual, and with the next forbade any Christian man to teach them, and by the same token, as he knew well, any Christian boy to learn them. Out of an assumed regard for Christian consciences he would decline to suffer that which their conscience did not disapprove. His objections may have been honest, but he was not in a proper position to object. Because Scripture *on Julian's showing* forbade all access to the classics, therefore Christians were denied that classical training which their own interpretation of Scripture allowed. Julian, in the same sentence, enforces and ridicules the authority of the Bible. To such shifts had prejudice reduced the philosopher. And for the matter of

[1] Sok. III. 16.

conscience, who was Julian that he should be an arbiter among the people? What were his claims to sit in judgment on the Church, to pass a verdict on the liabilities of Christians? Christianity had dared long since to lay under contribution the treasures of the wisdom of the ancients, and in the name of Christ claimed philosophy and science, in joint possession with the heathen. As its hand passed along the chords it could evoke, says Gregory[1], new music of its own, and attune those grand old melodies to unison with the Gospel theme, which ruled the whole. Since the time of Origen and Clement at any rate no *Index Expurgatorius* laid its ban upon the myths of Pindar or the theology of Æschylus: no *Apage Satanas* closed the Phaedrus or the Ethics against the Christian student. The leaders of Christian thought had lacked the nice discernment, the wise vigilance, the scrupulous consistency, that would have shunned the polluting touch of unclean philosophies. They had not that Mohammedan zeal, which believed that all literature beyond the Bible was useless from its identity or baneful from its superfluity. They had not even the Pagan fervour, the counterpart of Julian's own, to desire the annihilation of all that heathen polytheistic lore. So in the latter days an Apostate Christian forsooth must arise and expound to them what it was fitting for a Christian to teach and what not. *Ep.* 9.

Cyr. 229 c

In this edict further lurks the fatal flaw that necessarily mars every edict of persecution. The blow would prostrate the honest conscious Christian, while the dishonest need but bow his head and he would remain unscathed. Though in this particular instance, where the aim was so unworthy, this might have proved a not undesired result. A percentage of false disloyal Christians might be no ill leaven among the teachers, whom it behoved to be a pattern of morals as well as learning. And once again it defeated its own ends in depriving Christian lads of the sole cure of their infatuation that Julian could offer. The merest tyro in politics could foresee that Christian parents would not send their sons to *as ineffectual,*

[1] Greg. Naz. *Or.* IV. 106, p. 135.

14—2

'denominational' schools, which were the confessed organs of Pagan proselytism; while that Julian was not in a position to enact a statute for compulsory state education[1], the insulting regret which closes his rescript frankly enough declares.

as short-sighted. Finally, the edict was unwise in its own interests. The law died with its author. But had its provisions endured and proved effective, it needs small wit to discern the result. The Church has never been backward in devising and executing schemes of education, the value of which she from the earliest days so fearlessly recognised. A displacement of all Christian teachers from State Schools would have been the signal for the rise of unnumbered Church Schools, which would soon have disarmed Paganism of its most effective weapon of offence. Even as it was efforts in this direction, though not of the wisest kind, were quickly made. The two Apollinares[2] devised a wholly new curriculum: the father not only composed a Christian Grammar, but turned the Pentateuch into twenty-four books of heroic verse, and selections from the historical books into tragedies, while the son reduced both Gospels and Epistles to the form of Platonic dialogues.

The Edict persecuting. Such was the edict which for his hero's sake Ammianus[3] says must be 'plunged into everlasting silence,' as the darkest blot left upon the reign of Justice that he tried to renovate on earth: and which more than one Christian writer settles upon as before all else entitling him to the name of persecutor. There is no one act, where his personal responsibility is clearly established, which does so more justly.

Practical scope of Edict. It is easier however to criticise the words and character of the decree than to estimate its exact practical effect. The June edict[4] certainly applies on the face of it to schools throughout all the municipal towns of the Empire. The rescript under discussion proclaims itself a general law for

---

[1] From a passage in *Misop.* 356 it seems that at Antioch at any rate Julian made futile efforts in this direction, to which the Christians, and not least the Christian women, made a determined opposition.

[2] Sok. III. 16, Soz. v. 18, combined at length by Nikeph. x. 25 sqq.

[3] Illud inclemens, obruendum perenni silentio. Amm. M. XXII. x. 7.

[4] Supr. p. 205.

all instructors and teachers[1]: as such it is treated by the Christian writers who animadvert upon it. Gregory of Nazianzus, a well-informed if partisan witness, writes thus: 'He ousted us from letters (λόγων) like so many pilferers,... fearing the confutation of heathen errors'; and adheres to the same language, when he speaks of the Christians being deprived, defrauded, or debarred from school learning[2]. Rufinus[3] testifies that Christians were forbidden to study Pagan authors, admission to the schools being confined to worshippers of the Gods and Goddesses. Sokrates[4] describes the law as one 'prohibiting the Christians from education'; Sozomen[5] states that Julian forbade the children of Christians to study the Greek poets and orators, or to attend Pagan schools: and Theodoret[6] invests the prohibition with a similar latitude. Ammian's[7] censure of the decree certainly implies no less gross a violation of the liberty of the subject, and in another passage[8] he states in the broadest way that public abjuration of their faith by Christian teachers and rhetoricians was indispensable to their continuance in office.

Were not the evidence so full, and on the whole so harmonious, it might plausibly be argued that Julian's legislation was applicable only to a definite class of State Professors. In favour of this might be urged, the peculiar form of the rescript itself; the difficulty of supposing that there was in existence any such complete and centralised system of Imperial education, as would admit of effective supervision and control by the Head of the State; lastly, the incontrovertible fact that the Christian subjects did at once design, if not institute, some form of voluntary schools, in

Its real limits.

---

[1] τοῖς καθηγεμόσι καὶ διδασκάλοις κοινὸς κεῖται νόμος, *Ep.* 42.
[2] τῶν λόγων ἡμᾶς ἀπήλασεν, Greg. Naz. *Or.* IV. 5, p. 79. Cf. τὸ λόγων ἀποστερῆσαι Χριστιανούς, *Or.* IV. 101, p. 132, with ensuing chapters, and so τῶν λόγων ἀποκλεισθέντες, *Or.* V. 39, p. 174.
[3] Ruf. I. 32.
[4] Χριστιανοὺς παιδεύσεως μὴ μετέχειν, Sok. III. 12; τοὺς Χριστιανοὺς Ἑλληνικῆς παιδείας μετέχειν ἐκώλυε, *ib.* III. 16.
[5] Soz. V. 18.
[6] Theod. III. 8, cf. too Nikeph. X. 25, 26, pp. 54—60.
[7] Amm. M. XXII. X. 7. [8] Ibid. XXV. IV. 20.

which works similar to those of the Apollinares would form a part of the curriculum.

Possible extenuation of the edict.

Had Julian limited his measure to that recognised class of Professors, who obtained their chairs and derived their emoluments direct from the state, that is to say from the imperial treasury, and not from the contributions of local tax-payers, his policy would deserve a milder censure. By such action he would merely have asserted a principle, which was later destined to obtain unquestioned acceptance: namely, that no heretical, still less atheistical, teaching could be authorised or supported by the state. To a sincere Pagan, whose hands ruled the machinery of state education with autocratic power, it might well seem legitimate to turn it to the end which he thought best[1]. It appeared unreasonable for the state to subsidise teachers for inculcating that the state Gods were devils, or for the Pagan parent to contribute towards the training of his son as a Pheidippides, to whom in old age he might play Strepsiades. What would make the particular application of the principle culpably gross in Julian's case is, first, that in his age, as necessarily under every extended polytheistic dispensation, religion, or at any rate the choice of a religion, was far more an open question than in medieval or even modern times; secondly, that it was a very large section, in many places an enormous majority of his subjects, in the teeth of whose convictions he legislated; and thirdly, that it was an entire innovation to make education at all a vehicle for religious proselytism.

The Edict genuine persecution.

Still had Julian stopped here, he would have deserved more tender condemnation. But a candid review of the language of the actual edict, of the testimonies of historians, and of the practical action taken by the Apollinares and other educational leaders, appears to supply demonstrative proof that Julian deliberately resolved not merely to purge the imperial Professorial chairs of unorthodox occupants, not merely to impose a conformity test on all teachers in the public municipal schools, but penally to prohibit Christians from teaching or publicly reading the master-pieces of Pagan

[1] Ullmann, *Greg. von Naz.* 85 pp. defends Julian's action.

literature, and thereby to cramp if possible and lastingly impair the training and intellect of Christian children. The act was one of genuine, if refined, persecution. Nothing could justify such a prohibition short of proof that the effects of Christian teaching were openly and scandalously immoral. If Julian at times hints, he never seriously offers to substantiate so untenable a charge. Prejudice in this instance betrayed him into sophistries, culminating in a form of persecution quite as unjustifiable as those coarser methods which in word and act he constantly repudiated.

How far the edict was executed, materials for forming an opinion are few. To judge from the outcry it caused among the Christians and the prominence accorded to it even in anti-Christian writers, it remained by no means a dead letter. Nor were its provisions evaded, as they might have been, by cowardly reticence. Doubtless not a few Christian professors, trimmers such as Hekebolius, must have preferred apostasy to ruin. The clause in Julian's edict which spoke of the removal of terrorism, and the free avowal of religious beliefs must have rung mockingly enough in their ears. But in the main the Christians seem to have met the challenge nobly: by general consent they chose to surrender their profession rather than their faith[1]: one or two conspicuous examples emerge from the number of unrecorded witnesses. At Rome Marius Victorinus could not forswear the God who had given his tongue its eloquence : at Laodicea the Apollinares, father and son, commenced their classical reconstructions of Scriptures: Musonius[2] proved staunch : Proæresius[3], first of the Athenian Professoriate, the former tutor of Julian, received from his ex-pupil an assurance that in his case the authorities would not enforce the decree, no doubt with some implied hope of reciprocal forbearance on his part. In a like spirit Constantius had offered money to Liberius to support him in the exile he had himself inflicted. Proæresius, like Liberius, rejected not without disdain the proffered gratuity.

Actual results of edict.

[1] *Or.* VII. 30.
[2] *Vita Iuliani* app. to Mamertinus' Panegyric in Migne, *Patrol. Lat.* vol. 18.
[3] Eunap. *Vit. Soph. Proaeresii,* Jer. Euseb. *Chron.*

Fame has recorded the doings of these Coryphæi of the Church: of many another true man, who faced temporal loss as nobly, no record is inscribed upon the tablets of history.

Section III.

Estimates of Julian.

The evidence of facts that have affixed the name of persecutor on Julian has now been so far as possible sifted. The upshot of the whole is, in a word, that Julian 'persecuted Christianity rather than the Christians[1],' and to the best of his strength, though with sporadic failures here and there, impressed a like policy upon the empire at large. His tolerance to the individual was, as his treatment of the system declares, in the main not a moral sentiment rooted in large-hearted equity, but a calculated system of policy. It will now be instructive to cite the more important testimonies that bear upon the point, and see how far they corroborate the conclusions drawn from the facts. For this purpose Julian's own works must be assigned the fullest weight, and consisting as in no small part they do of informal instructions to subordinates and of letters to personal friends, it is impossible to suppose that they contain only hypocritical representations of his true sentiments. In public documents such as the Epistle to the Athenians, a politic mask of toleration might be assumed; and no decisive stress could be laid on them. On the other hand despatches to offending towns or individuals are absolutely reliable evidence of Julian's public policy, and confidential letters to ministers and private friends no less so of his real intentions. In case of all historical characters the survival of their correspondence is the surest touchstone of their worth; Julian can happily be subjected to the ordeal, and issues from it, if not scatheless, yet cleared of the most damaging charges. Throughout

Julian's writings.

---

[1] Cf. Wiggers in *Zeitsch. für die Hist. Theol.* 1837. By this rather thin epigram, which is the text of his discourse, he means that Julian strove rather to dethrone the system than to do personal violence to the individual.

his letters there is on the whole nothing so blackening to his fame as the education rescript, which has just been so fully discussed. The general principles he avows are usually most irreproachable. He makes frequent appeal to the clemency of his enactments.

'So kindly and tenderly,' he writes to Hekebolius[1], 'have I dealt with all the Galileans, that I have suffered no man anywhere to be violently dragged to the temples or put to any other such despite against his own free choice.'

Again, in one of his most spiteful letters, writing to a city conspicuous for the turbulence engendered by religious factions, and writing too from Antioch when the year 362 was more than half spent, while forbidding riots and clerical mob-demonstrations, he expressly confirms to the Christians of Bostra their unrestricted right of assembling together, and practising all such devotions as they pleased. After rebuking sectarian animosities and reprisals, and calling on Pagan worshippers not to injure or plunder the houses of those who are led astray by ignorance rather than choice, he declares[2] that men should be convinced and instructed by reason, not by blows or assaults or bodily violence, and closes thus:

'Again and again I charge all votaries of the true worship to do no wrong to the Galilean masses, neither to raise hand nor direct insult against them. For those who go wrong in matters of the highest import deserve pity, not hatred, for religion is verily chiefest of goods, and irreligion the worst of evils.' *Ep.* 52. 438 B

Without qualification or misgiving he contrasts his own treatment of Christians with that of his Christian predecessor, and recites the sufferings of the heretics of Samosata and Kyzikus, and the depopulation of the fairest provinces of Asia, to make his own leniency stand in clearer light against that background of shadows: and in the *Misopogon*, the latest perhaps of all his works, written at Antioch in 363, he challenges the citizens to adduce against him a single *Ep.* 52. 436 A

---

[1] Not the Sophist (who was amongst Julian's correspondents, cf. *Ep.* 19), but the Governor of Edessa.

[2] Exactly similar sentiments are attributed to him. Liban. *Epitaph.* p. 562. On this topic, cf. Beugnot, 187 pp.

instance of religious persecution. One short letter[1] states his view so very frankly and succinctly, that it shall be rendered entire.

'*I*,' he begins emphatically, '*I* by the Gods want no Galileans killed, or wrongfully scourged, or otherwise injured. Godly[2] men I do desire to be encouraged, and plainly say they ought. This Galilean folly has turned almost everything upside down: nothing but the Gods' mercy has saved us all. Therefore we ought to honour the Gods and godly men and cities.'

It is perfectly true that there are passages in a different tone. In number they are comparatively few, and to each of them in their proper place, whether to domineering acrimoniousness towards Athanasius, or to malicious spite against Titus of Bostra, or to acrid gibes upon the Christians of Edessa, attention has been fully and faithfully called in the foregoing pages. It remains true that, the education rescript excepted, throughout the surviving works of Julian there remains not one passage counselling or legalising persecution, that on the contrary, in every case where his own tone is most bitter and might most seem to countenance, if not suggest, persecution, he is careful to say that neither theoretically nor practically does he regard it as a suitable engine of conversion. Higher praise cannot with justice be given. Julian neither practised nor claimed to practise an *impartial* toleration. He went as far as abstract justice seemed to demand; but not a step further. He recognised no call for generosity, no claim to a perfect equality of position for all creeds. In dealing with his Christian subjects, justice, a niggard justice, once satisfied, this is his tone—

Ep. 49. 432 A

> No law requires that they my care should prove
> Or pity, hated by the Gods above[3].

Christianity should exist on sufferance only.

---

[1] *Ep.* 7, addressed to a certain Artabius otherwise unknown.

[2] θεοσεβεῖς. Julian's 'godly men' (cf. Oliver Cromwell's phrase) are of course 'Pagans.' This official note is, by La Bleterie and others, attributed to Julian's earlier months. De Broglie (*L'Église &c.* IV. p. 277) is perhaps more correct in dating it from Antioch.

[3]
οὐ γάρ μοι θέμις ἐστὶ κομιζέμεν οὐδ' ἐλεαίρειν
ἀνέρας, οἵ κε θεοῖσιν ἀπέχθωντ' ἀθανάτοισιν.

The lines are quoted or rather perverted from *Od.* x. 73.

In the works of the historians there is much to lead to similar results. It would be idle work to rehearse the conventional praises of Pagans or the vague defamations of Christian writers. The admissions of both will be far more instructive. From the Pagan side there is little or no hint of guilt of persecution, but Ammian[1] does most emphatically, and not once only, except the education edict from his general verdict. Eutropius no doubt alludes to the same in his brief declaration that Julian persecuted the Christians, but refrained from shedding their blood. Praises of leniency are of course plentiful in the mouth of Mamertinus or Himerius, Libanius or Eunapius. *Julian's Historians. Pagan.*

Turning to Church writers as more copious mines of information on this point, amid Gregory's unrivalled violence of denunciation, passages of the following kind are to be found[2]. *Ecclesiastical. Greg. Naz.*

'Authority has two departments, persuasion and force; the more brute element of despotism Julian delegated to the populace, whose recklessness goes all lengths of unreasoning inconsiderate impulse. *He issued indeed no public ordinance;* but non-repression of excesses converted his wishes into unwritten law. *The milder and more royal department, of persuasion, he made his own prerogative:* yet did not adhere to it completely: for the leopard cannot change his spots, nor the Moor his skin, nor fire its burning, nor the Evil One, who is a murderer from the beginning, his malice, nor Julian his naughtiness.'

The quotation has been carried so far to avoid giving a mere garbled extract, and to show also that it was not some sudden weak relenting that betrayed Gregory into admissions which he elsewhere seems to forget. In other places he is evidently at a loss for charges to drive quite securely home the charge of persecution in its narrower sense. Such surely are the two following passages:

'Julian omitted no kind of impiety; by persuasion, by threats, by sophistries he drew men to himself, not only by guile but also

---

[1] If controversy has not demonstrated *pro* and *con* that Ammian was a Pagan, at least no intelligent Christian reader can doubt it.

[2] Greg. Naz. *Or.* IV. 61, p. 105.

by force[1]. But by no sophistical disguises could he conceal his persecution.'

Here the category of modes of persecution clearly needed some climax, which is certainly not supplied by the explanatory afterthought. In the last words too there is conscious weakness of accusation.

One passage more will suffice[2]:—

'Of all persecutions ever made, Julian devised the most inhuman: for he mingled persuasion with tyranny, grudging his victims the glory of martyrdom, and casting doubt upon the zeal of the fearless.'

This is a valuable comment on Gregory's poetical flights[3], when, after mention of Cain and the Sodomites, of Pharaoh, Ahab, and Herod, he apostrophises Julian thus:—

> Mid all that swell the persecutors' line,
> Early or late or in the after time,
> Latest yet first, preeminence is *thine*,
> Slayer of souls, Satan's foul sink of crime,
> Tyrant accursed!

Rufinus. Rufinus, whose writing, though full of hostility to Julian, bears generally an impress of honesty and veracity, says[4] that Julian,

'Craftier than all other persecutors, avoiding violence and tortures, by rewards and distinctions and flattery and persuasions wrought upon more part of the people than if he had made violent assault upon them. He forbade Christians to study Pagan authors, and admission to the schools was reserved for such only as worshipped the Gods and Goddesses.'

Sokrates. With this declaration Sokrates is in marked accord. Attention has been already directed to the distinction which he draws[5] between the outset of Julian's reign, when he was 'indulgent to all alike,' and the subsequent period when he 'began to display partialities'; but the historian, while dwell-

---

[1] Greg. Naz. *Or.* xviii. 32, p. 353. ἐβιάζετο is so far ambiguous that 'by constraint' would be as faithful a rendering as 'by force.'
[2] Greg. Naz. *Or.* xxi. 32.
[3] Poem. Lib. i. § ii. p. 323. *In Laud. Virg.* l. 454—458.
[4] Ruf. i. 32.
[5] Sok. iii. 11.

ing on his vehement encouragement of Paganism, speaks a little later thus in quite general terms[1]:—

'He went cleverly to work. Having seen what honour was paid to the confessors in the persecution of Diocletian, and knowing the forwardness of many to become confessors, he revenged himself by taking the other line. He eschewed Diocletian's harsher way, though he by no means kept clear of persecution; for all troubling whatsoever of peaceable men I call persecution; and he troubled the Christians thus:—by prohibitive educational laws; that they might not, as he said, whet their tongues and be a match for Pagan disputants.'

Thus Sokrates supports Rufinus in his general verdict, and in representing Julian's rescript on education as the crown of his persecutions.

Sozomen as usual goes farther still in candour of statement on Julian's behalf[2]. He says that the Emperor,

'while minded in every way to support Paganism, *accounted the compulsion or punishment of unwilling worshippers ill-advised;*'

and at greater length writes in these terms[3]:—

'From the first, though devoid of all feeling for the Christians, he showed himself more humane than preceding persecutors; their example proved that penalties were of no service to the establishment of Paganism; nay, were the surest promoters of Christianity, which won lustre from the courage of willing martyrs for the faith. In jealousy not in mercy, he thought it unnecessary to work conversions by fire or by sword or by mutilations, or by drowning or burying alive, or such like favourite means. He hoped to pervert the masses to Paganism by argument and exhortation, and expected easily to compass his end by eschewing violence and adopting an unexpected policy of indulgence.'

Theodoret is too consistently hostile to extenuate thus his *Theodoret.* bill of indictment, but S. Jerome[4] admirably sums up Julian's *Jerome.* system as 'a gentle violence that strove to win not drive,' while Orosius[5] finds the Apostate guilty of assailing Christi- *Orosius.* anity by craft rather than repression, making perverts by stimulating their ambition, not by playing upon their fears.

---

[1] Sok. III. 12.   [2] Soz. v. xv. 8.   [3] Soz. v. iv. 6, 7.
[4] Jer. *Euseb. Chron.* p. 504.   [5] Oros. VII. 30.

Summary. The allegations adduced to prove Julian a persecutor have now been fully marshalled. The bulk of them appeared, even in combination, insufficient to convict Julian of personal responsibility for persecution in its extreme forms; in individual cases he allowed justice to be overruled and as it were cozened by prejudice; more than once he winked at barbarities of Pagans more fanatical than himself; in one notable instance he degraded himself to genuine persecution, though the pains inflicted were not of a corporal kind. The evidence of reported facts has next been compared with confessions extracted from Julian's own writings, and with admissions extorted from the principal witnesses on either side: these have on the whole remarkably corroborated the previous conclusions; and if details here and there furnish matter for doubt, on the whole assurance of the main truth has been attained, and but few contradictions remain unreconciled.

Julian's intentions. Here then the inquiry would naturally end. But the writings of previous historians seem to force upon us the unwelcome question, 'Would Julian have become an open persecutor, had power remained longer in his grasp?' A complete answer would entail a thankless and distasteful discussion, necessarily arriving at no sure result. The evidence, if indeed it can be called evidence, is meagre enough. It consists of surmises and inferences and laborious deductions of Gregory and his copiers: Julian's vague menaces uttered, or maybe not even uttered, in moments of irritation, have been reported[1] and magnified. He was said to have threatened on his victorious return from Persia to proclaim war to the knife with all Christians: the hand of God was traced in the dart that pierced his side. But it is not before Jerome[2] that the precise statement occurs that Julian on marching against the Persians had devoted the blood of the Christians to the Gods after the victory: it was reserved for the insight of Jerome's pupil, Orosius[3], to lay bare the full

---

[1] E.g. cf. Ruinart, *Acta de Sancto Theodoro confessore.*
[2] Jer. Euseb. *Chron.* p. 504.   [3] Oros. vii. 30.

blackness of his guilt: reiterating the master's words, he corroborates them thus:

'For he actually ordered the restoration of the amphitheatre at Jerusalem, intending on his return from Parthia to cast the bishops and all the holy monks[1] of that district to the beasts and make a spectacle of their sufferings!'

Modern historians[2], with few exceptions, have argued in the same direction. Inference and assertion are as easy as they are unsafe; 'of all forms of lying prophecy is the most gratuitous.' There is no doubt not a little to be plausibly urged in support of such a view. Throughout Julian's tenure of power a growing bitterness of tone is patent, manifesting itself in act and word alike. It was from Antioch he chastised the Cæsareans, and wrote his contemptible letter to the Bostrenians; from Antioch that he penned his savage letters against Athanasius; at Antioch once more that he composed the *Misopogon*, commenced his work against the Christians, and wrote his satirical *jeu d'esprit* the *Cæsars*, which closes with the bitterest and most cold-blooded of all his scoffs at Christianity. Corresponding to this change in his own tone, increased remissness is displayed in curbing the excesses of imperial officers, and in one case at least deliberate connivance in the torture of Christians, which was warranted by suspicions only and not actual facts.

Accepted view.

Julian at Antioch.

But there remains on the other side the broad indisputable fact that throughout the empire at large religious toleration was both the law and the practice. In the West there was absolute freedom from persecution; in the East

---

[1] Compare the droll tale of Julian's tame devil and the monk Publius in Kedrenus i. p. 526, Glykas iv. p. 472. Cf. also Kedr. p. 531.

[2] Lamé, *Julien l'Apostat*, p. 163, goes perhaps furthest, and predicts with pleased assurance that Julian would have persecuted hard and persecuted successfully. 'Si les persécutions des autres empereurs n'avaient point empêché le nombre des chrétiens de s'accroître, c'est qu'ils frappaient les corps sans pourvoir aux besoins des esprits; Julien avait pris l'ordre inverse......Une persécution dirigée par Julien se fût donc accomplie dans les meilleures conditions pour le succès; l'extinction du paganisme par l'épée des empereurs chrétiens prouve qu'il est possible de supprimer une religion par la violence, pourvu qu'on ait su la remplacer en lui prenant tout ce qu'elle avait de bon.'

extremely little, and that little induced by local disturbances or the bias of individual magistrates. If it be true that a relentless doom would have driven Julian to the last huge wrong, it is beyond dispute that to the end he struggled hard against that Nemesis of apostasy. It would have been hard to devise a fiercer ordeal than a prolonged stay at Antioch. Alone in policy, in sympathies, in patient and heroic efforts to restore virtue to a soulless corpse, encircled by flatterers and deceived by knaves, secretly ridiculed by Pagans and openly defied by Christians, meeting with no allowance for mistakes and no response to leniency, the young impetuous Emperor might have been sick at heart and fretted into outrage, even in some secluded retreat. But at Antioch these feelings must have been aggravated to tenfold force. The town where men had been first called Christians retained its old character; it was a nucleus of Christianity still, the very core of Church life in Asia. But its Christianity was of a type specially offensive to a disbelieving philosopher. It was noisy, turbulent, demonstrative. Nowhere, unless at Alexandria, did party spirit run so high. The town was usually split into rival camps. Many a stormy council had met at Antioch. It was the nursing-mother of Arian[1] disputants, the prolific birthplace of heretic[2] creeds: not five years before Julian's arrival the most violent Anomœans of the East had chosen Antioch as the rendezvous from which to send their synodal congratulations to Valens the Anomœan of the West. The very year before his appearance the appointment of a non-Arian bishop[3] had caused a tumult in the open church and been the signal for a schism, which lasted out the century. Apart from religious feuds the mob ten years previously had first kicked

---

[1] Cf. Newman's *Arians of the Fourth Century*, Chap. I. § 1.

[2] At the Council of Dedication at Antioch 341 A.D. five new creeds were drawn up, succeeded in 345 by the so-called *macrostich*.

[3] Meletius, chosen by the Arians, disappointed his partisans by an orthodox confession. He was banished, and Euzoius elected in his stead. The unfortunate attempt of a commission headed by Lucifer of Cagliari to restore peace, ended in his setting up a new party, which bore his name and survived for fifty years.

the life out of an innocent governor, and then torn in pieces his mangled remains. Such scenes were hardly uncommon[1]. A spirit of rancour was abroad among all classes, high and low. Julian was constantly called to face and endure this. He was the butt of ribald jeers, of seditious libels[2], of curses, of damnatory prayers[3]. Publia and her virgins regaled him with abusive Psalms; irreligious wags nicknamed him 'Slaughterer'; rude scoffers at philosophy dubbed him 'Goat'[4]; squibs, lampoons, scurrilous rhymes ran riot. How galling these petty insults were it is not easy to picture: measures of conciliation, generous attempts to cripple extortion and alleviate distress, all met with a like response. Pagans and Christians, rich and poor, landowners and salesmen, combined[5] to hinder the Emperor's designs and thwart his measures of reform. He tried to stem vulgarity and immorality; to break the tyranny of capitalists, and check the noisy Sansculottism of the mob: jeers, misrepresentations, abuse, were all the thanks he got. The giddy populace were to be won only by frivolous and degrading exhibitions[6] such as their conscientious ruler declined to give. To them the Emperor, his friends, and his views were strangers and intruders. Much as he despised these 'frogs of the marsh,' Julian smarted sorely under the unpopularity and contempt with which his overtures were met. He felt himself unappreciated; he knew that he deserved better of the unworthy citizens. He was altogether misunderstood, underrated, despised, and he dwelt on it bitterly. Every line of the *Misopogon* is saturated with this feeling. He was aware moreover that it was the very elevation of his aims,

Mis. 364 B c, 366.

Mis. 365

355, 357 D, 365 A.

342 B

354 c

358 A

344 B

---

[1] Amm. M. xiv. vii. 6, *Mis.* 370 c, cf. Amm. M. xiv. vii. 16.

[2] *Mis.* 364 B, 361 A.

[3] *Mis.* 344 A, with which cf. Greg. Naz. *Or.* xviii, c. 32, and Soz. vi. 2 concerning Didymus.

[4] Θύτης, Τράγος, Zonar. xiii. 12. For the latter cf. *Mis.* 339 A.; for both, with others to boot, Amm. M. xxii. xiv. 3.

[5] Cf. specially the conduct of the merchants during the scarcity of provisions at Antioch. Sok. iii. 17, Soz. v. 19, *Mis.* 350, 368 c—370 D.

[6] *Mis.* 339 c, 340 A, 342 c, 354 c, 359 D, 365; cf. Liban. *Epit.* p. 579.

the sincere toleration, the self-imposed restraints of power[1], that reduced him to this predicament. It is hardly possible to conceive of stronger temptations to persecution: toleration for the intolerant, forbearance towards the overbearing, without even the recompence of gratitude, were incessantly required of him. He was himself being persecuted at every turn for his religion; that he knew well was the secret of his unpopularity; he had but to speak the word, and an ample harvest of retaliation could be reaped; and yet he refrained himself at the risk of alienating friends and with the certainty of emboldening enemies; he stedfastly set his face against persecution; and only once or twice, when exasperated beyond patience, deviated from the attitude he had taken up.

It is possible perhaps in this matter to go further still. If it is at all admitted that incitements to persecution, and aggravations to forbearance reached at Antioch a pitch that could hardly have become intensified however long Julian had retained imperial power, and that he nevertheless adhered to his policy of toleration, other consequences may perhaps be deduced. It will be granted that Julian would not have followed the blood-stained track of a Decius or a Diocletian: it will be admitted that he was at least too shrewd in statesmanship, if not too true to philosophical conviction, to renew against ever-swelling superiority of force a battle lost irrevocably half a century before[2]: and more, it will be remembered that too great breadth of toleration was one of the charges levelled against Julian; it will be noted with fresh interest that it was the dead, irresponsive sloth of Paganism that soured his blood more even than the antagonism of believers; it might in a sanguine moment be conjectured, or at least not dismissed from the region of hope, that, if eighteen months of rule had taught and disciplined and disenchanted Julian so much, added years

---

[1] *Mis.* 343 A, 357 D, &c. &c. &c.
[2] The toleration Edict of Galerius, 310 A. D.

might have strengthened him to probe the diseased lie, and forsake deluding shadows and fruitless hopes for a creed more solid and aspirations more satisfying. If the historian must silence such a hope, at least let Ausonius' kindly epitaph on Titus be vouchsafed to the Apostate too,

FELIX BREVITATE REGENDI.

CHAPTER IX.

JULIAN AND CHRISTIANITY.

> "Out of this stuff, these forces, thou art grown,
> And proud self-severance from them were disease."

Julian's idea of Christianity.

JULIAN'S treatment of the Christians has been investigated at length: the personal opinions that he entertained of Christianity and the Christians demand a separate examination. Obviously the two questions are different. In the first case he acted as Emperor: in the second he thought as an individual. In the former his hands were in great measure tied by the mixed responsibilities of power; in the latter he was free as the unlettered peasant or the cultured philosopher.

It is not too much to say that intellectually, morally and practically he totally misconceived Christianity. Before the death of Constantine, and in a still greater degree of course at the death of Constantius, Christianity had attained a position sufficient to prove that it was the conquering force then present in the world, that in its hands lay the future. During the half-century preceding Julian's accession it had gone forward with leaps and bounds: its numerical strength, its moral earnestness, its intellectual self-justification all entitled it to at least respect as an antagonist, if not to acceptance as a master. Yet Julian treated it with unconcealed and miscalculating contempt. He professed and probably felt disdain as much as dislike. How could this be? In the first place he was singularly unfortunate in his contact with it. Alike in the court of Constantius, and in his early education and youth, Christianity came before him in the person of most unworthy representatives[1]; on the throne hardly less than in the schoolroom the same ill-fortune dogged him. The cordiality and impartiality of his numerous invitations availed him nothing. It was high time to prove that not all bishops were dissimulators, and not all prelates politicians: so the worthier with one consent held aloof from the Apostate. Athanasius indubitably represents the highest consciousness of the Christian Church of Julian's day. If there was one episcopal appointment more grievous a scandal to the Church than another, that of Aetius might probably be singled out. First a peddling tinker, next a quack, next a sophist, the coryphæus of heretics and the bane of the Church, he had won his spurs as 'the Atheist[2]' before in Julian's reign he attained the bishopric of Constantinople. Such were the two men. Athanasius Julian can scarcely mention without bad language: Aetius[3] above every ecclesiastic he delighted to honour; not content with receiving him at court he conferred upon him in addition an estate in Mitylene. Can facts speak plainer? In this respect Julian certainly deserves commiseration, but must not therefore elude just blame. If not in boyhood, at least as a man he had ample opportunities for forming a judgment from fairer specimens of Christianity than an Aetius or a Hekebolius. Basil the Great and Gregory of Nazianzus were his college associates; will rather than occasion must have been lacking if he never met Christian leaders such as Hilary of Poitiers or Eusebius of Vercellæ: doubtless their society would have been distasteful to him. The sequel to Julian's vain endeavours to pervert the young Cæsarius[4] was his retirement from court, a practical commentary neutralising pages of trim professions.

Contact with Christians.

---

[1] Schlosser dwells on the rapid degeneracy of the Christian clergy after the accession of Constantine.

[2] He was surnamed Ἄθεος: he was the founder of the Anomœans, the most openly unchristian of Arian sects.

[3] Cf. Soz. v. v., and Jul., *Ep.* 31.   [4] Supr. p. 143.

Christianity a scheme.

Cyr. 333 B–D

Ep. 52. 436– 437 A

Frag. Ep. 288 B

Frag. Ep. 305 C

Julian's primary misconception of Christianity was in regarding it as a sheer contrivance[1], a kind of mutual benefit society set up solely in the interests of the managers. He had found so much hypocrisy among Christians that he assumed it of them all. S. John's attribution of divinity to Christ was a clever fraud: the whole fabric of sacerdotalism was so much ingenious mechanism: the clergy were ambitious schemers; if deprived of the power to tyrannise and dictate and appropriate other men's goods, they at once became centres of faction, professional incendiaries, whose work it was to inflame party against party in their own selfish interests. The monks—except indeed in those cases where they had been driven by devils into the wilderness and provided with manacles and collars[2]—were no better; their assumed self-renunciation was a sham. At a small sacrifice for the most part, they had made a lucrative investment. In exchange for the paltry property or positions they had surrendered, these so-called 'Renouncers[3]' were everywhere courted, caressed, and obsequiously followed, besides recouping themselves in hard cash into the bargain. Monasticism was in Julian's eyes a low type of the false Cynicism he so hotly denounced. To him almsgiving and charities were but ingenious devices to support the ascendancy of a ruling caste. He compares the Christians to kidnappers, who tempt children by mouthfuls of cake, and finally catch them and fling them into confinement, to spend a life of misery as the cost of the transient sweet that tickled their palate for the nonce. If Pagans did but imitate the cunning of the Christians on more magnanimous motives, they would soon occupy the same position of influence.

---

[1] *Frag. Ep.* 305 C D, *Ep.* 49. 429 D, *Ep.* 51. 435, and esp. Cyril 39 A τῶν Γαλιλαίων ἡ σκευωρία πλάσμα ἐστιν ἀνθρώπων, ὑπὸ κακουργίας συντεθέν· ἔχουσα μὲν οὐδὲν θεῖον, ἀποχρησαμένη δὲ τῷ φιλομύθῳ καὶ παιδαριώδει καὶ ἀνοήτῳ τῆς ψυχῆς μορίῳ, τὴν τερατολογίαν εἰς πίστιν ἤγαγεν ἀληθείας.

[2] Cf. Jerome *Ep.* 22, *Ad Eustoch.*, § 28 (Migne, vol. i.).

[3] ἀποτακτισταί, Or. 7. 224 n. Apparently all MSS. insert the σ. I do not know that the word occurs elsewhere. For ἀποτακτῖται, see *Epiphan.* II. 129. Presumably they are the ἀποταξάμενοι (cf. Bingham, *Ant.* VII. 2).

Besides this arrant and pervading duplicity with which he charges them, Julian attributed a variety of other vices to the Christians. Not content with condemning individuals, he regards envy, strife and slander as *characteristic* of the Christian profession, a mistake which cost him not a few practical blunders. He represents Christians as drawn from the lowest and most degraded portions of society. He extends this reproach to primitive Christians as well as his own contemporaries, and avails himself of S. Paul's[1] black catalogue of crimes to prove that from the very first the Church had been recruited from the criminal ranks. There was considerable truth in the remark as a fact. The lowest and the highest strata of society[2] were still, as at the first, those from which Christianity derived its strength. Content with this fact, and keenly alive to the shortcomings of Christians, Julian precipitately inferred a condemnation of the religion itself. He was blind to the moral power of Christianity upon the life. Bigotry and prejudice revealed to him only the narrowness, violence and duplicity so rife amid contemporary Christians. In his belief they greedily assimilated all that was bad, rejecting what was good: and this no less in the religious and intellectual than in the moral and social sphere. Having abandoned the worship of the eternal Gods they preferred to worship the Galilean carpenter who died as a felon: disdaining to adore King Sun, they deified a Jewish corpse; nay, not content with one man or one corpse, they worshipped many corpses and dead men's bones without number. As in worship, so too in ceremonial. Even in the law they still professed to revere, they rebelliously rejected all that was most venerable and estimable. Like leeches they sucked only the bad blood out of the Mosaic code, leaving the purer portion. The same principle of perverse assimilation ruled their intellectual tastes. To the Greeks belonged science and culture; to the Christians unreason and stolidity[3]. Their own literature was stuff fit only for slaves;

---

[1] Rom. i.
[2] Beugnot makes this remark, which Chastel endorses, p. 95: cf. also Lamé, p. 41.
[3] Greg. Naz. *Or.* IV. cii.

232   JULIAN.

Cyr. 238 B

Greek literature with all its exquisite beauties they at once reprobated and pursued; here as elsewhere, taking a perverse delight in culling from it what was worst instead of what was choicest, and so weaving therefrom a web of mischief.

Julian's Polemics against Christianity.

Not satisfied with such general denunciations, Julian probed deeper, and was at great pains to refute the Galileans by argument as well as abuse or contempt. His controversial objections to Christianity were committed to seven[1] books, denied to us by the orthodox anxieties of his successors[2]. Happily the three earlier books survive, embedded in the elaborate refutation by Cyril.

Metaphysical objections.
Cyr. 58. 65

To begin with the metaphysical objections, the origin of evil, the creation of matter, the creation of mortal natures directly by God are all handled, and contrasted unfavourably with the Platonic theory of creation by mediary agents. Between the Christian and the Neo-Platonist system lies the fundamental difference that whereas Christians regarded evil as entering into the world through the Fall, as a supervening accident therefore and not an inherent necessity in the constitution of things, Neo-Platonists accepted a Manichean belief in the precedent eternity and with it the final indestructibility of evil. The creation or even sufferance of evil in a world created by God they deemed incompatible with the absolute unity and holiness of the Godhead. This line of attack, however, is so slightly pressed, compared with what might naturally be expected, that it is a safe conjecture that either Cyril's report is imperfect or that the subject was reserved for treatment in one of the lost books[3].

---

[1] Three according to Cyril, but seven according to Jer. *Ep.* 70 *Ad Magnum* (Migne, vol. i.): perhaps Cyril formally refuted three only out of the seven; Herwerden, p. 45, finds in Theoph. *Chron.* p. 80, a slender confirmation of this theory. A passage quoted by Sok. III. 23 does not occur in Cyril's extracts. On this cf. Desjardins, 148 pp. The fullest and best arranged summary of their contents I have met with is in Herwerden's *De Iul. Imp.* pp. 41—83, 97—138.

[2] Law of Theodosius II.

[3] At the same time the remains of the work are almost entirely *destructive*. This quite accords with Sokrates' criticism (*H. E.* III. xxiii. 7). 'The books are too vituperative. They are purely combative, not argumentative. Not having truth on his side, he tried to discredit established facts by

Relying mainly on the anthropomorphisms of the Old Testament Julian further asserts the moral obliquity of the Christian conception of God. Human passions are assigned to him. He is represented as a jealous God, not above anger and indignation, as confounding the innocent with the guilty (Numb. xxv.); and in his blind passion taking an indiscriminate revenge upon tens and hundreds of thousands, out of all proportion to the offence committed, in retaliation for the sin of a few. Again, he is meanly envious; he forbade man to take of the tree of wisdom, and yet more reprehensibly tried to deny him the knowledge of *good* and evil. Truly the imitation of such a God (which philosophers commend) would have strange and disastrous results. The unsightly representation is doubtless due in part to wilful dissembling on the part of Moses.

Christian conception of God attacked as immoral, Cyr. 152 c

160 D—161 B

93 B—94 A

146 B

The Christian or Jewish God is not only immoral, but curiously impotent and short-sighted. He created Eve as man's helpmate, and she turned out his seducer and worst enemy. He tried to debar men from the knowledge of good and evil, and was then outwitted by them. Next, becoming frightened of men, he adopted the awkward device of producing a confusion of tongues. In his dealings with Gods he betrays equal helplessness: he cannot prevent that worship of false Gods of which he is said to be jealous. Once again the Jewish conception of God's partiality in confining his solicitude and government to a special people most injuriously limits both the power and the sphere of his working. To the enlightened philosopher such an idea must appear no less false in fact than it is petty in conception. The polytheistic[1] idea of God's superintendence of the whole world by appointed agents is a far nobler one. And what is more, it alone is borne out by history: if history proves any-

as unworthy. 75 A, 94 A.

89 A, 93 B.

134 D—135 C

155 C D

99 B, 100, 148 C.

115 D—116 B

---

sarcastic ridicule.' In Lamé's words, the proper title for the work is 'Refutation of Judaism and Galileism,' rather than 'Defence of Paganism.' (*Jul. l'Apost.* p. 149).

[1] In Cyr. 69, 72, 146 n, 155, 238, 253, Julian tries to fasten polytheism on O. T. writers by the help of Gen. xi. 7, Ex. xxii. 28, &c. Cf. also Cyr. 100, 238, 290, on Ex. iv. 22, 23, v. 3, vii. 16, Deut. xxxii. 9, Gen. vi. 2.

thing, it proves both in ancient and modern times that the Jews are a God-forsaken race, not the special favourites of the Deity. In material prosperity their career is little more than a succession of captivities; Egyptians, Philistines, Assyrians, Babylonians, Syrians, Romans have one after another triumphed over them; while as for general enlightenment they fall hopelessly behind the Chaldeans, the Greeks, and many other nations.

Defects of Scripture. Julian further impugning the defects of Scripture finds that the revelation of God therein contained is not only false and immoral, but also strangely incomplete. For instance there is hardly a word as to the creation or function of angels, and intermediary spirits. Though they are again and again mentioned—whether obscurely, as in Gen. vi. 2, 4, or directly—it is left altogether undetermined whether they are created by God, or emanant from some other source, or unbegotten. Neither are proper distinctions drawn between acts of creation and acts of arrangement of pre-existent material. Various rationalistic objections are next brought against the credibility of Scripture. In what language, it is scoffingly asked, did the serpent talk? How is the account of the tower of Babel less fabulous or ridiculous than Homer's myth of giants piling Pelion upon Ossa? In a similar tone the discordance between the genealogies in Matthew and Luke is commented on. Further the literary defects of Scripture receive severe animadversion, and are elaborately contrasted with the excellencies of Greek literature. The prophets are derided[1], and the Hebrew tongue maligned. Julian likewise assails the want of unity between the different parts of Scripture. The ceremonial law for instance was given by God. Moses expressly says that it is to be eternal; 'Ye shall keep it a feast to the Lord, *throughout your generations;* ye shall keep it a feast by an ordinance *for ever*[2];' and to the same sense elsewhere. Christ reiterated a similar injunction; 'Think not I am come to destroy the

---

[1] *Frag. Ep.* 294, 295, with which compare particular criticisms in Cyril, p. 253 (cf. 259), 262, and Theod. Mops. in Munter, I. p. 136.

[2] *Ex.* xii. 24.

law and the prophets; I am not come to destroy but to fulfil[1],' and yet Paul has the audacity to say that 'Christ is the end of the law,' and Christians with one consent systematically neglect every one of its provisions. Again, Moses' entire ignorance of Christ is obvious[2]; the supposed prophecies of Christ, whether in Moses or elsewhere, are completely at fault: and it is again and again repeated that the worship of Christ is a defiant breach of the first commandment of the Jewish Law. Passing to the New Testament, we find Julian persistently endeavouring to depreciate the character of the witnesses. He speaks scoffingly of Matthew[3] and Luke[4], and in more general terms of the fraudulent machinations of the Evangelists. While the Jewish prophets are in his eyes foolish babblers, who but chattered to old women, in S. John he discerns a scheming and audacious impostor, who ventured to intrude upon the credulity of Christians novel[5] and blasphemous beliefs as to the divinity of Christ, his person, and his relation to God the Father. S. Peter is a hypocrite, and the differences between him and S. Paul are enlarged upon, while the latter, the arch-impostor and magician, is said, 'as occasion suits, like a polypus on the rocks, to shift his doctrines about God.'

<small>Cyr. 320 A

299 A, 305 E—
306 A, 351 A—C.

159 E, 253 B C,
261 E—262 E.

Depreciation of the New Testament.
Ep. 42. 423 D,
Cyr. 218 A.

Frag. Ep. 295 b

Cyr. 213 B, 262 D, 327 A—C, 333 B—D.

325 C

99 B

106 B</small>

Of our Lord himself Julian speaks in a slighting rather than bitter or blasphemous tone. He recognises neither novelty, nor beauty, nor force in his teaching, comments on his ill success in converting his own kindred and nation, and concludes that he did nothing worthy of mention, except perhaps a few miracles of healing or exorcism in out-of-the-way villages of Palestine. He looked upon the 'carpenter's son' with an aristocratic disdain, that must for ever discredit

<small>*Julian's view of Christ.*

Ep. 51. 433 D,
Cyr. 213 A B.

191 E</small>

---

[1] Matt. v. 17.

[2] Cyril 262, 290 E. Elsewhere Julian insists on the verbal interpretation of the Messianic prophecy by Moses, 'The Lord our God will raise up a prophet for you among our brethren *like unto me*,' 253 C D.

[3] The call of Matthew he rejects on internal evidence. Jer. *ad Mat.* ix. 9.

[4] He refuses credit to Luke's account of the angelic apparition in Gethsemane, because (1) the disciples were asleep, (2) John makes no mention of it.

[5] Cf. Cyr. 327 A and 335 B where Julian explicitly says that neither Paul nor any of the three other evangelists dared to call Jesus God.

his power of moral insight. Christ's teaching appeared to him weak, unpractical, and subversive of society[1]. He did not think him a bad man, or a scheming man, or a deluded man, but just an unlettered peasant, who had lived some three hundred years ago, when Augustus and Tiberius were great. There are times when a peevish jealousy breaks out as though Christ were pitted in a personal rivalry against Caesar[2], and defrauding him of the tribute due; but ebullitions of that kind are casual and kept out of Julian's set polemics against Christianity.

Cyr. 206 B, 213 A.

Of Christian mysteries.

The highest mysteries of the Christian faith he treats with unsparing contempt. He of course rejects the divinity of Christ; he unsparingly denounces the whole doctrine of the Trinity[3], which originated in the obscure imagination of 'the good John[4]'; and special taunts are directed against the dogma of the Miraculous Conception, of Atonement by Christ's death, and of the premundane existence of Christ. Christian 'faith' put him out of all patience[5]. Against the sacramental[6] efficacy of baptism he indulges a special spite: in his satirical Caesars he jeers at the thought of Constantine deserting the ideal of holy life, and after being lapped in the arms of luxury and self-indulgence, turning at last to Jesus, and being washed in baptismal water pure from the taint of sin. 'Baptism,' he exclaims in his work against the Christians, 'does not take away the scales of leprosy, nor ringworm, nor scurvy, nor warts, nor gout, nor dysentery, nor dropsy, nor the whitlow, nor bodily ailments small or great, but will clean drive out adultery and theft, and moral transgressions one and all.' The taint of his own baptism he endeavoured, we have seen, to wash out by initiatory rites,

194, 201, 206, 253 B, 262 D E.
213 B

Caes. 336 A B

Cyr. 245 D

---

[1] Sok. III. 14, *Ep.* 43, 79, Cyril 335.

[2] Henrik Ibsen introduces this effectively in the closing act of his *Julian the Emperor*.

[3] This is interesting as showing how widely apart the Christian and Neo-Platonic ideas of the Trinity were.

[4] ὁ χρηστὸς Ἰωαννῆς, Cyr. 327 A.

[5] Greg. Naz. *Or.* IV. c. 102, p. 637 A.

[6] Herwerden, p. 82 and 135, detects an uncertain allusion to the Lord's Supper in the word θυσίαν, Cyr. 306 A.

and each Christian pervert was bidden to undergo some such purificatory process. *Ep. 52. 436 c*

Thus Julian's formal objections to Christianity, so far as they have been preserved, are less metaphysical in kind than might be anticipated. Many of them represent a low range of thought[1], such as far worse and far duller men of the present epoch would disdain. Large extracts from Julian's works are well suited to the *National Reformer*, and might even repay translation. Briefly his intellectual attitude may be described as that of modern rationalism of the coarser kind with the following modifications. First, in common with almost all thinkers of his day, and more particularly as himself a Neo-Platonist, he takes no exception to the records of miracles in Scripture. Exhibitions of miraculous power were in his view hardly worth notice, much less evidences of divine agency. Secondly, the class of objections commonly called scientific were necessarily as yet undeveloped, though discernible in germ, for instance in the asserted inadequacy of the legend about Babel to explain the diversity of languages found on the earth. Thirdly, criticism had not yet commenced its destructive work; partly that the science was as yet but little advanced; and still more perhaps that at that day materials of proof were too abundant to admit of such statements or theories as at the present day can be plausibly supported, so as at times, even if untrue, to defy refutation. Be that as it may, Julian accepts both Old and New Testament intact, and in particular refers to S. John's Gospel throughout as the undoubted testimony of the apostle. On the other hand, Julian could press far more forcibly than the modern rationalist the recentness of the rise of Christianity and the lateness of its appearance in the world's history; nor had he to deal in the same way with Church life and development as an evidence for the truth of the religion. He does not fail to taunt Christians with 'having invented new-fangled rites of sacrifice.' His view of the moral character both of Christ and his disciples is rather

Julian's intellectual attitude towards Christianity.

Cyr. 191 B

306 A

---

[1] Neander, *Church Hist.* III. 112 pp., with his usual just discrimination, points out the weakness and insufficiency of much of Julian's attack.

that of the school of Voltaire, than of the more enlightened scepticism of Strauss or Renan.

Julian's unfairness to Christianity.

Underlying almost all Julian's polemics against Christianity there is a covert comparison between it and the Neo-Platonist religion which he desired to substitute. The biblical account of creation is contrasted disadvantageously with that found in Plato: the Jewish idea of God with the philosopher's. The statement that the God of Moses is less gentle than Lykurgus, less forbearing than Solon, less just or benign than Numa, is a typical one. Jewish wisdom, Jewish law, Jewish literature, Jewish history, Jewish life, social or political, are set side by side with their counterparts, as most favourably represented, in Greece or Rome or Egypt. Throughout there is a certain, and in part it must be owned, conscious unfairness. Not only does Julian misunderstand the anthropomorphisms of the Old Testament, not only does he fail to see the principle of progressiveness in God's self-revelation to mankind, not only does he argue sophistically or mock unkindly or blaspheme offensively, but there is this pervading injustice in his attack, that he compares ideal Paganism with ordinary secular Christianity. For the Pagan he assumes that the philosopher's secret is the peasant's creed; for the Christian that the individual's failure is the system's condemnation.

Cyr. 168 b

Julian's bitterness towards Christianity.

In a word in Julian's judgment of Christians candour is no match for prejudice. He misrepresents their character; he denies them the name they adored[1]; in his mouth they are 'Galileans,' or 'infidels,' or 'atheists,' and their religion is the plague-spot of the Galilean mispersuasion; he profanes or curses all they hold most sacred: he breathes a wish that all their literature could be expunged from existence. This bitterness could not but engage him in serious errors: it warped his judgment, and dulled his observation. He saw their factiousness and augured their ruin; he imagined that

Ep. 63. 454 b

Ep. 9. 378 b

Its result.

---

[1] Once only does the word Χριστιανοί occur in Julian's writings, and on that occasion it is in a quotation from a bishop's letter: cf. *Ep.* 52. 437 D. According to Greg. Naz. *Or.* IV. c. lxxvi. p. 602, Julian prescribed the use of the term 'Galilean' by law.

the interpositions of Constantine and Constantius had alone frustrated suicide: he gave them rope to hang themselves.

Deceived by external symptoms he missed the internal solidity of their religion: he did not comprehend the hold it had upon men's hearts: it appealed, he thought, to all that was puerile, superficial, transient, in the nature of man. He supposed it to be a charlatanism, better contrived than most, which imposed upon mankind by assumed authority, by stilted gravity, by frowns and by tears, by bribery and by caresses, by mysterious threats and by delusive promises, by all the paraphernalia with which designing men can catch the popular taste. 'He fell into the error, to which in all ages men of the world are exposed, of mistaking whatever shows itself on the surface of the Apostolic Community, its prominences and irregularities, all that is extravagant, and all that is transitory, for the real moving principle and life of the system[1].' The truth is that he was continually looking backwards, not forwards[2]. Hellenism and the Roman Empire were the two colossal objects that blocked his line of vision. He failed to discern that their day was done, their strength worn out. In the midst of that world-heaving period of storm and stress, he miscalculated all the most valid forces. Christianity was to his vision a disintegrating power, fatal alike to the power of Rome and the power of Paganism. He was so far right[3]. But he did not discern that it was the force of the future: that if now it rocked the mountains that pressed upon it, it would shortly hurl them to the ground, and freed from the incubus walk forth erect amid the ruins, busy at its nobler creative work of planting the desolate places and renewing the face of the earth. He knew nothing of the struggle he had undertaken.

Miscalculation of contemporary forces.

Ep. 49.

---

[1] Newman, *Arians, &c.*, p. 354.
[2] Chateaubr. *Étud. Hist.* ii. p. 57.
[3] Cf. Montalembert, *Monks of the West*, Bk. i.

CHAPTER X.

JULIAN AND HELLENISM.

> "Schöne Welt, wo bist du? Kehre wieder
> Holdes Blüthenalter der Natur!
> Ach, nur in dem Feenland der Lieder
> Lebt noch deine fabelhafte Spur.
> Ausgestorben trauert das Gefilde,
> Keine Gottheit zeigt sich meinem Blick,
> Ach, von jenem lebenwarmen Bilde
> Blieb der Schatten nur zurück."

Julian misunderstands the Pagans.

IF Julian misinterpreted Christianity, his initial misconception of Paganism was as grotesquely complete. His reaction is the picture of a man plunging deeper and deeper into an impassable morass. Little by little the truth dawned upon him that he was a general without soldiers, and that no inch of ground he won could be permanently retained.

Julian as Hellenist.

It was from the literary side, in other words as Hellenism, that Paganism first fascinated Julian[1]. By inheritance, by instinct, and by training, he was possessed with a singular appetite for culture. From childhood, he says, he was smitten with a devouring passion for books. His beau-ideal of life was that of the student[2]. At an early age he became an ardent book-collector. The happiest remembrance of his youth was that of days when in sight of the blue Propontis and dancing sails, he reclined on beds of convolvulus and thyme and clover *with his eyes upon his book*, able in the pauses of

---

[1] Naville, p. 6 pp.
[2] Supr. p. 128, cf. Amm. M. xvi. 5, Lib. *Ad Iul. Hyp.* p. 376, Jul. *Ep.* 9. 378 A.

reading to feast upon the beauties of the scene[1]. Of all his wedding presents none charmed him so much as the library with which the Empress enriched him. Through his Gallic campaigns and in his Persian expedition his books 'followed him everywhere like his shadow[2].' On hearing of the death of Bishop George, it was Julian's chief solicitude that the prelate's library, with which in old days he had made acquaintance, should not be broken up or spoiled. Of all his letters, Naville remarks, two only are to ladies; the one promotes Kallixene the priestess; the other thanks 'the most worshipful' Theodora for a present of books! His knowledge of literature was most extensive[3]; not one of his associates, he says, had perused more volumes than himself. His own pages prove the intimacy of his knowledge of Greek authors[4], before all others Homer and Plato. He himself was Greek to the core—'enamoured of Greece,' writes Libanius[5], 'above all of Athens the eye of Greece, Athene's town, the mother of Plato, Demosthenes and wisdom.' His pages[6] teem with loving laudation most exactly corresponding to this description. 'Though a Thracian maybe by birth, I count myself Greek by vocation' are his own words. He learnt of Greek teachers, selected Greek friends, wrote and thought in the Greek tongue, moved in a world of Greek ideas. Yet essentially Greek as he was, so wide was his literary range that he did not, like the disdainful schoolmen[7] of his time, wholly ignore the language and literature of Rome. In Gaul he humorously laments that he had 'almost forgotten his Greek,' and not only could he talk Latin, but harangue

Or. 3. 124 A B

Ep. 27. 402 B

Ep. 9, *Ep.* 36.

Ep. 21, *Ep.* 5.

Mis. 347 A

Mis. 367 C

---

[1] *Ep.* 46. 427 B C. Cf. too *Ep.* 72, probably a spurious letter, in which Julian during a river-voyage expatiates in the freedom from dust and noise, as he passes '*his Phaedrus or some dialogue of Plato in his hand*' beneath groves of plane or cypress.

[2] Cf. Lib. *Epit.* p. 546.   [3] Amm. M. XVI. v. 7.

[4] More than 30 different Greek authors are quoted in his pages. Quotations from Homer alone considerably exceed 100.

[5] Lib. *Epit.* 531.

[6] *Or.* III. 119 A—C, *Or.* IV. 152 D—153 A, *Or.* V. 159 A, *Or.* VIII. 252 B, *Mis.* 348 C, and *passim* in *Ep. ad Ath.*

[7] Capes, *Univ. of Anc. Athens*, p. 82.

publicly in that language with sufficient ease[1]. His extensive knowledge of Roman History old and new, and of anecdotes and sayings of Roman statesmen and emperors makes it certain that he indulged himself on occasion with Latin authors[2].

Literary power.

Nor did he possess merely literary appreciation. He was endowed with literary faculties of no mean order. In Niebuhr's judgment 'he was a true Attic, unequalled for elegance since the day of Dion Chrysostom.' He moulded his style on that of Libanius; but the judgment of posterity[3] is unanimous that the pupil surpassed the master. He did not emancipate himself from all the rhetorical vices of his age, from frigid affectations, from conceits, flourishes, and plethoric use of quotations, but these are most rank in his more youthful rhetorical exercises[4], and under the breezier influence of practical activity disappeared: at his worst he displays less verbosity and meretriciousness than Libanius. In writing he had the most astonishing fertility[5], coupled with powers of expression, of illustration, of humour, and of irony, entitling him to take place beside Lucian, and higher than all his immediate contemporaries. In his writings, considering the occasions which gave them birth, and remembering that they are

---

[1] Amm. M. xvi. i. 4. 5, v. 7. Julian's Law Latin, the only surviving remains of his Latin work, is by no means bad. 'Forcible and elaborate, though much less pure than his Greek' is La Bleterie's judgment, who quotes his funeral decree as a sample. Eutrop. x. 16 is somewhat depreciatory.

[2] Duncombe, I. p. 187 n., quotes La Bleterie's note on the *Cæsars*, 'It is plain Julian had read the Epistles of Cicero to Atticus.' Naville, p. 14, evidently doubts his acquaintance with Latin literature.

[3] So expressly La Bleterie, Gibbon, De Broglie iv. p. 24, Naville p. 11, Mücke p. 152, &c., and, no doubt with less sincerity, Libanius himself in *Ep.* 372. Spanheim ranks him in literary power above all imperial predecessors.

[4] Especially his three panegyrics on Constantius and Eusebia, and a few letters, e.g. *Epp.* 19, 54, and *par excellence Ep.* 24. In the *Ep. ad Ath.*—a fair enough field for pedantry—there is not one quotation.

[5] For instance, *Or.* iv. (37 pages in Hertlein) was written in three evenings (157 c), *Or.* v. (27 pages) in part of one night without previous preparation (178 D). *Or.* vi. (30 pages) in the leisure moments of two occupied days (203 c).

the products for the most part of sleepless nights snatched from the midst of a life of restless and incessant activities, we are amazed at the retentiveness of memory, the rapidity of composition, the fecundity of allusion with which they bristle at every page.

All this literary fervour was enlisted on the side of Paganism. Hellenism was the name he gave to Paganism. It appeared to him inseparably bound up with old Greek form of belief[1]: it was the fruit or the flower which would inevitably perish if the roots were exposed or even seriously disturbed. Julian did his utmost to encourage the Sophists[2], because he regarded them as the exponents and representatives of Hellenic education. And this[3], the study of the great poets and historians and orators of Greece, he believed to be the sole mental discipline which could induce virtuous and intelligent habits of mind, and achieve the intellectual regeneration of his fellow-men. Piety and Greek culture he regarded as synonymous. Mingling with the *literary* value that he attached to Paganism was its *philosophical* importance. Neo-Platonism as a philosophic system claimed to unravel the difficulties of life and belief: and Julian accepted it as the most satisfactory solution of the mysteries of existence. It taught him, writes Libanius[4] in his account of Julian's conversion, the nature of the soul, its origin and destiny, the means by which it is humbled and abased, or exalted and lifted up, the meaning of spiritual bondage and spiritual liberty, with the way to escape the one and attain the other. It initiated him into the love of gods and dæmons. This same philosophy, while definitely supporting Paganism, inferred

Hellenism.

Philosophy.

---

[1] πρὸς τὴν τιμὴν τῶν θεῶν ὑπ' αὐτῶν ἐκινήθης τῶν λόγων Liban. *Prosph.* I. p. 405. Cf. οἰκεῖα καὶ συγγενῆ ταῦτα ἀμφότερα, ἱερὰ καὶ λόγοι in the Πρὸς τοὺς εἰς τὴν παιδ. &c., III. p. 437; and νομίζων ἀδελφὰ λόγους τε καὶ θεῶν ἱερά *Epit.* p. 574, c. 77.

[2] Lib. *Epit.* p. 574, 575.

[3] This idea pervades the rescript on Education translated supr. p. 207—9. Cf. *Ep.* 51. 433 D. For reiterated insistence on culture, and more particularly Greek culture, as a 'Pagan Evidence,' cf. Cyril, 176 B C, 178 B C, 184 D, 221 E, 224 C, 229 C—230 A, 235 C.

[4] *Epitaph.* p. 528.

from its existence and its diversities an underlying unity. The outward differences of expression were to the Neo-Platonist only less important than the hidden unity on which they were based. Special characteristics of belief, worship, morals, are permanently fixed in nations, ingrained in their mental or moral structure. They are not random or evanescent: they correspond to archetypal ideas. They are due to the action of the deities of polytheism, whose existence is inferred and demonstrated by precisely the same line of argument as that which led Plato to his Ideal theory[1]. Thus Neo-Platonism and polytheism each leant upon the other, and it is not wonderful that Julian identified philosophy and religion. Knowledge of the Gods and similitude to the Gods were his favourite definitions of philosophy. He was the best philosopher who most approximated to their likeness. 'Julian believed that science and religion were sisters[2].' He was at great pains, and indeed would strain all historical evidence, to show that all the great philosophers were devout Pagans too[3]. Philosophy, and as associated with it Paganism, had proved to himself a purifying and expanding power, and he believed it would prove the same to others. He was in no small measure the victim of delusion. The earlier phases of his acquaintance with Pagan philosophers need not here be retraced. Friendless and forlorn he had found in them guides, teachers, admirers, and, what he most needed, sympathising friends. Intellectually Julian was a born hero-worshipper. With all his quickness and vivacity, he fell short in genuine original power. He became a child in the hands of men by no means his superiors in mental calibre. His exaggerated admiration of Maximus, the fulsome effusiveness of his compliments to Iamblichus pass from the sublime to the ridiculous. They betray a certain shallowness of judgment, and amount to almost an hallucination. In broad and hyperbolic expressions of regard Julian's breadth of reading and fertility of imagination enabled him to outmatch his contemporaries.

---

[1] Cf. Naville, p. 71.
[2] Liban. *Epit.* i. p. 574, and Πρὸς τοὺς εἰς τὴν παιδ. αὐτὸν ἀποσκ. III. p. 437.
[3] Naville, pp. 26, 27, notices this.

To the ancient Maximus he writes with the ardour of some youthful lover. His letters he places under his pillow as a healing charm on which his head may rest; only by virtue of them in the absence of the author can he be said truly to live. When Maximus[1] arrived at court, no sooner was he announced than Julian left the throne of judgment; and passing down the hall publicly embraced and kissed the philosopher, to the mixed amusement and contempt of the assembled court. Not only is Iamblichus[2] a second Plato; not only are his letters the swallows of spring, and the harbingers of calm, but he himself, considering Julian's own religious creed, is almost blasphemously styled a Helios, shedding abroad on earth pure rays of celestial light, an Æsculapius of reasoning souls, in whose absence the Emperor is wrapped in Cimmerian darkness, and consumed with a fever of desire. When he lay ill the letters of Iamblichus could recover him from sickness, nor could he peruse their contents till he had covered with kisses the envelope that brought them, and feasted his eyes and lips on the seal which the philosopher's own hand had stamped[3]. Here again is a sample letter to Libanius, extracted in full.

Ep. 15.

Ep. 59, 53.

Ep. 40, 419 A B
Ep. 34, 406 C D
Cf. *Ep.* 27.
401 B

Ep. 53, 439 C

Ep. 60

'Yesterday I read your essay almost through before breakfast; and after breakfast without a moment's rest completed the reading. Happy art thou who canst so indite, nay happy rather who canst so think. What language! what wit! what combination! what discrimination! what treatment! what arrangement! what periods! what language! what harmony! what a *tout ensemble*[4]!'

Ep. 14.

Such excessive adulation betrays a weakness of temperament, which fatally crippled Julian's independence of judgment. In sending a composition of his own to Maximus, Julian compares himself to the eagle that teaches her un-

Ep. 16.

---

[1] Amm. M. xxii. vii. 3, Liban. *Epit.* p. 574, Eunap. *Vit. Max.*

[2] And this be it remembered not the well-known Neo-Platonist philosopher, but a younger Iamblichus, contemporary with Julian himself. Some historians treat all the correspondence with Iamblichus as suppositious.

[3] Semisch, p. 13, finds truly affecting what to many will seem maudlin.

[4] For the same tone the close of *Ep.* 44 may be compared, but it is rejected by various editors as spurious.

fledged young to face the sun's full beams, and still more submissively to the Celtic mother who delivers her babes to the mercy of the Rhine to prove whether they be bastards or no. A word from Maximus should be the verdict of death. Thus Julian committed his intellectual belief, bound hand and foot, into the keeping of others. Excusably if erroneously he made up his mind on the merits of Christianity and Paganism in the favour of the latter. The misfortune was that he never reconsidered his decision when longer thought and broader experience might have enabled him to rectify it. Once made he laid it on the shelf; he accepted the teaching of others, and when come to man's estate, in reality never scrutinised its real value.

Julian overrates Hellenism

The fact is that in his estimate both of contemporary Hellenism and of Neo-Platonism Julian went wofully astray. There was no germ of recreative life in the Hellenic culture which Julian so admired and strove to foster. Already its cheek was hectic with approaching death. The arts and skill—such as they were—which it most boasted, were symptoms of mortification. Already in the schools the sophist and the rhetorician had dispossessed the philosopher[1]: in other words form had superseded substance; the health of the body was neglected, nay forgotten, for the cut of the figure and the beautification of the clothes: the day of doom was very close. Julian lived during the short breathing-space which was granted to the Sophists before they too made their bow, and were hissed off the stage. The schools of Rhetoric were decaying fast: enervation of moral teaching and laxity of discipline were undermining the whole system of education[2]. Men were already turning from the polished periods and complacent pedantry of Athens and Antioch to the rising law schools of Rome and Berytus[3]. Libanius and other neglected favourites were already beginning to bemoan the wane of enthusiasm, the deterioration of intellectual earnestness and power, the increase of fastidiousness and the

---

[1] Cf. Capes, *University Life at Ancient Athens*, p. 52.
[2] *Ib.* p. 90.   [3] *Ib.* p. 129.

decrease of students[1]. Himerius, the last of the great holders of the chair of Rhetoric at Athens, died within five years of Julian himself. Void of its old strength but maintaining all its old pretensions, 'Hellenism headed by an Emperor was matched against Christianity unsupported by the state, but with the blood of martyrs in her veins, and truth for standard-bearer[2].' And if Julian misread the immediate future in store for Hellenic culture, still more was he at fault in the necessary connexion that he assumed between it and Paganism. The truth was that there was no chance for Hellenic culture, unless it were divorced from Paganism and married to the religion of Christ. For that the times were not yet ripe; but Julian only necessitated and precipitated its extinction by widening the existing breach, and doing his utmost to make the union impossible.

Nor was Julian less hopelessly mistaken in his estimate of Neo-Platonism. There is more excuse for him here; for it undeniably was the best and greatest, because the only philosophy of his day. It had too the merit of being in possession. Still he vastly overrated its achievements. A little more penetration might have placed Julian nearer the level of the modern student. It did not require fifteen centuries to prove that Iamblichus was something lower than Plato, any more than that Libanius did not cast Demosthenes altogether into the shade. It was true that some brilliant lights and hues hovered around the sunset of Greek philosophy[3]; but when Julian mistook the evening glow for the fresh radiance of morning he made a gigantic mistake. The last of the great Neo-Platonists had lived and died before Julian ascended the throne; the Neo-Platonists of his own day were none of them gifted with genius, and most of them were credulous and dissembling charlatans. From Iamblichus onwards philosophy was posting to ruin and self-annihilation: it was yet to boast a Proclus and an Hypatia: but its age-

and Neo-Platonism.

---

[1] Capes, p. 111, 112, 123. [2] Mangold, p. 26.
[3] Not a few, like Schlosser in *Jenaisch. allg. Lit.* p. 131, will not allow so much as this: to him the Sophists have nothing of value but the precious remnants botched into their patchwork.

long decrepitude had begun, the protracted enfeeblement which waited two hundred years[1] for the fiat of destruction to fall, when the sorry remnant, 'the last Seven Sages of Greece,' turned their backs on Athens and crept away eastward, vainly hoping to find in heathen Persia a respect which Christian Europe had refused. All this was dark to Julian; a fundamental error beset his whole mental constitution, a fatal transposition of actual truth, which led him to miscalculate all the forces at work around him. Among dying embers he watched and wondered at the lingering sparks; they gained a brightness from the growing darkness, but they could not light up the old fires that had smouldered out[2].

Julian's evidences of Paganism.

But Julian found subsidiary evidences of Paganism besides those of a literary and philosophical character. It is beyond question that he looked upon the truth and laws of theurgic art as scientifically demonstrable, and their validity as proved by the experience of generations of men. From the history of Cain and Abel, from the usage of Abraham downwards, divination, rightly conducted, had received the approval and unmistakably revealed the will of the Deity. Apart from this mysterious lore, a crowd of historical evidences attested the truth of Paganism. Some were of a material kind: witness the heaven-descended Ancilia! Some prophetic: witness the inspired predictions of the Sybil! Some personal: witness the wisdom of virtuous legislators of the past, of Lykurgus, of Solon, of Numa 'the most wise'! Some national: witness Greece! witness Rome! Last link in this long chain of historical evidences stood Julian himself. For he, like his supporters, appealed to his own career as most decisive testimony to the power and interference of the Gods. It was as their champion that he had been delivered in childhood from the murderer, guarded and guided and promoted in youth, and in the prime of his days set without a struggle sole on the seat of Empire.

Theurgy.

Cyr. 346—7, 356—358.

Historical Evidences.

194 c
194 d
141 d, 168 b, 193 b—d.

It must seem strange at first sight that Julian should

---

[1] Justinian's edict for closing the schools of Athens, issued 529 A.D.

[2] Cf. words much to the point in Mücke, *Jul. Leben und Schriften*, pp. 71, 72.

have appealed with the persistency he does to historical evidences of Paganism. How, it will be said, could Paganism have historical evidences to allege? It was well enough for Christianity born in obscurity and only struggling by hard-won inches to toleration and pre-eminence to claim on its side the verdict of history: but Paganism was never pitted against a rival: in various shapes it parted out the whole world; Paganism triumphant was but the reverse side of Paganism overcome: one element dispossessed another, and that was all. The answer to this is, what must be once more reaffirmed, that to Julian Paganism was Hellenism. And this Julian conceived to have everywhere prevailed. It had moulded, trained and immortalised Greece: it had subjugated the East: it had taken captive Rome its conqueror; it had now learned how to combine in a connected whole the religions of the world. It had one last foe to conquer, Galileism, and would then take its rightful sceptre of universal sovereignty. In this estimate Julian had some facts to bear him out; others he imported into history. Hellenic colonies he argued *Or. 4. 152 D* had civilised the world, and prepared it for obedience to Rome: Rome was Hellenic in origin, Hellenic in rites, and *Caes. 324 A* Hellenic in faith. Romulus was sprung of Ares, Numa received his revelations from Sun direct, Cæsar could trace *Or. 4. 154, 155.* descent to Æneas son of Aphrodite.

On the same side, and bound up with these historical *Conserva-* beliefs, were enlisted all Julian's conservative instincts. These *tism.* were necessarily strong. The greatness of Rome was in the past: her choicest rulers he could aspire only to imitate not to surpass. Marcus Aurelius[1] as virtuous ruler, Trajan as military leader, he could not scale sublimer heights. His policy and the entire movement which he headed were reactionary. The 'dear dead light' was that to which he looked back, that which he strove to rekindle. He was in one word a Romanticist[2]. He undertook conservation and reconstruc-

---

[1] Amm. M. xvi. i. 4, as well as *Jul. ad Them.* 253 A, and many passages in the *Caesares*.

[2] 'The Romanticist,' to borrow the *Edinburgh Review* paraphrase of Strauss' explanation of his term, 'is one who, in literature, in the arts, in

tion, but not origination. Return seemed to him the sole salvation. This was true of religion above all else. 'Innovation I shun in all things, most of all in what concerns the Gods,' is his own declaration. The prime impulsive or subversive forces of his time were the Christians and the barbarians. Julian's public life was one sustained struggle against these two. One threatened the outward, the other the inward unity of the Empire. The Christians were the 'spiritual barbarians' of the day. Their innovating, progressive, revolutionary character was in Julian's estimation one of their most flagrant demerits. In his eyes nothing was more heinous than abandonment of traditional law. Observance of law was by his teaching a part of religion. It had a positive religious as well as moral significance. Each national difference and peculiarity, laws, morals, customs, and rites alike, were characters impressed by the presiding deity, and the dereliction of any one of these was rebellion and apostasy from revealed truth.

margin: Ep. 63. 453 D
margin: Ep. 25. 397 D
margin: Cyr. 238, 306 A.

margin: Julian mistakes moral power of Paganism.

Such then were the principal grounds on which Julian based his enthusiastic devotion to Hellenism. Living in immediate contact, and for the most part in personal intercourse with the most gifted Pagans of his day, it was intelligible and perhaps natural that Julian should exaggerate the intellectual merits of Neo-Platonism and expiring Hellenism. His deductions even from its past history are explicable enough, illogical as they may appear from a modern standpoint. That he should have so completely

religion, or in politics, endeavours to revive the dead past; one who refuses to accept the fiat of history; refuses to acknowledge that the past *is* past, that it has grown old and obsolete; one who regards the present age as in a state of chronic malady, curable only by a reproduction of some distant age, of which the present is not the *child*, but the *abortion*. Poets who see poetry only in the Middle Ages, who look upon fairy tales and legends as treasures of the deepest wisdom; painters, who can see nothing pictorial in the world around them; theologians, who see no faith equal to the deep reverence of saint-worship, who see no recognition of the Unspeakable except in superstition, who acknowledge no form of worship but the ceremonies of the early church; politicians, who would bring back "merrie England" into our own sad times by means of ancient pastimes and white waistcoats:—these are all Romanticists.'

misapprehended its moral powers is far more amazing. He did go so far as to recognise some at least of its actual moral deficiencies; he allowed for instance that the Jews _{Cyr. 202.} exhibited superior purity and religious scrupulousness; but the wonderful thing is that he should have supposed Paganism capable of reform; that he should have attributed so much potential energy and recuperative power to a system which really possessed none. It has been paradoxically declared[1] that no Pagan would conceive of reforming Paganism; and if reformation be limited to its strict sense of correction of supervenient abuses and return to some primitive uncontaminated model, the remark is strictly true. There was no model, neither personal exemplar nor authoritative tradition, to which to return. Paganism might be amended, it could not be reformed. Neither would it admit of the transformation to which Julian endeavoured to subject it. It may have been one weakness of the scheme that the welfare, nay existence of the religious organisation was inseparable from that of the empire[2], but assuredly it showed other and more fatal flaws. We have seen the kind of revival contemplated, the creation, namely, of a Pagan Church Catholic. The notion originated with the Neo-Platonists. It was a stupendous folly. If it needed a clever man to frame the conception, a far duller one might have recognised the utter impracticability of carrying it into effect. None but a pedant could have supposed the strange jumble of poetry, philosophy, mysticism and witchcraft which commended itself to Julian, a religion capable of being popularized[3]. Still 'it laid hold on the minds of the Hellenist philosophers of the day with a strange fascination.' It was perhaps worth while that once for all the feasibility of the attempt should be disproved to demonstration.

To summarise once more results already attained, Julian, *Julian's Reformation.* following the general Neo-Platonist rebound from the sceptical materialism that preceded it, assumed the religious in-

---

[1] Beugnot, p. 199.
[2] Lamé, *Julian l'Apost.* caps. II. and VI., pp. 123, 124, treats this as *the one fatal weakness.*
[3] Schlosser, *Uebersicht der Gesch.* III. ii. pp. 312, 408.

stinct; asserted in unqualified terms man's intuitive apprehension of God; recognised in religion the support of morality, the sustainer of law, the author and preserver of Hellenic culture. The truth of Paganism as against Christianity was substantiated by its antiquity and universality as witnessed by the scattered but confluent testimonies of the various nations of mankind; by the historical success which had attended the propagation of the religions of Greece and Rome; by the evidences of prophecy and divination; by visible tokens of the Gods' presence among men; last and most chiefly by the full ripe clusters of poetry and philosophy that graced the old religion. Keenly alive to the imperfections of contemporary Paganism Julian strove to eradicate them. Looking around him and taking note of the rapid growth and prevalence of Christianity he proceeded to emend Paganism on that model. He has been called 'the ape of Christianity.' Gregory of Nazianzus elaborates his metaphor at length. Impressed with the belief that Christianity was a mere scheme, and blind to the genuine enthusiasm that animated it, Julian fancied that Paganism had merely *doceri ab hoste*, to learn from its worst enemy, to adopt its tactics, to follow its example in some details, and that forthwith it would step into its place and everywhere supplant its influence. The first thing necessary was a purified morality; the second an organised church. To these ends the 'Luther of Paganism'[1] constantly strove. He introduced an elaborate sacerdotal system. The practices of sacred reading, preaching, praying, antiphonal singing, penance, and a strict ecclesiastical discipline[2] were all innovations in Pagan ritual. Added to these was a system of organised almsgiving, to which Julian attributed so much of the success of Christianity; with the proceeds temples might be restored, the poor succoured, the sick and destitute relieved. Nay if Gregory's words are more than rhetoric, even monasteries and nunneries, refuges and hospitals were reared in the name of Paganism.

Its futility.

But attempts like these necessarily and irremediably

[1] Chateaubr. *Étud. Hist.* II. 107.   [2] Greg. Naz. *Or.* IV. cxi. p. 648.

failed. The alms which were to be the panacea for infidelity *Frag. Ep.* 305 B
were not forthcoming. Julian spared neither private purse
nor public funds, but though he might rebuild temples he
could not provide a congregation. State endowment never
yet created spiritual life. It was a more hopeless attempt
than a restoration of medieval monasticism in the nineteenth
century[1]. The real fact was that every element of permanent vitality was hopelessly wanting to this revival. It
may have been the last resort of both Neo-Platonism and
Paganism: if so, it was the knell of both. A Pagan Catholic
Church was a contradiction in terms. For first a visible
unity was absolutely impossible. For convenience sake Paganism has been treated as a system; and as though it formed
a compact whole: and for certain purposes such language
is perfectly legitimate. It is convenient to group the Opposition in Parliament as a single party; to class Dissenters as
a common society. But regarded in their positive and proper
selves, both split into numberless divisions, possessed of no
common principle save that of joint antagonism to a common
foe. Far more is this the case with Paganism. Its name
was legion. There was no pretence in it of unity. Nay its
whole strength lay in disunion. It possessed not a single
element of cohesion. No common parent, no primitive stock:
no authoritative sanction, no common creed, no symbol of
faith, not even a common God. It was simply a conglomera-
tion of fragments, that had neither natural affinity nor
artificial connexion. To proclaim the oneness of these, to
rally them into a single whole, was wantonly to make a
decisive blow possible. Paganism might perhaps for long
wage a successful guerilla warfare with Christianity, now
advancing, now receding, cutting off troops here or supplies
there, but to meet it in the open field was to court defeat.

And if the want of unity in Paganism made catholicity
unattainable, sacerdotalism became by virtue of that fact
an impossibility. Julian might frame rules and spin theories,
but a sacerdotal system devoid of all basis except arbitrary
state enactment was the baldest folly. To have conceived

[1] Schlosser, *Uebers. der Gesch.* III. ii. p. 411.

the possibility of realising such does small credit to Julian's sagacity. The essence of sacerdotalism consists in the possession of certain mystical and transmitted, and it may perhaps be added inalienable, powers. To such Julian's priests could not make pretence. By simplest Pagan use a citizen was made priest in the same fashion as he was made magistrate: it was an affair of election; and his tenure and terms of office were similarly regulated. A man became priest for one festival, for one day, or for one year, as utility demanded. The idea of such a priesthood could not of a sudden be revolutionised to order. It is true that under most if not all forms of mystery-worship, priests became a trained and consecrated caste. But even such a priesthood could only base its prerogative on very arbitrary and undefined claims, while between the various priest-castes there was not only no realised unity, but not even a potential bond of connexion. What theory was there or could there be in Paganism analogous to that of Apostolic transmission? What power of absolution, or ordination or administration of holy mysteries was vested in their hands? and by what virtue? or by whose warrant? from whence derived? Their office was a mere caricature of the Christian priesthood. Their services and prayers were but mumming ritual. Their initiations and their sacrifices unmeaning parodies, or unholy sorceries, fit only to tickle the foolish or awe the superstitious. When Felix[1] the youthful martyr of Abitina, having confessed himself a Christian, was asked whether he had attended meetings, he replied with an explosion of scorn, 'As if a Christian could live without the Lord's ordinance! Knowest thou not, Satan, that the Christian's whole being is in the sacrament?' The very thought was unintelligible to a Pagan worshipper. Just as in the past there was neither bond of union nor historical foundation, so in the present there was no active spiritual fellowship with believers or with God, no feeding on a present Saviour and no communion with the saints.

---

[1] The incident belongs to the time of Diocletian. Mason, *Persecution of Diocletian*, p. 157.

Turn we to morality, and the case stands hardly any *Paganism immoral.* better. The Paganism of Julian's time was incurably corrupt[1]. It was immoral to the core. Many sanctuaries existed as dens of debauchery. Prostitutes were priestesses, and temple was cant name for brothel. The essence of worship was the satisfaction of lust[2]. When on days of high festival Julian royally attired passed through the streets of Constantinople to solemn celebration of the feast, it was no decorous procession of venerable priests or modest virgins that followed in his steps: around the chaste grave young Emperor thronged a drunken rout[3]: among those that bore the insignia of sacerdotal pomp were mutilated priests of Cybele, priestess-courtesans of Venus, immodest screaming bacchants catching the public gaze by their obscene cries and antics. And this immorality was not only on the surface, or confined to certain public resorts. It was far more than skin-deep. It pervaded and poisoned the very springs of home life: it violated the sanctity of the domestic hearth. It cannot be grossly unfair to select the darling festival of Antioch as in some measure typical of eastern Paganism. This was the so-called Maiuma feast. Julian[4] takes the dissolute townspeople to task for the vast sums they lavished on carouses during its celebration. Nominally it was a religious festival. What then was its character? In the great amphitheatre, in an open reservoir filled with water, the common women of the town swam and gambolled in public. A resident at Antioch, and no less firm a Pagan than Libanius, declares that the essence of the Maiuma was 'not to abstain from any kind of abomination.' It remains one proof of Julian's weakness that he had to license this annual degradation, which his predecessor had suppressed. There was not wanting a moral element among Pagans; but it was too feeble to protest. Even when it found a voice, it had nothing

---

[1] Compare De Broglie, *L'Église*, IV. p. 151.
[2] Julian's fifty-eighth letter gives some hint of the form of 'adoration' in vogue about the obelisk of Alexandria.
[3] Amm. M. XXII. xii. 6, Eunap. *Vit. Max.*, Chrys. *in Iul. et Gent.* II. pp. 667, 668.
[4] *Mis.* 362 D, cf. La Bleterie's note *in loc.* Also Chastel, p. 213 n.

much to say. The Neo-Platonists, as moral or religious philosophers, were practically a close sect. They did not aspire to moral propagandism. Their creed was a hothouse plant. The leading sophists did indeed undertake to expound ethics; it was one of their main pretensions, no less than of the older sophists, to teach young men virtue. Each had his clientèle of students, for whose conduct he accounted himself responsible hardly less than for their intellectual training. But the moral hold of the sophists was steadily relaxing; their utterances are burdened with regrets and complaints anent the decay of discipline. It was no wonder. Their lectures were no better than dull sermons. 'As preachers of righteousness the schoolmen were easily surpassed by the great doctors of the church, who like themselves had mastered all the rules of rhetoric and used them in a nobler cause[1].' They were not like their great predecessors, men of daring and incisive intellect, the free-thinkers of Greece exposing conventional untruth, and excogitating doctrines destined to revolutionise or rather recreate ethics. These wrangling Diadochi could but hark back with stale iterations and vapid moralising to lifeless or exploded theories, and bring to disrepute the world-renowned forces which had given them birth.

Paganism callous.

Again, Paganism was in matter of religion immovably callous. There are times when the most odious moral corruption coexists with fanatical religious fervour. But this was not the case with the Pagans of Julian's day. Among them religious indifference reigned supreme. Where Paganism retained an outward ascendancy, where, as at Rome, the aristocracy of wealth and fashion remained adherents of the old cults, it had lulled itself into the most complete nonchalance of fancied security. There is no attempt at self-defence, much less at missionary vigour. No Pagan priest[2] comes forward as an apologist for his faith; there too

[1] Capes, *Univ. Life in Anc. Athens*, p. 90, an interesting sketch to which I owe much at this point. Cf. Chastel, 343 pp.

[2] The dialogue *Philopatris* forms at best a very unimportant exception, if it is to be excepted at all. For the statement in the text Neander, *Church History* III. p. 112—124, may be compared.

Julian must in person and alone bear the brunt of the fray. With a comatose inactivity Paganism accepted or adopted a policy of absolute and culpable *laissez-faire*. It was in its dotage and simply asked to be let alone to its torpor and imbecility and folding of the hands in sleep. The Pagans themselves only laughed at Julian's zeal, or stared at it in dull undisguised amazement: then after the first moment of amused surprise yawned themselves to sleep again. It was the same among the educated and the uneducated, among the rich as among the poor. Julian alone was impervious to the comic aspect of his proceedings, and his gravity heightened the joke. The Sophists no doubt as a body warmly supported him; for while Constantius had treated them with marked coolness and ousted them from court, Julian had restored to them more than their previous privileges. But their support was strictly limited to the sphere of self-interest, and guaranteed no devotion or self-sacrifice. Basking in court sunshine, they sponged upon their patron's liberality[1], but were mere spectators of his attempt to reanimate religion. Many were time-servers not at all anxious to commit themselves too deeply against the Christians. Some, like Chrysanthius and Aristomenes, and perhaps too Libanius, were so incredulous of Julian's success, as actually to shrink from appearing at court at all. That however was a refinement of prudence discarded by most. As a body the Sophists were only too glad to sip the sweets of power while the sun shone. They even urged the reformer to steps against which his own sense of justice revolted. They welcomed the triumph of Hellenism, but in their own person would face no risk nor privation to promote it. They applauded the combatants and egged them on, but did not come down into the arena. Indeed throughout the correspondence and speeches of Sophists contemporary with Julian, few features are more marked than their pervading religious indifferentism. Such indifferentism was in point of fact inevitable: and for this reason, that there was no *essential* antagonism between Hellenism and Christianity. When Paganism

---

[1] Cf. supr. p. 155—6, and also Liban. *Ep.* 372.

became Hellenism the essential hostility between it and Christianity ceased. And it was of Hellenism, of intellectual culture that is to say and not of moral or theological beliefs, that the Sophists were apostles. Gregory and Basil were firm Christians, as students at Athens: Libanius numbered among his pupils Theodore of Mopsuestia, Maximus Bishop of Seleucia and John Chrysostom himself[1]. The same indifferentism (which appears a juster term than tolerance) was not confined to the great educators, but affected the cultured classes at large. To quote one palmary instance:— *the* great historian of Julian's age was Ammianus Marcellinus: he was soldier and officer of state as well as student: notwithstanding the unusually full materials for judgment that he left behind him, there are still students and readers of his works who remain unsatisfied that he was a Pagan. Neither he nor any other profane historian has thought it worth while to record the exact time or circumstances of Julian's profession of apostasy. As with the higher classes so was it with the lower, save that the latter showed a little more of boorish curiosity. The rich spectacles provided for their edification soon lost the charm of novelty; if they attended the temple at all, it was with the object of securing a good view of the lord of the world, and enjoying the unwonted spectacle of an emperor butchering beasts, handling entrails, or distending his cheeks to kindle the altar-fire[2]. Again and again does Julian reiterate the complaint that people came to the temples to see him, not to do worship to the Gods. Even when the outward show was unimpeachable, when in externals decorousness and zeal were everywhere apparent, Julian at last could not resist the suspicion that it was due solely to a desire to win his approbation and with it some substantial reward.

Ep. 27. 400.

Paganism at Antioch.

If Paganism was languid where as at Rome it was in the ascendant, it was not less so where it with difficulty held its

---

[1] Sok. vi. 3, Soz. viii. 2. The latter, but for his religion, he would have selected as his successor. Chastel, 344 pp., gives a good selection of extracts showing the intimate relations maintained between the leaders of Christian and Pagan education.

[2] Liban. *Ad Iul. Hyp.* p. 394, 395.

own. Antioch was a metropolis of the East: it was fourth city in the Empire, third patriarchate in the Church; including native Syrians, Greek colonists, and Roman officials, it had a large Pagan population, and party-spirit was brisk. The first sound (it had been noted as of ominous significance) that fell upon the Emperor's ear, as he approached the town, was the wild summer wailing for the lost Adonis. Adonis was indeed dead and his fellows! In spite of all Julian's efforts and exhortation, in spite of his own devotion, in spite of his restoration of Apollo's shrine at Daphne, when he came to celebrate with renovated pomp the annual festival of the town's patron deity, the sole representative of all the wealth and prosperity of that great city was a single priest with a solitary goose, who could scarcely prevail on his own son to serve him as acolyte. No wonder that Julian turned away sick at heart, to vent his spleen in indignant objurgations to the council. But it was everywhere the same. 'Everywhere,' says Libanius[1], 'were altars and fires and blood and fat of sacrifice and smoke and sacred rites, and diviners fearlessly performing their functions. And on the mountain-tops were pipings and processions, and the sacrificial ox, which was at once an offering to the Gods and a banquet to men.' Ah yes, everywhere were these things, but where were the genuine worshippers, who could make them all significant?

Mis. 362.

Paganism was thus profoundly indifferent, because it was not only hopelessly and mortally corrupt, but also because it was yet more hopelessly and recklessly frivolous. There was probably less of flagrant wickedness at Rome than at the time when in the words of her great historian the imperial city was 'the common sink and rendezvous of every atrocity and abomination[2].' But it will be worth while to scan the somewhat less dark portraiture[3] of a later age, and see reflected in the microcosm of Rome the outward spirit of the age of Julian. The trials of infancy, the stalwart pride

Frivolity of Paganism.

---

[1] Liban. *Epitaph.* I. p. 564.
[2] Tac. *Ann.* xv. 44.
[3] As rendered by Amm. Marc. xiv. 6, of which the following lines are a close paraphrase, almost deserving inverted commas.

of youth, the strength of maturity, the venerable tranquillity of a green old age were all past. It was the acme of genius now to invent a more stylish phaeton, a daintier fringe, or a more transparent gossamer stuff. The rich man rattled along the basalt-paved streets at the head of a miniature army; not a scullion was left behind: grooms and lacqueys led the van: grimy cooks and hired loungers filled the ranks, while lines of sallow and ill-favoured eunuchs brought up the rear: in every direction troops of ballet-girls with wanton ringlets tripped or waltzed along the pavements, showing their ancles in true theatrical fashion. Meanwhile the libraries were deserted as graveyards. The philosopher's chair was taken by the choir-master, and professors of broad farce filled the ancient seats of professors of rhetoric. While the growth of celibacy and rapid physical degeneracy threatened to extirpate the higher classes, the lower spent all their time, gambling and betting, in low and immoral resorts. Turbulence, taverns, and vulgarity according to Ammian were the three prominent characteristics of Rome. No wonder that in such a society science, poetry and art were obsolete. Constantine, master of the resources of the world, had not been able to deck his arch of Triumph, except by decorations pilfered from his great predecessor's trophy; while all Europe and Asia had to be rifled to supply statues for the requirements of the new metropolis that bore its founder's name. Poetry had died after the ill treatment accorded it by Silius Italicus and succeeding poetasters; Claudian was in his nursery, and the Muses had not yet been christened and begun to lisp again in Prudentius[1]. Alike in art, in intellect, and in morals, every spark of interest or earnestness had died out at Rome[2]. She was in a state of such hopeless moral debauch that to Ammian[3] it

[1] Ausonius I omit, as so very questionable a Christian or poet. The expression used of Claudian is not meant to be more than vague, the date of his birth being so uncertain.

[2] Haec similiaque memorabile nihil vel serium agi Romae permittunt. Amm. M. xiv. vi. 26.

[3] Amm. M. xxviii. iv. 5, a chapter in which the Rome of sixteen years later (369 A.D.) is painted in even more sinister colours than above.

seemed that though Epimenides of Crete had risen from the dead, he could not have purged her uncleanness. Religion, morality, law alike pronounced her disease incurable. While the plague was upon her, the Imperial city, in thoughtless frivolity or giddy intoxication, was dancing her carnival of death, till the fierce Visigoth knocked at the gates and burst sword in hand upon the awe-struck revellers.

Rome then, as depicted to us by a contemporary, was a city given over to the pursuit of pleasure, a fourth century Paris. Rome too was the acknowledged stronghold of Paganism. The coincidence is not fortuitous: between the two facts there exists a natural correlation of idea. True that Paganism owed something to the legal sanction, the official garb in which it walked; true too that the influence of the schools, and the preaching of the Sophists, by no means altogether failed in their advocacy of Paganism; true once more that where the instinct of legality failed, or intellectual appreciativeness was absent, divination and sorcery, with their subtle organisation of mixed terrorism and winningness, their shrewd frauds of menace or promise or present delusion, enchained many victims of superstition; but yet, bearing in mind the activity and efficacy of these varied forces, and the yet more degraded allurements by which Paganism seduced the affections of its votaries, we may confidently affirm that the true basis of Paganism was not law, not culture, not superstition, not lust, much less of course religion, but in one word *pleasure*. The maintenance of Paganism was consciously identified with the maintenance of pleasure, in its existing public forms. And if there is one right which a corrupt and fallen nation or populace asserts with devoted tenacity, it is the right to be amused. It was so with the people of Rome. Long after they had surrendered their free rights to the minions of emperors, they delighted still to call themselves lord in the amphitheatre, to scream for *circenses* as vociferously as for *panem*. Forms of civic election were gone through for this end. It was the one duty and reward of the elective magistrates to provide their constituents with suitable and sufficient amusements. The splendour of

Paganism the religion of Pleasure.

the games was the measure of his merit. It has become a modern commonplace to oppose the spirit of Hebraism to that of Hellenism. The antithesis has been often criticised, and may be defective, but if there is one form of Hellenism to which more than another so-called Hebraism is antagonistic, it was the popular Hellenism of Julian's own day. It was easy-going, giddy, sensual, gregarious. This Hellenism Julian tried to Hebraise[1]—to make it earnest, grave, chaste, self-contained. It declined to 'put on the new man.' It was too merry and wayward to attempt any such thing. Like Undine, it had not taken a soul—and winced and shrank away from the thought of it. Living and letting live, it had no heart to be sober or sad. It danced its innocent revel or rioted in dissolute delights, or thrilled to weird enchantments. From all these Julian thought to wean it. It is no marvel that he was left without encouragement and without support. The one marvel is that he should have attempted at all to spin ropes of this waste sand with no better cement than Iamblichus' patent.

Paganism was doomed, and Neo-Platonism could but precipitate eventual ruin. The moral sense of mankind had revolted long since against the gross conceptions of pristine theology. When Neo-Platonism espoused its allegorical method of interpretation, it was a confession that no supporter of Paganism, however ardent, could any longer adhere to its doctrines. The new orthodoxy was too capricious in method, too arbitrary in result, and too devoid of authoritative sanction ever to command assent. The moral regeneration of Paganism was in even worse case than the intellectual. The local and national and patriotic associations, which of old had served Paganism so well, were all

[1] Cf. Mücke, *Julian's Leben und Schriften*, p. 93. Julian täuschte sich nicht bloss über die Natur des Christenthums sondern auch über die des Hellenismus, indem er dieser Religion, der alles Asketische, alles Entsagen und Verzichten auf den heiteren Genuss einer schönen Sinnenwelt ganz fern lag, christliche Enthaltsamkeit und Demuth, ununterbrochene Bekämpfung der Sinnlichkeit, Verläugnung des eigenen Willens und fügsame Unterordnung unter ein strenges Sittengesetz zumuthete, das alle Freude aus dem menschlichen Dasein auf immer zu verbannen schien.

stricken with death. Those who needed the consolation of religion at all, instinctively felt that that religion must be universal not partial, a religion not of clans or peoples, but of mankind. Julian and the Neo-Platonists realised the truth ; but their misty, impersonal assurances of life to come, their 'ecstacy' so confined and unattainable, their empty formalities of worship could in the end satisfy none whom Christianity failed to allure.

CHAPTER XI.

VICISTI GALILAEE!

Basilius. Here lies a splendid broken tool of God.
THE EMPEROR JULIAN, Act v. H. Ibsen (transl. by C. Ray).

Estimates of Julian.

THERE are few principal actors on the great world-stage on whom history has passed more discordant verdicts than on Julian. In the case of those few it is generally true either that the records of their lives are meagre and conflicting, that they lived in a dark age, or else that the very profundity of their aims or maybe some inscrutable blending of good and evil purposes have wrapped them in impenetrable obscurity. They have lived and died enigmas which defied the skill of the historian to produce an authoritative solution. Neither excuse can be pleaded in the instance of Julian. Contemporary records are superabundant. Histories, speeches, letters alike of friends and enemies, throw on him a glare of light from every side. His laws, his written or reported orations, his public despatches and private correspondence are a body of evidence of the best kind, and of unimpeachable veracity. These exhibit Julian as no bewildering oracular genius, driven like Mohammed by fitful gusts of inspiration, or remorselessly 'ploughing his way' like Cromwell unscrupulous in his means from intensity of belief in his end, but rather as a sincere busy garrulous ruler, whose whole life nothing but self-deceiving subtlety could fail to construe aright. Prejudice and intense religious bias have certainly done their utmost to misstate or misinterpret simple truths.

It would be more amusing than instructive to compare venom from Gregory's 'Invective' with flowers from the 'Panegyric' of Libanius. It would be easy to quote from writers, whom lapse of time might have made impartial, strange contrarieties of judgment the fruit of theological prepossessions. But what shall we say to more deeply-seated contradictions? If it is explicable that Schlosser[1] should detect only the inveterate dissembler, where Hase[2] discovers next to Athanasius the greatest figure of his century, how explain that while the most eminent of English Roman Catholics[3] allows the Apostate to have been 'all but the pattern man of philosophical virtue,' in whom must be recognised 'a specious beauty and nobleness of moral deportment which combines in it the rude greatness of Fabricius or Regulus with the accomplishments of Pliny or Antoninus,' the founder and high priest of Positivism has linked his name with Napoleon Buonaparte's to denote in the Comtist calendar one day of solemn reprobation[4]. To have attained this twofold distinction argues something remarkable in the man. Nor is it solely modern caprice straining after originality, nor any spurious flourish of tolerance that has dictated these judgments. It was a Christian successor of Julian's, who chose for his epitaph Homer's[5] tribute to Agamemnon lord of man,

ἀμφότερον, βασιλεύς τ' ἀγαθὸς κρατερός τ' αἰχμητής,

and well-nigh the earliest of Christian poets to whom Julian seemed
ductor fortissimus armis,
conditor et legum, celeberrimus ore manuque[6].

At Julian's accession to the throne, for the second time in the history of the Roman Empire, Plato's darling wish was *The combat of faiths.*

---

[1] Schlosser, *Jena. Lit.-Zeit., Jan.* 1813, pp. 122—135, and *Univ.-hist. Ueb. der Gesch. der alt. Welt.* III. §§ 2, 3.
[2] *Kirchengeschichte*, p. 124.
[3] J. H. Newman, *Idea of a University*, p. 194.
[4] Naville, *Jul. l'Apost.* Pref. p. vii. Another writer has already contrasted the pious Gottfried Arnold's doubt 'whether Julian persecuted the Christians or the Christians Julian,' with Gibbon's audible undertone of depreciation.—*Zeitschr. für wiss. Theol.* p. 96.
[5] Hom. *Il.* III. 179. [6] Prud. *Apoth.* 450.

gratified, 'a philosopher was made king.' Nor as Emperor did he show himself untrue to his professions: he was but too eager and proud to carry out his philosopher's convictions, little by little approximating Rome to the Ideal State. The movement which he headed ought to be one of profound historic and even dramatic interest. For the last time for more than fourteen centuries civilised Europe by state decree proclaimed Christianity a lie, and deified Wisdom in its stead. It was the final stand made by Hellenism against its great rival. Hellenism was represented at its best, the best at any rate of which it was at that age capable; Christianity, when the conflict began, in some respects at its worst. It had lost its pristine earnestness: it was giddy at its new and dangerous elevation: in its new development as connected with the state, it was still in infancy; and was suffering from all the maladies to which such an infancy was necessarily prone: it had not yet had space or experience to learn wisdom; nor was its constitution yet formed to natural robustness. The combatants then might seem well-matched, the naturally weaker having on his side the advantage of age and experience and past prestige. There might have been expected a struggle of prolonged and thrilling interest, a battle of giants, a rocking to and fro of battalions locked in the death-grip as on Julian's own field of Strasburg, where the din of fight grew ever louder and louder, 'fierce as waves beating upon rocks,' where daring outdid daring and courage rose with failure hardly less than with success, and every gap was filled by a more impetuous foe[1]. As a matter of fact the drama presented to us is nothing of the kind. It is flat and tame: the result is foreseen from the beginning. There is not even incident enough to construct an exciting plot to postpone the irreversible denouement. There is more sober truth than usual in Gregory's declamation when he describes Julian's revival as 'a tragic burlesque[2].' And this not because opportunity failed, still less because Julian's own powers were slight or efforts feeble.

---

[1] Amm. M. xvi. xii. 43, &c.
[2] Greg. Naz. Or. iv. 79, p. 605 B.

His opportunity was nothing short of magnificent. The curse of the race of Pelops had seemed to dog the doomed house of Constantius Chlorus. The death of Gallus in 354 A.D. left Julian, except the reigning Emperor, sole male survivor of that great stock. Thereupon the fortune of the house seemed to accumulate all her bounties for his service. Fortune won to his cause Eusebia's heart: she tamed the jealous savagery of Constantius himself: she invested her darling with the purple: she mated him with an imperial consort: she led him past perils of false friends and perils of indomitable foes; she stood by him at the council board and in the field of battle; she wafted him on wings of victory from Strasburg and the lower Main to the German Ocean and the Zuider Zee: she crowned him with honour and glory and the gifts of good government: she named him sovereign Augustus: not even then did she desert him. Seldom has pretender thrown a more desperate stake than when in violence to his own judgment and against his will[1] Julian was forced to play for Empire, and plunged through the Black Forest eastward. But Fortune was not wearied: for Julian she seemed furnished with a cornucopia of blessings. Ere the crisis came, the crisis whose approach was to be measured by weeks not months, Constantius lay dead, Julian was lord of the world. And his power lay not in sounding titles: he was dowered with a magnificent prestige: he was the leader of a devoted army. Six years before, almost to a day[2], the soldiers at the coronation ceremony had rattled their shields[3] upon their knees in enthusiasm for their new *Imperator:* in the interval every promise, every hope had been more than realised. Julian was now the emperor of their own choice and manufacture; Celts and Petulants were eager to follow the star of their Augustus even to the hot and hated East. Nor did the army alone exult. Hellene philosophers maybe or grateful Gaul or harried Nisibis and

Julian's opportunity.

---

[1] De Broglie errs, I think, in denying this, though his remarks and note (*L'Église, &c.*, IV. 82) deserve careful consideration. To his quotations add Eunap. *Hist.* XIX. 70.

[2] Julian was crowned Cæsar, Nov. 6, 355: Constantius died, Nov. 3, 361.

[3] Amm. M. xv. viii. 15.

Mesopotamia praised God more loud than others, but a chorus of universal acclamation went up throughout the empire. Its echo reached further still. Southward from the unknown regions of the Phasis, westward from Armenia and beyond the Tigris, northward from the tracts of Mauretania, nay even from Ceylon and the Maldive Isles, hurried embassies to do homage to the risen Sun[1]. There was not one boon left to crave from fortune.

Julian's capacity.

So much for Julian's opportunity. What of his own powers, and earnestness of purpose? It would be idle repetition to dilate again upon these[2]. He was a brilliant general, whose Gallic and German campaigns for largeness of result as contrasted with paucity of means might compare with those of the great Cæsar, or of Gustavus Adolphus. He was a successful financier, an industrious and conscientious ruler; he was endowed with rare intellectual gifts, and unfailing fixity of moral purpose. Taken all in all he possessed a combination of qualities such as might have secured him a place more than respectable among the world's great rulers. He bent every faculty of body and mind, every energy of his richly endowed nature, towards the end in which he sincerely believed. He spared no pains; grudged no outlay; held nothing in reserve; spent and was spent for his cause. More than this, he worked with singular wisdom and moderation. It is easy to say that in particular instances a little extra leniency or some additional severity would have been more judicious: but on the whole it would be hard to point out any salient defects either in the plan proposed or the execution effected.

Julian compared with Constantine.

Whether then we look at the start accorded to Julian by fortune, or at his own personal powers, he must be allowed to have the advantage over the great Constantine. He surpassed him in validity and security of title, in strategic

---

[1] Amm. M. xxii. vii. 7, 10.

[2] Here for once Auer waxes eloquent in the Apostate's praise. "Julian seemed a divinely chosen instrument to prove that not even *the combination of the highest physical moral and intellectual powers* (!) could any longer dog the triumph of the invisible forces of Christianity." De Broglie's summary *L'Église &c.*, iv. 405 pp. seems admirably just.

ability, in financial skill, in literary and intellectual power, in capacity for application, in moral purity. Yet in spite of all Julian failed egregiously where Constantine splendidly succeeded; failed not only eventually and in the long run, but visibly there and then. There was one quality in which Julian did not surpass Constantine, in common sense and the power to read the spirit of his age. Constantine was the first Christian, Julian the last Pagan Emperor.

The numerical details of his success[1] or failure offer matter for endless contention. No certain statistics are procurable. The truth must be gathered from *a priori* reasoning, eked out by scattered hints in the pages of contemporary writers. There are authors[2] who represent Julian's efforts as triumphantly successful. Such a view appears unhistorical. It is true that there were perverts. Hekebolius the apostate Sophist represents to some extent a class[3]; Julian, uncle to the Emperor, another; he earned by his compliance the Prefecture of the East: and there was no doubt many another man who found it as easy to shift his religion as his dress[4].' It appears that Julian once found even in a bishop[5] a Pagan

Limits of success.

---

[1] The matter has been already touched on supr. p. 258—9.

[2] Cf. Lamé, pp. 40, 161, with whom Mücke, pp. 78, 91, though more soberly, agrees in the main.

[3] Julian's raptures over 'the conversion of one Sophist' do not tally with any very constant occurrence of the event. Cf. Greg. Naz. *Or.* IV. 5 and 65, Sok. III. 13.

[4] So Asterius of Amasea, *Adv. Avar.* p. 208. I owed the quotation to Neander, but find Johnson quoting the passage at length in his *Julian's Arts to extirpate Christianity*, p. 16. His preceding classification of renegades is racy enough. 'First; The Volant Squadron, that running Camp, which immediately wheels about upon the least signal of a Change of Religion. Those very forward People, who as soon as they knew what *Julian* would be at, presently took the Hint, and were special good Heathens in an Instant... Secondly, A sort of simple, unthinking and stupid Men, who...no more scruple the Prince's Religion than they doubt whether his Coin be lawful Money. They count it...very ill manners to think themselves wiser than their betters, concluding that God and the *Czar* know all &c., &c.'

[5] For the story of Pegasius at Ilium see Julian's seventy-eighth letter. Bishop Heron of Thebes may be added if Philost. VII. 13 and *Chron. Pasch.* I. p. 548 are to be trusted, and with him a minor dignitary the Presbyter Theoteknus, but their apostasy appears to belong to the persecution under Maximinus.

in disguise. But to jump from these individual instances to the facile generalisation[1] that all soldiers and civil functionaries who, to please the sons of Constantine went over *en masse* to Galileism, during Julian's eighteen months of empire returned *en masse* to Hellenism, is quite inadmissible. The facts belie it. If it comes to mere counting of pips, there are a Proaeresius and a Victorinus to set against Hekebolius, a Valentinian and a Valens against Count Julian. From Julian's own works quite another impression is derivable. A growing despondency pervades them. The boast to Maximus about the public celebration of services and the religious disposition of the soldiers may count for nothing, for it was penned from Illyria when Julian was little better than an adventurer, fighting for empire with a halter round his neck, and heading soldiers of fortune who would as lief serve Gods as God, or the devil as either, if he proved the best paymaster. There is indeed one utterance, to which undeserved weight has been attached. It runs:—'the gifts of the Gods are great and splendid, passing all prayer and all hope; for (be Nemesis propitious to my words[2]) a short while back none would have dared pray for so complete a change in so short a time.' Taken alone the words seem strong. But what is the context? The statement which these words are used to enforce is—'*Hellenism does not yet succeed as I reckoned, from the fault of those who profess it.*' The 'great gifts of the Gods' are put in contrast to the little use made of them: the 'complete change' alluded to is evidently, as elsewhere[3], the liberty of worship now allowed to Pagans, of which unfortunately they availed themselves so meagrely. The letter itself is on the surface of it an address to the high priest of Galatia, meant to encourage him and give suggestions in his uneven struggle with Christianity. It is really in complete accord with other more despondent notices preserved. Few of Julian's letters can be localised with certainty at Constantinople: such as do demonstrably belong to

Ep. 38.

Ep. 49.

---

[1] For which see Lamé p. 40, as supr.
[2] The parenthesis itself implies a misgiving.
[3] Cf. *Ep.* XLII. 423 BC.

that first six months of sovereign power are in great part invitations to Court[1] or complimentary notes[2] or official despatches[3], containing not much of interest—unless indeed it be their silence—concerning the Hellenic reaction. Perhaps the Eastern capital[4] was too Christian by tradition and every antecedent to offer a fair field. When Julian set out on his progress through Asia Minor, he perhaps hoped that Pagan indifference had been merely local. If so he must have been not a little chagrined. From Cappadocia comes a plaintive lament that there is not one 'genuine Hellene' to be found; 'most won't sacrifice, and the few who will don't know how.' Julian writes expressly to his friend Aristoxenus, begging him to import himself and show them the way. At Pessinus, though Julian promoted a faithful priestess, though he praised her zeal with his own hand royal, though he religiously kept the fast of Cybele, though he indited for the use of devotees a pious charge, yet faith was not to be elicited from Pessinus, nay not even to be purchased by the promise of hard cash[5]. At Antioch things were worse still: to restore Paganism was 'to turn the world upside down:' the *Chi* and the *Kappa*, Christ and Constantius, were everywhere rampant: the issue of Julian's endeavours was a priest and one goose at the high festival of that wealthy city[6]. The post from Alexandria[7] brought news of nothing but reverses: the council of Berœa openly turned the cold shoulder to their sovereign's exhortations: not even little Batnae could quite conceal the hypocrisy of efforts prompted by loyalty or self-

Ep. 4.

Ep. 21.

Or. 5. 161 c
Or. 5.

Mis. 360 D
Mis. 363 B
Mis. 362.

Ep. 27.

---

[1] e.g. *Epp.* 23, 31

[2] e.g. *Epp.* 15, 39, 69.

[3] e.g. *Epp.* 25 b, 58. *Ep.* 25 to the Jews is of great interest but belongs probably to the Antioch period.

[4] Himerius is witness of Julian's efforts to introduce Polytheism and Mithras worship there. Cf. Sok. III. 11.

[5] *Ep.* 49. 431 D. The letter must certainly I think be of later date than Julian's own visit to Pessinus in or about June, 362.

[6] Rode, p. 96—97, conceives that stiff-necked Antioch quite repented herself, when brought to reason by Julian's morose nominee Alexander. His quotations are well marshalled, but his conclusions, if space allowed, might well be controverted.

[7] Supr. 190 pp.

interest. The records of persecution under Julian prove not a few ebullitions of local anti-Christian spite, but none at all of Pagan devotion[1]. When priests could not keep their own wives and children in the path of outward orthodoxy[2], it could hardly be expected of the laity to make sacrifices for the cause. If there was any one class with whom as a whole Julian was successful, it was the army[3]. He petted it, he bribed it[4], he purged it, he made it to a man his own. That very army, albeit with slaughter of victims and inspection of entrails[5], elected a Christian his successor.

Julian's failure.

It is no hard problem to diagnose his failure. Christians by instinct grasped the truth. They fabled how, when Julian had taken the fatal step, and declared himself apostate, there appeared in the entrails that he was inspecting the Cross encircled in a crown: how on his march from Gaul, as he passed by the ripening vineyards, the dew that fell upon his chlamys took drop by drop the form of the Holy Sign: how, once again, as the blood spurtled from the fatal javelin-wound, he took of it, and flinging it away as the emblem of the wasted life, cried *Vicisti, Galilaee!* 'Galilean, thou hast conquered[6]!' Fantastic tales like these embody a pictured truth. In the fulness of the promise, as in the weariness of the disappointments of imperial sway, Julian was constantly haunted by that mysterious ever-present power, which though he reverenced it not, by the spell of its dominion frustrated all his most cherished hopes. Against it he fought well, but fought in vain. The legends parable aright. From the first day of professed apostasy, from the

---

[1] Chap. viii.   [2] *Ep.* 49, 430 A B. Cf. Soz. v. 16.

[3] In this all authorities agree. Among other passages, cf. Iul. *Ep.* 38. 415 c, Amm. M. xxii. xii. 6, Liban. *ad Iul. Hyp.* p. 399, Greg. Naz. *Or.* iv. c. 64—66, 80—84, Sok. iii. 13, Leo Gram. p. 95.

[4] Soz. v. 17, Greg. Naz. *Or.* iv. 82, Liban. *Epit.* p. 578.

[5] Amm. M. xxv. vi. 1. S. Johnson, *Answer to Jovian* 105 pp. vigorously contends that *all* the army—except Jovian and Valens and Libanius' hypothetical murderer of Julian—were *professed* heathens, and quotes Theod. iv. 1. The facts are against the theory.

[6] This famous story first given by Theod. iii. 25, and diversified into a variety of shapes, is no doubt unhistorical. Νενίκηκας Γαλιλαιε are the words, of which the *Latin* has become the traditional form of quotation.

hour when he instituted aggressive tactics against Christianity, at his departure from Vienne no less truly than at that later departure from Antioch, already 'the carpenter's son' was at work 'making a coffin[1].' Fortune might still lavish gifts, but all were useless, so long as the fundamental weakness was uneradicated. The Apostate's powers remained all they had been; his energy grew with the increased demands upon it. Yet a vital paralysis laid hold of all his schemes and efforts. He threatened and he thrust at an enemy or rather enemies that seemed slow and yielding and not always brave; yet the despised antagonists needed hardly so much as to parry the thrusts; they fell innocuous, exhausting chiefly the strength of the assailant. Weight of numbers and some secret impetus kept pressing them forward. It was hard work for the attack to gain a single inch, while confidence, harbinger of victory, waned visibly. Sooner or later too the solitary fighter must retire, and leave the arena to his adversaries. Failure was indeed a foregone conclusion. The cause was already lost when Julian took up cudgels for it. He might make proselytes, even in some numbers, of a more or less worthless kind: ambition, self-interest, superstition, hatred of Christianity, and a hundred other motives were busy tempting men to avow the Imperial creed. But into not one of his proselytes could he infuse the genuine sincerity and enthusiasm which animated himself. A pedant dreamer still, even in the stir and push of busy action, he lived in a past world. His thoughts, beliefs, aspirations, all belonged to another date, and centered in a bygone age. He cast in his lot with all that was in the truest sense stale and unprogressive[2]. Less practical and clear-sighted than his great exemplar, Marcus Aurelius, he made a gross miscalculation of the forces round about him: he transposed and inverted them every one. 'He turned his face to the past, and his back upon the future[3].' No wonder that he failed so unequivocally and irremediably. He supposed that Hellenism was a principle of recreative life, whereas in reality its roots were all decayed,

[1] For the well-known story cf. Soz. VI. 2, Theod. III. 23, Nikeph. x. 35.
[2] Cf. Naville, *Jul. l'Apost.* pp. 83, 84, Mangold, p. 27, Lasaulx, p. 59.
[3] Chateaubr. *Étud. Hist.* II. p. 57.

and its last flowers already beginning to droop. 'Christianity was a living plant, which imparted its vitality to the foreign suckers grafted upon it; the dead and sapless trunk of Paganism withered even the living boughs which were blended with it, by its own inevitable decay[1]. Julian essayed to head a reaction which if successful would have revolutionised the world's history. So disastrous would it have been that it becomes difficult even to figure the result to the imagination. Had Julian's cultured Hellenism triumphed over despised and rejected Galileism, the sole power would have been annihilated, which was destined to tame the barbarian, establish law, save learning, elevate humanity, and construct from the debris of the empire European civilisation. No greatness, no self-sacrifice, no singleness of aim, no accumulation of merit in the leader can atone for the demerits of his cause. Newman's eulogium and Comte's imprecation are alike justified. Julian was as near as might be the *vir sapiens;* Julian's cause was Antichrist. Herein lies the infinite pathos of his career[2]. Viewed on the religious side it must remain always *manqué,* abortive, disappointing whether to pourtray or to ponder. History shows few sadder samples of noble views distorted, great powers misapplied, and high aims worse than wasted. There is a twice-told tale[3] how in youth Julian essayed to raise a memorial shrine to the holy Mamas; but as he built, the earth at the foundations crumbled, for God and his holy martyr deigned not to accept the labour and offering of his hands. It is an allegory of his life. He toiled on rotten foundations. The edifice tumbled before it could be reared; nay its weight sapped the substructure.

'Julian's life was an accident, and at his death events reverted to their natural channel.' Such is the brief summary of Julian's reign which a calm and generous writer[4] has set down. Of the main issue involved the words are

[1] Milman, *Hist. Christ.* II. 453.
[2] Mangold, p. 27.
[3] Cf. Greg. Naz. *Or.* v. 24—29, p. 88—90, rehearsed in Theod. III. 2, Soz., Sok., &c. How the anecdote laid hold of Christian imagination is seen by its repetition in Leo Gram., Glykas, &c.
[4] Beugnot, p. 221.

literally true. But it is impossible that no side-issues should have been determined by so pretentious and so decisive a conflict. The more important of these may be briefly indicated.

First then, on the negative side, Hellenism as a religious creed was finally discredited. It was tried and found wanting. It was well—perhaps necessary—that this should be so. Above all it was well that it should receive a *fair* trial: that Neo-Platonism should rally all the available forces of intellect and religion for a life and death struggle, fought under a captain of such consummate power and discretion as Julian. In that way Pagans learnt quicker and more conclusively that it was irretrievably doomed, that all hope of restoration was chimerical: in that way Christians attained to more solid assurance that God's cause was their own. Short as was Julian's reign it was long enough to make its verdict most explicit. Dreamers to be sure there were, fatuous pedants self-blinded by their own conceits, who against hope, almost against light and knowledge, hoped still that Hellenism had a future in store; who persisted that nothing but Julian's death had postponed the eventual triumph; who hugged the baseless fancy that the accident of some new Emperor's creed could change the current of history[1], and traced in Julian the antitype of the coming Messiah of Neo-Platonism. But such fools or fanatics dwindled fast. It would have been too much to hope that one individual could at a stroke disenchant a whole world of its folly. As it was Julian's career taught all sober Hellenes from Libanius downwards the needed truth that their creed was doomed. It soon slunk away from the towns, and as the reader of Libanius' Oration for the Temples may see, lingered on in harvest-homes and vintage-feasts, and immemorial festivals of peasant folk, till it could incorporate itself unsuspected with Christian observances. Within ten years of Julian's death Hellenism is first officially called 'Paganism.' A longer reign could have scarcely served the purpose better. Increased pressure, or active persecution (had Julian been

Hellenism discredited as a religion;

[1] Kingsley in his *Hypatia* harps often on this string.

driven into such a course) might have multiplied proselytes and perverts; but assuredly faithful martyrs would have matched their witness against false apostates. Julian did not err in thinking that his death came at a happy hour. Fortune continued kind to the last. The Gods loved him when they suffered him to die young. He had lived years enough to show how futile an attempt, nay rather how irretrievable a failure, was the consummation of his schemes. Life prolonged could have proved but prolonged disappointment, and perhaps too sullied fame.

and intellectually. Julian's failure did not merely discredit Hellenism as a creed. It also precipitated its fall as an intellectual system. It is instructive to note how Julian's one salient act of distinct persecution recoiled upon itself, not without reflex mischief to the world at large. Before his time the breach between Christianity and the schools had not become impassable. More than once Christian hands had reached across and taken of their hid treasures, and displayed and praised aloud their beauty and cunning. Julian in shortsighted jealousy repelled and prohibited all such advances. To do so was to sign the death-warrant of Hellenism. He exposed his unshattered aspirations, and opened Christian eyes to their real strength. He 'made men feel how intensely anti-christian was the spirit of the schools, and how great was the possible danger of a like revival[1].' As Hellenic faith died, the sole hope for Hellenic culture was that as the adopted child of Christianity it might find a safe and honoured home. It may have been that the times were not yet ripe for such a connexion, and that under no circumstances it could have been realised, but at least Julian did his worst to render it for ever impossible, when he imposed premature disabilities, and barred every advance under ban of excommunication.

Effects of reaction on the Christian Church. Incidentally however Julian's endeavours were fraught with certain good results. Morally, except by making the unworthiness of Paganism more palpable, they left it little

[1] Capes, *Univ. Life &c.*, p. 126. Herwerden, pp. 93, 94 (I think more superficially) takes the opposite view.

better and little worse than before. Not so with Christianity. For the Church Julian's reign was an unmixed benefit. At his accession it was in terrible distress. The bi-partite Acacian Councils of Seleucia and Ariminum had already (359 A.D.) surrendered the *Homoüsion* of Nicæa. Had Constantius gone on to reign much longer, orthodoxy, humanly speaking, would have been extinct. Rapid and unlooked-for success had soiled the Church's purity. The chiefest Christian virtues had fallen into obscurity, or transformed themselves to vices. Humility, charity, forbearance, simplicity and unassuming piety retired from the world's gaze; in times of religious even more than of political embroilment simplicity, however noble, is laughed out and hides its head[1]; too often zeal turned to bigotry, firmness to intolerance, fearless patience to domineering arrogance. In the plenitude of new-won power, the Church was rioting in all the inebriation of success. Julian broke in upon the revels, a monitor no less salutary than unwelcome. His reign acted upon Christianity as an invaluable purge or disinfectant. Directly and indirectly, in morals and in dogma, it purified the Church, both laity and clerics; it shamed or frightened not a few from their absorption in cavilling disputations[2]; it brought back the orthodox from their banishment to guide once more the helm of council. Even in the short space allowed him by Julian's irritation, Athanasius was able to preside at the Council of Alexandria. If the Emperor had harboured a shrewd hope that the return of the exiles would be the renewal of squabbles, the verdict of that Council must have been a mortification. All Bishops who had been cowed or surprised into Arianism were suffered to rehabilitate themselves by virtue of simple signature of the Nicene formulary. The Councils that preceded Julian's accession mark the high

---

[1] διὰ τὰς στάσεις τὸ εὔηθες οὗ τὸ γενναῖον πλεῖστον μετέχει, καταγελασθὲν ἠφανίσθη. Thuk. III. 83.

[2] Mücke, II. pp. 74, 79, 80, quite neglects Church history when he represents Christian rancour as undiminished. Lasaulx, p. 89, argues that increased mutual forbearance between Christians and Pagans was also one result of Julian's reaction, but this I doubt.

tide of encroaching Arianism: his reign[1] sees it waver; the first council that followed his death, when at Lampsacus the Homœan symbol of Ariminum was condemned and fifty-nine semi-Arian Bishops openly subscribed the Homoüsion, marks its decided refluence. Julian's reign not only sobered factions, and developed reconciliation: it also separated the worldly and the hypocrite from the true man and the believer, sorting and sifting out a purified residue. It proved that though overlaid with error, and stifled by foul excrescences, and charged with heavy vapours, the vital forces of Christianity were potent still. And one other service it partly did. Premature recognition by the State had damagingly paganised Christianity. In art, in ritual and in politics the Church showed traces of too facile accommodation to heathen modes of thought. Men were abruptly reminded that the distinctions between heathenism or Hellenism and Christianity were something more than verbal differences. Even at the cost of some irritation of susceptibilities, and some narrowing of sympathies, it was a lesson most needful to learn. Julian had not lived in vain.

[1] The provincial synod of Gallic prelates, who excommunicated Saturninus and rejected the formula of Ariminum, took place after Julian was proclaimed Augustus, though before his accession to sole power. (De Broglio IV. 93.)

APPENDICES.

APPENDIX A.

GENEALOGICAL TABLE OF THE FAMILY OF CONSTANTIUS CHLORUS.

The names of Caesars are printed in Italics.
" " Augusti " Capitals.

```
FLAV. VAL. CONSTANTIUS CHLORUS
=(1) Helena  =(2) Theodora (daughter of Maximianus Caesar)
      |                    |
      |         ┌──────────┼──────────┬─────────────┬──────────────┬──────────────┐
      |    Constantius  Dalm. Iul. Fl. Annibalianus  Fl. Iul. Constantius  Fl. Val. Constantia  Anastasia  Eutropia
      |                                              =(1) Galla              =LICINIUS         =Bassianus Caesar  =Nepotianus
      |                    |                         =(2) Basilina
      |         Fl. Iul. Dalmatius   Fl. Cl. Annibalianus   (Son)² Fl. Iul. Gallus  (Daughter)³  FL. CL. IULIANUS  Fl. L. Licinius  Nepotianus
      |                               =Constantina                 =Constantina                 =Helena
      |                                                                (Daughter)
      |
FLAV. VAL. AUR. CONSTANTINUS MAGNUS
=(1) Minervina  =(2) Fausta (daughter of the Emp. GALERIUS)
      |                    |
┌─────┴────┬───────────────┼──────────────────┬──────────────────┬───────────────┐
Fl. Iul. Crispus,  FL. CL. CONSTANTINUS II.  FL. IUL. CONSTANTIUS II.  FL. IUL. CONSTANS I.  Fl. Iul. Constantina¹  ?Constantia¹  Fl. Max. Helena¹
                                              =(1) (?Fausta)³                                 =(1) Annibalianus                   =IULIANUS Imp.
                                              =(2) Fl. Aur. Eusebia                           =(2) Gallus
                                              =(3) Max. Faustina
                                                      |
                                              Fl. Max. Constantia
                                              =GRATIANUS Imp.
```

¹ Between these three there is a frequent confusion of names. In Amm. M. (cf. xv. viii. 18, &c.), Sok. (cf. iii. i.), Philost. (cf. iv. ii.), Zos. (cf. iii. ii. &c.) Helena is the invariable name for Julian's spouse; in Soz. v. ii. Nikeph. x. i. this is transmuted into Constantia. Constantina also, by a more natural confusion, sometimes appears as Constantia. There was one Constantia, half-sister to Constantine the Great, and another daughter to Constantius II. I cannot answer for the reality of the supposed Constantia, daughter to the great Constantine, and sister to Constantius and Helena. I find the name given in genealogical tables, one of which states that she was a nun.
² The existence of this son of unknown name, the eldest of the family, murdered at the accession of Constantius, is vouched for by Jul. *Ep. ad Ath.* 270 D.
³ That Constantius II. married as his first wife a sister of Gallus is plainly stated in Jul. *Ep. ad Ath.* 272 D. The name Galla is, so far as I know, assigned for convenience only by modern authorities. A more ingenious conjecture is that her name was Fausta. This name appears on one or two coins, closely connected in type with those bearing the name of Gallus, of Julian, and of Helena the wife of Julian. These last appear to have been struck in Gaul at the time of Julian's elevation to the Caesarship. (See King's *Early Christian Numismatics*, pp. 37—8.) The N. P. of the superscription, i.e. *Nobilissima Femina*, causes a difficulty. *Nobilissima Femina* appears to be the technical counterpart of *Nobilissimus Caesar*, and as such would be applied only to the wife or near relative of a *Caesar*. Now before Fausta's alliance with Constantius, she had no claim to any such title, for Julian had not yet been elevated to the Caesarship: after her marriage she would naturally be styled *Augusta*. Hence Mr King (following Banduri) assumes Fausta to have been a second otherwise unknown sister—or perhaps cousin—of Julian, a somewhat unsatisfactory solution of her identity.

APPENDIX B.

CHRONOLOGICAL TABLES OF JULIAN'S LIFE.

A.D.
331 *Nov.* 6. Birth of Julian, son of Iul. Constantius and Basilina, at Constantinople. (*Note* 1.)
332 Death of Julian's mother Basilina.
332—336 According to Teuffel's probable conjecture, suggested by *Ep.* 46, Julian spent these years on his mother's estate at Bithynia.

337 · Julian, concealed by Mark, Bp. of Arethusa, escapes the massacre of his relatives, which followed the death of the great Constantine.
Julian is entrusted to the care of the family eunuch Mardonius.
337—344 Residence at Constantinople. (In the earlier part of this period must be placed a hypothetical stay at Nikomedia. *Note* 2.)
J. attends school under charge of Mardonius; is instructed in religion by Eusebius, Bp. first of Nikomedia, subsequently of Constantinople.

344 to commencement of 350. (*Note* 3.) Residence at Macellum in Cappadocia, with his brother Gallus.

A.D.
331

332 Constantius conducts war with Sarmatians.
333 *Dec.* 25. Constans made Cæsar.
335 Constantine celebrates his *tricennalia.*
Sept. Dalmatius made Cæsar. Hannibalianus set over Pontic district, and married to Constantia.
336 Constantius marries (Galla) Fausta. (*App.* A, *n.* 3.)
337 *May* 22. Death of the great Constantine. Joint rule of Constantine II., Constans and Constantius commences.
Murder of Iul. Constantius, Dalmatius[1], Hannibalianus, &c.
Sapor ravages Mesopotamia.
338—339 First siege of Nisibis by Sapor. Constantius at head of army in East.
340 Constantine II. defeated and killed by Constans near Aquileia.
(? perhaps in 339) Eusebius transferred from the see of Nikomedia to Constantinople.
341 Constans at war in Gaul, continued into next year. Athanasius deposed by Arian synod at Antioch.
342 Constans victorious in Gaul.
Death of Eusebius of Nikomedia.
343 Constans in Britain.
345 Libanius commences work at Nikomedia.
346 Second (three months) siege of Nisibis by Sapor.
347 Council of Sardica and Philippopolis.
348 Indecisive engagement of Constantius with Persians at Singara.
349 Athanasius returns to Alexandria.

---

[1] Perhaps early in 338.

A.D.
350 Julian is recalled to Constantinople, where he attends lectures.

A.D.
350 *Jan.* Magnentius assumes Empire in the West, and kills Constans. *March.* Vetranio proclaimed at Mursia, and (*June*) Nepotianus at Rome. Nepotianus is killed: Vetranio deposed by Constantius.

Gallus recalled from Macellum owing to Persian difficulties. Sapor's third (four months) siege of Nisibis.

During the spring of this year Libanius lectured at Constantinople, returning in summer to Nikomedia.

351 Julian removes to Nikomedia, where Libanius was lecturing: During his stay here has an interview with Gallus, now Cæsar, *en route* for the East.
351—354 At Nikomedia Julian becomes acquainted with many leading Neo-platonists of the day, e. g. .Libanius, Aedesius, Chrysanthius, Priscus, Eusebius, &c. To prosecute his studies travels through Asia Minor, visiting Pergamus, Ephesus, &c., where prob. he first met the philosopher Maximus. Some (but see *Note* 4) assume here a residence at the University of Athens.
354 Julian is summoned from Ionia to Milan after the execution of Gallus. Seven months of semi-imprisonment, divided between Milan and Comum.
355 Through Eusebia's good offices Julian is permitted about the beginning of July to leave Milan for Greece, to resume his studies there. Julian goes to Athens.
Oct. Julian is recalled suddenly from Athens, and reaches Milan.
Nov. 6. Julian publicly made Cæsar.
Julian's marriage with Helena.
Orat. 1. *Panegyric on Constantius.*
Dec. 1. Julian, with small escort, leaves Milan for Gaul.
356 Julian's first Consulship as colleague to Constantius. J. winters at Vienne.
First campaign in Gaul. Julian, having, *June* 24, relieved Augustodunum (Autun), fights his way by Autosiodorum (Auxerre), and Tricasæ (Troyes), and occupies Brotomagus (Brümath), Rigomagum (Re-

351 *March.* Gallus becomes Cæsar.
Sept. Defeat of Maguentius at Mursa by Constantius.

352 Constantius gets the mastery of Magnentius, who retires into Gaul.

Gallus suppresses Jewish insurrection: plays the tyrant at Antioch.
353 *Aug.* Magnentius, defeated in Gaul, commits suicide at Lugdunum.

Constantius marries Eusebia: repairs to Gaul in the autumn.

Gallus continues his misgovernment at Antioch.
354 Gallus in obedience to Constantius' desire repairs to Europe: is put to death at Flanona near Pola.

355 Constantius at war with the Alamanni.

Sylvanus' abortive insurrection and fall.

Synod of Milan condemns Athanasius.

Liberius banished.

356 George of Cappadocia, with help of Syrianus, takes possession of the see of Alexandria. Athanasius conceals himself in the Thebais.

A.D.	
magen), Confluentes (Coblenz), and Colonia Agrippina (Köln). He marches by way of the Treveri (Trèves) to the territory of the Senones (Sens), where he is besieged in winter quarters. In this year his first-born son died at time of birth. Helena, J.'s wife, repairs to Rome.	
357 Julian's second Consulship with Constantius. *Orat.* II. III. *Panegyrics to Constantius*[1] *and Eusebia.* Helena goes to Rome—becomes mother of a son still-born. *Orat.* VIII. *On the departure of Salustius.* *Second campaign in Gaul.* Marred at the outset by Barbatio's treachery. Defeat of Barbatio on right bank of Rhine, and his departure for Court. Julian's great victory over King Chnodomar at Argentoratum (Strasburg). J. crossing the Rhine ravages the territory of the Alamanni to the lower Main.	357 *May.* Constantius' triumphal entry into Rome. At the end of May Constantius marches against Suevi and Quadi in Rhœtia.
358 *Jan.* Goes into winter quarters at Paris. *Third campaign in Gaul.* J. reduces the Salian and Chamavian Franks. Crosses the Rhine, and humbles Suomar and Hortar kings of the Alamanni.	358 Negotiations with Persia. Sapor advances haughty pretensions. Constantius' successful Quadian and Sarmatian war. *Aug.* Liberius returns to Rome. *Aug.* Earthquake at Nikomedia.
359 J. strengthens the Rhine fortifications, &c., and finally humbles the restless Alamanni chiefs.	359 Sapor invades the Empire. Prolonged siege and capture of Amida. *July* 27—*Oct.* 7. Synods of Ariminum and Seleucia.
360 Julian's third Consulship with Constantius. Administrative and financial reforms in Gaul. Julian is proclaimed Augustus by his troops at Paris. Crosses the Rhine, and chastises the Attuarii. Julian winters at Vienne and there celebrates his *quinquennalia.* Death of Helena, and conveyance of her remains to Rome.	360 Synod of Constantinople, and deposition of Bp. Macedonius. Sapor re-invades Mesopotamia. Capture of Singara and Bezabde (Phœnice). Constantius marches eastwards, and tries in vain to retake Bezabde. Death of Eusebia[2]. Constantius winters at Antioch. Constantius' marriage with Faustina.
361 *Jan.* Julian at Vienne. Julian having provided for order in Gaul, at the opening of summer	361 Synod at Antioch. Constantius from Edessa watches Sapor's movements. Eventually

---

[1] So Desjardins, p. 202, n. xxiv.; Mücke, p. 161, supposes it put forth at Constantinople in 361 A.D. as a kind of olive-branch to the adherents of Constantius.
[2] I do not remember any precise chronological notice of Eusebia's death. In the middle of 357 she was alive and well. In recording Constantius' marriage with Faustina at the end of 360, Amm. M. 21. 6. 4 speaks of Eusebia as *iam pridem amissam.* The date 360 is only fairly probable; De Brog. IV. p. 91.

A.D.	A.D.
crossed the Rhine, and followed the Ister down to Sirmium, where he took up his abode, and reorganised Illyria, Dalmatia, &c. *Letter to the Senate and People of Athens.* Two legions, faithful to Constantius, hold Aquileia. On the borders of Thrace Julian receives news of Constantius' death; enters Constantinople as sole Emperor (*Dec.*), and takes up his residence there. Aquileia surrenders. *Letter to Themistius the Philosopher.*	
362 Julian at Constantinople. *Orat.* VII. *Against Heraklius the Cynic.* *May.* Julian leaves Constantinople — journeys eastward by Libyssa, Nikomedia, Nikæa, Pessinus, and Ankyra — passes Taurus by Pylæ and so by Tarsus to Antioch. *Orat.* V. *In honour of the Mother of the Gods*[1]. (*June* or) *July.* Julian reaches Antioch (*Note* 7). *Orat.* VI. *Against ill-taught Cynics.* *Dec. Orat.* IV. *To King Sun.*	*Nov.* 3 (See *Note* 5). Death of Constantius at Mopsukrenæ: followed by state funeral at Constantinople. Chalcedon Commission commences sittings.
	362 Artemius executed; Bp. George murdered at Alexandria. (See *Note* 6.) Athanasius at once reappears in Alexandria. *Sept.* Council of Alexandria. *Oct.* 22. Temple of Daphne burnt. *Nov.* J. banishes Athanasius from Egypt. Subsequently, in reply to an embassy from Alexandria pleading the cause of their Bp, declines to reconsider his decision.
363 *Fragment of a Letter.* *Misopogon.* *Books against the Christians.* *Mar.* 5. Julian sets out from Antioch. *April.* Julian invades Persian territory.	363 Athanasius leaves Alexandria.

[1] Desjardins, p. 62, supposes it composed at Pessinus; Mücke, p. 171, would transfer it to Kallinikon on Euphrates, *March* 363 A.D. Clinton oddly localises it at Constantinople.

NOTES.

[*The fullest discussion of the Chronology of Julian's youth is to be found in an article by Teuffel in Schmidt's Zeitsch. für Geschichtswissenschaft. 1845. Vol. IV. pp. 143—156.*]

Note 1. Date of Julian's Birth.

Though the authorities are by no means in exact agreement, the year 331 A.D. seems tolerably certain as the date of Julian's birth, though some historians prefer to place it in 332 A.D., agreeing with Victor's (*Epit.* 42) saying that he was nearly[1] 23 when made Cæsar, sc. 355 A.D.

The day of his birth was *Nov.* 6.

At Constantius' accession, sc. *May* 337, he was 'not yet eight,' Sok. III. 1; 'still in his 8th year,' Soz. v. 2; both which are in favour of 331 as against 332, though Nikeph. X. 1. 6 is more correct still in saying that he had not yet reached his 6th year.

Writing to the Alexandrians (*Ep.* 51) at the close of 362 Julian speaks of himself as 20 years a Christian, and now in his 12th year of Paganism; this accords with his being born in 331.

In Feb. 363 (*Misop.* 353 A) 'more than thirty' is Julian's own indecisive expression.

Julian's death took place *June* 363. Eutr. X. 16 says correctly that he was 31, Jer. *Euseb: Chron.* 'in his 32nd year,' and so Amm. M. XXV. iii. 23, if indeed that be the correct rendering of *anno aetatis altero et tricensimo.* Sok. III. 21 and *Chron. Edess.* make the slip of saying 'in the 31st year of his life,' by which they probably mean 'not yet 32,' as Sok. has already himself supplied us with an earlier date.

Note 2. Residence at Nikomedia.

From Amm. M. XXII. 9. 4 it appears proper to assume here a residence of Julian at Nikomedia. Mücke, p. 24, wishes to set aside the statement of Ammian, and to suppose that Eusebius superintended Julian's education only during a visit to Constantinople. But the context in Ammian removes all possibility of an accidental misstatement of place, as it turns upon Julian's recognition of friends and scenes in Nikomedia familiar to him in boyhood. [On the other hand we may remember that Julian certainly knew Nikomedia from a subsequent residence there, about which Amm. is silent, and therefore, so Rode (p. 22) rather harshly argues, unin-

---

[1] The *fere* is absurd, seeing that Julian assumed the Cæsarship actually on his birthday.

formed.] Neander (*The Emperor Julian*, &c.) finds chronological difficulties in the statement that Eusebius instructed him at Nikomedia. But Eusebius' translation to the see of Constantinople did not take place till 339 A.D. No *positive* evidence forbids our supposing that Julian migrated to Nikomedia at the end of 337, or in 338 A.D. Indeed he may have been there at the time of Constantine's death. The historians pass but lightly over Julian's early years. Part of this period preceding the residence at Macellum he no doubt spent at Constantinople. May he not have followed Eusebius there, if that Bishop was indeed entrusted with the lad's education?

Desjardins, p. 8, untenably makes Julian reside throughout with Mardonius at Nikomedia.

Note 3. Residence at Macellum.

That this residence extended over six consecutive years (cf. *ad Ath.* 271 c) is consentiently affirmed by our authorities, and unquestioned by modern writers. But as to the exact date of these six years (which Liban. and Sok. curiously ignore) there is great variety of opinion. Mücke, p. 11, endorses the blunder of Theod. IV. 2, and makes the Macellum exile ensue directly upon the murder of J.'s relatives, so as to occupy 339—345. Against this there are decisive arguments. 1. There is nothing in the history of Julian or Gallus satisfactorily to fill the years 345—351. 2. This early date, covering Julian's boyhood from eight to fourteen, does not tally with expressions used concerning Julian, nor with accounts of his doings at Macellum. In *Ad Ath.* 271 B Julian speaks of himself as κομιδῇ μειράκιον at the time of his transference: the expression accords quite as well with eleven or twelve as with eight. But Theod. III. 2 is more precise; Julian is ἄνηβος at the commencement, rising to πρόσηβος and ἔφηβος during the term of the residence; the earliest age allowed by these expressions is eleven to seventeen. Greg. Naz.'s language εἰς ἄνδρας προϊόντες (*Or.* IV. 556 c) is inapplicable to a boy of fourteen. Further, the account of rhetorical themes written for or against Christianity, and still more the reading in Church, favour strongly the later date. Would a boy of 13 or 14 have already fulfilled the functions of *lector?* 3. From *Ad Ath.* 274 A it appears that Constantius saw Julian in Cappadocia. This must in all probability have been in March 347, when alone Constantius was in Cæsarea: but the year 347 falls outside Mücke's limits. (Cf. Sievers, *Studien,* &c., p. 228.) 4. It may be added that the going to school, the attendance at theatres &c., under the regime of Mardonius imply a more continuous residence in Constantinople than Mücke allows for.

The correct date for the Macellum residence must be 344—350. For Julian it probably came to an end about the middle of 350; Gallus *perhaps* left earlier in the year. Any later date, e.g. Teuffel, who adopts 345—351,

Lamé, who (p. 28) speaks of Julian as 'going on for fifteen' when he reached Macellum, and Chastel, who (p. 126) says 'already fifteen,' seems incorrect. The residence certainly terminated before Gallus' elevation to the Cæsarship, which took place early in 351, not 350 as Auer p. 2, Mücke p. 15, &c., wrongly put it. Further, though Julian, *Ad Ath.* 272 A, speaks rhetorically of Gallus as going 'straight from the wilds to the palace,' a not inconsiderable interval must be allowed between the departure from Macellum and the exaltation to the Cæsarship. Gallus, according to Soz. v. 2, on his departure from Macellum went to Ephesus for a while: in this statement (see Rode's criticisms (p. 27 n.) on Mücke's chronology) Soz. is probably only redishing Sok.'s correct account of Gallus' stay in Ionia after the 337 A.D. assassinations; but in any case time must be allowed for Gallus to go to Court (Constantius was at the time involved in his troubles with Magnentius), there marry Constantina, and come back as Cæsar to the East. Julian's proceedings—(for it seems on the whole, notwithstanding Teuffel's arguments, most natural to refer the confused accounts of Constantius' jealousy in Lib. *Epitaph.* 525 and Sok. III. 1 to this and not the earlier stay in Constantinople, to Julian the young man of 18, not Julian the boy of 12)—require an equally long period. He came from Macellum to Constantinople, attended lectures there evidently for some little time, became the mark for gossip, roused the Emperor's jealousies, received orders to betake himself to Nikomedia, and was already established there (Liban. *Epit.* p. 527) when Gallus passed eastward as Cæsar in the spring of 351. [This argument falls to the ground if Ammian's statement (see note 2 on p. 54; Teuffel trips strangely in saying the question is chronologically indifferent) that J.'s interview with Gallus took place at *Constantinople* be preferred to Libanius'. It may be added however that Sievers, *Studien*, &c. p. 229, supposes the interview recorded by Ammian to be a different interview occurring on Gallus' *return* from the East, and supports this theory by rather elaborate conjectures.]

Rode, p. 25, suggests 349 as quite as probable a date for the departure from Macellum as 350, but wrongly. It is fairly clear that Nikomedia, not Constantinople, is where Julian first came in contact with Libanius' lectures. Now Libanius (cf. Clinton, *Fasti Romani*) removed from Nikomedia to Constantinople early in 350, and returned to Nikomedia in the summer. Julian arrived at Constantinople after his departure (sc. summer, 350), when his praises were still in every one's mouth.

Note 4. Visits to Athens.

The number of Julian's visits to Athens is a very moot point. Neander in his monograph on Julian postulates three separate visits, but as no successor has defended his error, does not require particular refutation.

288   APPENDIX B.

The real controversy lies between two visits and one visit. On the historicity of the visit to Athens after the release from Comum in 355 all are agreed (cf. *Ad Ath.* 273 B, Amm. M. xv. ii. 8, Liban. *Epit.* p. 531, &c.); the question is, Did Julian resort to Athens in the interval between his arrival at Nikomedia in 351, and his sudden summons from Ionia to Milan in 354? Wiggers, in *Zeitschr. für die hist. Theol.*, 1837, p. 131, ignores any such visit; so too does Lamé, who is however no guide to accurate chronology. Teuffel, Desjardins, Richter and Rode all reject the first visit, which other writers, except Sievers, who gives arguments but suspends judgment, assume, and which Mücke, p. 28, untenably extends over three years, 358—354. The objections alleged are (1) That Julian would not have spoken (*Or.* III. p. 118 D) of 'a *long-cherished desire*' to see Greece, had he resided there previously. (2) That Julian does not discriminate two visits in his manifesto addressed to the Athenians. (3) That the theory of two visits cannot be extracted from Libanius or Greg. Naz., while any visit defined by them is that which took place after the death of Gallus. To (1) it may be replied that the πάλαι can be referred without violence to the seven months of semi-captivity: to (2) that between the recall of Gallus from Macellum and his execution no note of time or circumstance is given: to (3) that the evidence though weighty is negative in character. Negative it must of necessity be, if in truth there were but one visit. That neither Julian, nor any of the best-informed writers, should have explicitly alluded to the double residence, if historical, appears to me incredible. But I subjoin the strongest case that can be made out on the other side.

1. Eunap. *Vit. Max.* connects Julian's visit to Athens (he speaks of only one) immediately with his intercourse with Maximus. 2. The πάλιν in *Ad Them.* 260 A, where Julian speaks of taking his departure *again* (πάλιν), sc. a second time, for Greece, receives a scarcely natural explanation from the upholders of a single residence only. 3. The term 'his mother's hearth' in *Ad Ath.* 273 B, still more the οἴκαδε (if rightly referable to Athens) of *Or.* III. 118 B, imply a previous acquaintance with Athens (for the passages cf. note 4 on p. 56), but Teuffel interprets them naturally of Julian's *intention* to repair to Bithynia or Ionia. 4. The residence at Athens in 355 seems singularly brief, if it be the only one, for the importance constantly attached to it. Gallus' execution took place in *Dec.* 354. Julian was then sent for, and could not have arrived at Milan before the end of 354 at earliest. There he was kept in durance seven months, which bring us to at least the beginning of *July* 355. He became Cæsar *Nov.* 6, having already been some weeks at Milan. Thus into July, August and Sept. (Mücke's idea that he returned to Milan by June 1 is based on a misunderstanding) must be crowded the roundabout journey from Milan into Greece (J. went by Sirmium, as we learn from *Ad Ath.* 273 C, and then probably indirect), the residence at Athens, and the journey to Italy.

Note 5. Death of Constantius.

Constantius died on *Nov.* 3 according to Sok. II. xlvii. 4, III. i. 1, and Idatius *Fasti*. Ammian's *abiit e vita tertium nonarum Octobrium* is a slip, to be corrected into *Novembrium* (see Clinton, *Fasti Rom.*).

Note 6. Death of Bp. George.

About George's death Gibbon, chap. 23, is exceedingly precise with what appears to me hopelessly wrong chronology. According to him Julian's accession is proclaimed at Alexandria, *Nov.* 30, 361. The archbishop George is at once dragged to prison, and after 24 days, viz. on Dec. 24 the prison is broken open and the prisoner lynched. Athanasius returns in triumph Feb. 21, 362. Having by no means mastered the requisite authorities I criticise with the greatest deference chronology so precise, the evidence for which I have not unravelled [1]. I can only say that Amm. M. XXII. xi. 3 distinctly attributes the fall of George to the sentence and execution of Artemius, which took place about the time (Amm. M. XXII. xi. 2) of Julian's arrival at Antioch, sc. the end of June 362. Julian's *Epp.* 26, 6, 51 will then belong naturally enough to the later months of 362. Gibbon objects that the events thus become crowded, but July, August and September allow abundant time for Athanasius to re-establish himself, and call out *Ep.* 26 and 6 in October: indeed to postpone these to a period eight or nine months after Athanasius' return seems *un*natural. Tillemont adopts a like arrangement.

Note 7. Julian's Visit to Antioch.

Julian certainly reached Antioch in July, and probably early in that month.

Until the beginning of May he was legislating (cf. *Theod. Cod.* XI. xii. 2) at Constantinople. The date of his edict from Nikomedia (*Theod. Cod.* VII. iv. 8) is unfortunately not preserved. Now on July 28 we find him issuing laws (*Theod. Cod.* I. xvi. 8) from Antioch, and his letter to the Bostrenians, written from Antioch, is expressly dated August 1. That he was at Constantinople in May and at Antioch in July is thus clear. Two other notes of time occur. Julian appears to have been at Pessinus during the festival of Cybele: he certainly reached Antioch (Amm. M. XXII. ix. 15) during the Adonis feast, which throughout the East had been fused

---

[1] I imagine they are from the Veronese fragment published by the Marquis Maffei, to which Gibbon refers in a note.

with the wailing for Tammuz. Some (cf. Macrob. *Sat.* I. 21) place these celebrations after the autumnal equinox; in reality they took place at or immediately after the summer solstice (cf. Amm. M. XXII. 9, Jul. *Or.* IV. 155 C, and see Clinton's *Fast. Rom.*, Jondot's *Hist. de l'Emp. Jul.* II. p. 130, Desjard. p. 48, De Brog. IV. 226 n., Rode p. 68. 72, Baring Gould's *Curious Myths* &c., p. 286), and fix Julian's arrival to the end of June, or very beginning of July. Libanius not only says that Julian stayed at Antioch 'the *whole* summer and winter,' but attests still more precisely (*Epitaph.* p. 578) that he resided there 'nine months.' To satisfy this even roughly, seeing that he left Antioch on March 5, he must have arrived earlier than July 5.

Mücke p. 105—6 and Auer p. 262 follow the incorrect assertion of Zos. III. 11 that Julian stayed ten months at Constantinople, and thus postpone his departure for Antioch till September.

APPENDIX C.

SYNOPSIS OF LITERATURE UPON JULIAN.

SECTION I. BIBLIOGRAPHY OF JULIAN'S WORKS.

ALDUS MANUTIUS. Some of the *Letters* in Ἐπιστολαὶ διαφόρων φιλοσόφων ῥητόρων σοφιστῶν, &c. Part 2. Venice, 1499.

PET. MARTINIUS. *Misopogon and Letters*, with Lat. trans.: prefaced by a life of Julian. Paris, 1566.

C. CANTOCLARUS. *Cæsars*, with Lat. trans., &c. Paris, 1577.

B. GRANGIER. French trans. of *Cæsars*, with abridged *Vie de Julien*. Paris, 1580.

DUVAL published in a collected shape the *Cæsars* by Cantoclarus, the *Misopogon* and *Letters* by Martin, together with *Orat.* II. edited by Cantoclarus, and *Orat.* IV. by Th. Marcilius, who added a Commentary. Paris, 1583.

F. SYLBURG. *Cæsars*. Frankfort, 1590.

P. CUNAEUS. *Cæsars*, with Lat. trans., at end of his *Sardi Venales, &c.* Leyden, 1612. Trans. republished 1632, and with his other writings, Leipsic, 1693.

D. PETAU. *Oratt.* I. II. III. with Lat. trans. and Commentary. Flèche, 1614. All the *Orations and Letters*, with Lat. trans. and Commentary. Paris, 1630.

V. MARINERIUS. Lat. trans. &c. of *Orat.* IV. Madrid, 1625.

J. F. RIST. *Cæsars*, with German trans. and notes. Hamburg, 1663.

E. SPANHEIM. (1) *Cæsars* trans. into French, with Notes. Heidelberg, 1660; with additions, Paris, 1683; and further, Amsterdam, 1728. (2) Petau's text (emended) and Lat. trans. of the *Eight Orations*, the *Letter to Themistius, Letter to the Athenians*, and *Fragment of a Letter; Cæsars*, with Cantoclarus' Lat. trans.; *Misopogon and Letters*, with Martin's Lat. trans.; Cyril's 10 books of Refutation, reprinted from Aubert's 1638 Ed.; Prefaces and Commentaries of Martin, Cantoclarus, Petau and Aubert; and an enormous Commentary on *Orat.* I. by Spanheim himself. Leipsic, 1696.

M. P. MORET. French trans. of *Cæsars*, &c. Paris, 1682.

J. A. FABRICIUS. Unedited *Letters* of Jul. in *Salutaris Lux Evangelii*. Hamburg, 1731.

J. M. HEUSINGER. *Cæsars* (with Cunäus' and Spanheim's translations) with Commentary, and a dissertation by Spon on Julian's coins. Gotha, 1736.

292   APPENDIX C.

LA BLETERIE. *Histoire de l'Empereur Jovien et Traductions de quelques ouvrages de l'Empereur Julien.* Paris, 1748. (The whole of this is practically translated by J. DUNCOMBE. See *infr.*)

MARQUIS D'ARGENS. *Julian against the Christians*, with French trans., pref. and notes. Berlin, 1764.

G. F. ZANNETTO. *Cæsars* in Italian. Triuigi, 1764.

D. WYTTENBACH. *Epistola Critica ad Ruhnkenium.* 1769.

H. J. LASIUS. *Cæsars and Misopogon*, with Spanheim's pref., German trans. and notes. Greifswald, 1770.

T. C. HARLES. *Cæsars*, with Commentary, &c. Erlangen, 1785.

T. TAYLOR. *Oratt.* IV. V. English trans. with notes. London, 1793.

J. DUNCOMBE. Translation of the *Cæsars, Misopogon, Letters*, and various selections from Julian's works, with notes from Petau, La Bleterie, Gibbon, &c. (Some pieces of Libanius are added, and also La Bleterie's 'Life of Jovian,' all in English.) 2 vols. London, 1798.

G. H. SCHAEFER. Text and Commentary of *Orat.* I., with Petau's trans., and reprint of D. Wyttenbach's *Epist. Critica.* Leipzig, 1802.

T. TAYLOR. *Arguments of the Emp. Julian against the Christians translated*, &c. 25 copies privately printed, London, 1809, but reprinted by Nevins. London, 1873.

A. F. STELLA. *Cæsars*, with Italian trans. and commentary. Milan, 1820.

R. TOURLET. French trans. of Complete Works with notes, &c., and a prefatory life of Julian. Paris, 1821.

L. H. HEYLER. *Letters* and *Fragments*, with full commentary. Mainz, 1828.

Arguments of Celsus, Porphyry, and the Emperor Julian against the Christians (with extracts from Lardner's and Bingham's translations). London, 1830.

J. HORKEL. *Emendationes Iulianeae.* Berlin, 1841.

F. C. HERTLEIN. (1) *Emendationes Iulianeae.* 1847. (2) *Kritische Bemerkungen zu Julian's Schriften.* 1850. (3) *Coniectanea Critica in Iuliani orationes atque epistolas.* 1856. (4) *Specimen novae Iuliani Caesarum editionis.* 1857. (5) *Conjecturen zu Griechischen Prosaikern*, p. 15—22. 1861. (6) *Variae lectiones ad Iuliani Caesares e codd. Parisinis enotatae.* Wertheim, 1863. (7) In *Hermes* Vol. III. 309 pp. 1868, Vol. VIII. 167 pp. 1874. (8) *Iuliani*[1] *Imperatoris quae supersunt praeter reliquias apud Cyrillum omnia* for the Teubner series. Leipsic, 1875.

C. G. COBET. In *Mnemosyne* (Leyden) for 1855, *Variae Lectt.* 312 pp.; *ibid.* for 1859, *Annott. crit. et palaeogr. ad Iulianum*, 341 pp.; *ibid.* for 1860, *Annott. critt. &c. ad Iulianum*, 1 pp., and *Ad Iuliani* συμπόσιον ἢ Κρόνια *vulgo Caesares*, 249 pp.; *ibid.* for 1861, *Annot. crit. et palaeogr. ad*

---

[1] The references throughout have been made to this edition: for the fragments contained in Cyril I have used Spanheim's 1696 ed.-

Iul. oratt.; Ad orat. quae inscribitur Ἀντιοχικὸς ἢ Μισοπώγων, 164 pp.; *ibid.* for 1874, *Iul. locus correctus*, p. 27 and p. 346 ; *Novae lectt. quibus continentur observ. crit. in scrip. Graecos repetitae ex Mnemosyne.* Leyden, 1858.

E. CAUER. *Caesars*, with Commentary. Breslau, 1856.

E. TALBOT. French trans. of Julian's Works, complete, with notes, &c., preceded by a 'Study' or Essay upon Julian. Paris, 1863.

C. SINTENIS in *Hermes*. Vol. I. 1866. 69 pp., p. 144.

R. HERCHER (1) in *Hermes*. Vol. I. 1866, p. 474; Vol. II. 1867, 457 pp.; Vol. XII. 1877, 145—6. (2) *Letters* in the *Epistolographi Graeci*. Paris, 1873.

C. HENNING in *Hermes*. Vol. IX. 1875, 257 pp.

SECTION II. ANCIENT AUTHORITIES FOR THE HISTORY OF JULIAN.

(In this even more than in the other sections of this Appendix I must express my great obligations to Dr J. F. Mücke for his useful and thorough Appendix upon the sources for the History of Julian.)

§ 1. CONTEMPORARY WRITERS.

Dates affixed to the names cover in all cases the time during which the work referred to must have been written. The editions set down are those employed for reference in the body of this work. The arrangement in each department is, so far as may be, chronological.

A. *Orators, &c.*

MAMERTINUS, 362 A.D. *Gratiarum Actio Iuliano Augusto* (Migne, *Patrologia Lat.* Vol. 18). Mamertinus (Consul for 362) returns thanks to Julian for his nomination to the Consulship. [The Latin Life of Julian appended, is I suppose by the Jesuit DE LA BAUNE, appearing in his *Panegyrici Veteres*. Paris, 1686.]

HIMERIUS. Panegyric delivered at Constantinople, Dec. 362. Wernsdorf's texts and notes, re-edited with preface by T. C. Harles. Erlangen, 1785.

LIBANIUS. (1) *Orationes et Declamationes*. Ed. Reiske. Altenburg, 1791. The Περὶ τῆς τιμωρίας Ἰουλιανοῦ, the Πρὸς τοὺς βαρὺν αὐτὸν καλέσαντας, the Πρὸς Ἀντιοχέας περὶ τῆς τοῦ βασιλέως ὀργῆς, the Ἐπιτάφιος Ἰουλιανῷ and a letter or two to Julian are Latinised in Fabricius, *Bibliotheca Graeca*, Vol. VII.; the Ὑπὲρ τῶν ἱερῶν is Englished in Lardner's *Testimonies*, Vol. IV., and the two *Monodies* on *Nikomedia* and *The Temple of Daphne* in Duncombe's *Julian* and *Libanius*. (2) *Epistolae*. Ed. J. C. Wolf. Amsterdam, 1738. (Letters to Julian are translated in Duncombe.)

GREGORIUS NAZIANZENUS. Esp. *Oratt.* IV. V. *Contra Iulianum.* Ed. Migne, *Patrologia Graeco-Lat.* Vol. 35.

B. *Historians.*

AMMIANUS MARCELLINUS. *Rerum Gestarum Libri.* 2 vols. Ed. Gardthausen. Leipsic, 1874. Far the fullest and best of the old histories.

EUTROPIUS (circ. 365 A.D.). *Breviarium Historiae Romanae.* Lib. X. xiv—xvi. Ed. Havercamp. Leyden, 1729.

SEXTIUS AURELIUS VICTOR. *De Caesaribus* c. 42, and *Epitome de Vita et Moribus Imperatorum Romanorum*, c. 42. 43. Ed. Sam. Pitiscus, 1696.

SEXTUS RUFUS, alias RUFUS FESTUS, alias SEXTUS RUFUS FESTUS (circ. 372 A.D.). *Breviarium*, c. 28. Ed. Havercamp with Eutropius, 1729.

JEROME (4th Cent., last half). *Translatio Chronicorum Eusebii.* Lib. II. Ed. Migne, *Patrologia Lat.* Vol. 27.

RUFINUS (end of 4th Cent.). *Historia Ecclesiastica* I. Ed. Migne, *Patrologia Lat.* Vol. 21.

§ 2. WRITERS OF THE 5TH TO THE 14TH CENTURY.

A. *Codes.*

Codex Theodosianus. G. Hänel. Bonn, 1842.
Codex Justinianus.

B. *Historians.*

EUNAPIUS (born 347, outlived 415). (1) *Vitae Sophistarum et Fragmenta Historiarum.* Ed. J. F. Boissonade, with notes by D. Wyttenbach. 2 vols. Amsterdam, 1822. (2) *Excerpta ex Historia* and *Fragmenta* in Niebuhr's *Corpus Script. Hist. Byz.* Ed. I. Bekker and Niebuhr. Bonn, 1829.

CYRIL[1] of Alexandria (circ. 410 A.D.). *Pro Christiana Religione adversus Iulianum Imperatorem.* Ed. with Julian's works by E. Spanheim. Leipsic, 1696.

PHILOSTORGIUS (368—430 A.D.). *Ecclesiasticae Historiae*, esp. Lib. VII. Ed. Migne, *Patrologia Graeco-Lat.* Vol. 65.

OROSIUS (5th Cent. first half). *Historiae adv. Paganos.* Lib. VII. xxix. xxx. Ed. Migne, *Patrol. Lat.* Vol. 31.

SOKRATES (5th Cent. first half). *Ecclesiastica Historia*, esp. Lib. III. 3 vols. Ed. R. Hussey. Oxford, 1853.

SOZOMEN (5th Cent. first half). *Ecclesiastica Historia*, esp. Lib. V. VI. 3 vols. Ed. R. Hussey. Oxford, 1860.

[1] I have not thought well to include Church Writers (e. g. Chrysostom, Augustine, Sulpicius Severus, &c.) or others (e. g. Prudentius) who allude only incidentally to Julian and his times.

ZOSIMUS (5th Cent. first half). *Historia* Lib. III., in Niebuhr's *Corpus Script. Hist. Byz.* Ed. I. Bekker. Bonn, 1837. The best and most independent of Byzantine accounts.

THEODORET (circ. 450 A.D.). *Ecclesiastica Historia.* Ed. T. Gaisford. Oxford, 1853.

CASSIODORUS (6th Cent. first half). *Historia Ecclesiastica Tripartita.* (sc. from Soz. Sokr. and Theod.) Ed. Migne, *Patrologia Lat.* Vol. 69.

IOANNES LYDUS (490—565 A.D.). *De Mensibus* IV. 75, in Niebuhr's *Corpus Script. Hist. Byz.* Ed. I. Bekker. Bonn, 1837.

IOANNES MALALAS (6th[1] Cent.). *Chronographia* Lib. XIII. pp. 325—334, in Niebuhr's *Corpus Script. Hist. Byz.* Ed. Dindorf. Bonn, 1831.

THEOPHANES (6th Cent. second half). *Chronographia* I. pp. 68—82, 3 vols. in Niebuhr's *Corpus Script. Hist. Byz.* Ed. J. Classen. Bonn, 1839.

Chronicon Paschale (7th Cent. first half). Lib. I. pp. 541—552, 2 vols. in Niebuhr's *Corpus Script. Hist. Byz.* Ed. L. Dindorf. Bonn, 1832.

IOANNES ANTIOCHENUS (7th Cent.). Fragments in Müller, *Fragm. Hist. Graec.* IV. Paris, 1851.

LEO GRAMMATICUS (10th Cent.). *Chronographia*, pp. 91—95, in Niebuhr's *Corpus Script. Hist. Byz.* Ed. I. Bekker. Bonn, 1842.

GEORGIUS KEDRENUS (11th Cent.). *Historiarum Compendium* I. pp. 521—539, in Niebuhr's *Corpus Script. Hist. Byz.* 2 vols. Ed. I. Bekker. Bonn, 1838.

MICH. GLYKAS (12th Cent.). *Annales* IV. pp. 466—473, in Niebuhr's *Corpus Script. Hist. Byz.* Ed. I. Bekker. Bonn, 1836.

ZONARAS (12th Cent.). *Annales* XIII. x—xiii. Ed. Migne *Patrologia Graeco-Lat.* Vol. 134.

NIKEPHORUS (Kallistus) (14th Cent. first half). *Ecclesiastica Historia* Lib. X. Ed. Migne, *Patrologia Graeco-Lat.* Vol. 146.

Acta Martyrum. Ed. Ruinart. Verona, 1731.

SECTION III. MODERN AUTHORITIES.

A. *Monographs upon Julian.*

S. JOHNSON[2] (Rector of Corringham) under *nom de plume* PHILARETUS ANTHROPOPOLITA. *Some Seasonable Remarks upon the Deplorable Fall of the Emperor Julian, &c.* London, 1681.

S. JOHNSON. *Julian the Apostate being A Short Account of his Life,* of which a considerable portion is polemic on Divine Right and Passive Obedience. London, 1682. To this *A Lover of* TRUTH, VIRTUE *and* JUS-

---

[1] Some place him as late as the 9th century.
[2] For an account of "Julian Johnson," in which this controversy is touched, see Chap. VI. of Macaulay's *Hist. of England.*

TICE replied in *Some Remarques upon a late Popular Piece of Nonsense, Called* JULIAN *the* APOSTATE. This rejoinder elicited an angry *Vindication* (with a long abusive title) of 40 pages; issuing from *A true Lover of his* KING, *his* COUNTRY, *and the* PROTESTANT RELIGION. London, 1682. This was not all the stir made by the original work. *Constantius the Apostate* appeared (London, 1683), examining and rewriting the history to support by it the theory of Divine Right: while shortly after *A Minister of Religion* (in reality G. HICKS) replied at greater length and with more learning both to the historical and other matter with *Jovian, or An Answer to Julian the Apostate.* London, 1683. *Jovian* received a meagre criticism in *A Letter of Remarks upon Jovian by A Person of Quality*—(A. Annesley, Earl of Anglesey).

Further, T. LONG published (London, 1683), *A Vindication of the Primitive Christians...against...the Life of Julian written by Ecebolius the Sophist;* and J. DOWELL, *The Triumph of Christianity; or the Life of Cl. Fl. Julian the Apostate.* London, 1683.

S. JOHNSON issued in Dutch *Julianus den Apostaat, of Kort begrijp van zijn Leven.* Vrystad, 1688. In 1689—(the book was ready 1683, but publication was prohibited)—he retaliated on opponents with *Julian's Arts to undermine and extirpate Christianity,* followed by *An Answer to Constantius the Apostate* and *An Answer to Jovian.* Victory rested with Mr Johnson, and further tracts *Animadversions on Mr Johnson's Answer to Jovian* by W. HOPKINS, D.D. (London, 1691), and in 1692 *A Letter to Mr S. Johnson* from SIR R. HOWARD occasioned by the *Animadversions* concern Julian very little.

J. P. OHEIM. *De Iuliani Imperatoris Apostasia.* Leipsic, 1684.

J. A. FABRICIUS. *Salutaris Lux Evangelii, &c.* Cap. XIV., 294 pp. Hamburg, 1731.

P. GAUDENTIUS. *Iulianus Imp. Philosophus* in Meuschen's *Vitae Summorum Virorum,* II. 65 pp. Coburg, 1735.

LA BLETERIE. *Vie de l'Empereur Julien.* Paris, 1735. The book was translated (? by Bower) into English, and published in London, 1746.

G. F. GUDE. *De artibus Iuliani apostatae paganam superstitionem instaurandi.* Jena, 1739.

W. WARBURTON. *Julian, or A Discourse concerning the Earthquake &c.* London, 1750.

ABBÉ DE LA PORTE. *L'esprit de Julien* in his *L'Esprit des Monarques Philosophes.* Amsterdam, 1764.

MARQUIS D'ARGENS. *Defense du paganisme par l'empereur Julien, &c.* Berlin, 1764. Criticised by G. F. MEIER in *Beurtheilung der Betrachtungen des Herrn Marquis von Argens über den Kayser Julian* (Halle, 1764), and by W. CRICHTON *Betrachtungen über des Kayser Julian's Abfall von der christlichen Religion und Vertheidigung des Heidenthums* (Halle, 1765). A second enlarged edition appeared in 1767, but the 'new edition' of 1768 yielded to his critics and comprised little more than a trans. of Julian's attack on Christianity with not very voluminous notes. Third edition of the *Defense du Pag.* again augmented, in 2 vols. Berlin 1769.

H. P. C. HENKE. *De Theologia Iuliani Imperatoris Philosophi* in *Opusc. Acad.* p. 353—379. Leipsic, 1802.

G. F. WIGGERS. (1) *De Iuliano Apostata, religionis Christianae et Christianorum persecutore.* Rostock, 1810. (2) *Julian der Abtrünnige,* in *Zeitschr. für die Hist. Theologie.* (Illgen. vol. 7.) Leipsic, 1837.

S. T. MUECKE. *De Iuliano imperatore scholis Christianorum infesto.* Schleusinger Programm, 1811.

A. NEANDER. *Der Kaiser Julian und sein Zeitalter.* Leipsic, 1813. Translated into English by G. V. Cox, and published by Parker, 1850.

F. C. SCHLOSSER. (1) A criticism on Neander's work in the *Jenaïsche Allgemeine Litteratur-Zeitung,* Jan. 1813, 121 pp. Jena and Leipsic. (2) *Universalhistorische Uebersicht der Geschichte der alten Welt,* III. ii. 316 pp., 408 pp., and iii. 1—151. *Frankfurt am Main,* 1830. (3) Article in *Archiv für Geschichte und Literatur,* Vol. I. 217—272, on *Univ., Stud. u. Prof. der Griechen zu Julian's u. Theodosius' Zeit,* &c. Frankfurt am Main, 1830.

M. JONDOT. *Histoire de l'Empereur Julien.* 2 vols. Paris, 1817.

C. H. VAN HERWERDEN. *De Iuliano Imp., religionis Christianae hoste eodemque vindice.* Leyden, 1827.

H. SCHULZE. *De Philosophia et Moribus Iuliani Apostatae.* Stralsund, 1839.

TEUFFEL. (1) *De Iuliano Christianismi contemptore et osore.* Tubingen, 1844. (2) 2 Arts. *Zur Geschichte des Kaisers Julian* in *Zeitschrift für Geschichtswissenschaft,* ed. by Dr W. A. Schmidt, Vol. IV. pp. 143—161. Berlin, 1845. (3) Article *Iulianus Apostata* in Pauly's *Realencyclopädie*[1].

A. DESJARDINS. *L'Empereur Julien.* Paris, 1845.

D. F. STRAUSS. *Der Romantiker auf dem Throne der Cäsaren* oder *Julian der Abtrünnige,* 1847. Part V. in the *Gesammelte Schriften,* I. p. 174—216. Bonn, 1876. (An article containing the gist of the above appeared in the *Edinburgh Review,* July, 1848.)

J. WOLF. *Kaiser Julian.* Teschener Programm, 1855.

J. E. AUER. *Kaiser Julian der Abtrünnige im Kampfe mit den Kirchenvätern seiner Zeit.* Vienna, 1855.

H. FRANC. *Nature et caractères de la polémique de l'Empereur Julien contre le Christianisme.* Paris, 1857.

E. LAMÉ. *Julien l'Apostat.* Paris, 1861.

Kaiser Julianus der Abtrünnige, two anonymous articles in Hilgenfeld's *Zeitsch. für wissenschaftliche Theologie.* Halle, 1861.

W. MANGOLD. *Julian der Abtrünnige,* ein Vortrag den 19. Feb. 1861 in Marburg gehalten. Stuttgart, 1862.

[1] I have not gone through the superfluous labour of inserting a list of Encyclopaedia Articles, with the names of their authors.

C. SEMISCH. *Julian der Abtrünnige. Ein Charakterbild.* Breslau, 1862.

J. F. A. MUECKE. *Flavius Claudius Iulianus.* Abth. I. *Julian's Kriegsthaten.* Gotha, 1867. Abth. II. *Julian's Leben und Schriften.* Gotha, 1869.

E. ZEIDLER. *Julian.* 1869.

A. KELLERBAUER. *Kaiser Julian's Regierung.* Kempten, 1876.

F. RODE. *Geschichte der Reaction K. Julians gegen die christliche Kirche.* Jena, 1877.

H. A. NAVILLE. *Julien l'Apostat et sa Philosophie du Polythéisme.* Paris, 1877.

B. *Histories, &c.*

(*This list does not of course pretend to completeness. I have only set down the most important authorities, adding such of the multitudinous text-books of Ecclesiastical or Secular History, 'Welt-Geschichten,' &c., as I have chanced to find most useful or accessible.*)

C. BARONIUS. *Annales Ecclesiastici.* Lucae, 1739.

GOTTFR. ARNOLD. *Unparteiische Kirchen- und Ketzerhistorien.* Vol. I. Bk. IV. i. § 11 ff. Frankfurt am Main, 1699.

TILLEMONT. (1) *Histoire des Empereurs, &c.* Vol. IV. of 5 vol. Ed. Paris, 1700—1704. (2) *Mémoires pour servir à l'histoire Ecclésiast.* Vol. VII. of the second (16 vol.) Ed. Paris, 1701—1712.

C. DE S. MONTESQUIEU. *Considérations sur les Causes de la Grandeur des Romains et de leur Décadence.* Paris, 1734.

J. M. SCHROECKH. *Christliche Kirchengeschichte.* Part 6. Leipsic, 1774.

E. GIBBON[1]. *Decline and Fall of the Roman Empire.* 1787.

TZSCHIRNER. *Der Fall des Heidenthums.* Leipsic, 1829.

A. NEANDER. *Church History*, translated by J. Torrey in Clark's Foreign Theol. Library. Edinburgh, 1851.

RUEDIGER. *De statu et conditione Paganorum sub Impp. Christ. post Constantinum magnum.* Warsaw, 1825.

J. H. NEWMAN. *Arians of the Fourth Century* (1833), 4th ed. London, 1876.

A. BEUGNOT. *Hist. de la destruction du Paganisme en Occident.* Paris, 1835.

E. CHASTEL. *Hist. de la destruction du Paganisme dans l'Empire d'Orient.* Paris, 1850.

E. V. LASAULX. *Der Untergang des Hellenismus, &c.* München, 1854.

H. KELLNER. *Hellenismus und Christenthum, &c.* Köln, 1866.

A. DE BROGLIE. *L'Église et l'Empire Romain au IVe Siècle* (1856). 5th Ed. in 6 vols. Paris, 1867.

---

[1] *Hermathena*, Part 5 (for 1877) devotes an article to Gibbon's treatment of Julian.

H. H. MILMAN. *Hist. of Latin Christianity.* Vol. I. 4th Ed. in 9 vols. London, 1867.

J. C. ROBERTSON. *Hist. of the Christian Church.* Vol. I. of 8 vol. Ed. London, 1874.

W. BRIGHT. *Hist. of the Church*, 313—451. London, 1860.

J. W. DRAPER. *Hist. of the Intellectual Development of Europe.* Revised ed. in 2 vols. London, 1875.

C. A. HASE. *Kirchengeschichte.* 10th Ed. Leipsic, 1877.

P. SMITH. *Student's Ecclesiastical History.* London, 1878.

As useful subsidiary aids may be mentioned:

ULLMANN. *Gregorius von Nazianz der Theologe.* Darmstadt, 1825.

G. R. SIEVERS. *Studien zur Geschichte der römischen Kaiser.* Berlin, 1870. *Das Leben des Libanius.* Berlin.

W. W. CAPES. *University Life in Ancient Athens.* London, 1877.

C. *Neo-Platonism.*

E. ZELLER. *Die Philosophie der Griechen in ihrer geschichtlichen Entwicklung*, III. 2, (Leipzig, 1868), and F. UEBERWEG, *Hist. of Philosophy*, (transl. by G. S. Morris and N. Porter, London, 1872), give all the necessary authorities.

D. *Fiction.*

H. IBSEN. *Keyser og Galilæer* (1873), translated as *The Emperor and the Galilean*, by C. Ray. London, 1876.

C. KINGSLEY's *Hypatia* perhaps deserves to be added.

March, 1879.

A CLASSIFIED LIST
OF
EDUCATIONAL WORKS
PUBLISHED BY
GEORGE BELL & SONS.

Full Catalogues will be sent post free on application.

BIBLIOTHECA CLASSICA.

A Series of Greek and Latin Authors, with English Notes, edited by eminent Scholars. 8vo.

Æschylus. By F. A. Paley, M.A. 18s.
Cicero's Orations. By G. Long, M.A. 4 vols. 16s., 14s., 16s., 18s.
Demosthenes. By R. Whiston, M.A. 2 vols. 16s. each.
Euripides. By F. A. Paley, M.A. 3 vols. 16s. each.
Homer. By F. A. Paley, M.A. Vol. I. 12s.; Vol. II. 14s.
Herodotus. By Rev. J. W. Blakesley, B.D. 2 vols. 32s.
Hesiod. By F. A. Paley, M.A. 10s. 6d.
Horace. By Rev. A. J. Macleane, M.A. 18s.
Juvenal and Persius. By Rev. A. J. Macleane, M.A. 12s.
Plato. By W. H. Thompson, D.D. 2 vols. 7s. 6d. each.
Sophocles. By Rev. F. H. Blaydes, M.A. Vol. I. 18s.
────── Philoctetes. By F. A. Paley, M.A. [*In the Press.*
Tacitus: The Annals. By the Rev. P. Frost. 15s.
Terence. By E. St. J. Parry, M.A. 18s.
Virgil. By J. Conington, M.A. 3 vols. 12s., 14s., 14s.
An Atlas of Classical Geography; Twenty-four Maps. By W. Hughes and George Long, M.A. New edition, with coloured outlines. Imperial 8vo. 12s. 6d.

Uniform with above.

A Complete Latin Grammar. By J. W. Donaldson, D.D. 3rd Edition. 14s.
A Complete Greek Grammar. By J. W. Donaldson, D.D. 3rd Edition. 16s.

GRAMMAR-SCHOOL CLASSICS.

A Series of Greek and Latin Authors, with English Notes. Fcap. 8vo.

Cæsar: De Bello Gallico. By George Long, M.A. 5s. 6d.
────── Books I.-III. For Junior Classes. By G. Long, M.A. 2s. 6d.
Catullus, Tibullus, and Propertius. Selected Poems. With Life. By Rev. A. H. Wratislaw. 3s. 6d.

Cicero: De Senectute, De Amicitia, and Select Epistles. By George Long, M.A. 4s. 6d.
Cornelius Nepos. By Rev. J. F. Macmichael. 2s. 6d.
Homer: Iliad. Books I.–XII. By F. A. Paley, M.A. 6s. 6d.
Horace. With Life. By A. J. Macleane, M.A. 6s. 6d. [In 2 parts. 3s. 6d. each.]
Juvenal: Sixteen Satires. By H. Prior, M.A. 4s. 6d.
Martial: Select Epigrams. With Life. By F. A. Paley, M.A. 6s. 6d.
Ovid: the Fasti. By F. A. Paley, M.A. 5s.
Sallust: Catilina and Jugurtha. With Life. By G. Long, M.A. 5s.
Tacitus: Germania and Agricola. By Rev. P. Frost. 3s. 6d.
Virgil: Bucolics, Georgics, and Æneid, Books I.–IV. Abridged from Professor Conington's Edition. 5s. 6d.
(The Bucolics and Georgics in one volume. 3s.)
—— Æneid, Books V.–XII. Abridged from Professor Conington's Edition. 5s. 6d.
Xenophon: The Anabasis. With Life. By Rev. J. F. Macmichael. 5s.
—— The Cyropædia. By G. M. Gorham, M.A. 6s.
—— Memorabilia. By Percival Frost, M.A. 4s. 6d.
A Grammar-School Atlas of Classical Geography, containing Ten selected Maps. Imperial 8vo. 5s.

Uniform with the Series.

The New Testament. in Greek. With English Notes, &c. By Rev. J. F. Macmichael. 7s. 6d.

———

CAMBRIDGE GREEK AND LATIN TEXTS.

Æschylus. By F. A. Paley, M.A. 3s.
Cæsar: De Bello Gallico. By G. Long, M.A. 2s.
Cicero: De Senectute et de Amicitia, et Epistolæ Selectæ. By G. Long, M.A. 1s. 6d.
Ciceronis Orationes. Vol. I. (in Verrem.) By G. Long, M.A. 3s. 6d.
Euripides. By F. A. Paley, M.A. 3 vols. 3s. 6d. each.
Herodotus. By J. G. Blakesley, B.D. 2 vols. 7s.
Homeri Ilias. I.–XII. By F. A. Paley, M.A. 2s. 6d.
Horatius. By A. J. Macleane, M.A. 2s. 6d.
Juvenal et Persius. By A. J. Macleane, M.A. 1s. 6d.
Lucretius. By H. A. J. Munro, M.A. 2s. 6d.
Sallusti Crispi Catilina et Jugurtha. By G. Long, M.A. 1s. 6d.
Terenti Comœdiæ. By W. Wagner, Ph.D. 3s.
Thucydides. By J. G. Donaldson, D.D. 2 vols. 7s.
Virgilius. By J. Conington, M.A. 3s. 6d.
Xenophontis Expeditio Cyri. By J. F. Macmichael, B.A. 2s. 6d.
Novum Testamentum Græcum. By F. H. Scrivener, M.A. 4s. 6d. An edition with wide margin for notes, half bound, 12s.

CAMBRIDGE TEXTS WITH NOTES.

A Selection of the most usually read of the Greek and Latin Authors, Annotated for Schools. Fcap. 8vo. 1s. 6d. each.

Euripides. Alcestis. By F. A. Paley, M.A.
—— Medea. By F. A. Paley, M.A.
—— Hippolytus. By F. A. Paley, M.A.
—— Hecuba. By F. A. Paley, M.A.
—— Bacchæ. By F. A. Paley, M.A.
—— Ion. By F. A. Paley, M.A. [Price 2s.]
Æschylus. Prometheus Vinctus. By F. A. Paley, M.A.
—— Septem contra Thebas. By F. A. Paley, M.A.
Ovid. Selections. By A. J. Macleane, M.A.

PUBLIC SCHOOL SERIES.

A Series of Classical Texts, annotated by well-known Scholars. Crown 8vo.

Aristophanes. The Peace. By F. A. Paley, M.A. 4s. 6d.
—— The Acharnians. By F. A. Paley, M.A. 4s. 6d.
—— The Frogs. By F. A. Paley, M.A. 4s. 6d.
Cicero. The Letters to Atticus. Bk. I. By A. Pretor. M.A. 4s. 6d.
Demosthenes de Falsa Legatione. By R. Shilleto, M.A. 6s.
—— The Law of Leptines. By B. W. Beatson, M.A.
Plato. The Apology of Socrates and Crito. By W. Wagner, Ph.D. 4th Edition. 4s. 6d.
—— The Phædo. By W. Wagner, Ph.D. 5s. 6d.
—— The Protagoras. By W. Wayte, M.A. 4s. 6d.
Plautus. The Aulularia. By W. Wagner, Ph.D. 2nd edition. 4s. 6d.
—— Trinummus. By W. Wagner, Ph.D. 2nd edition. 4s. 6d.
—— The Menaechmei. By W. Wagner, Ph.D. 4s. 6d.
Sophoclis Trachiniæ. By A. Pretor, M.A. 4s. 6d.
Terence. By W. Wagner, Ph.D. 10s. 6d.
Theocritus. By F. A. Paley, M.A. 4s. 6d.

Others in preparation.

CRITICAL AND ANNOTATED EDITIONS.

Ætna. By H. A. J. Munro, M.A. 3s. 6d.
Aristophanis Comœdiæ. By H. A. Holden, LL.D. 8vo. 2 vols. 23s. 6d. Plays sold separately.
—— Pax. By F. A. Paley, M.A. Fcap. 8vo. 4s. 6d.
Catullus. By H. A. J. Munro, M.A. 7s. 6d.
Horace. Quinti Horatii Flacci Opera. By H. A. J. Munro, M.A. Large 8vo. 1l. 1s.
Livy. The first five Books. By J. Prendeville. 12mo. roan, 5s. Or Books I.-III. 3s. 6d. IV. and V. 3s. 6d.

Lucretius. Titi Lucretii Cari de Rerum Natura Libri Sex. With a Translation and Notes. By H. A. J. Munro, M.A. 2 vols. 8vo. Vol. I. Text, 16s. Vol. II. Translation, 6s. (Sold separately.)

Ovid. P. Ovidii Nasonis Heroides XIV. By A. Palmer, M.A. 8vo. 6s.

Propertius. Sex Aurelii Propertii Carmina. By F. A. Paley, M.A. 8vo. Cloth, 9s.

Sophocles. The Ajax. By C. E. Palmer, M.A. 4s. 6d.

Thucydides. The History of the Peloponnesian War. By Richard Shilleto, M.A. Book I. 8vo. 6s. 6d. (Book II. *in the press.*)

Greek Testament. By Henry Alford, D.D. 4 vols. 8vo. (Sold separately.) Vol. I. 1l. 8s. Vol. II. 1l. 4s. Vol. III. 18s. Vol. IV. Part I. 18s.; Part II. 14s.; or in one Vol. 32s.

LATIN AND GREEK CLASS-BOOKS.

Auxilia Latina. A Series of Progressive Latin Exercises. By Rev. J. B. Baddeley, M.A. Fcap. 8vo. 2s.

AN INTRODUCTORY PART to the above on Accidence. [*In the Press.*]

Latin Prose Lessons. By A. J. Church, M.A. 2nd Edit. Fcap. 8vo. 2s. 6d.

Latin Exercises and Grammar Papers. By T. Collins, M.A. 2nd Edition. Fcap. 8vo. 2s. 6d.

Analytical Latin Exercises. By C. P. Mason, B.A. 2nd Edit. 3s. 6d.

Scala Græca: a Series of Elementary Greek Exercises. By Rev. J. W. Davis, M.A., and R. W. Baddeley, M.A. 3rd Edition. Fcap. 8vo. 2s. 6d.

Greek Verse Composition. By G. Preston, M.A. Crown 8vo. 4s. 6d.

BY THE REV. P. FROST, M.A., ST. JOHN'S COLLEGE, CAMBRIDGE.

Eclogæ Latinæ; or, First Latin Reading-Book, with English Notes and a Dictionary. New Edition. Fcap. 8vo. 2s. 6d.

Materials for Latin Prose Composition. New Edition. Fcap. 8vo. 2s. 6d. Key, 4s.

A Latin Verse-Book. An Introductory Work on Hexameters and Pentameters. New Edition. Fcap. 8vo. 3s. Key, 5s.

Analecta Græca Minora, with Introductory Sentences, English Notes, and a Dictionary. New Edition. Fcap. 8vo. 3s. 6d.

Materials for Greek Prose Composition. New Edit. Fcap. 8vo. 3s. 6d. Key, 5s.

Florilegium Poeticum. Elegiac Extracts from Ovid and Tibullus. New Edition. With Notes. Fcap. 8vo. 3s.

BY THE REV. F. E. GRETTON.

A First Cheque-book for Latin Verse-makers. 1s. 6d.

A Latin Version for Masters. 2s. 6d.

Reddenda; or Passages with Parallel Hints for Translation into Latin Prose and Verse. Crown 8vo. 4s. 6d.

Reddenda Reddita (*see next page*).

BY H. A. HOLDEN, LL.D.

Foliorum Silvula. Part I. Passages for Translation into Latin Elegiac and Heroic Verse. 8th Edition. Post 8vo. 7s. 6d.

——— Part II. Select Passages for Translation into Latin Lyric and Comic Iambic Verse. 3rd Edition. Post 8vo. 5s.

——— Part III. Select Passages for Translation into Greek Verse. 3rd Edition. Post 8vo. 8s.

Folia Silvulæ, sive Eclogæ Poetarum Anglicorum in Latinum et Græcum conversæ. 8vo. Vol. I. 10s. 6d. Vol. II. 12s.

Foliorum Centuriæ. Select Passages for Translation into Latin and Greek Prose. 6th Edition. Post 8vo. 8s.

TRANSLATIONS, SELECTIONS, &c.

_{*} Many of the following books are well adapted for School Prizes.

Æschylus. Translated into English Prose by F. A. Paley, M.A. 2nd Edition. 8vo. 7s. 6d.

———— Translated into English Verse by Anna Swanwick. Crown 8vo. 2 vols. 12s.

———— Folio Edition, with 33 Illustrations after Flaxman. 2l. 2s.

Anthologia Græca. A Selection of Choice Greek Poetry, with Notes. By F. St. John Thackeray. 4th and Cheaper Edition. 16mo. 4s. 6d.

Anthologia Latina. A Selection of Choice Latin Poetry, from Nævius to Boëthius, with Notes. By Rev. F. St. John Thackeray. Fcap. 8vo. 6s. 6d.

Aristophanes: The Peace. Text and Metrical Translation. By B. B. Rogers, M.A. Fcap. 4to. 7s. 6d.

———— The Wasps. Text and Metrical Translation. By B. B. Rogers, M.A. Fcap. 4to. 7s. 6d.

Corpus Poetarum Latinorum. Edited by Walker. 1 vol. 8vo. 18s.

Horace. The Odes and Carmen Sæculare. In English Verse by J. Conington, M.A. 7th edition. Fcap. 8vo. 5s. 6d.

———— The Satires and Epistles. In English Verse by J. Conington, M.A. 4th edition. 6s. 6d.

———— Illustrated from Antique Gems by C. W. King, M.A. The text revised with Introduction by H. A. J. Munro, M.A. Large 8vo. 1l. 1s.

Mvsæ Etonenses, sive Carminvm Etonæ Conditorvm Delectvs. By Richard Okes. 2 vols. 8vo. 15s.

Propertius. Verse translations from Book V., with revised Latin Text. By F. A. Paley, M.A. Fcap. 8vo. 3s.

Plato. Gorgias. Translated by E. M. Cope, M.A. 8vo. 7s.

———— Philebus. Translated by F. A. Paley, M.A. Small 8vo. 4s.

———— Theætetus. Translated by F. A. Paley, M.A. Small 8vo. 4s.

———— Analysis and Index of the Dialogues. By Dr. Day. Post 8vo. 5s.

Reddenda Reddita: Passages from English Poetry, with a Latin Verse Translation. By F. E. Gretton. Crown 8vo. 6s.

Sabrinæ Corolla in hortulis Regiæ Scholæ Salopiensis contexuerunt tres viri floribus legendis. Editio tertia. 8vo. 8s. 6d.

Sertum Carthusianum Floribus trium Seculorum Contextum. By W. H. Brown. 8vo. 11s.

Theocritus. In English Verse, by C. S. Calverley, M.A. Crown 8vo. 7s. 6d.

Translations into English and Latin. By C. S. Calverley, M.A. Post 8vo. 7s. 6d.

———— By R. C. Jebb, M.A.; H. Jackson, M.A., and W. E. Currey, M.A. Crown 8vo. 8s.

———— into Greek and Latin Verse. By R. C. Jebb. 4to. cloth gilt. 10s. 6d.

REFERENCE VOLUMES.

A Latin Grammar. By T. H. Key, M.A. 6th Thousand. Post 8vo. 8s.
A Short Latin Grammar for Schools. By T. H. Key, M.A., F.R.S. 11th Edition. Post 8vo. 3s. 6d.
A Guide to the Choice of Classical Books. By J. B. Mayor, M.A. Crown 8vo. 2s.
The Theatre of the Greeks. By J. W. Donaldson, D.D. 8th Edition. Post 8vo. 5s.
A Dictionary of Latin and Greek Quotations. By H. T. Riley. Post 8vo. 5s. With Index Verborum, 6s.
A History of Roman Literature. By W. S. Teuffel, Professor at the University of Tübingen. By W. Wagner, Ph.D. 2 vols. Demy 8vo. 21s.
Student's Guide to the University of Cambridge. Revised and corrected. 3rd Edition. Fcap. 8vo. 6s. 6d.

CLASSICAL TABLES.

Greek Verbs. A Catalogue of Verbs, Irregular and Defective; their leading formations, tenses, and inflexions, with Paradigms for conjugation, Rules for formation of tenses, &c. &c. By J. S. Baird, T.C.D. 2s. 6d.
Greek Accents (Notes on). By A. Barry, D.D. New Edition. 1s.
Homeric Dialect. Its Leading Forms and Peculiarities. By J. S. Baird, T.C.D. New edition, revised by W. Gunion Rutherford. 1s.
Greek Accidence. By the Rev. P. Frost, M.A. New Edition. 1s.
Latin Accidence. By the Rev. P. Frost, M.A. 1s.
Latin Versification. 1s.
Notabilia Quædam; or the Principal Tenses of most of the Irregular Greek Verbs and Elementary Greek, Latin, and French Construction. New edition. 1s.
Richmond Rules for the Ovidian Distich, &c. By J. Tate, M.A. 1s.
The Principles of Latin Syntax. 1s.

CAMBRIDGE SCHOOL AND COLLEGE TEXT-BOOKS.

A Series of Elementary Treatises for the use of Students in the Universities, Schools, and Candidates for the Public Examinations. Fcap. 8vo.

Arithmetic. By Rev. C. Elsee, M.A. Fcap. 8vo. 7th Edit. 3s. 6d.
Algebra. By the Rev. C. Elsee, M.A. 4th Edit. 4s.
Arithmetic. By A. Wrigley, M.A. 3s. 6d.
——— A Progressive Course of Examples. With Answers. By J. Watson, M.A. 3rd Edition. 2s. 6d.
Algebra. Progressive Course of Examples. By Rev. W. F. M'Michael, M.A., and R. Prowde Smith, M.A. 3s. 6d.

Plane Astronomy, An Introduction to. By P. T. Main, M.A. 3rd Edition. [*In the Press.*]

Conic Sections treated Geometrically. By W. H. Besant, M.A. 2nd Edition. 4s. 6d.

Elementary Conic Sections treated Geometrically. By W. H. Besant, M.A. [*In the Press.*]

Statics, Elementary. By Rev. H. Goodwin, D.D. 2nd Edit. 3s.

Hydrostatics, Elementary. By W. H. Besant, M.A. 7th Edit. 4s.

Mensuration, An Elementary Treatise on. By B. T. Moore, M.A. 5s.

Newton's Principia. The First Three Sections of, with an Appendix; and the Ninth and Eleventh Sections. By J. H. Evans, M.A. 5th Edition, by P. T. Main, M.A. 4s.

Trigonometry, Elementary. By T. P. Hudson, M.A. 3s. 6d.

Optics, Geometrical. With Answers. By W. S. Aldis, M.A. 3s. 6d.

Analytical Geometry for Schools. By T. G. Vyvyan. 3rd Edit. 4s. 6d.

Greek Testament, Companion to the. By A. C. Barrett, A.M. 3rd Edition. Fcap. 8vo. 5s.

Book of Common Prayer, An Historical and Explanatory Treatise on the. By W. G. Humphry, B.D. 5th Edition. Fcap. 8vo. 4s. 6d.

Music, Text-book of. By H. C. Banister. 7th Edit. revised. 5s.

——— Concise History of. By H. G. Bonavia Hunt, B. Mus. Oxon. 3rd Edition revised. 3s. 6d.

ARITHMETIC AND ALGEBRA.

Principles and Practice of Arithmetic. By J. Hind, M.A. 9th Edit. 4s. 6d.

Elements of Algebra. By J. Hind, M.A. 6th Edit. 8vo. 10s. 6d.

Choice and Chance. A Treatise on Permutations and Combinations. By W. A. Whitworth. 2nd Edition. Crown 8vo. 6s.

See also foregoing Series.

GEOMETRY AND EUCLID.

Text-Book of Geometry. By T. S. Aldis, M.A. Small 8vo. 4s. 6d. Part I. 2s. 6d. Part II. 2s.

The Elements of Euclid. By H. J. Hose. Fcap. 8vo. 4s. 6d. Exercises separately, 1s.

——— The First Six Books, with Commentary by Dr. Lardner. 10th Edition. 8vo. 6s.

——— The First Two Books explained to Beginners. By C. P. Mason, B.A. 2nd Edition. Fcap. 8vo. 2s. 6d.

The Enunciations and Figures to Euclid's Elements. By Rev. J. Brasse, D.D. 3rd Edition. Fcap. 8vo. 1s. On Cards, in case, 5s. 6d. Without the Figures, 6d.

Exercises on Euclid and in Modern Geometry. By J. McDowell, B.A. Crown 8vo. 2nd Edition revised. 6s.

Geometrical Conic Sections. By W. H. Besant, M.A. 3rd Edit. 4s. 6d.

Elementary Geometrical Conic Sections. By W. H. Besant, M.A. [*In the Press.*

The Geometry of Conics. By C. Taylor, M.A. 2nd Edit. 8vo. 4s. 6d.

Solutions of Geometrical Problems, proposed at St. John's College from 1830 to 1846. By T. Gaskin, M.A. 8vo. 12s.

TRIGONOMETRY.

The Shrewsbury Trigonometry. By J. C. P. Aldous. Crown 8vo. 2s.

Elementary Trigonometry. By T. P. Hudson, M.A. 3s. 6d.

Elements of Plane and Spherical Trigonometry. By J. Hind, M.A. 5th Edition. 12mo. 6s.

An Elementary Treatise on Mensuration. By B. T. Moore, M.A. 5s.

ANALYTICAL GEOMETRY AND DIFFERENTIAL CALCULUS.

An Introduction to Analytical Plane Geometry. By W. P. Turnbull, M.A. 8vo. 12s.

Treatise on Plane Co-ordinate Geometry. By M. O'Brien, M.A. 8vo. 9s.

Problems on the Principles of Plane Co-ordinate Geometry. By W. Walton, M.A. 8vo. 16s.

Trilinear Co-ordinates, and Modern Analytical Geometry of Two Dimensions. By W. A. Whitworth, M.A. 8vo. 16s.

An Elementary Treatise on Solid Geometry. By W. S. Aldis, M.A. 2nd Edition revised. 8vo. 8s.

Geometrical Illustrations of the Differential Calculus. By M. B. Pell. 8vo. 2s. 6d.

Elementary Treatise on the Differential Calculus. By M. O'Brien, M.A. 8vo. 10s. 6d.

Notes on Roulettes and Glissettes. By W. H. Besant, M.A. 8vo. 3s. 6d.

Elliptic Functions, Elementary Treatise on. By A. Cayley, M.A. Demy 8vo. 15s.

MECHANICS & NATURAL PHILOSOPHY.

Statics, Elementary. By H. Goodwin, D.D. Fcap. 8vo. 2nd Edition. 3s.

Statics, Treatise on. By S. Earnshaw, M.A. 4th Edition. 8vo. 10s. 6d.

Dynamics, A Treatise on Elementary. By W. Garnett, B.A. 2nd Edition. Crown 8vo. 6s.

Statics and Dynamics, Problems in. By W. Walton, M.A. 8vo. 10s. 6d.

Theoretical Mechanics, Problems in. By W. Walton. 2nd Edit. revised and enlarged. Demy 8vo. 16s.

Mechanics, An Elementary Treatise on. By Prof. Potter. 4th Edition revised. 8s. 6d.

Hydrostatics, Elementary. By Prof. Potter. 7s. 6d.

Hydrostatics By W. H. Besant, M.A. Fcap. 8vo. 7th Edition. 4s.

Hydromechanics. A Treatise on. By W. H. Besant, M.A. 8vo. New Edition revised. 10s. 6d.

Dynamics of a Particle, A Treatise on the. By W. H. Besant, M.A. [*Preparing*.

Dynamics of a Rigid Body. Solutions of Examples on the. By W. N. Griffin, M.A. 8vo. 6s. 6d.

Motion, An Elementary Treatise on. By J. R. Lunn, M.A. 7s. 6d.

Optics, Geometrical. By W. S. Aldis, M.A. Fcap. 8vo. 3s. 6d.

Double Refraction, A Chapter on Fresnel's Theory of. By W. S. Aldis, M.A. 8vo. 2s.

Optics, An Elementary Treatise on. By Prof. Potter. Part I. 3rd Edition. 9s. 6d. Part II. 12s. 6d.

Optics, Physical; or the Nature and Properties of Light. By Prof. Potter, A.M. 6s. 6d. Part II. 7s. 6d.

Heat, An Elementary Treatise on. By W. Garnett, B.A. Crown 8vo. 2nd Edition revised. 3s. 6d.

Geometrical Optics, Figures Illustrative of. From Schelbach. By W. B. Hopkins. Folio. Plates. 10s. 6d.

Newton's Principia, The First Three Sections of, with an Appendix; and the Ninth and Eleventh Sections. By J. H. Evans, M.A. 5th Edition. Edited by P. T. Main, M.A. 4s.

Astronomy. An Introduction to Plane. By P. T. Main, M.A. Fcap. 8vo. cloth. 4s.

Astronomy, Practical and Spherical. By R. Main, M.A. 8vo. 14s.

Astronomy, Elementary Chapters on, from the 'Astronomie Physique' of Biot. By H. Goodwin, D.D. 8vo. 3s. 6d.

Pure Mathematics and Natural Philosophy, A Compendium of Facts and Formulæ in. By G. R. Smalley. Fcap. 8vo. 3s. 6d.

Elementary Course of Mathematics. By H. Goodwin, D.D. 6th Edition. 8vo. 16s.

Problems and Examples, adapted to the 'Elementary Course of Mathematics.' 3rd Edition. 8vo. 5s.

Solutions of Goodwin's Collection of Problems and Examples. By W. W. Hutt, M.A. 3rd Edition, revised and enlarged. 8vo. 9s.

Pure Mathematics. Elementary Examples in. By J. Taylor. 8vo. 7s. 6d.

Euclid, Mechanical. By the late W. Whewell, D.D. 5th Edition. 5s.

Mechanics of Construction. With numerous Examples. By S. Fenwick, F.R.A.S. 8vo. 12s.

Anti-Logarithms, Table of. By H. E. Filipowski. 3rd Edition. 8vo. 15s.

Mathematical and other Writings of R. L. Ellis. M.A. 8vo. 16s.

Pure and Applied Calculation, Notes on the Principles of. By Rev. J. Challis, M.A. Demy 8vo. 15s.

Physics, The Mathematical Principle of. By Rev. J. Challis, M.A. Demy 8vo. 5s.

HISTORY, TOPOGRAPHY, &c.

Rome and the Campagna. By R. Burn, M.A. With 85 Engravings and 26 Maps and Plans. With Appendix. 4to. 3*l*. 3*s*.

Modern Europe. By Dr. T. H. Dyer. 2nd Edition revised and continued. 5 vols. Demy 8vo. 2*l*. 12*s*. 6*d*.

The History of the Kings of Rome. By Dr. T. H. Dyer. 8vo. 16*s*.

A Plea for Livy. By Dr. T. H. Dyer. 8vo. 1*s*.

Roma Regalis. By Dr. T. H. Dyer. 8vo. 2*s*. 6*d*.

The History of Pompeii: its Buildings and Antiquities. By T. H. Dyer. 3rd Edition, brought down to 1874. Post 8vo. 7*s*. 6*d*.

Ancient Athens: its History, Topography, and Remains. By T. H. Dyer. Super-royal 8vo. Cloth. 1*l*. 5*s*.

The Decline of the Roman Republic. By G. Long. 5 vols. 8vo. 14*s*. each.

A History of England during the Early and Middle Ages. By C. H. Pearson, M.A. 2nd Edition revised and enlarged. 8vo. Vol. I. 16*s*. Vol. II. 14*s*.

Historical Maps of England. By C. H. Pearson. Folio. 2nd Edition revised. 31*s*. 6*d*.

History of England, 1800-15. By Harriet Martineau, with new and copious Index. 1 vol. 3*s*. 6*d*.

History of the Thirty Years' Peace, 1815-46. By Harriet Martineau. 4 vols. 3*s*. 6*d*. each.

A Practical Synopsis of English History. By A. Bowes. 4th Edition. 8vo. 2*s*.

Student's Text-Book of English and General History. By D. Beale. Crown 8vo. 2*s*. 6*d*.

Lives of the Queens of England. By A. Strickland. Library Edition, 8 vols. 7*s*. 6*d*. each. Cheaper Edition, 6 vols. 5*s*. each. Abridged Edition, 1 vol. 6*s*. 6*d*.

Eginhard's Life of Karl the Great (Charlemagne). Translated with Notes, by W. Glaister, M.A., B.C.L. Crown 8vo. 4*s*. 6*d*.

Outlines of Indian History. By A. W. Hughes. Small post 8vo. 3*s*. 6*d*.

The Elements of General History. By Prof. Tytler. New Edition, brought down to 1874. Small post 8vo. *s*. 6*d*.

ATLASES.

An Atlas of Classical Geography. 24 Maps. By W. Hughes and G. Long, M.A. New Edition. Imperial 8vo. 12*s*. 6*d*.

A Grammar-School Atlas of Classical Geography. Ten Maps selected from the above. New Edition. Imperial 8vo. 5*s*.

First Classical Maps. By the Rev. J. Tate, M.A. 3rd Edition. Imperial 8vo. 7*s*. 6*d*.

Standard Library Atlas of Classical Geography. Imp. 8vo. 7*s*. 6*d*.

PHILOLOGY.

WEBSTER'S DICTIONARY OF THE ENGLISH LAN-
GUAGE. Re-edited by N. Porter and C. A. Goodrich. With Dr. Mahn's Etymology. 1 vol. 21s. With Appendices and 70 additional pages of Illustrations, 31s. 6d.
'THE BEST PRACTICAL ENGLISH DICTIONARY EXTANT.'—*Quarterly Review.*
Prospectuses, with specimen pages, post free on application.

New Dictionary of the English Language. Combining Explanation with Etymology, and copiously illustrated by Quotations from the best Authorities. By Dr. Richardson. New Edition, with a Supplement. 2 vols. 4to. 4l. 14s. 6d.; half russia, 5l. 15s. 6d.; russia, 6l. 12s. Supplement separately. 4to. 12s.
An 8vo. Edit. without the Quotations, 15s.; half russia, 20s.; russia, 24s.

The Elements of the English Language. By E. Adams, Ph.D.
15th Edition. Post 8vo. 4s. 6d.

Philological Essays. By T. H. Key, M.A., F.R.S. 8vo. 10s. 6d.

Language, its Origin and Development. By T. H. Key, M.A., F.R.S. 8vo. 14s.

Synonyms and Antonyms of the English Language. By Archdeacon Smith. 2nd Edition. Post 8vo. 5s.

Synonyms Discriminated. By Archdeacon Smith. Demy 8vo. 16s.

Etymological Glossary of nearly 2500 English Words in Common Use derived from the Greek. By the Rev. E. J. Boyce. Fcap. 8vo. 3s. 6d.

A Syriac Grammar. By G. Phillips, D.D. 3rd Edition, enlarged. 8vo. 7s. 6d.

A Grammar of the Arabic Language. By Rev. W. J. Beaumont. M.A. 12mo. 7s.

Who Wrote It? A Dictionary of Common Poetical Quotations. Fcap. 8vo. 2s. 6d.

DIVINITY, MORAL PHILOSOPHY, &c.

Novum Testamentum Græcum. Textus Stephanici, 1550. By F. H. Scrivener, A.M., LL.D. New Edition. 16mo. 4s. 6d. Also on Writing Paper, with Wide Margin. Half-bound. 12s.

By the same Author.

Codex Bezæ Cantabrigiensis. 4to. 26s.

A Full Collation of the Codex Sinaiticus with the Received Text of the New Testament, with Critical Introduction. 2nd Edition, revised. Fcap. 8vo. 5s.

A Plain Introduction to the Criticism of the New Testament. With Forty Facsimiles from Ancient Manuscripts. 2nd Edition. 8vo. 16s.

Six Lectures on the Text of the New Testament. For English Readers. Crown 8vo. 6s.

The New Testament for English Readers. By the late H. Alford, D.D. Vol. I. Part I. 3rd Edit. 12s. Vol. I. Part II. 2nd Edit. 10s. 6d. Vol. II. Part I. 2nd Edit. 16s. Vol. II. Part II. 2nd Edit. 16s.

The Greek Testament. By the late H. Alford, D.D. Vol. I. 6th Edit. 1l. 8s. Vol. II. 6th Edit. 1l. 4s. Vol. III. 5th Edit. 18s. Vol. IV. Part I. 4th Edit. 18s. Vol. IV. Part II. 4th Edit. 14s. Vol. IV. 1l. 12s.

Companion to the Greek Testament. By A. C. Barrett, M.A. 3rd Edition. Fcap. 8vo. 5s.

Liber Apologeticus. The Apology of Tertullian, with English Notes, by H. A. Woodham, LL.D. 2nd Edition. 8vo. 8s. 6d.

The Book of Psalms. A New Translation, with Introductions, &c. By Very Rev. J. J. Stewart Perowne, D.D. 8vo. Vol. I. 4th Edition, 18s. Vol. II. 4th Edit. 16s.

—— Abridged for Schools. 2nd Edition. Crown 8vo. 10s. 6d.

History of the Articles of Religion. By C. H. Hardwick. 3rd Edition. Post 8vo. 5s.

Pearson on the Creed. Carefully printed from an early edition. With Analysis and Index by E. Walford, M.A. Post 8vo. 5s.

Doctrinal System of St. John as Evidence of the Date of his Gospel. By Rev. J. J. Lias, M.A. Crown 8vo. 6s.

An Historical and Explanatory Treatise on the Book of Common Prayer. By Rev. W. G. Humphry, B.D. 5th Edition, enlarged. Small post 8vo. 4s. 6d.

The New Table of Lessons Explained. By Rev. W. G. Humphry, B.D. Fcap. 1s. 6d.

A Commentary on the Gospels for the Sundays and other Holy Days of the Christian Year. By Rev. W. Denton, A.M. New Edition. 3 vols. 8vo. 54s. Sold separately.

Commentary on the Epistles for the Sundays and other Holy Days of the Christian Year. By Rev. W. Denton, A.M. 2 vols. 36s. Sold separately.

Commentary on the Acts. By Rev. W. Denton, A.M. Vol. I. 8vo. 18s. Vol. II. 14s.

Notes on the Catechism. By Rev. A. Barry, D.D. 5th Edit. Fcap. 2s.

Catechetical Hints and Helps. By Rev. E. J. Boyce, M.A. 3rd Edition, revised. Fcap. 2s. 6d.

Examination Papers on Religious Instruction. By Rev. E. J. Boyce. Sewed. 1s. 6d.

Church Teaching for the Church's Children. An Exposition of the Catechism. By the Rev. F. W. Harper. Sq. fcap. 2s.

The Winton Church Catechist. Questions and Answers on the Teaching of the Church Catechism. By the late Rev. J. S. B. Monsell, LL.D. 3rd Edition. Cloth, 3s.; or in Four Parts, sewed.

The Church Teacher's Manual of Christian Instruction. By Rev. M. F. Sadler. 16th Thousand. 2s. 6d.

Short Explanation of the Epistles and Gospels of the Christian Year, with Questions. Royal 32mo. 2s. 6d.; calf, 4s. 6d.

Butler's Analogy of Religion; with Introduction and Index by Rev. Dr. Steere. New Edition. Fcap. 3s. 6d.

—— **Three Sermons** on Human Nature, and Dissertation on Virtue. By W. Whewell, D.D. 4th Edition. Fcap. 8vo. 2s. 6d.

Lectures on the History of Moral Philosophy in England. By W. Whewell, D.D. Crown 8vo. 8s.

Elements of Morality, including Polity. By W. Whewell, D.D. New Edition, in 8vo. 15s.

Astronomy and General Physics (Bridgewater Treatise). New Edition. 5s.

Kent's Commentary on International Law. By J. T. Abdy, LL.D. New and Cheap Edition. Crown 8vo. 10s. 6d.

A Manual of the Roman Civil Law. By G. Leapingwell, LL.D. 8vo. 12s.

FOREIGN CLASSICS.

A series for use in Schools, with English Notes, grammatical and explanatory, and renderings of difficult idiomatic expressions. Fcap. 8vo.

Schiller's Wallenstein. By Dr. A. Buchheim. New Edit. 6s. 6d. Or the Lager and Piccolomini, 3s. 6d. Wallenstein's Tod, 3s. 6d.
——— **Maid of Orleans.** By Dr. W. Wagner. 3s. 6d.
——— **Maria Stuart.** By V. Kastner. 3s.
Goethe's Hermann and Dorothea. By E. Bell, M.A., and E. Wölfel. 2s. 6d.
German Ballads. from Uhland, Goethe, and Schiller. By C. L. Bielefeld. 3s. 6d.
Charles XII., par Voltaire. By L. Direy. 3rd Edition. 3s. 6d.
Aventures de Télémaque, par Fénélon. By C. J. Delille. 2nd Edition. 4s. 6d.
Select Fables of La Fontaine. By F. E. A. Gasc. New Edition. 3s.
Picciola, by X. B. Saintine. By Dr. Dubuc. 4th Edition. 3s. 6d.

FRENCH CLASS-BOOKS.

Twenty Lessons in French. With Vocabulary, giving the Pronunciation. By W. Brebner. Post 8vo. 4s.
French Grammar for Public Schools. By Rev. A. C. Clapin, M.A. Fcap. 8vo. 6th Edit. 2s. 6d. Separately, Part I. 2s.; Part II. 1s. 6d.
French Primer. By Rev. A. C. Clapin, M.A. 3rd Edition. Fcap. 8vo. 1s.
Primer of French Philology. By Rev. A. C. Clapin. Fcap. 8vo. 1s.
Le Nouveau Tresor; or, French Student's Companion. By M. E. S. 16th Edition. Fcap. 8vo. 3s. 6d.

F. E. A. GASC'S FRENCH COURSE.

First French Book. Fcap 8vo. New Edition. 1s. 6d.
Second French Book. New Edition. Fcap. 8vo. 2s. 6d.
Key to First and Second French Books. Fcap. 8vo. 3s. 6d.
French Fables for Beginners, in Prose, with Index. New Edition. 12mo. 2s.
Select Fables of La Fontaine. New Edition. Fcap. 8vo. 3s.
Histoires Amusantes et Instructives. With Notes. New Edition. Fcap. 8vo. 2s. 6d.

Practical Guide to Modern French Conversation. Fcap. 8vo. 2s. 6d.

French Poetry for the Young. With Notes. Fcap. 8vo. 2s.

Materials for French Prose Composition; or, Selections from the best English Prose Writers. New Edition. Fcap. 8vo. 4s. 6d. Key, 6s.

Prosateurs Contemporains. With Notes. 8vo. New Edition, revised. 5s.

Le Petit Compagnon: a French Talk-Book for Little Children. 16mo. 2s. 6d.

An Improved Modern Pocket Dictionary of the French and English Languages. 25th Thousand, with additions. 16mo. Cloth. 4s. Also in 2 vols., in neat leatherette, 5s.

Modern French-English and English-French Dictionary. 2nd Edition, revised. In 1 vol. 12s. 6d. (formerly 2 vols. 25s.)

GOMBERT'S FRENCH DRAMA.

Being a Selection of the best Tragedies and Comedies of Molière, Racine, Corneille, and Voltaire. With Arguments and Notes by A. Gombert. New Edition, revised by F. E. A. Gasc. Fcap. 8vo. 1s. each; sewed, 6d.   CONTENTS.

MOLIERE:—Le Misanthrope. L'Avare. Le Bourgeois Gentilhomme. Le Tartuffe. Le Malade Imaginaire. Les Femmes Savantes. Les Fourberies de Scapin. Les Précieuses Ridicules. L'Ecole des Femmes. L'Ecole des Maris. Le Médecin malgré Lui.

RACINE:—Phèdre. Esther. Athalie. Iphigénie. Les Plaideurs. Thébaïde; or, Les Frères Ennemis. Andromaque. Britannicus.

P. CORNEILLE:—Le Cid. Horace. Cinna. Polyeucte.

VOLTAIRE:—Zaïre.

GERMAN CLASS-BOOKS.

Materials for German Prose Composition. By Dr Buchheim. 5th Edition, revised, with an Index. Fcap. 4s. 6d.

A German Grammar for Public Schools. By the Rev. A. C. Clapin and F. Holl Müller. Fcap. 2s. 6d.

Kotzebue's Der Gefangene. With Notes by Dr. W. Stromberg. 1s.

ENGLISH CLASS-BOOKS.

The Elements of the English Language. By E. Adams, Ph.D. 15th Edition. Post 8vo. 4s. 6d.

The Rudiments of English Grammar and Analysis. By E. Adams, Ph.D. New Edition. Fcap. 8vo. 2s.

BY C. P. MASON, B.A. LONDON UNIVERSITY.

First Notions of Grammar for Young Learners. Fcap. 8vo. Cloth. 8d.

First Steps in English Grammar for Junior Classes. Demy 18mo. New Edition. 1s.

Outlines of English Grammar for the use of Junior Classes. Cloth. 5th Edition. 1s. 6d.

English Grammar, including the Principles of Grammatical Analysis. 22nd Edition. Post 8vo. 3s. 6d.

Shorter English Grammar, with copious carefully graduated Exercises. Crown 8vo. 3s. 6d. [*Just published.*

English Grammar Practice, being the Exercises from the above, in a separate volume. 1s. [*Just published.*

The Analysis of Sentences applied to Latin. Post 8vo. 1s. 6d.

Analytical Latin Exercises: Accidence and Simple Sentences, &c. Post 8vo. 3s. 6d.

Edited for Middle-Class Examinations.

With Notes on the Analysis and Parsing, and Explanatory Remarks.

Milton's Paradise Lost, Book I. With Life. 3rd Edit. Post 8vo. 2s.

―――― **Book II.** With Life. 2nd Edit. Post 8vo. 2s.

―――― **Book III.** With Life. Post 8vo. 2s.

Goldsmith's Deserted Village. With Life. Post 8vo. 1s. 6d.

Cowper's Task, Book II. With Life. Post 8vo. 2s.

Thomson's Spring. With Life. Post 8vo. 2s.

―――― **Winter.** With Life. Post 8vo. 2s.

Practical Hints on Teaching. By Rev. J. Menet. M.A. 4th Edit. Crown 8vo. cloth, 2s. 6d.; paper, 2s.

Test Lessons in Dictation. Paper cover, 1s. 6d.

Questions for Examinations in English Literature. By Rev. W. W. Skeat. 2s. 6d.

Drawing Copies. By P. H. Delamotte. Oblong 8vo. 12s. Sold also in parts at 1s. each.

Poetry for the School-room. New Edition. Fcap. 8vo. 1s. 6d.

Select Parables from Nature, for Use in Schools. By Mrs. A. Gatty. Fcap. 8vo. Cloth. 1s.

School Record for Young Ladies' Schools. 6d.

Geographical Text-Book; a Practical Geography. By M. E. S. 12mo. 2s.

The Blank Maps done up separately, 4to. 2s. coloured.

A First Book of Geography. By Rev. C. A. Johns, B.A., F.L.S. &c. Illustrated. 12mo. 2s. 6d.

Loudon's (Mrs.) Entertaining Naturalist. New Edition. Revised by W. S. Dallas, F.L.S. 5s.

―――― **Handbook of Botany.** New Edition, greatly enlarged by D. Wooster. Fcap. 2s. 6d.

The Botanist's Pocket-Book. With a copious Index. By W. R. Hayward. 2nd Edit. revised. Crown 8vo. Cloth limp. 4s. 6d.

Experimental Chemistry, founded on the Work of Dr. Stöckhardt. By C. W. Heaton. Post 8vo. 5s.

Double Entry Elucidated. By B. W. Foster. 7th Edit. 4to. 8s. 6d.

A New Manual of Book-keeping. By P. Crellin, Accountant. Crown 8vo. 3s. 6d.

Picture School-Books. In Simple Language, with numerous Illustrations. Royal 16mo.

School Primer. 6d.—School Reader. By J. Tilleard. 1s.—Poetry Book for Schools. 1s.—The Life of Joseph. 1s.—The Scripture Parables. By the Rev. J. E. Clarke. 1s.—The Scripture Miracles. By the Rev. J. E. Clarke. 1s.—The New Testament History. By the Rev. J. G. Wood, M.A. 1s.—The Old Testament History. By the Rev. J. G. Wood, M.A. 1s.—The Story of Bunyan's Pilgrim's Progress. 1s.—The Life of Christopher Columbus. By Sarah Crompton. 1s.—The Life of Martin Luther. By Sarah Crompton. 1s.

BOOKS FOR YOUNG READERS.

In 8 vols. Limp cloth, 6d. each.

The New-born Lamb; Rosewood Box; Poor Fan; Wise Dog——The Cat and the Hen; Sam and his Dog Red-leg; Bob and Tom Lee; A Wreck——The Three Monkeys——Story of a Cat, told by Herself——The Blind Boy; The Mute Girl; A New Tale of Babes in a Wood——The Dey and the Knight; The New Bank-note; The Royal Visit; A King's Walk on a Winter's Day——Queen Bee and Busy Bee——Gull's Crag, a Story of the Sea.

BELL'S READING-BOOKS.

FOR SCHOOLS AND PAROCHIAL LIBRARIES.

The popularity which the 'Books for Young Readers' have attained is a sufficient proof that teachers and pupils alike approve of the use of interesting stories, with a simple plot in place of the dry combination of letters and syllables, making no impression on the mind, of which elementary reading-books generally consist.

The Publishers have therefore thought it advisable to extend the application of this principle to books adapted for more advanced readers.

Now Ready. Post 8vo. Strongly bound.

Masterman Ready. By Captain Marryat, R.N. 1s. 6d.
The Settlers in Canada. By Captain Marryat, R.N. 1s. 6d.
Parables from Nature. (Selected.) By Mrs. Gatty. 1s.
Friends in Fur and Feathers. By Gwynfryn. 1s.
Robinson Crusoe. 1s. 6d.
Andersen's Danish Tales. (Selected.) By E. Bell, M.A. 1s.
Southey's Life of Nelson. (Abridged.) 1s.
Grimm's German Tales. (Selected.) By E. Bell, M.A. 1s.
Life of the Duke of Wellington, with Maps and Plans. 1s.

Others in Preparation.

London: Printed by JOHN STRANGEWAYS, Castle St. Leicester Sq.

www.ingramcontent.com/pod-product-compliance
Lightning Source LLC
Chambersburg PA
CBHW030742230426
43667CB00007B/812